MY SiDEWALKS ON
SCOTT FORESMAN
READING STREET

Early Reading Intervention

Part 1

Teacher's Guide

Learning Letters and Sounds

PEARSON

Scott Foresman

scottforesman.com

Editorial Offices: Glenview, Illinois • Parsippany, New Jersey • New York, New York
Sales Offices: Boston, Massachusetts • Duluth, Georgia • Glenview, Illinois
Coppell, Texas • Sacramento, California • Mesa, Arizona

References

The following resources provide a foundation for the research upon which this program is based.

Adams, M. J., Foorman, B. R., Lundberg, I., and Beeler, T. (1998b). *Phonemic awareness in young children.* Baltimore, MD: Paul H. Brookes.

Ball, E. W., and Blachman, B. A. (1991). "Does Phoneme Awareness Training in Kindergarten Make a Difference in Early Word Recognition and Developmental Spelling?" *Reading Research Quarterly, 26(1),* 49–66.

Blachman, B. A. et al., (2000). *Road to the code: A phonological awareness program for young children.* Baltimore, MD: Paul H. Brookes.

Blevins, W. (1999). *Phonemic awareness activities.* New York, NY: Scholastic.

Byrne, B. and Fielding-Barnsley, R. (1993). *Sound foundation kit.* Artarmon, Australia: Peter Lynden Publishing.

Carnine, D. W., Silbert, J., and Kame'enui, E. J. (1997). *Direct instruction reading (3rd ed.).* Upper Saddle River, NJ: Merrill/Prentice-Hall.

Cunningham, P. M. (1991a). *Phonics they use: Words for reading and writing.* New York: HarperCollins.

Cunningham, P. M. (1991b). "Research Directions: Multimethod, Multilevel Literacy Instruction in First-Grade." *Language Arts, 68,* 578–584.

Cunningham, P. M. and Hall, D. P. (1994). *Making words: multilevel, hands-on, developmentally appropriate spelling and phonics activities.* Torrance, CA: Good Apple.

Engelmann, S. and Bruner, E. C. (1995). *Reading mastery I* (Rainbow edition). Columbus, OH: SRA/McGraw-Hill.

Gaskings, I. et al., (1997). "Procedures for Word Learning: Making Discoveries About Words." *The Reading Teacher, 50,* 312–327.

Henderson, E. (1990). *Teaching spelling.* Boston: Houghton Mifflin.

Lindamood, P. and Lindamood, P. (1998). *Lindamood phonemic sequencing program for reading, spelling, and speech: Teacher's manual for the classroom and the clinic.* Austin, TX: PRO-ED.

Notari-Syverson, A., O'Connor, R. E., and Vadasy, P. F. (1998). *Ladders to literacy: A kindergarten activity book.* Baltimore, MD: Paul H. Brookes.

Smith, S. B. et al., (2001). "An Analysis of Phonological Awareness Instruction in Four Kindergarten Basal Reading Programs." *Reading and Writing Quarterly, 17,* 25–51.

Smith, S., Simmons, D. C., and Kame'enui, E. J. (1998). "Phonological awareness: Research bases." In D. C. Simmons and E. J. Kame'enui (Eds.), *What reading research tells us about children with diverse learning needs: Bases and basics* (pp. 61–127). Mahwah, NJ: Lawrence Erlbaum Associates.

Smith, S., Simmons, D. C., and Kame'enui, E. J. (1998). "Phonological Awareness: Instructional and Curricular Basics and Implications." In D. C. Simmons and E. J. Kame'enui (Eds.), *What reading research tells us about children with diverse learning needs: Bases and basics* (pp. 129–140). Mahwah, NJ: Lawrence Erlbaum Associates.

Torgesen, J. K. and Bryant, B. T. (1994). *Phonological awareness training for reading.* Austin, TX: PRO-ED.

Yopp, H. K. (1992) "Developing Phonemic Awareness in Young Children." *The Reading Teacher, 45(9),* 696–703.

Activity Acknowledgments

The authors of this program would like to acknowledge the people who developed the following activities used in the program:

First Sound Song, H.K. Yopp, 1992. Part 1: 36, 52, 128, 154, 178, 204, 237; Part 3: 107.

If You Land on Me, Say My First Sound, modified from Blevins's (1977) *Phonemic Awareness Activities for Early Reading Progress.* Part 1: 290; Part 2: 50, 107, 147, 157.

Say It and Move It with Two-Square Strips, based on an activity from Ball and Blachman, 1999. Part 2: 12.

Regular and Irregular Words, modification of an activity from Carnine, Silbert, and Kame'enui, 1977. Part 3: 5, 17, 29, 41, 53, 75, 85, 97, 109, 121, 151, 161, 171, 181, 199, 211, 223, 235, 245, 254, 255; Part 4: 5, 6, 18, 19, 30, 31, 43, 44, 56, 57, 68, 78, 90, 91, 102, 103, 115, 126, 127, 138, 147, 148, 157, 158, 169, 170, 181, 193, 205, 215, 225, 226, 235, 236, 245, 246, 255, 256, 265, 273, 283, 293, 303, 304, 313, 325.

Sentence Page, modification of an activity from Carnine, Silbert, and Kame'enui, 1977. Part 4: 9, 22, 34, 47, 60, 81, 93, 106, 118, 129, 151, 161, 173, 185, 198, 218, 228, 238, 248, 258, 276, 286, 296, 306, 317.

Illustrations by Karen Bell

About the illustrator: Karen Bell and her family live on a ranch in Malibu, California, with a large collection of assorted dogs, cats, chickens, goats, turtles, and horses. Unfortunately, there are no dinosaurs.

MY SIDEWALKS ON
SCOTT FORESMAN
READING STREET
Early Reading Intervention

Scott Foresman Sidewalks: Early Reading Intervention is based on Project Optimize, a five-year longitudinal research study by Dr. Edward J. Kame'enui and Dr. Deborah C. Simmons. The program helps you identify at-risk children in kindergarten and provide intervention to improve reading achievement.

Scientifically Research-Based

Research shows that 97% of kindergarten children who were taught with *Scott Foresman Sidewalks: Early Reading Intervention* experienced faster achievement rates and were able to sustain that level of achievement into second grade.

Comprehensive Assessment

Scott Foresman Sidewalks: Early Reading Intervention helps you make placement decisions and monitor progress, so you can focus instruction based on children's needs.

Validated Instructional Design ✓

The instructional design of *Scott Foresman Sidewalks: Early Reading Intervention* ensures the time, duration, and instructional delivery necessary for student success.

Program Authors

Deborah C. Simmons, Ph.D.

Associate Professor and Co-Director

Institute for the Development of Educational Achievement
University of Oregon

Dr. Simmons is a well-respected researcher in the areas of literacy acquisition and development and intervention for children at risk of reading failure. Over the years, she has published numerous books, book chapters, and research articles, with her articles appearing in *The Journal of Educational Psychology, Reading and Writing Quarterly, Reading Today*, the *Journal of Learning Disabilities*, and the *Journal of Educational Research*.

Dr. Simmons serves on editorial boards for several professional journals, including the *Journal of Special Education, Learning Disabilities Quarterly, Exceptional Children,* and *Reading and Writing Quarterly*. She also served on the Assessment Group of the Reading First Initiative for the U.S. Department of Education.

PROJECT OPTIMIZE

Project Optimize, which has become *Scott Foresman Sidewalks: Early Reading Intervention*, is just one of many collaborations between Dr. Simmons and Dr. Kame'enui. They are currently working on several research projects concentrating on accelerating literacy and improving reading competence for at-risk children.

Edward J. Kame'enui, Ph.D.

Professor and Director

Institute for the Development of Educational Achievement
University of Oregon

Dr. Kame'enui has published several college textbooks on various topics related to teaching reading and curriculum design. He also has published research and issue articles in publications including *The Exceptional Child, Reading Research Quarterly*, the *Journal of Educational Research*, and the *Journal of Reading Behavior*.

Dr. Kame'enui serves on editorial boards for several professional journals, including *Reading Research, Learning Disabilities Research and Practice,* and the *Journal of Special Education*. He has served as the team leader of the Assessment Group of the Reading First Initiative for the U.S. Department of Education and has also served on advisory boards for the PBS television show *Between the Lions* and the International Dyslexia Association.

Authors and Consultants

CONSULTING AUTHORS

Michael D. Coyne, Ph.D.
Neag School of Education
University of Connecticut

Lana Edwards, Ph.D.
Assistant Professor
Lehigh University, Bethlehem, Pennsylvania

Carrie Thomas-Beck, Ph.D.
Curriculum Specialist
Springfield Public Schools, Springfield, Oregon

SPECIAL THANKS

This program reflects the collaboration of researchers and practitioners and the contributions of many. The authors gratefully acknowledge and sincerely appreciate the effort, input, and support of the following individuals and organizations:

Bethel School District (Eugene, Oregon) Administrators, Principals, Teachers, Educational Assistants, and Students

Springfield School District (Springfield, Oregon) Principals, Kindergarten Teachers, Educational Assistants, and Students

Additionally, the authors would like to thank the following individuals for their continued and significant contributions:
Amy Riepma, Rhonda Wolter, and **Melissa Allen**

CONSULTANTS

Beth Harn, Ph.D.
Assistant Professor of Psychology
California State University, Fresno

Diane O'Keefe
Business Manager
Institute for the Development
of Educational Achievement
University of Oregon

Naomi Rahn, M.S.
Instructor/Field Experience Coordinator
Early Intervention Program
University of Oregon

Tanya Sheehan
Research Assistant
Institute for the Development
of Educational Achievement
University of Oregon

Sylvia Barrus Smith, Ph.D.
Research Associate
Institute for the Development
of Educational Achievement
University of Oregon

Katie Tate
Editor
Institute for the Development
of Educational Achievement
University of Oregon

Joshua Wallin
Research Assistant
Institute for the Development
of Educational Achievement
University of Oregon

Scientifically Research-Based

Project Optimize

Project Optimize is a five-year longitudinal research study investigating the effectiveness of instructional emphasis and specificity on the early reading and vocabulary development of kindergarten children.

What prompted the study?

National Education Reform

The President has mandated that all children should read at or above grade level by Grade 3.
We need proven instruction to help struggling readers meet that goal.

Findings of Other Researchers

Interventions delivered in Grade 3 and beyond fail to close the achievement gap.
The later the onset of intervention, the poorer the probability that children will read at Grade 3.

Research Questions

What types of instruction and intervention strategies are most effective
with the bottom 25% of kindergartners?
How intensive should the intervention be (time, duration, and instructional delivery)
to reach satisfactory goals and maintain them over time?

Funding

Project Optimize was funded by the U.S. Department of Education
and the Office of Special Education Programs.

Corporate Sponsors

Pacific Corporation and Washington Mutual

THE SAMPLE

- 441 kindergarten children from seven schools in the Pacific Northwest were screened on onset recognition fluency and letter naming fluency.

- The bottom 25% on both criteria were invited to participate in an "extended-day" kindergarten intervention.

- Children were randomly assigned to one of the three interventions.

THE DEMOGRAPHICS

- All Title I schools

- Free and reduced lunch: 37% to 63%

- District mobility: 15% to 20%

- Gender mix: 58% male, 42% female

- Sample size: 112 beginning sample, 96 end of kindergarten, 77 end of Grade 1

THE INTERVENTIONS

- 30 minutes of additional instruction per day

- Instruction was delivered in small groups of 2–5 children.

- Instruction was delivered by either a certified teacher or a teaching assistant.

- Pre- and post-data were collected.

- Progress was monitored monthly.

Instructional Interventions

Intervention A
Scott Foresman Sidewalks:
Early Reading Intervention

**Code Emphasis/
High Specificity**

- 15 minutes of instruction on select phonological awareness skills, alphabetic understanding, and word reading

- 15 minutes of instruction on further development of phonological awareness, writing development, and integrating phonologic awareness and orthography (letter-sound to whole word writing)

Intervention B
*Phonological Awareness/
Vocabulary Comprehension*

**Code and Comprehension
Emphasis/High Specificity**

- 5 minutes of instruction on select phonological awareness skills, alphabetic understanding, and word reading

- 15 minutes focused on literature development, repeated reading procedure, explicit vocabulary instruction, and explicit story grammar and retell instruction

Intervention C
Basal Publisher:
Sounds and Letters Module

**Code Emphasis/
Moderate Specificity**

- 30 total minutes of instruction focusing on a range of phonological awareness skills, alphabetic understanding, and word reading, plus writing instruction

Results

GROWTH IN PHONOLOGICAL AWARENESS

Test: Phonemic Segmentation Fluency **Benchmark:** 35 Phonemes per Minute

Children in all three interventions exceeded the benchmark. Children in Intervention A exceeded the benchmark at least two months earlier and showed greater achievement than children in Interventions B and C.

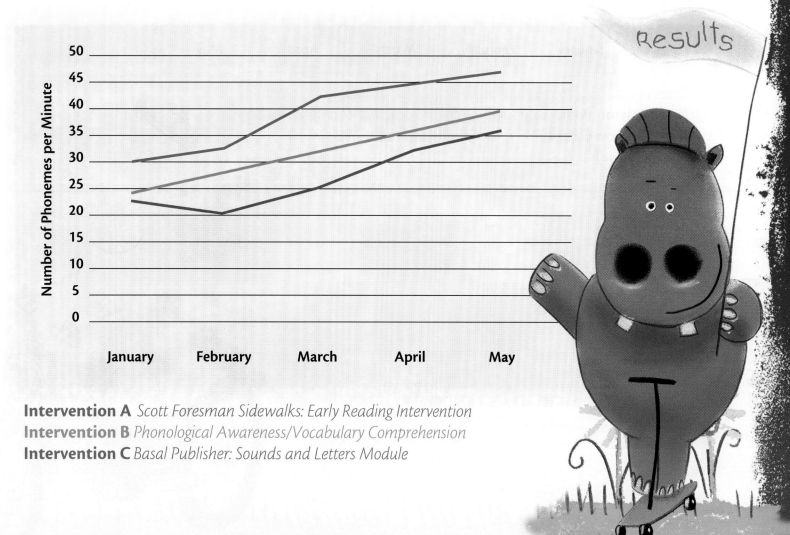

Intervention A *Scott Foresman Sidewalks: Early Reading Intervention*
Intervention B *Phonological Awareness/Vocabulary Comprehension*
Intervention C *Basal Publisher: Sounds and Letters Module*

Results

GROWTH IN ALPHABETIC PRINCIPLE

Test: Nonsense Word Fluency **Benchmark:** 25 Letter-Sound Correspondences per Minute

Children in Interventions A and B exceeded the benchmark. Children in Intervention A showed the greatest achievement, surpassing the benchmark by 56%.

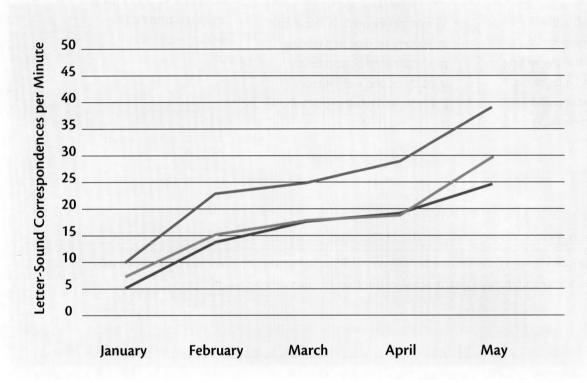

Intervention A *Scott Foresman Sidewalks: Early Reading Intervention*
Intervention B *Phonological Awareness/Vocabulary Comprehension*
Intervention C *Basal Publisher: Sounds and Letters Module*

Results

WHERE STUDENTS WITH SIMILAR ENTRY LEVELS FINISHED KINDERGARTEN

Test: Phonemic Segmentation Fluency (PSF) **Median:** 21–30

87% of the children who received Intervention A achieved the benchmark. In most districts with similar children who did not receive an intervention, fewer than 30% of the children achieved the benchmark.

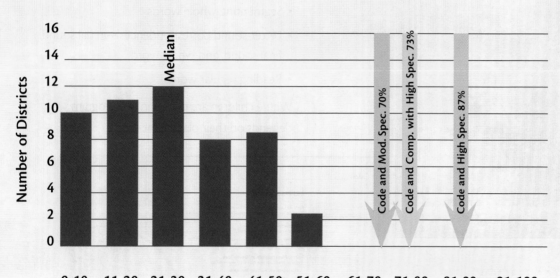

Intervention A *Scott Foresman Sidewalks: Early Reading Intervention*
Intervention B *Phonological Awareness/Vocabulary Comprehension*
Intervention C *Basal Publisher: Sounds and Letters Module*

Research Conclusions

Research shows that 97% of kindergarten children who were taught with *Scott Foresman Sidewalks: Early Reading Intervention* experienced faster achievement rates and were able to sustain that level of achievement into second grade.

SPECIFICITY MATTERS

Children in Interventions A and B, who received 15 minutes of highly specified instruction, made gains compared to those in Intervention C, who received a full 30 minutes of less specific instruction.

EMPHASIS MATTERS

How instructional time is used affects outcomes in consequential ways. Emphasis on phonologic and alphabetic tasks affected achievement.

EMPHASIS AND SPECIFICITY MATTER

The combination of emphasis and specificity resulted in greater levels of early reading achievement than either of the factors alone.

Comprehensive Assessment

ASSESSMENT HANDBOOK

The Assessment Handbook helps you make placement decisions and monitor progress, so you can focus instruction based on children's needs.

Everything teachers need to place and monitor students in the program is contained in the Assessment Handbook.

- Placement Test with directions
- Four Progress-Monitoring Tests
- Progress-Monitoring Checklists
- Exit Test to ensure mastery of skills

Before

PLACEMENT TEST

The Placement Test is used to determine where a child best fits within the program. Children are assessed in the following areas:

- Letter names and sounds
- Isolating initial sounds
- Segmenting whole words
- Letter-sound correspondences—initial sound, final sound, and whole word
- Reading regular words

Where children are placed in the program depends on their placement scores.

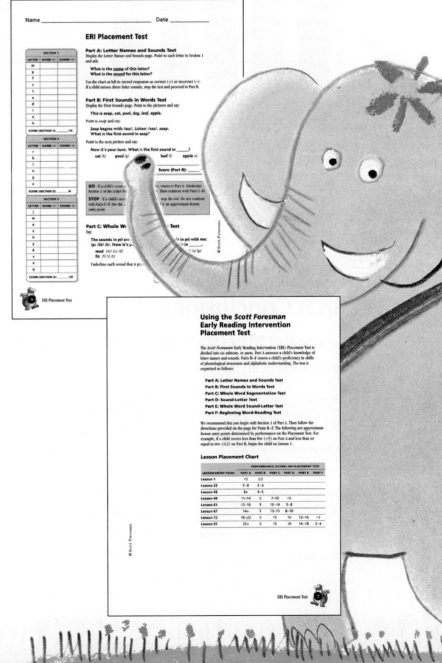

During

ONGOING ASSESSMENT

Ongoing assessment features appear routinely throughout the Teacher's Guide. You can use these features to:

- Quickly assess whether children have learned a skill
- Correctly determine the appropriate instructional strategy to help children learn

PROGRESS-MONITORING TESTS

There are four progress-monitoring tests, one for each part of the program. Administering these tests lets you know:

- If children are ready to move on to the next part of the program
- If children need any additional instruction

STUDENT PROGRESS CHECKLISTS

There are progress-monitoring checklists for every six lessons. Use the checklists:

- To monitor progress on a weekly basis
- As a record of skills that children have learned
- To determine if children may need more intensive instruction

After

EXIT TEST

The Exit Test allows you to determine whether or not your children have appropriately mastered the skills in the program and are ready to end their intervention lessons. During the Exit Test, children are assessed on:

- Letter names and sounds
- Isolating initial sounds
- Segmenting whole words
- Letter-sound correspondences—initial sound, final sound, and whole word
- Reading regular words
- Reading irregular words

Components

Teacher Resources

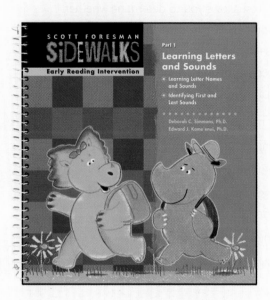

TEACHER'S GUIDES

A proven research base ensures success for
at-risk readers. 126 lessons in an easy-to-follow
format give you the flexibility to teach one
30-minute or two 15-minute sessions. (4 volumes)

TEACHER RESOURCE PACKAGE

A wealth of additional resources for every lesson!
These heavy-duty cards have a teacher-friendly design
that makes managing materials even easier.

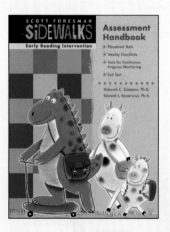

Hi, I'm Diz and I'm a
Stegosaurus. Meet me and my
friends Nat the Triceratops, Ron
the Brontosaurus, and Rex the
Tyrannosaurus Rex.

ASSESSMENT HANDBOOK

The materials you need to accurately assess all
your students are conveniently located in one book.
Contains the Placement Test, four Progress-Monitoring
Tests, Progress-Monitoring Checklists, and an Exit Test.

DIZ THE DINOSAUR

This plush puppet with a moveable
mouth and arms allows you to implement
instruction from any lesson.

Student Materials

DIZ STUDENT STORYBOOKS

These 10 decodable storybooks use engaging recurring characters
to blend practice and application of sound-spelling patterns. (6 copies of each)
Also available in a take-home version.

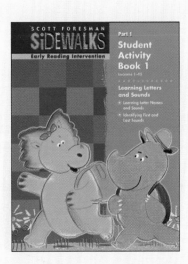

WRITE-ON/WIPE-OFF CARDS

These cards have a write-on/wipe-off surface on the
lined front side for practicing careful writing and a blank
reverse side for writing large letters.

STUDENT ACTIVITY BOOKS

No more photocopying! The student resources
for every lesson include separate D'Nealian®
and ball-and-stick pages. (4 volumes, 6 copies each)

Components

Manipulatives

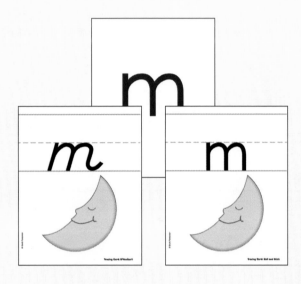

ALPHABET CARD PACKAGE
This unique package contains Alphabet Cards for learning letter names and sounds, Tracing Cards for connecting sounds to letters and learning letter shapes, and a Teacher's Sound Production Cue Card for prompting sound production.

LETTER AND WORD CARDS PACKAGE
Use Letter Cards in D'Nealian® and ball-and-stick formats for naming and tracing letters, Game Cards for games that practice letter names and sounds, and Word Cards to practice word reading strategies.

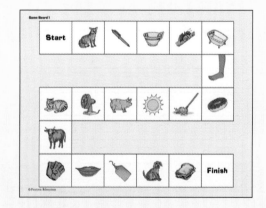

LETTER TILES
Sturdy, plastic, manipulative tiles are easy for little fingers to handle and allow children to practice segmenting and blending.

PICTURE CARDS
Identify and isolate initial and final sounds with these full-color photographs.

GAME BOARDS AND 2- AND 3-SQUARE STRIPS
Game boards help students identify initial and final sounds in an engaging format while the 2- and 3-Square Strips assist them in segmenting, blending, and reading words.

Instructional Design: Components

Professional Development Videos

Scott Foresman Sidewalks: Early Reading Intervention videos are ideal for staff training and/or teacher in-service.

RESEARCH: A MESSAGE FROM THE AUTHORS

Featuring program authors Dr. Deborah Simmons and Dr. Edward Kame'enui, this video discusses the scientific research foundation for the program and displays the results of Project Optimize, showing the remarkable achievements of children using *Scott Foresman Sidewalks: Early Reading Intervention.*

CLASSROOM DEMONSTRATION LESSON

View real-time video lessons of a real teacher and students using actual lessons from *Scott Foresman Sidewalks: Early Reading Intervention* and then hear reactions to the program from real teachers and administrators.

Program Contents

Use the *Sidewalks* boxes to organize all of your materials and create a colorful classroom display.

- Teacher's Guides:
  Part 1: Learning Letter Names and Sounds
  Part 2: Segmenting, Blending, and Integrating
  Part 3: Word Reading
  Part 4: Sentence Reading
- Teacher's Resource Packages (4)
- Student Activity Books (4 titles, 6 copies of each)
- Assessment Handbook
- Diz Student Storybooks (10 titles, 6 copies of each)
- Diz Take-Home Storybooks (6 books, 10 titles in each)
- Diz Dinosaur Puppet
- Picture Cards (174)
- Write-on/Wipe-off Cards (6)
- Letter Tiles (26)

- Alphabet Card Package (26 D'Nealian® Tracing Cards, 26 ball-and-stick Tracing Cards, 26 Alphabet Cards, and a Sound Production Cue Card)
- Letter and Word Cards Package (158 Letter Cards, 229 Word Cards, and 156 Game Cards)

Management

Getting Started

Scott Foresman Sidewalks: Early Reading Intervention contains everything you need to intervene early and successfully.

IDENTIFY AT-RISK CHILDREN

The beginning of the school year is the best time to informally assess which children are at risk for reading difficulties. At some point during the fourth to sixth week of the year, take the time to administer a formal screening assessment to determine which children fall into the bottom 25% of all readers. These children are the most at risk of experiencing reading difficulties. *Scott Foresman Sidewalks: Early Reading Intervention* allows you to intervene and dramatically increase these children's chance for reading success.

DIBELS

When using a screening test at the beginning of the year, you may want to consider DIBELS— Dynamic Indicators of Basic Early Literacy Skills. This test may be downloaded from the Internet for free. For the test and scoring information, see **dibels.uoregon.edu.**

FORM INTERVENTION GROUPS

The Placement Test must be administered to each child individually and only takes a few minutes per child. It will allow you to determine the entry point in the program for each student. Once all the children have been assessed, you can place them into groups. Each group should be made up of two to five children. After you have determined where children fit into the program, they will receive the instruction as a supplement to their regular reading and literacy instruction.

Half-Day or Whole-Day Environment

Scott Foresman Sidewalks: Early Reading Intervention is appropriate for small-group instruction and is designed for flexible use based on the structure of your school day. You can choose to give the instruction in one 30-minute period or in two 15-minute periods. The instruction can come either before or after school or as part of an extended-day program.

Daily Preparation

Scott Foresman Sidewalks: Early Reading Intervention is designed to streamline the time that it takes to prepare for each group.

DAILY PREPARATION

Every lesson starts with a lesson overview with this important planning information:

- The activities children will engage in that day
- A list of materials needed for each activity
- A time estimate for each activity

All are designed to make daily preparation easier. When you first begin the program, preparation time should be approximately 15 minutes. That amount will significantly decrease as you and your students become more familiar with the program.

The program boxes are designed to be both a storage system and an organizational system. Labeled compartments inside the boxes indicate where to find the materials needed for the day's instruction.

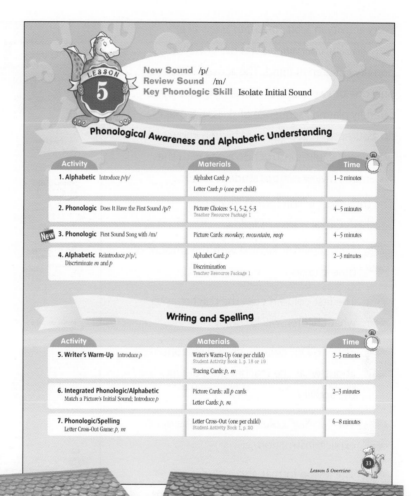

Management

Daily Instruction

Scott Foresman Sidewalks: Early Reading Intervention is an activity-based program proven to have the right instruction for at-risk children.

Every activity in *Scott Foresman Sidewalks: Early Reading Intervention* was designed with primary children in mind. The activities last only one or two minutes and are organized in a carefully planned sequence of skills that makes no assumptions about what children know. This direct, explicit instruction along with the systematic review ensures student success.

The three-part lesson format inside each Teacher's Guide is easy to follow.

1. Each activity is labeled with the amount of time it takes.

2. The first column cues the teacher as to what children will be doing.

3. The "To Do" column gives directions about what the teacher does during the activity.

4. The "To Say" column contains the direct, explicit instruction.

5. The lesson format also includes opportunities for Ongoing Assessment and gives an immediate reteaching strategy for children who don't grasp the material the first time through.

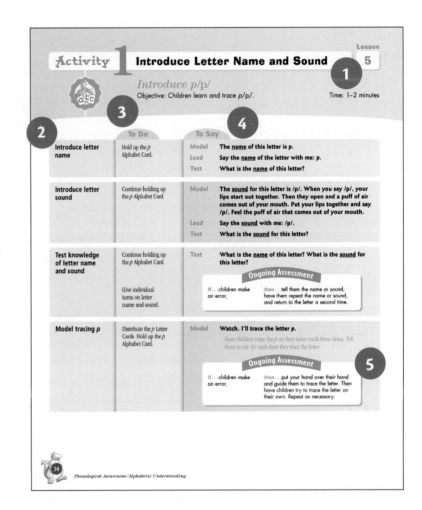

Professional Development

Professional development is an important component of *Scott Foresman Sidewalks: Early Reading Intervention*. We offer two professional development videos to help teachers get the best results from the program.

RESEARCH: A MESSAGE FROM THE AUTHORS

This 15-minute video introduces program authors Dr. Deborah Simmons and Dr. Edward Kame'enui. Dr. Simmons and Dr. Kame'enui discuss Project Optimize, the longitudinal research study that served as the basis for *Scott Foresman Sidewalks: Early Reading Intervention*. You can use this video:

- As an overview of early reading intervention
- To get background information on the design of the research study
- To learn the amazing results after the first year
- To assess prior knowledge and experiences related to early reading intervention

CLASSROOM DEMONSTRATION LESSON

This 30-minute demonstration shows teacher Amy Riepma teaching a *Scott Foresman Sidewalks: Early Reading Intervention* lesson with a group of her students. Use this video:

- To see what 30 minutes of instruction look like
- To get a feel for the pace and flow of a lesson
- As part of instructor training
- As a refresher for program training
- As a model for classroom management methodology
- As a model for evaluating the program and determining the most effective use in your school

Scope and Sequence

Part 1   Learning Letters and Sounds

- Learning Letter Names and Sounds
- Identifying First and Last Sounds

- Monitor Progress
  Use the Assessment Handbook to monitor children's progress.
  Use the Reteaching and Acceleration Plan as necessary.

Lesson	New Phonological Awareness Skill	New Phoneme	Review Phonological Awareness Skill
1	Identify initial sound	*m*/m/	
2		*m*/m/	
3		*m*/m/	
4		*p*/p/	
5		*p*/p/	
6		*p*/p/	
7	Identify initial sound	*f*/f/	Identify initial sound
8		*f*/f/	
9		*f*/f/	
10		*c*/k/	
11		*c*/k/	
12		*c*/k/	
13	Identify initial sound	*t*/t/	Identify initial sound
14		*t*/t/	
15		*t*/t/	
16		*s*/s/	
17		*s*/s/	
18		*s*/s/	
19	Identify initial sound	*d*/d/	Identify initial sound
20		*d*/d/	
21		*d*/d/	
22		*l*/l/	
23		*l*/l/	
24		*l*/l/	
25	Identify initial sound	*a*/a/	Identify initial sound
26		*a*/a/	
27		*a*/a/	
28		*a*/a/	
29		*a*/a/	
30		*a*/a/	
31	Identify final sound	*o*/o/	Identify initial sound
32		*o*/o/	
33	Initial and final sound discrimination	*o*/o/	
34		*o*/o/	
35		*o*/o/	
36		*o*/o/	
37	Identify final sound	*r*/r/	Identify initial sound and final sound
38		*r*/r/	
39		*r*/r/	
40		*r*/r/	
41		*r*/r/	
42		*r*/r/	

Part 2 Segmenting, Blending, and Integrating

- Segmenting and Blending Sounds in Words
- Integrating Sounds and Letters

- Monitor Progress
  Use the Assessment Handbook to monitor children's progress.
  Use the Reteaching and Acceleration Plan as necessary.

Lesson	New Phonological Awareness Skill	New Phoneme	Review Phonological Awareness Skill
43	Segmenting	*b*/b/	Identify initial and final sound
44		*b*/b/	
45		*b*/b/	
46		*b*/b/	
47		*b*/b/	
48		*b*/b/	
49	Segmenting with letter tiles:	*i*/i/	Identify initial and final sound
50	initial sound	*i*/i/	Segmenting
51		*i*/i/	
52		*i*/i/	
53		*i*/i/	
54		*i*/i/	
55	Segmenting with letter tiles:	*n*/n/	Identify initial and final sound
56	final sound	*n*/n/	Segmenting with letter tiles: initial sound
57		*n*/n/	
58		*n*/n/	
59		*n*/n/	
60		*n*/n/	
61	Segmenting with letter tiles:	*g*/g/	Identify initial and final sound
62	initial and final sound	*g*/g/	Segmenting with letter tiles: initial or final sound
63		*g*/g/	
64		*g*/g/	
65		*g*/g/	
66		*g*/g/	
67	Segmenting with letter tiles:	*u*/u/	Identify initial and final sound
68	initial, medial, and final sound	*u*/u/	
69	Combined oral segmenting	*u*/u/	
70	and blending	*u*/u/	
71		*u*/u/	
72		*u*/u/	

Part 3 Reading Words

- Segmenting and Blending Sounds in Words
- Reading Simple Words

- Monitor Progress
  Use the Assessment Handbook to monitor children's progress.
  Use the Reteaching and Acceleration Plan as necessary.

Lesson	Skill	New Phoneme	# of Words	Word Type	Continuous Sounds vs. Stop Sounds in the Words
73	Review combined oral segmenting and blending	*j*/j/	10	VC and CVC	All continuous sounds for L73–L75
74		*j*/j/			
75	Sounding out words	*j*/j/			Initial continuous sound for L76–L77
76		*w*/w/			
77		*w*/w/			A combination of the above for L78
78		*w*/w/			
79	Review combined oral segmenting and blending	*e*/e/	15	VC and CVC	Initial continuous sound
80		*e*/e/			
81	Sounding out words	*e*/e/			
82		*e*/e/			
83		*e*/e/			
84		*e*/e/			
85	Review combined oral segmenting and blending	*z*/z/	20	VC and CVC	Initial continuous sound
86		*z*/z/			
87	Sounding out words	*z*/z/			
88		*b*/h/			
89		*b*/h/			
90		*b*/h/			
91	Review combined oral segmenting and blending	*y*/y/	21	VC and CVC	Initial continuous sound or initial stop sound
92		*y*/y/			
93	Sounding out words	*y*/y/			
94		*y*/y/		Irregular	
95	Introduce one irregular word	*y*/y/			
96		*y*/y/			

Scope and Sequence

Part 4 Reading Sentences and Storybooks

- Segmenting and Blending Sounds in Words
- Reading Sentences

- Monitor Progress
  Use the Assessment Handbook to monitor children's progress.
  Use the Reteaching and Acceleration Plan as necessary.

Lesson	Skill	New Phoneme	# of Words	Word Type	Continuous Sounds vs. Stop Sounds
97	Sounding out words:	k/k/	25	VC and CVC	Initial continuous sound or initial stop sound
98	• Overtly sound out some words	k/k/	2–4 words per sentence (1 sentence at a time)		
99	• Introduce sounding out "in your head"	k/k/			
100	Read four irregular words	v/v/		Irregular	
101	Sentence reading (overt sounding out)	v/v/			
102	Storybook reading	v/v/			
103	Sounding out words:	x/ks/	30	VC and CVC	Initial continuous sound or initial stop sound
104	• Overtly sound out some words	x/ks/	3–6 words per sentence (2 sentences at a time)		
105	• Introduce "Big Kid Reading"	x/ks/			
106	Read seven irregular words	q/kw/		Irregular	
107	Sentence reading (sound out each word "in your head")	q/kw/			
108	Storybook reading	q/kw/			
109	Sounding out words:	none	37	VC and CVC	Initial continuous sound or initial stop sound
110	• Overtly sound out a few words	none	3–7 words per sentence (1–2 sentences at a time)		
111	• "Big Kid Reading"	none			
112	Read eight irregular words	none		Irregular	
113	Sentence reading ("Big Kid Reading")	none			
114	Storybook reading	none			
115	Sounding out words:	none	36	VC and CVC	Initial continuous sound or initial stop sound
116	• Overtly sound out CVCC words	none	4–6 words per sentence (2 sentences at a time)		
117	• "Big Kid Reading"	none			
118	Read eight irregular words	none		VCC and CVCC	Initial continuous sound
119	Sentence reading ("Big Kid Reading")	none			
120	Storybook reading	none		Irregular	
121	Sounding out words:	none	43	VC and CVC	Initial continuous sound or initial stop sound
122	• Overtly sound out CVCC words	none	4–8 words per sentence (3 sentences at a time)		
123	• "Big Kid Reading"	none			
124	Read eight irregular words	none		VCC and CVCC	Initial continuous sound
125	Sentence reading ("Big Kid Reading")	none			
126	Storybook reading	none		Irregular	

Contents
Part 1 Learning Letters and Sounds

- Learning Letter Names and Sounds
- Identifying First and Last Sounds

New Sound /m/
Key Phonologic Skill Isolate Initial Sound

Phonological Awareness and Alphabetic Understanding

Activity	Materials	Time
New **1. Alphabetic** Introduce *m*/m/	Alphabet Card: *m* Letter Card: *m* (one per child)	2–3 minutes
New **2. Phonologic** Does It Have the First Sound /m/?	Picture Cards: *man, fin, map, mouse, sun, mud*	6–7 minutes
New **3. Alphabetic** Reintroduce *m*/m/	Alphabet Card: *m*	2–3 minutes

Writing and Spelling

Activity	Materials	Time
New **4. Writer's Warm-Up** Introduce *m*	Tracing Card: *m* Writer's Warm-Up (one per child) Student Activity Book 1, p. 5 marker (not provided)	2–3 minutes
New **5. Integrated Phonologic/Alphabetic** Match a Picture's Initial Sound; Introduce *m*	Picture Cards: all *m* cards Letter Cards: *m*, "star," "heart"	2–3 minutes
New **6. Phonologic/Spelling** Letter Cross-Out Game: *m*	Letter Cross-Out (one per child) Student Activity Book 1, p. 6	6–8 minutes

Activity  1 Introduce Letter Name and Sound

Introduce m/m/

Objective: Children learn and trace m/m/.

Time: 2–3 minutes

	To Do	**To Say**	
Introduce letter name	Hold up the *m* Alphabet Card.	Model	**The <u>name</u> of this letter is *m*.**
		Lead	**Say the <u>name</u> of the letter with me: *m*.**
		Test	**What is the <u>name</u> of this letter?**
Introduce letter sound	Continue holding up the *m* Alphabet Card.	Model	**The <u>sound</u> for this letter is /mmm/. When you say /mmm/, your lips come together. Put your lips together and say /mmm/.**
		Lead	**Say the <u>sound</u> with me: /mmm/.**
		Test	**What is the <u>sound</u> for this letter?**
Test knowledge of letter name and sound	Continue holding up the *m* Alphabet Card.	Test	**What is the <u>name</u> of this letter? What is the <u>sound</u> for this letter?**
	Give individual turns on letter name and sound.		**Ongoing Assessment** If...children make an error, then...tell them the name or sound, have them repeat the name or sound, and return to the letter a second time.
Model tracing *m*	Distribute the *m* Letter Cards. Hold up the *m* Alphabet Card.	Model	**Everyone, watch. I'll trace the letter *m*.** Have children trace the *m* on their letter cards three times. Tell them to say /mmm/ each time they trace the letter. **Ongoing Assessment** If...children make an error, then...put your hand over their hand and guide them to trace the letter. Then have children try to trace the letter on their own. Repeat as necessary.

Phonological Awareness/Alphabetic Understanding

 2 Isolate Initial Sound

Does It Have the First Sound /m/?

Objective: Children isolate initial /m/.

Time: 6–7 minutes

	To Do		**To Say**	
Model names of pictures	Gather the picture cards. Place the *man* Picture Card on the table.	**Model**	**This is *man*. What is this?** Continue with *fin*, *map*, *mouse*, *sun*, and *mud*.	
			Test children on the picture names by placing the cards on the table one at a time and asking: **What is this?**	
Introduce the game Does It Have the First Sound /m/?	Practice production of target sound.		Tell children they will play a game. They will find the pictures with the first sound /mmm/.	
			Let's say /mmm/. Remember, when you say /mmm/, your lips come together. Put your lips together and say /mmm/.	
Model the game	Place the *man* Picture Card on the table.	**Model**	**My turn. I'll say the name of the picture and then tell whether it has the first sound /mmm/: *man*** (exaggerate the first sound). ***Man* has the first sound /mmm/. My lips are together when I say /mmm/, *man*. Next picture: *fin*** (exaggerate the first sound). ***Fin* does not have the first sound /mmm/.**	
Play the game to test knowledge of /m/	Place the *map* Picture Card on the table.	**Test**	**This is *map*. What is this? Does *map* have the first sound /mmm/?** Confirm correct responses and prompt sound production: **Yes, *map* has the first sound /mmm/.**	
			Let's say /mmm/. When you say /mmm/, your lips come together. Put your lips together and say /mmm/, *map*.	
			Test children with three other examples: *mouse*, *sun*, and *mud*.	
	Give individual turns.			

Ongoing Assessment

If...children make incorrect responses,	**then**...model the correct answer. Review the sound production cue. Have children repeat the correct answer. Go back to the example a second time.

3

Phonological Awareness/Alphabetic Understanding

Activity  Reintroduce Letter Name and Sound

Reintroduce m/m/

Objective: Children practice letter name and sound: m/m/.

Time: 2–3 minutes

	To Do	**To Say**	
Introduce letter name	Hold up the *m* Alphabet Card.	Model	The <u>name</u> of this letter is *m*.
		Lead	Say the <u>name</u> of the letter with me: *m*.
		Test	What is the <u>name</u> of this letter?
Introduce letter sound	Continue holding up the *m* Alphabet Card.	Model	The <u>sound</u> for this letter is /mmm/. When you say /mmm/, your lips come together. Put your lips together and say /mmm/.
		Lead	Say the <u>sound</u> with me: /mmm/.
		Test	What is the <u>sound</u> for this letter?
Test knowledge of initial /m/	Hold up the *m* Alphabet Card.	Test	What is the <u>name</u> of this letter? What is the <u>sound</u> for this letter?

Ongoing Assessment

If…children make incorrect responses,

then…tell them the name or sound, have them repeat the name or sound, and return to the letter a second time.

Give individual turns.

Phonological Awareness/Alphabetic Understanding

Introduce m

Objective: Children trace and write *m*.

Time: 2–3 minutes

	To Do	To Say	
Review letter name and sound	Hold up the *m* Tracing Card.	**Test**	**What is the <u>name</u> of this letter? What is the <u>sound</u> for this letter?**
Model tracing *m*	Distribute a Writer's Warm-Up to each child. Hold up the *m* Tracing Card.	**Model**	**Watch as I trace the letter *m* with my finger.**
		Lead	**Now you trace the first two *m*'s on your warm-up sheet.**
	Model tracing *m* again.	**Model**	**Watch as I trace *m* again.**
		Lead	**Now use your pencil to trace the next two *m*'s.**
Model writing *m*	Hold up the lined side of the *m* Tracing Card.	**Model**	**Watch as I write the letter *m*. I start at the dot and write the letter.**

Have children write the letter *m* two times on their warm-up sheets. Remind them to write their letters carefully.

Ongoing Assessment

If...children make an error,	then...have them write the letter again. If needed, put your hand over their hand and guide them to write the letter. Then have them write the letter on their own. Repeat as necessary.

Test knowledge of writing *m*	Model writing *m* again.	Have children cover the letters they traced and wrote. Have them write the letter *m* two times from memory. Then have them uncover their papers and compare the letters.

Do your letters look the same? Circle the letter that is your best work.

Activity **5** Connect Sound to Letter

*Match a Picture's Initial Sound;
Introduce m*

Objective: Children connect /m/ to *m*.

Time: 2–3 minutes

	To Do	**To Say**	
Introduce the activity	Gather the *m* Picture Cards and the *m*, "star," and "heart" Letter Cards.	Tell children that they are going to choose the letter that matches the first sound of some pictures.	
Model the activity	Place the *mop* Picture Card on the table.	**Model**	**My turn. This is *mop*. The first sound in *mop* is /mmm/.** Place the *m* and "heart" Letter Cards under the picture.
			I'm going to choose the letter that matches this picture's first sound. Point to the correct letter: ***m* is the letter for /mmm/ like the /mmm/ in *mop*.**
Test knowledge of initial sound	Place the *man* Picture Card on the table.	**Test**	**This is *man*. What is this? The first sound in *man* is /mmm/. What is the first sound in *man*? That's right, /mmm/ is the first sound in *man*.** Place two letter cards under the picture. Vary the choice and order.
			Your turn. Choose the letter that matches this picture's first sound. Everyone, think of which letter has the same sound as the /mmm/ in *man*. Does everyone know?
			Call on a child to point to the correct letter. **What's the <u>name</u> of the letter you pointed to? What's the <u>sound</u> for that letter? That's right; *m* is the letter for /mmm/ like the /mmm/ in *man*.** Reinforce the letter name and sound with the group: **Everyone, what's the <u>name</u> of this letter? What's the <u>sound</u> for this letter?** Continue with the remaining cards.

Ongoing Assessment

If . . . children make an error,

then . . . model the answer, have them repeat it, and return to the picture card a second time.

Activity 6 Connect Sound to Letter

New

Letter Cross-Out Game: m

Objective: Children connect /m/ to m.

Time: 6–8 minutes

	To Do	**To Say**
Introduce the Letter Cross-Out Game	Distribute a Letter Cross-Out to each child.	Tell children that they are going to cross out letters that go with sounds. **Let's see if we can cross out all of the letters on the sheet!**
Model the game	Hold up a Letter Cross-Out sheet.	**Model** **My turn. The first sound is /mmm/. I'm going to cross out a letter for the sound /mmm/.** Cross out one of the *m*'s on your cross-out sheet. **Now you cross out a letter for the sound /mmm/. That's right, *m* is the letter for the sound /mmm/.**
Play the game to test knowledge of /m/		**Test** **The next sound is /mmm/. Everyone, what is the next sound? Cross out the letter for the sound /mmm/.** Reinforce the group on the letter name and sound: **Everyone, what's the <u>name</u> of the letter you crossed out? What's the <u>sound</u> for the letter?** Continue until all of the *m*'s have been crossed out.

Ongoing Assessment

If...children make an error,

then...point to the correct letter and model its sound. Have children repeat the sound and cross out the correct letter.

LESSON 2

New Sound /m/
Key Phonologic Skill Isolate Initial Sound

Phonological Awareness and Alphabetic Understanding

Activity	Materials	Time
1. Alphabetic Introduce *m*/m/	Alphabet Card: *m* Letter Card: *m* (one per child)	2–3 minutes
2. Phonologic Which Picture Has the First Sound /m/?	Picture Choices: 2-1, 2-2, 2-3 Teacher Resource Package 1	6–7 minutes
3. Alphabetic Reintroduce *m*/m/; Discriminate *m*	Alphabet Card: *m* Discrimination Teacher Resource Package 1	2–3 minutes

Writing and Spelling

Activity	Materials	Time
4. Writer's Warm-Up Introduce *m*	Tracing Card: *m* Writer's Warm-Up (one per child) Student Activity Book 1, p. 7 marker (not provided)	2–3 minutes
5. Integrated Phonologic/Alphabetic Match a Picture's Initial Sound; Introduce *m*	Picture Cards: all *m* cards Letter Cards: *m*, "star," "heart"	2–3 minutes
6. Phonologic/Spelling Letter Cross-Out Game: *m*	Letter Cross-Out (one per child) Student Activity Book 1, p. 8	6–8 minutes

Activity 1 — Introduce Letter Name and Sound

Introduce m/m/

Objective: Children learn and trace m/m/.

Time: 2–3 minutes

	To Do	**To Say**	
Introduce letter name	Hold up the *m* Alphabet Card.	Model	The <u>name</u> of this letter is *m*.
		Lead	Say the <u>name</u> of this letter with me: *m*.
		Test	What is the <u>name</u> of this letter?
Introduce letter sound	Continue holding up the *m* Alphabet Card.	Model	The <u>sound</u> for this letter is /mmm/. When you say /mmm/, your lips come together. Put your lips together and say /mmm/.
		Lead	Say the <u>sound</u> with me: /mmm/.
		Test	What is the <u>sound</u> for this letter?
Test knowledge of letter name and sound	Continue holding up the *m* Alphabet Card.	Test	What is the <u>name</u> of this letter? What is the <u>sound</u> for this letter?

Ongoing Assessment

If...children make an error,	then...tell them the name or sound, have them repeat the name or sound, and return to the letter a second time.

Give individual turns on letter name and sound.

Model tracing *m*	Distribute an *m* Letter Card to each child. Hold up the *m* Alphabet Card.	Model	Watch. I'll trace the letter *m*.

Have children trace the *m* on their letter cards three times. Tell them to say /mmm/ each time they trace the letter.

Ongoing Assessment

If...children make an error,	then...put your hand over their hand and guide them to trace the letter. Then have children try to trace the letter on their own. Repeat as necessary.

Activity 2 Isolate Initial Sound

Which Picture Has the First Sound /m/?

Objective: Children isolate initial /m/.

Time: 6–7 minutes

	To Do		**To Say**
Model names of pictures	Gather the picture choices. Display Picture Choice 2-1. Point to *map*.	Model	**This is *map*. What is this?** Continue with the remaining pictures: *cone, fish; fin, sandwich, moon.* Then test children on the picture names by pointing to the pictures one at a time and asking: **What is this?**
Introduce the game Which Picture Has the First Sound /m/?	Practice production of target sound.		Tell children they will play a game. You will show them three pictures. They will find the picture with the first sound /mmm/. **Let's say /mmm/. When you say /mmm/, your lips come together. Put your lips together and say /mmm/.**
Model the game	Display Picture Choice 2-1. Cover the bottom row.	Model	**My turn. I'll show you how to play the game. This is *map, cone, fish*. I'll find the picture with the first sound /mmm/: *map*** (exaggerate the initial sound). ***Map* has the first sound /mmm/.** Model another example using *fin, sandwich, moon*.
Play the game to test knowledge of /m/	Display Picture Choice 2-2. Cover the bottom row.	Test	Have children name each picture: *saw, cat, mitt*. **Which picture has the first sound /mmm/?** Confirm correct responses and prompt sound production: **Yes, *mitt* has the first sound /mmm/. Let's say /mmm/. Remember, when you say /mmm/, your lips come together. Put your lips together and say /mmm/, *mitt*.** Continue with the bottom row of pictures (*cut, mop, fan*) and Picture Choice 2-3 (*sun, maze, coat; man, fox, sit*).
	Give individual turns.		

Ongoing Assessment

If...children make incorrect responses,	**then**...model the correct answer. Review the sound production cue. Have children repeat the correct answer. Go back to the example a second time.

  **Reintroduce Letter Name and Sound**

New

Reintroduce m/m/;
Discriminate m
Objective: Children practice letter name and sound: *m/m/*.   Time: 2–3 minutes

	To Do	**To Say**	
Introduce letter name	Hold up the *m* Alphabet Card.	Model	The <u>name</u> of this letter is *m*.
		Lead	Say the <u>name</u> of the letter with me: *m*.
		Test	What is the <u>name</u> of this letter?
Introduce letter sound	Continue holding up the *m* Alphabet Card.	Model	The <u>sound</u> for this letter is /mmm/. When you say /mmm/, your lips come together. Put your lips together and say /mmm/.
		Lead	Say the <u>sound</u> with me: /mmm/.
		Test	What is the <u>sound</u> for this letter?
Test knowledge of letter name and sound	Hold up the *m* Alphabet Card.	Test	What is the <u>name</u> of this letter? What is the <u>sound</u> for this letter?
	Give individual turns.		**Ongoing Assessment** If…children make an error, then…tell them the name or sound, have them repeat the name or sound, and return to the letter a second time.
Discriminate *m*	Hold up the *m* Discrimination sheet. Point to the first letter or symbol.	Test	What is the <u>name</u> of this? If it is a letter, also ask for the sound: What is the <u>sound</u> for this letter? Continue with the remaining letters and symbols. **Ongoing Assessment** If…children make an error, then…tell them the name or sound and have them repeat it. Return to the beginning of the row for that letter or symbol. If children make no errors on the row, move on to the next row.

Activity 4 Writer's Warm-Up

Introduce m

Objective: Children trace and write *m*.

Time: 2–3 minutes

	To Do	To Say	
Review letter name and sound	Hold up the *m* Tracing Card.	Test	**What is the <u>name</u> of this letter? What is the <u>sound</u> for this letter?**
Model tracing *m*	Distribute a Writer's Warm-Up to each child. Hold up the *m* Tracing Card. Model tracing *m* again.	Model Lead Model Lead	**Watch as I trace the letter *m* with my finger.** **Now trace the first two *m*'s on your warm-up sheet.** **Watch as I trace the letter *m* again.** **Now use your pencil to trace the next two *m*'s.**
Model writing *m*	Hold up the lined side of the *m* Tracing Card.	Model	**Watch as I write the letter *m*. I start at the dot and write the letter.** Have children write the letter *m* two times on their warm-up sheets. Remind them to write their letters carefully.

Ongoing Assessment

If... children make an error,	then... have them write the letter again. If needed, put your hand over their hand and guide them to write the letter. Then have them write the letter on their own. Repeat as necessary.

Test knowledge of writing *m*	Model writing *m* again.	Have children cover the letters they traced and wrote. Have them write *m* two times from memory. Then have them uncover their papers and compare the letters. **Do your letters look the same? Circle your best *m*.**

Match a Picture's Initial Sound;
Introduce m

Objective: Children connect /m/ to *m*.

Time: 2–3 minutes

	To Do	**To Say**
Introduce the activity	Gather the *m* Picture Cards and the *m*, "star," and "heart" Letter Cards.	Tell children that they are going to choose the letter that goes with the first sound of some pictures.
Model the activity	Place the *moon* Picture Card on the table.	**Model** **This is *moon*. The first sound in *moon* is /mmm/.** Place the *m* and "heart" Letter Cards under the picture. **I'm going to choose the letter that matches this picture's first sound.** Point to the correct letter: ***m* is the letter for /mmm/ like the /mmm/ in *moon*.**
Test knowledge of initial sound	Place the *map* Picture Card on the table.	**Test** **This is *map*. What is this? The first sound in *map* is /mmm/. What is the first sound in *map*? That's right, /mmm/ is the first sound in *map*.** Place two letter cards under the picture. Vary the choice and order. **Your turn. Choose the letter that matches this picture's first sound. Everyone, think of which letter has the same sound as the /mmm/ in *map*. Does everyone know?** Call on a child to point to the correct letter. **What's the <u>name</u> of the letter you pointed to? What's the <u>sound</u> for the letter? That's right; *m* is the letter for the sound /mmm/ like the /mmm/ in *map*.** Reinforce the letter name and sound with the group: **Everyone, what's the <u>name</u> of the letter? What's the <u>sound</u> for the letter?** Continue with the remaining cards.

Ongoing Assessment

If...children make an error,	then...model the answer, have them repeat it, and return to the picture card a second time.

Letter Cross-Out Game: m

Objective: Children connect /m/ to *m*.

Time: 6–8 minutes

	To Do	To Say
Introduce the game Letter Cross-Out	Distribute a Letter Cross-Out to each child.	Tell children that they are going to cross out letters that go with sounds. **Let's see if we can cross out all of the letters on the sheet!**
Model the game	Hold up a Letter Cross-Out.	Model **My turn. The first sound is /mmm/. I'm going to cross out a letter for the sound /mmm/.** Cross out one of the *m*'s on your cross-out sheet. **Now you cross out a letter for the sound /mmm/. That's right; *m* is the letter for /mmm/.**
Play the game to test knowledge of /m/		Test **The next sound is /mmm/. Everyone, what's the next sound? Now cross out the letter for the sound /mmm/.** Reinforce the group on the letter name and sound: **Everyone, what's the <u>name</u> of the letter you crossed out? What's the <u>sound</u> for the letter?** Continue until all of the *m*'s are crossed out.

Ongoing Assessment

If... children make an error,	**then...** point to the correct letter and model its sound. Have children repeat the sound and cross out the correct letter.

15

Writing/Spelling

New Sound /m/
Key Phonologic Skill Isolate Initial Sound

Phonological Awareness and Alphabetic Understanding

Activity	Materials	Time
1. Alphabetic Introduce *m*/m/	Alphabet Card: *m* Letter Card: *m* (one per child)	2–3 minutes
2. Integrated Phonologic/Alphabetic Which Picture Has the First Sound /m/?	Alphabet Card: *m* Picture Choices: 3-1, 3-2, 3-3 Teacher Resource Package 1	6–7 minutes
3. Alphabetic Reintroduce *m*/m/; Discriminate *m*	Alphabet Card: *m* Discrimination Teacher Resource Package 1	2–3 minutes

Writing and Spelling

Activity	Materials	Time
4. Writer's Warm-Up Introduce *m*	Tracing Card: *m* Writer's Warm-Up: (one per child) Student Activity Book 1, p. 9	2–3 minutes
5. Integrated Phonologic/Alphabetic Match a Picture's Initial Sound; Introduce *m*	Picture Cards: all *m* cards Letter Cards: *m*, "star," "heart"	2–3 minutes
New **6. Phonologic/Spelling** First Sounds: *m*	First Sounds (one per child) Student Activity Book 1, p. 10	6–8 minutes

Activity 1 · Introduce Letter Name and Sound

Introduce m/m/
Objective: Children learn and trace m/m/.

Time: 2–3 minutes

	To Do	**To Say**	
Introduce letter name	Hold up the *m* Alphabet Card.	Model	The <u>name</u> of this letter is *m*.
		Lead	Say the <u>name</u> of the letter with me: *m*.
		Test	What is the <u>name</u> of this letter?
Introduce letter sound	Continue holding up the *m* Alphabet Card.	Model	The <u>sound</u> for this letter is /mmm/. When you say /mmm/, your lips come together. Put your lips together and say /mmm/.
		Lead	Say the <u>sound</u> with me: /mmm/.
		Test	What is the <u>sound</u> for this letter?
Test knowledge of letter name and sound	Continue holding up the *m* Alphabet Card.

Give individual turns on letter name and sound. | Test | What is the <u>name</u> of this letter? What is the <u>sound</u> for this letter? |

Ongoing Assessment
If...children make incorrect responses, then...tell them the name or sound, have them repeat the name or sound, and return to the letter a second time.

| **Model tracing *m*** | Distribute an *m* Letter Card to each child. Hold up the *m* Alphabet Card. | Model | Everyone, watch as I trace the letter *m*.

Have children trace the *m* on their letter cards three times. Tell them to say /mmm/ each time they trace the letter. |

Ongoing Assessment
If...children make an error, then...put your hand over their hand and guide them to trace the letter. Then have the children try to trace the letter on their own. Repeat as necessary.

Activity 2 Isolate Initial Sound

Which Picture Has the First Sound /m/?

Objective: Children isolate /m/ and connect to letter.   Time: 6–7 minutes

	To Do	**To Say**	
Model names of pictures	Gather the picture choices. Display Picture Choice 3-1. Point to *mop*.	Model	**This is *mop*. What is this?** Continue with the remaining pictures: *cat, fire; foot, mow, cup.* Then test children on the picture names by pointing to the pictures one at a time and asking: **What is this?**
Introduce the game Which Picture Has the First Sound /m/?	Hold up the *m* Alphabet Card.		**We're going to play a game. I'll show you a letter and three pictures. You'll find the picture that has the first sound of the letter.** **The <u>name</u> of this letter is *m*. The <u>sound</u> for this letter is /mmm/. Remember, when you say /mmm/, your lips come together. Put your lips together and say /mmm/.**
		Test	**What is the <u>sound</u> for this letter?**
Model the game	Display Picture Choice 3-1. Cover the bottom row.	Model	**My turn. I'll show you how to play the game. This is *mop, cat, fire*. I'll find the picture with the first sound /mmm/.** Point to the *m* Alphabet Card. ***Mop* has the first sound /mmm/.** Exaggerate the first sound and say the word: **/mmm/, *mop*.** Model another example using *foot, mow, cup.*
Play the game to test knowledge of /m/	Hold up the *m* Alphabet Card. Display Picture Choice 3-2. Cover the bottom row. (The pictures are: *paw, cap, mouse; maze, pool, food.*)	Test	**What is the <u>sound</u> for this letter?** Have children name each picture. **Which picture has the first sound /mmm/?** Confirm correct responses and prompt sound production: **Yes, *mouse* has the first sound /mmm/. Let's say /mmm/. Remember, when you say /mmm/, your lips come together. Put your lips together and say /mmm/, *mouse*.** Continue with the bottom row of pictures and Picture Choice 3-3 (*pig, man, fan; can, pie, mitt*).
	Give individual turns.		

Ongoing Assessment

If... children make incorrect responses,	**then...** model the correct answer. Review the sound production cue. Have children repeat the correct answer. Go back to the example a second time.

Phonological Awareness/Alphabetic Understanding

Activity 3 Reintroduce Letter Name and Sound

Reintroduce m/m/; Discriminate m

Objective: Children practice letter name and sound: *m/m/*.   Time: 2–3 minutes

	To Do	**To Say**	
Introduce letter name	Hold up the *m* Alphabet Card.	Model	The <u>name</u> of this letter is **m**.
		Lead	Say the <u>name</u> of the letter with me: **m**.
		Test	What is the <u>name</u> of this letter?
Introduce letter sound	Continue holding up the *m* Alphabet Card.	Model	The <u>sound</u> for this letter is /mmm/. When you say /mmm/, your lips come together. Put your lips together and say /mmm/.
		Lead	Say the <u>sound</u> with me: /mmm/.
		Test	What is the <u>sound</u> for this letter?
Test knowledge of letter name and sound	Continue holding up the *m* Alphabet Card. Give individual turns on letter name and sound.	Test	What is the <u>name</u> of this letter? What is the <u>sound</u> for this letter?

Ongoing Assessment

If...children make incorrect responses, **then**...tell them the name or sound, have them repeat the name or sound, and return to the letter a second time.

Discriminate *m*	Hold up the Discrimination sheet. Point to the first letter or symbol.	Test	What is the <u>name</u> of this? If it is a letter, also ask for the sound: **What is the <u>sound</u> for this letter?** Continue with the remaining letters and symbols.

Ongoing Assessment

If...children make an error, **then**...tell them the name or sound and have them repeat it. Return to the beginning of the row for that letter or symbol. If children make no errors on the row, move on to the next row.

Phonological Awareness/Alphabetic Understanding

Activity 4 Writer's Warm-Up

Introduce m

Objective: Children trace and write m.

Time: 2–3 minutes

	To Do	To Say	
Review letter name and sound	Hold up the *m* Tracing Card.	**Test**	**What is the <u>name</u> of this letter? What is the <u>sound</u> for this letter?**
Model tracing m	Distribute a Writer's Warm-Up to each child. Hold up the *m* Tracing Card.	**Model**	**Everyone, watch as I trace the letter m with my finger.**
		Lead	**Now you trace the first two m's on your warm-up sheet.**
	Model tracing *m* again.	**Model**	**Everyone, watch as I trace the letter m again.**
		Lead	**Now use your pencil to trace the next two m's.**
Model writing m	Hold up the lined side of the *m* Tracing Card.	**Model**	**Everyone, watch as I write the letter m. I start at the dot and write the letter.**
			Have children write *m* two times on their warm-up sheets. Remind them to write their letters carefully.

Ongoing Assessment

If...children make an error,	**then**...have them write the letter again. If needed, put your hand over their hand and guide them to write the letter. Then have them write the letter on their own. Repeat as necessary.

Test knowledge of writing m	Model writing *m* again.	Have children cover the letters they traced and wrote. Have them write the letter *m* two times from memory. Then have them uncover their papers and compare the letters.
		Do your letters look the same? Circle your best m.

Activity 5

Match a Picture's Initial Sound;
Introduce m

Objective: Children connect /m/ to *m*.

Time: 2–3 minutes

	To Do		**To Say**
Introduce the activity	Gather the *m* Picture Cards and the *m*, "star," and "heart" Letter Cards.		Tell children that they are going to choose the letter that matches the first sound of some pictures.
Model the activity	Place the *moon* Picture Card on the table.	Model	**This is *moon*. The first sound in *moon* is /mmm/.** Place the *m* and "star" Letter Cards under the picture. **I'm going to choose the letter that matches this picture's first sound.** Point to the correct letter: ***m* is the letter for /mmm/ like the /mmm/ in *moon*.**
Test knowledge of initial sound	Place the *monkey* Picture Card on the table.	Test	**This is *monkey*. What is this? The first sound in *monkey* is /mmm/. What is the first sound in *monkey*? That's right, /mmm/ is the first sound in *monkey*.** Place two letter cards under the picture. Vary the choice and order. **Your turn. Choose the letter that matches this picture's first sound. Everyone, think of which letter has the same sound as the /mmm/ in *monkey*. Does everyone know?** Call on a child to point to the correct letter. **What's the <u>name</u> of the letter you pointed to? What's the <u>sound</u> for the letter? That's right, *m* is the letter for /mmm/ like the /mmm/ in *monkey*.** Reinforce the letter name and sound with the group: **Everyone, what's the <u>name</u> of the letter? What's the <u>sound</u> for the letter?** Test children on the remaining cards.

Ongoing Assessment

If . . . children make an error,	then . . . model the answer, have them repeat it, and return to the picture card a second time.

22

Writing/Spelling

Activity 6 Connect Sound to Letter

First Sounds: m

Objective: Children connect /m/ to *m*.

Time: 6–8 minutes

	To Do	**To Say**	
Introduce the activity	Distribute a First Sounds page to each child.		Tell children that they are going to write the letter that goes with the first sound of some pictures.
Model the activity	Hold up a First Sounds page. Point to the first picture.	Model	Everyone, this is *mitt*. The first sound in *mitt* is /mmm/. I'm going to write the letter for the sound /mmm/ like the /mmm/ in *mitt*. Write the letter *m* under the picture.
		Lead	Now you write the letter for the sound /mmm/ like the /mmm/ in *mitt*. Start at the dot and write the letter. That's right, *m* is the letter for the sound /mmm/.
Test knowledge of /m/	Point to the next picture on the First Sounds page.	Test	Everyone, this is *man*. What is this? The first sound in *man* is /mmm/. What is the first sound in *man*? That's right, /mmm/ is the first sound in *man*.
			Your turn. Write the letter that matches this picture's first sound. Everyone, write the letter for the same sound as the /mmm/ in *man*. Start at the dot and write the letter. Reinforce the group on the letter name and sound: Everyone, what's the <u>name</u> of the letter you wrote? What's the <u>sound</u> for the letter? Continue with the remaining pictures.

Ongoing Assessment

If...children make an error,	**then**...model the letter name and sound and have children repeat them. Have children write the correct letter.

LESSON 4

New Sound /p/
Review Sound /m/
Key Phonologic Skill Isolate Initial Sound

Phonological Awareness and Alphabetic Understanding

Activity	Materials		Time
New **1. Alphabetic** Introduce *p/p/*	Alphabet Card: *p*	Letter Card: *p* (one per child)	1–2 minutes
2. Phonologic Does It Have the First Sound /p/?	Picture Cards: *pin, man, pail, pig, five, pan*		4–5 minutes
New **3. Integrated Phonologic/Alphabetic** Picture Scene Search: /m/	Alphabet Card: *m* Picture Scene /m/ Teacher Resource Package 1		4–5 minutes
4. Alphabetic Reintroduce *p/p/*; Discriminate *p*	Alphabet Card: *p* Discrimination Teacher Resource Package 1		2–3 minutes

Writing and Spelling

Activity	Materials	Time
5. Writer's Warm-Up Introduce *p*	Writer's Warm-Up (one per child) Student Activity Book 1, p. 11 Tracing Cards: *p, m*	2–3 minutes
6. Integrated Phonologic/Alphabetic Match a Picture's Initial Sound; Introduce *p*	Picture Cards: all *p* cards Letter Cards: *p, m*	2–3 minutes
7. Phonologic/Spelling First Sounds: *p*	First Sounds (one per child) Student Activity Book 1, p. 12	6–8 minutes

25

Lesson 4 Overview

Activity **1** Introduce Letter Name and Sound

New

Introduce p/p/
Objective: Children learn and trace p/p/.

Time: 1–2 minutes

	To Do	**To Say**	
Introduce letter name	Hold up the *p* Alphabet Card.	Model	The <u>name</u> of this letter is *p*.
		Lead	Say the <u>name</u> of the letter with me: *p*.
		Test	What is the <u>name</u> of this letter?
Introduce letter sound	Continue holding up the *p* Alphabet Card.	Model	The <u>sound</u> for this letter is /p/. When you say /p/, your lips start out together. Then they open and a puff of air comes out of your mouth. Put your lips together and say /p/. Feel the puff of air that comes out of your mouth.
		Lead	Say the <u>sound</u> with me: /p/.
		Test	What is the <u>sound</u> for this letter?
Test knowledge of letter name and sound	Continue holding up the *p* Alphabet Card. Give individual turns on letter name and sound.	Test	What is the <u>name</u> of this letter? What is the <u>sound</u> for this letter?

Ongoing Assessment

If...children make an error,   then...tell them the name or sound, have them repeat the name or sound, and return to the letter a second time.

Model tracing *p*	Distribute the *p* Letter Cards. Hold up the *p* Alphabet Card.	Model	Watch. I'll trace the letter **p**.

Have children trace the *p* on their letter cards three times. Tell them to say /p/ each time they trace the letter.

Ongoing Assessment

If...children make an error,   then...put your hand over their hand and guide them to trace the letter. Then have children try to trace the letter on their own. Repeat as necessary.

Activity 2 Isolate Initial Sound

Does It Have the First Sound /p/?

Objective: Children isolate initial /p/.

Time: 4–5 minutes

	To Do	**To Say**	
Model names of pictures	Gather the picture cards. Place the *pin* Picture Card on the table.	Model	**This is *pin*. What is this?** Continue with *man, pail, pig, five,* and *pan*. Test children on the picture names by placing the cards on the table one at a time and asking: **What is this?**
Introduce the game Does It Have the First Sound /p/?	Practice production of target sound.		Tell children they will play a game. They will find the pictures with the first sound /p/. **Let's say /p/. When you say /p/, your lips start out together. Then they open and a puff of air comes out of your mouth. Put your lips together and say /p/. Feel the puff of air that comes out of your mouth.**
Model the game	Place the *pin* Picture Card on the table.	Model	**My turn. I'll say the name of the picture and then tell whether the first sound is /p/: *pin*** (exaggerate the first sound). ***Pin* has the first sound /p/. A puff of air comes out of my mouth when I say /p/, *pin*. Next picture: *man*** (exaggerate the first sound). ***Man* does not have the first sound /p/.**
Play the game to test knowledge of initial /p/	Place the *pail* Picture Card on the table.	Test	**Your turn. This is *pail*. What is this? Is the first sound in *pail* /p/?** Confirm correct responses and prompt sound production: **Yes, the first sound in *pail* is /p/.** **Let's say /p/. Remember, when you say /p/, your lips start out together. Then they open and a puff of air comes out of your mouth. Put your lips together and say /p/. Feel the puff of air that comes out of your mouth.** Continue with *pig, five,* and *pan*.
	Give individual turns.		**Ongoing Assessment** If...children make incorrect responses, then...model the correct answer. Review the sound production cue. Have children repeat the correct answer. Go back to the example a second time.

Phonological Awareness/Alphabetic Understanding

Activity  Isolate Initial Sound

Picture Scene Search: /m/

Objective: Children isolate initial /m/.

Time: 4–5 minutes

	To Do	**To Say**	
Introduce the game	Hold up the picture scene.		Today we have a new game. I'm going to show you a picture. You're going to find things in the picture that have the first sound /mmm/.
Test knowledge of /m/	Hold up the *m* Alphabet Card.	**Test**	The <u>name</u> of this letter is *m*. What is the <u>sound</u> for this letter? Confirm correct responses: **Yes, /mmm/. When you say /mmm/, your lips come together. Put your lips together and say /mmm/.**

> ### Ongoing Assessment
>
> **If...** children make incorrect responses,   **then...** model the correct sound and have children repeat it. Review the sound production cue. Repeat the test.

	To Do	**To Say**	
Model and play the game	Hold up the picture scene.	**Model**	**My turn. I'll find something in the picture with the first sound /mmm/.** Point to and name something with the first sound /mmm/: **mountain has the first sound /mmm/.**
	Give individual turns.	**Lead**	**Your turn. Find something with the first sound /mmm/.** Confirm correct responses and have the group repeat it: **Yes, the first sound in moon is /mmm/. Everyone say /mmm/, moon.**
			Target words: *mountain, moon, merry-go-round, monkey, mustache, mouse, money, mustard, muffin, mop, man, milk.*

Phonological Awareness/Alphabetic Understanding

Activity 4 Reintroduce Letter Name and Sound

Reintroduce p/p/; Discriminate p

Objective: Children practice letter name and sound: p/p/.

Time: 2–3 minutes

	To Do	To Say	
Introduce letter name	Hold up the *p* Alphabet Card.	Model	The <u>name</u> of this letter is **p.**
		Lead	Say the <u>name</u> of the letter with me: **p.**
		Test	What is the <u>name</u> of this letter?
Introduce letter sound	Continue holding up the *p* Alphabet Card.	Model	The <u>sound</u> for this letter is /p/. When you say /p/, your lips start out together. Then they open and a puff of air comes out of your mouth. Put your lips together and say /p/. Feel the puff of air that comes out of your mouth.
		Lead	Say the <u>sound</u> with me: /p/.
		Test	What is the <u>sound</u> for this letter?
Test knowledge of letter name and sound	Hold up the *p* Alphabet Card.	Test	What is the <u>name</u> of this letter? What is the <u>sound</u> for this letter?
	Give individual turns.	**Ongoing Assessment** **If...**children make incorrect responses,	**then...**tell them the name or sound, have them repeat the name or sound, and return to the letter a second time.
Discriminate p	Hold up the Discrimination sheet. Point to the first letter or symbol.	Test	**What is the <u>name</u> of this?** If it is a letter, also ask for the sound: **What is the <u>sound</u> for this letter?** Continue with the remaining letters and symbols.
		Ongoing Assessment **If...**children make incorrect responses,	**then...**tell them the name or sound and have them repeat it. Return to the beginning of the row for that letter or symbol. If children make no errors on the row, move on to the next row.

Activity 5 Writer's Warm-Up

Introduce p

Objective: Children trace and write *p* and review writing *m*.   Time: 2–3 minutes

	To Do	**To Say**	
Review letter name and sound	Hold up the *p* Tracing Card.	Test	**What is the <u>name</u> of this letter? What is the <u>sound</u> for this letter?**
Model tracing *p*	Distribute a Writer's Warm-Up to each child. Hold up the *p* Tracing Card.	Model	**Watch as I trace the letter *p* with my finger.**
		Lead	**Now you trace the first two *p*'s on your warm-up sheet with your finger.**
	Model tracing *p* again.	Model	**Everyone, watch as I trace *p* again.**
		Lead	**Now use your pencil to trace the next two *p*'s.**
Model writing *p*	Hold up the lined side of the *p* Tracing Card.	Model	**Watch as I write the letter *p*. I start at the dot and write the letter.**
		Lead	**Now you write two *p*'s. Start at the dot as I did. Write carefully.**

Ongoing Assessment

If...children make an error,   **then**...have them write the letter again. If needed, put your hand over their hand and guide them to write the letter. Then have them write the letter on their own. Repeat as necessary.

Test knowledge of writing *p*	Model writing *p* again.	Have children cover the letters they traced and wrote. Have them write *p* two times from memory. Then have them uncover their papers and compare the letters. **Do your letters look the same? Circle your best letter.**
Review writing *m*		Have children trace and write *m* on their warm-up sheets.

Ongoing Assessment

If...children make an error,   **then**...model tracing the letter on the tracing card and then have them write the letter again. If needed, put your hand over their hand and guide them to write the letter. Then have them write the letter on their own. Repeat as necessary.

 **Connect Sound to Letter**

*Match a Picture's Initial Sound;
Introduce p*

Objective: Children connect /p/ to p.

Time: 2–3 minutes

	To Do	**To Say**	
Introduce the activity	Gather the *p* Picture Cards and the *p* and *m* Letter Cards.	**You're going to choose the letter that goes with the first sound of some pictures.**	
Model the activity	Place the *pig* Picture Card on the table.	**Model**	**This is pig. The first sound in pig is /p/.** Place the *p* and *m* Letter Cards under the picture. **I'm going to choose the letter that matches this picture's first sound.** Point to the correct letter: **p is the letter for /p/ like the /p/ in pig.**
Test knowledge of initial sound	Place the *pan* Picture Card on the table.	**Test**	**This is pan. What is this? The first sound in pan is /p/. What is the first sound in pan? That's right, /p/ is the first sound in pan.** Place the *p* and *m* Letter Cards under the picture. **Your turn. Choose the letter that matches this picture's first sound. Think. Which letter is the letter for the sound /p/ in pan? Do you think you know?** Call on a child to point to the correct letter. **What's the <u>name</u> of the letter you pointed to? What's the <u>sound</u> for that letter? That's right; p is the letter for the sound /p/ like the /p/ in pan.** Reinforce the letter name and sound with the group: **Everyone, what's the <u>name</u> of the letter? What's the <u>sound</u> for the letter?** Continue with the remaining cards.

Ongoing Assessment

If...children make an error,	then...model the answer, have them repeat it, and return to the picture card a second time.

Activity 7 Connect Sound to Letter

First Sounds: p

Objective: Children isolate initial sound and write the corresponding letter.

Time: 6–8 minutes

	To Do	**To Say**	
Introduce the activity	Distribute a First Sounds page to each child.	Tell children they are going to write the letter that goes with the first sound of some pictures.	
Model the activity	Hold up a First Sounds page. Point to the first picture.	**Model**	**This is *pig*. The first sound in *pig* is /p/. I'm going to write the letter for /p/ like the /p/ in *pig*.** Write a *p* under the picture.
		Lead	**Now you write the letter for /p/ like the /p/ in *pig*. Start at the dot and write the letter. That's right, *p* is the letter for /p/.**
Test knowledge of /p/	Point to the next picture on the First Sounds page.	**Test**	**This is *pie*. What is this? The first sound in *pie* is /p/. What is the first sound in *pie*? That's right, /p/ is the first sound in *pie*.**
			Your turn. Write the letter for this picture's first sound. Everyone, write the letter for the same sound as the /p/ in *pie*. Start at the dot and write the letter. Reinforce the group on the letter name and sound: **Everyone, what's the <u>name</u> of the letter you wrote? What's the <u>sound</u> for the letter?** Continue with the remaining pictures: *pen, paw, pan*.

Ongoing Assessment

If...children make an error,	then...model the letter name and sound and have children repeat them. Have children write the correct letter.

New Sound /p/
Review Sound /m/
Key Phonologic Skill Isolate Initial Sound

Phonological Awareness and Alphabetic Understanding

Activity	Materials	Time
1. Alphabetic Introduce *p*/p/	Alphabet Card: *p* Letter Card: *p* (one per child)	1–2 minutes
2. Phonologic Does It Have the First Sound /p/?	Picture Choices: 5-1, 5-2, 5-3 Teacher Resource Package 1	4–5 minutes
New **3. Phonologic** First Sound Song with /m/	Picture Cards: *monkey, mountain, mop*	4–5 minutes
4. Alphabetic Reintroduce *p*/p/; Discriminate *m* and *p*	Alphabet Card: *p* Discrimination Teacher Resource Package 1	2–3 minutes

Writing and Spelling

Activity	Materials	Time
5. Writer's Warm-Up Introduce *p*	Writer's Warm-Up (one per child) Student Activity Book 1, p. 13 Tracing Cards: *p, m*	2–3 minutes
6. Integrated Phonologic/Alphabetic Match a Picture's Initial Sound; Introduce *p*	Picture Cards: all *p* cards Letter Cards: *p, m*	2–3 minutes
7. Phonologic/Spelling Letter Cross-Out Game: *p, m*	Letter Cross-Out (one per child) Student Activity Book 1, p. 14	6–8 minutes

Activity 1 — Introduce Letter Name and Sound

Introduce p/p/

Objective: Children learn and trace p/p/.

Time: 1–2 minutes

	To Do	**To Say**	
Introduce letter name	Hold up the *p* Alphabet Card.	Model	The <u>name</u> of this letter is *p*.
		Lead	Say the <u>name</u> of the letter with me: *p*.
		Test	What is the <u>name</u> of this letter?
Introduce letter sound	Continue holding up the *p* Alphabet Card.	Model	The <u>sound</u> for this letter is /p/. When you say /p/, your lips start out together. Then they open and a puff of air comes out of your mouth. Put your lips together and say /p/. Feel the puff of air that comes out of your mouth.
		Lead	Say the <u>sound</u> with me: /p/.
		Test	What is the <u>sound</u> for this letter?
Test knowledge of letter name and sound	Continue holding up the *p* Alphabet Card.	Test	What is the <u>name</u> of this letter? What is the <u>sound</u> for this letter?

Ongoing Assessment

If...children make an error,	**then**...tell them the name or sound, have them repeat the name or sound, and return to the letter a second time.

Test knowledge of letter name and sound (cont.)	Give individual turns on letter name and sound.		
Model tracing *p*	Distribute the *p* Letter Cards. Hold up the *p* Alphabet Card.	Model	Watch. I'll trace the letter *p*.
			Have children trace the *p* on their letter cards three times. Tell them to say /p/ each time they trace the letter.

Ongoing Assessment

If...children make an error,	**then**...put your hand over their hand and guide them to trace the letter. Then have children try to trace the letter on their own. Repeat as necessary.

Phonological Awareness/Alphabetic Understanding

Activity 2 Isolate Initial Sound

Does It Have the First Sound /p/?

Objective: Children isolate initial /p/.

Time: 4–5 minutes

	To Do	**To Say**	
Model names of pictures	Gather the picture choices. Display Picture Choice 5-1. Point to *coat*.	Model	**This is *coat*. What is this?** Continue with the remaining pictures: *pen, mouse; pool, fire, man.* Test children on the picture names by pointing to the pictures one at a time and asking: **What is this?**
Introduce the game Does It Have the First Sound /p/?	Practice production of target sound.		Tell children they will play a game. You will show them three pictures. They will find the picture with the first sound /p/. **Let's say /p/. Remember, when you say /p/, your lips start out together. Then they open and a puff of air comes out of your mouth. Put your lips together and say /p/. Feel the puff of air that comes out of your mouth.**
Model the game	Display Picture Choice 5-1. Cover the bottom row.	Model	**My turn. This is *coat, pen, mouse*. I'll find the picture with the first sound /p/: *pen*** (exaggerate the first sound). ***Pen* has the first sound /p/.** Exaggerate the first sound and say the word: **/p/, *pen*.** Model another example with *pool, fire,* and *man*.
Play the game to test knowledge of /p/	Display Picture Choice 5-2. Cover the bottom row. Give individual turns.		Have children name each picture *(cane, mitt, peas; pin, can, fox)*. **Which picture has the first sound /p/?** Confirm correct responses and prompt sound production: **Yes, *peas* has the first sound /p/. Let's say /p/. Remember, when you say /p/, your lips start out together. Then they open and a puff of air comes out of your mouth. Put your lips together and say /p/. Feel the puff of air that comes out of your mouth.** Continue with the bottom row of pictures and Picture Choice 5-3 *(pie, fish, moon; fan, paw, cut)*.

Ongoing Assessment

If... children make incorrect responses,	**then...** model the correct answer. Review the sound production cue. Have children repeat the correct answer. Go back to the example a second time.

Phonological Awareness/Alphabetic Understanding

Activity 3 Isolate Initial Sound

First Sound Song with /m/

Objective: Children isolate initial /m/ in a song.

Time: 4–5 minutes

	To Do	**To Say**	
Introduce the song		Today you're going to learn a song. I'll show you three pictures with the first sound /mmm/. These pictures will be in the song.	
	Display the *monkey, mountain,* and *mop* Picture Cards.	Model	**This is *monkey, mountain, mop.***
		Lead	**Say the names of the pictures with me: *monkey, mountain, mop.***
		Model	***Monkey, mountain,* and *mop* all have the first sound /mmm/. Say /mmm/ with me. Remember, when you say /mmm/, your lips come together. Put your lips together and say /mmm/.**
Model the song	Continue to display the *monkey, mountain,* and *mop* Picture Cards.	Model	Sing the following words to the tune of "Old MacDonald Had a Farm," pointing to the pictures whenever you sing the name of the picture. **What is the first sound of these words: *monkey, mountain, mop?* /mmm/ is the first sound of these words: *monkey, mountain, mop.* With a /mmm/, /mmm/ here and a /mmm/, /mmm/ there, here a /mmm/, there a /mmm/, everywhere a /mmm/, /mmm/. /mmm/ is the first sound of these words: *monkey, mountain, mop.***
Lead the song	Lead children through the song several times, pointing to the pictures as they sing.	Lead	**Now sing the song with me.**
Test knowledge of initial /m/	Display the picture cards. Point to *monkey.*	Test	**Your turn. Say the first sound in *monkey.*** Confirm correct responses and prompt sound production. Continue with *mountain* and *mop.*
	Give individual turns.		

Ongoing Assessment

If... children make incorrect responses,	**then...** model the correct answer and have children repeat it. Return to the example a second time.

This activity was adapted from H. K. Yopp (1992).

Activity 4 — Reintroduce Letter Name and Sound

Reintroduce p/p/;
Discriminate m and p

Objective: Children practice letter name and sound: *p/p/*.   Time: 2–3 minutes

	To Do	To Say	
Introduce letter name	Hold up the *p* Alphabet Card.	**Model**	The <u>name</u> of this letter is *p*.
		Lead	Say the <u>name</u> of the letter with me: *p*.
		Test	What is the <u>name</u> of this letter?
Introduce letter sound	Continue holding up the *p* Alphabet Card.	**Model**	The <u>sound</u> for this letter is /p/. Remember, when you say /p/, your lips start out together. Then they open and a puff of air comes out of your mouth. Put your lips together and say /p/. Feel the puff of air that comes out of your mouth.
		Lead	Say the <u>sound</u> with me: /p/.
		Test	What is the <u>sound</u> for this letter?
Test knowledge of letter name and sound	Continue to hold up the *p* Alphabet Card.	**Test**	What is the <u>name</u> of this letter? What is the <u>sound</u> for this letter?
	Give individual turns.		**Ongoing Assessment** **If...** children make incorrect responses, **then...** tell them the name or sound, have them repeat the name or sound, and return to the letter a second time.
Discriminate *m* and *p*	Hold up the Discrimination sheet. Point to the first letter or symbol.	**Test**	**What is the <u>name</u> of this?** If it is a letter, also ask for the sound: **What is the <u>sound</u> for this letter?** Continue with the remaining letters and symbols.
			Ongoing Assessment **If...** children make an error, **then...** tell them the name or sound and have them repeat it. Return to the beginning of the row for that letter or symbol. If children make no errors on the row, move on to the next row.

Activity 5 Writer's Warm-Up

Introduce p

Objective: Children trace and write *p* and review writing *m*.

Time: 2–3 minutes

	To Do	To Say	
Review letter name and sound	Hold up the *p* Tracing Card.	Test	**What is the <u>name</u> of this letter? What is the <u>sound</u> for this letter?**
Model tracing p	Distribute a Writer's Warm-Up to each child. Hold up the *p* Tracing Card. Model tracing *p* again.	Model	**Watch as I trace the letter p with my finger.**
		Lead	**Now you trace the first two p's on your warm-up sheet with your finger.**
		Model	**Everyone, watch as I trace p again.**
		Lead	**Now use your pencil to trace the next two p's.**
Model writing p	Hold up the lined side of the *p* Tracing Card.	Model	**Watch as I write the letter p. I start at the dot and write the letter.**
			Have children write the letter *p* two times on their warm-up sheets. Remind them to write their letters carefully.

Ongoing Assessment

If...children make an error,	then...have them write the letter again. If needed, put your hand over their hand and guide them to write the letter. Then have them write the letter on their own. Repeat as necessary.

Test knowledge of writing p	Model writing *p* again.	Have children cover the letters they traced and wrote. Have them write *p* two times from memory. Then have them uncover their papers and compare the letters.
		Do your letters look the same? Circle the p that is your best work.

Review writing m		Have children trace and write *m* on their warm-up sheets.

Ongoing Assessment

If...children make an error,	then... model tracing the letter on the tracing card and then have them write the letter again. If needed, put your hand over their hand and guide them to write the letter. Then have them write the letter on their own. Repeat as necessary.

Writing/Spelling

Activity **6** Connect Sound to Letter

Match a Picture's Initial Sound; Introduce p

Objective: Children connect /p/ to p.

Time: 2–3 minutes

	To Do	**To Say**	
Introduce the activity	Gather the *p* Picture Cards and the *p* and *m* Letter Cards.		Tell children that they are going to choose the letter that goes with the first sound of some pictures.
Model the activity	Place the *pig* Picture Card on the table.	Model	**This is *pig*. The first sound in *pig* is /p/.** Place the *p* and *m* Letter Cards under the picture. **I'm going to choose the letter that matches this picture's first sound.** Point to the correct letter: **p is the letter for /p/ like the /p/ in *pig*.**
Test knowledge of initial /p/	Place the *pen* Picture Card on the table.	Test	**This is *pen*. What is this? The first sound in *pen* is /p/. What is the first sound in *pen*? That's right, /p/ is the first sound in *pen*.** Place two letter cards under the picture. Vary the choice and order. **Your turn. Choose the letter that matches this picture's first sound. Everyone, think of which letter has the same sound as the /p/ in *pen*. Does everyone know?** Call on a child to point to the correct letter. **What's the <u>name</u> of the letter you pointed to? What's the <u>sound</u> for the letter? That's right; p is the letter for /p/ like the /p/ in *pen*.** Reinforce the letter name and sound with the group: **Everyone, what's the <u>name</u> of the letter? What's the <u>sound</u> for the letter?** Continue with the remaining cards.

Ongoing Assessment

If...children make an error,	**then**...model the answer, have them repeat it, and return to the picture card a second time.

 **Connect Sound to Letter**

Letter Cross-Out Game: p, m

Objective: Children connect /p/ to p and /m/ to m.

Time: 6–8 minutes

	To Do	To Say	
Introduce the activity	Distribute a Letter Cross-Out to each child.	Tell children that they are going to cross out letters that go with sounds. **Let's see if we can cross out all of the letters on the sheet!**	
Model the activity	Hold up a Letter Cross-Out.	Model	**The first sound is /p/. I'm going to cross out a letter for the sound /p/.** Cross out one of the *p*'s on your cross-out sheet.
		Lead	**Now you cross out a letter for the sound /p/. That's right; p is the letter for the sound /p/.**
Test knowledge of p/p/ and m/m/	Continue to hold up a Letter Cross-Out.	Test	**The next sound is /mmm/. Everyone, what is the sound? Now cross out the letter for the sound /mmm/.** Reinforce the group on the letter name and sound: **Everyone, what's the <u>name</u> of the letter you crossed out? What's the <u>sound</u> for the letter?** Continue with the remaining sounds until all of the letters have been crossed out.

Ongoing Assessment

If… children make an error,   **then…** point to the correct letter and say its sound. Have children repeat the sound and cross out the correct letter.

Writing/Spelling

New Sound /p/
Review Sound /m/
Key Phonologic Skill Isolate Initial Sound

Phonological Awareness and Alphabetic Understanding

Activity	Materials		Time
1. Alphabetic Introduce *p*/p/	Alphabet Card: *p*	Letter Card: *p* (one per child)	1–2 minutes
2. Integrated Phonologic/Alphabetic Which Picture Has the First Sound /p/?	Alphabet Card: *p* Picture Choices: 6-1, 6-2, 6-3 Teacher Resource Package 1		4–5 minutes
New 3. Integrated Phonologic/Alphabetic First Sound Mix-Up Game with /m/ and /p/	Letter Cards: *p, m* Picture Cards: all *m* and *p* cards (except *mop* and *map*)	Sound Production Cue Card	4–5 minutes
4. Alphabetic Reintroduce *p*/p/; Discriminate *m* and *p*	Alphabet Card: *p* Discrimination Teacher Resource Package 1		2–3 minutes

Writing and Spelling

Activity	Materials		Time
5. Writer's Warm-Up Introduce *p*	Tracing Cards: *p, m* Writer's Warm-Up (one per child) Student Activity Book 1, p. 15		2–3 minutes
6. Integrated Phonologic/Alphabetic Match a Picture's Initial Sound; Introduce *p*	Picture Cards: all *p* cards	Letter Cards: *p, m*	2–3 minutes
New 7. Phonologic/Spelling Letter Race Game: *p, m*	Alphabet Cards: *p, m* Letter Race (one per child) Student Activity Book 1, p. 16		6–8 minutes

Activity **1** Introduce Letter Name and Sound

Introduce p/p/

Objective: Children learn and trace p/p/.

Time: 1–2 minutes

	To Do	To Say	
Introduce letter name	Hold up the *p* Alphabet Card.	Model	The <u>name</u> of this letter is *p*.
		Lead	Say the <u>name</u> of the letter with me: *p*.
		Test	What is the <u>name</u> of this letter?
Introduce letter sound	Continue holding up the *p* Alphabet Card.	Model	The <u>sound</u> for this letter is /p/. When you say /p/, your lips start out together. Then they open and a puff of air comes out of your mouth. Put your lips together and say /p/. Feel the puff of air that comes out of your mouth.
		Lead	Say the <u>sound</u> with me: /p/.
		Test	What is the <u>sound</u> for this letter?
Test knowledge of letter name and sound	Continue holding up the *p* Alphabet Card. Give individual turns on letter name and sound.	Test	What is the <u>name</u> of this letter? What is the <u>sound</u> for this letter?

Ongoing Assessment

If...children make an error,	then...tell them the name or sound, have them repeat the name or sound, and return to the letter a second time.

Model tracing *p*	Distribute the *p* Letter Cards. Hold up the *p* Alphabet Card.	Model	Everyone, watch. I'll trace the letter *p*.
			Have children trace the *p* on their letter cards three times. Tell them to say /p/ each time they trace the letter.

Ongoing Assessment

If...children make an error,	then...put your hand over their hand and guide them to trace the letter. Then have children try to trace the letter on their own. Repeat as necessary.

Phonological Awareness/Alphabetic Understanding

Activity 2 — Isolate Initial Sound

Which Picture Has the First Sound /p/?

Objective: Children isolate /p/ and connect to letter.

Time: 4–5 minutes

	To Do		**To Say**
Model names of pictures	Gather the picture choices. Display Picture Choice 6-1. Point to *pan*.	Model	**This is *pan*. What is this?** Continue with *fish, maze; cut, pie,* and *moon.* Test children on each picture name. Ask: **What is this?**
Introduce the game Which Picture Has the First Sound /p/?	Hold up the *p* Alphabet Card and point to the letter.	 Model Test	**Now we're going to play a game. I'll show you a letter and three pictures. You'll find the picture with the first sound /p/.** **The <u>name</u> of this letter is *p*. The <u>sound</u> for this letter is /p/. Remember, when you say /p/, your lips start out together. Then they open and a puff of air comes out of your mouth. Put your lips together and say /p/. Feel the puff of air that comes out of your mouth.** **What is the <u>sound</u> for this letter?**
Model the game	Display Picture Choice 6-1. Cover the bottom row.	Model	**My turn. I'll show you how to play. This is *pan*, *fish*, *maze*. I'll find the picture with the first sound /p/.** Point to the *p* Alphabet Card. **Pan** (exaggerate the first sound). **Pan has the first sound /p/.** Exaggerate the first sound and say the word: **/p/, pan.** Model another example: *cut, pie, moon.*
Play the game to test knowledge of /p/	Hold up the *p* Alphabet Card. Display Picture Choice 6-2. Cover the bottom row (pictures for PC 6-2: *cone, peas, fan; mow, coat, pen* and 6-3: *fire, mitt, paw; pool, cane, fork*). Give individual turns.	Test	**What is the <u>sound</u> for this letter?** Have children name each picture. **Which picture has the first sound /p/?** Confirm correct responses and prompt sound production: **Yes, *peas* has the first sound /p/. When you say /p/, your lips start out together. Then they open and a puff of air comes out of your mouth. Put your lips together and say /p/. Feel the puff of air that comes out of your mouth: /p/, peas.** Continue with the bottom row of pictures and Picture Choice 6-3.

Ongoing Assessment

If...children make incorrect responses,	**then**...model the correct answer. Review the sound production cue. Have children repeat the correct answer. Go back to the example a second time. If this activity is too difficult for children, use two pictures instead of three.

 **Activity**  **3** **Isolate Initial Sound**

First Sound Mix-Up Game
with /m/ and /p/

Objective: Children connect initial sound to letter: m/m/, p/p/.   Time: 4–5 minutes

	To Do	**To Say**	
Review names of pictures	Gather the *m* and *p* Picture Cards.	Hold up each picture card. Ask: **What is this?**	
Introduce the game First Sound Mix-Up	Mix up the picture cards. Place the *m* and *p* Letter Cards on the table.	**We're going to play a game called First Sound Mix-Up. I'll hold up a picture. You'll say the name of the picture and tell me its first sound. You'll have to be careful, though, because the pictures are all mixed up. Some of the pictures have the first sound /mmm/ and some have the first sound /p/.**	
Model the game	Display the *man* Picture Card.	**Model**	**My turn. I'll show you how to play. This is *man*. I'll say the first sound in *man*: /mmm/. Now I'll put *man* next to the letter for the sound /mmm/.** Place the picture next to the *m* Letter Card. **Remember, the <u>name</u> of this letter is *m*. The <u>sound</u> for the letter is /mmm/.**
	Display the *pie* Picture Card.		**I'll do one more. This is *pie*. I'll say the first sound in *pie*: /p/. Now I'll put *pie* next to the letter for the sound /p/.** Place the picture next to the *p* Letter Card. **Remember, the <u>name</u> of this letter is *p*. The <u>sound</u> for the letter is /p/.**
Play the game to test knowledge of initial sounds	Display the next picture.	**Test**	**What is this? Say the first sound in _____.** Confirm correct responses and prompt sound production for /mmm/ or /p/. (Use the Sound Production Cue Card.) Have a child place the picture next to the letter for its first sound.

Ongoing Assessment

If...children make incorrect responses,	**then**...tell them the answer and have them repeat it. Put the picture back in the pile so that you can return to it a second time.

(Give individual turns.)

Phonological Awareness/Alphabetic Understanding

Activity 4 Reintroduce Letter Name and Sound

Reintroduce p/p/; Discriminate m and p

Objective: Children practice letter name and sound: p/p/.   Time: 2–3 minutes

	To Do	To Say	
Introduce letter name	Hold up the *p* Alphabet Card.	Model	**The <u>name</u> of this letter is *p*.**
		Lead	**Say the <u>name</u> of the letter with me: *p*.**
		Test	**What is the <u>name</u> of this letter?**
Introduce letter sound	Continue holding up the *p* Alphabet Card.	Model	**The <u>sound</u> for this letter is /p/. When you say /p/, your lips start out together. Then they open and a puff of air comes out of your mouth. Put your lips together and say /p/. Feel the puff of air that comes out of your mouth.**
		Lead	**Say the <u>sound</u> with me: /p/.**
		Test	**What is the <u>sound</u> for this letter?**
Test knowledge of letter name and sound	Hold up the *p* Alphabet Card.	Test	**What is the <u>name</u> of this letter? What is the <u>sound</u> for this letter?**
	Give individual turns.		**Ongoing Assessment** If...children make incorrect responses, then...tell them the name or sound and have them repeat it. Return to the alphabet card a second time and repeat the test.
Discriminate *m* and *p*	Hold up the Discrimination sheet. Point to the first letter or symbol.	Test	**What is the <u>name</u> of this?** If it is a letter, also ask for the sound: **What is the <u>sound</u> for this letter?** Continue with the remaining letters and symbols.
			Ongoing Assessment If...children make an error, then...tell them the name or sound and have them repeat it. Return to the beginning of the row for that letter or symbol. If children make no errors, move on to the next row.

Activity 5 — Writer's Warm-Up

Introduce p

Objective: Children trace and write *p* and review writing *m*.   Time: 2–3 minutes

	To Do	To Say	
Review letter name and sound	Hold up the *p* Tracing Card.	**Test**	**What is the <u>name</u> of this letter? What is the <u>sound</u> for this letter?**
Model tracing *p*	Distribute a Writer's Warm-Up to each child. Hold up the *p* Tracing Card.	**Model**	**Watch as I trace the letter *p* with my finger.**
		Lead	**Now trace the top two *p*'s on your warm-up sheet with your finger.**
	Model tracing *p* again.	**Model**	**Everyone, watch as I trace the letter *p* again.**
		Lead	**Now use your pencil to trace the two *p*'s on the next line.**
Model writing *p*	Hold up the lined side of the *p* Tracing Card.	**Model**	**Everyone, watch as I write the letter *p*. I start at the dot and write the letter.**
		Lead	**Now you write two *p*'s. Start at the dot like I did. Write carefully.**

Ongoing Assessment

If...children make an error,	then...have them write the letter again. If needed, put your hand over their hand and guide them to write the letter. Then have them write the letter on their own. Repeat as necessary.

Test knowledge of writing *p*	Model writing *p* again.		Have children cover the letters they traced and wrote. Have them write *p* two times from memory. Then have them uncover their papers and compare the letters. **Do all of your *p*'s look the same? Circle the letter that is your best work.**
Review writing *m*			**Trace the letter *m* with your pencil. Now write *m*. Remember to start at the dot.**

Ongoing Assessment

If...children make an error,	then...model writing the letter using the tracing card and have them write the letter again. If needed, put your hand over their hand and guide them to write the letter. Then have them write the letter on their own. Repeat as necessary.

Activity 6 Connect Sound to Letter

Match a Picture's Initial Sound; Introduce p

Objective: Children connect initial /p/ to *p*.

Time: 2–3 minutes

	To Do	To Say
Introduce the activity	Gather the *p* Picture Cards and the *p* and *m* Letter Cards.	**You're going to choose the letter that goes with the first sound of some pictures.**
Model the activity	Place the *pail* Picture Card on the table.	**Model** **My turn. This is *pail*. The first sound in *pail* is /p/.** Place the *p* and *m* Letter Cards under the picture. **I'm going to choose the letter that matches this picture's first sound.** Point to the correct letter: *p* **is the letter for the sound /p/ like the /p/ in *pail*.**
Test knowledge of initial sound	Place the *pan* Picture Card on the table.	**Test** **This is *pan*. What is this? The first sound in *pan* is /p/. What is the first sound in *pan*? That's right, /p/ is the first sound in *pan*.** Place the *m* and *p* Letter Cards under the picture. **Your turn. Choose the letter that matches this picture's first sound. Think. Which letter is the letter for the sound /p/ in *pan*? Do you think you know?** Call on a child to point to the correct letter. **What's the <u>name</u> of the letter you pointed to? What's the <u>sound</u> for that letter? That's right,** *p* **is the letter for /p/ like the /p/ in *pan*.** Reinforce the letter name and sound with the group: **Everyone, what's the <u>name</u> of the letter? What's the <u>sound</u> for the letter?** Continue with the remaining cards.

Ongoing Assessment

If...children make an error,	**then**...model the answer, have them repeat it, and return to the picture card a second time.

Activity 7 — Connect Sound to Letter

Letter Race Game: p, m

Objective: Children connect /p/ to p and /m/ to m.

Time: 6–8 minutes

	To Do	To Say	
Review letter names and sounds	Gather the alphabet cards. Hold up the *p* Alphabet Card.	**What is the <u>name</u> of this letter? What is the <u>sound</u> for this letter?** Repeat for *m*/m/.	
Introduce the Letter Race Game	Distribute a Letter Race to each child.	**We're going to have a letter race. I'm going to tell you the sound for one of the letters on your sheet. You're going to write the letter on the right racetrack. Which letter do you think will win?**	
Model the game	Hold up a Letter Race.	Model	**Let's do one together. The first sound is /p/. I'm going to write the letter for /p/ on the racetrack for /p/.** Write a *p* on the *p* racetrack.
		Lead	**Now you write the letter for /p/ on the right racetrack. Start at the dot and write the letter. That's right, *p* is the letter for the sound /p/.**
Play the game to test knowledge of /p/ and /m/	Say /mmm/ or /p/, and have children write the letter for the sound on the correct racetrack. Vary the order. Continue until one letter wins.		**The next sound is /_/. Write the letter for that sound on the right racetrack. Start at the dot and write the letter.** Reinforce the group on the letter name and sound: **Everyone, what's the <u>name</u> of the letter you just wrote? What's the <u>sound</u> for that letter?**

Ongoing Assessment

If... children make an error,	then... model the letter name and sound and have children repeat them. Have children write the correct letter.

New Sound /f/
Review Sounds /p/, /m/
Key Phonologic Skill Isolate Initial Sound

Phonological Awareness and Alphabetic Understanding

Activity	Materials	Time
1. Alphabetic Introduce *f*/f/	Alphabet Card: *f* Letter Card: *f* (one per child)	1–2 minutes
2. Phonologic Does It Begin with /f/?	Picture Cards: *fan, pig, five, fish, fin, man* Alphabet Card: *f*	4–5 minutes
3. Phonologic First Sound Song with /p/	Picture Cards: *puzzle, pail, pin*	4–5 minutes
4. Alphabetic Reintroduce *f*/f/; Discriminate *m* and *p*	Alphabet Card: *f* Discrimination Teacher Resource Package 1	2–3 minutes

Writing and Spelling

Activity	Materials	Time
5. Writer's Warm-Up Introduce *f*	Writer's Warm-Up (one per child) Student Activity Book 1, p. 17 Tracing Cards: *f, m, p*	2–3 minutes
6. Integrated Phonologic/Alphabetic Match a Picture's Initial Sound; Introduce *f*	Picture Cards: all *f* cards Letter Cards: *f, p, m*	2–3 minutes
New **7. Phonologic/Spelling** Letter Tag: *p, m*	Letter Tag (one per child) Student Activity Book 1, p. 18	6–8 minutes

Activity **1** Introduce Letter Name and Sound

Introduce f/f/

Objective: Children learn and trace f/f/.

Time: 1–2 minutes

	To Do	To Say	
Introduce letter name	Hold up the *f* Alphabet Card.	Model	**The name of this letter is *f*.**
		Lead	**Say the name with me: *f***
		Test	**What is the name of this letter?**
Introduce letter sound	Continue holding up the *f* Alphabet Card.	Model	**The sound for this letter is /fff/. When you say /fff/, your top teeth touch your bottom lip. Say /fff/ and feel your top teeth touch your bottom lip.**
		Lead	**Say the sound with me: /fff/.**
		Test	**What is the sound for this letter?**
Test knowledge of letter name and sound	Continue holding up the *f* Alphabet Card.	Test	**What is the name of this letter? What is the sound for this letter?**
	Give individual turns on letter name and sound.		

Ongoing Assessment

If... children make an error,	**then...** tell them the name or sound and have them repeat it. Return to the letter a second time.

Model tracing *f*	Distribute the *f* Letter Cards. Hold up the *f* Alphabet Card.	Model	**Everyone, watch. I'll trace the letter *f*.**
			Have children trace the *f* on their letter cards three times. Tell them to say /fff/ each time they trace the letter.

Ongoing Assessment

If... children make an error,	**then...** put your hand over their hand and guide them to trace the letter. Then have the children try to trace the letter on their own. Repeat as necessary.

Activity 2 Isolate Initial Sound

Does It Begin with /f/?

Objective: Children isolate initial /f/.

Time: 4–5 minutes

	To Do	To Say	
Model names of pictures	Gather the picture cards. Place *fan* on the table.	**Model**	**This is *fan*. What is this?** Continue with *pig, five, fish, fin,* and *man*. Test children on the picture names by placing the cards on the table one at a time and asking: **What is this?**
Introduce the game Does It Begin with /f/?	Hold up the *f* Alphabet Card.		We're going to play a game. I'll show you a picture. You'll tell me if the picture begins with /fff/. Let's say /fff/. When you say /fff/, your top teeth touch your bottom lip. Say /fff/ and feel your top teeth touch your bottom lip.
Model the game	Place the *fan* Picture Card on the table.	**Model**	**My turn. I'll say the name of the picture and then tell whether it begins with /fff/: *fan*** (exaggerate the first sound). ***Fan* begins with /fff/. My top teeth touch my bottom lip when I say /fff/, *fan*. Next picture: *pig*** (exaggerate the first sound). ***Pig* does not begin with /fff/.**
Play the game to test knowledge of /f/	Display the *five* Picture Card.	**Test**	**This is *five*. What is this? Does *five* begin with /fff/?** Confirm correct responses and prompt sound production: **Yes, *five* begins with /fff/. Let's say /fff/. When you say /fff/, your top teeth touch your bottom lip. Say /fff/ and feel your top teeth touch your bottom lip: *five*.** Continue with *fish, fin,* and *man*.
	Give individual turns.		

Ongoing Assessment

If... children make incorrect responses,	**then**... model the correct answer. Review the sound production cue. Have children repeat the correct answer. Go back to the example a second time.

 **Activity** **3** **Isolate Initial Sound**

First Sound Song with /p/

Objective: Children isolate initial /p/ in a song.

Time: 4–5 minutes

	To Do	**To Say**	
Introduce the First Sound Song	Display the *puzzle, pail,* and *pin* Picture Cards.		**We're going to learn a song. I'll show you three pictures that begin with /p/. These pictures will be in the song.**
		Model	**This is *puzzle, pail, pin.***
		Lead	**Say the names of the pictures with me: *puzzle, pail, pin. Puzzle, pail,* and *pin* all begin with /p/. Say the sound /p/ with me. Remember, when you say /p/, your lips start out together. Then they open and a puff of air comes out of your mouth. Put your lips together and say /p/. Feel the puff of air that comes out of your mouth.**
Model the song	Continue to display the *puzzle, pail,* and *pin* Picture Cards.	Model	**My turn. I'll sing the song for you.** Sing the following words to the tune of "Old MacDonald Had a Farm," pointing to the pictures whenever you sing the names of the pictures. **What is the sound that begins these words: *puzzle, pail, pin?* /p/ is the sound that begins these words: *puzzle, pail, pin.* With a /p/, /p/ here and a /p/, /p/ there, here a /p/, there a /p/, everywhere a /p/, /p/. /p/ is the sound that begins these words: *puzzle, pail, pin.***
		Lead	**Your turn. Sing the song with me.** Lead children through the song several times, pointing to the pictures as they sing.
Test knowledge of initial /p/	Hold up the *puzzle* Picture Card.	Test	**Your turn. Say the first sound in *puzzle.*** Confirm correct responses and prompt sound production: **Yes, the first sound in *puzzle* is /p/. Remember, when you say /p/, your lips start out together. Then they open and a puff of air comes out of your mouth.** Continue with *pail* and *pin.*
	Give individual turns.		

Ongoing Assessment

If... children make incorrect responses,	**then**... model the correct answer and have children repeat it. Return to the example a second time.

Reintroduce f/f/; Discriminate m and p

Objective: Children practice letter name and sound: f/f/.   Time: 2–3 minutes

	To Do	**To Say**	
Introduce letter name	Hold up the *f* Alphabet Card.	Model	**The <u>name</u> of this letter is *f*.**
		Lead	**Say the <u>name</u> with me: *f*.**
		Test	**What is the <u>name</u> of this letter?**
Introduce letter sound	Continue holding up the *f* Alphabet Card.	Model	**The <u>sound</u> for this letter is /fff/. When you say /fff/, your top teeth touch your bottom lip. Say /fff/ and feel your top teeth touch your bottom lip.**
		Lead	**Say the <u>sound</u> with me: /fff/.**
		Test	**What is the <u>sound</u> for this letter?**
Test knowledge of letter name and sound	Continue holding up the *f* Alphabet Card.	Test	**What is the <u>name</u> of this letter? What is the <u>sound</u> for this letter?**

Ongoing Assessment

If . . . children make incorrect responses,   **then . . .** tell them the name or sound, have them repeat the name or sound, and return to the letter a second time.

	To Do	**To Say**	
Give individual turns on letter name and sound.			

	To Do	**To Say**	
Discriminate *m* and *p*	Hold up the Discrimination sheet. Point to the first letter or symbol.	Test	**What is the <u>name</u> of this?** If it is a letter, also ask for the sound: **What is the <u>sound</u> for this letter?** Continue with the remaining letters and symbols.

Ongoing Assessment

If . . . children make incorrect responses,   **then . . .** tell them the name or sound and have them repeat it. Return to the beginning of the row for that letter or symbol. If children make no errors on the row, move on to the next row.

Activity 5 Writer's Warm-Up

Introduce f

Objective: Children trace and write f and review writing m and p.

Time: 2–3 minutes

	To Do	**To Say**	
Review letter name and sound	Hold up the f Tracing Card.	**What is the <u>name</u> of this letter? What is the <u>sound</u> for this letter?**	
Model tracing f	Distribute a Writer's Warm-Up to each child. Hold up the f Tracing Card.	Model	**Everyone, watch as I trace the letter f with my finger.**
		Lead	**Now you trace the first two f's on your warm-up sheet with your finger.**
	Model tracing f again.	Model	**Everyone, watch as I trace the letter f again.**
		Lead	**Now use your pencil to trace the next two f's.**
Model writing f	Hold up the lined side of the f Tracing Card.	Model	**Everyone, watch as I write the letter f. I start at the dot and write the letter.**

Have children write the letter f two times on their warm-up sheets. Remind them to write their letters carefully.

Ongoing Assessment

If... children make an error,	then... have them write the letter again. If needed, put your hand over their hand and guide them to write the letter. Then have them write the letter on their own. Repeat as necessary.

Test children on writing f	Model writing f again.	Have children cover the letters they traced and wrote. Have them write f two times from memory. Then have them uncover their papers and compare the letters.

Do your letters look the same? Circle your best f.

Have children trace and write each review letter on their warm-up sheets.

Review m and p

Ongoing Assessment

If... children make an error,	then... model tracing the letter with the tracing card and have them write the letter again. If needed, put your hand over their hand and guide them to write the letter. Then have them write the letter on their own. Repeat as necessary.

Activity 6 Connect Sound to Letter

Match a Picture's Initial Sound; Introduce f

Objective: Children connect /f/ to f.

Time: 2–3 minutes

	To Do		To Say
Introduce the activity	Gather the picture cards and the letter cards.		Tell children that they are going to choose the letter that matches the first sound of some pictures.
Model the activity	Place the *fish* Picture Card on the table.	Model	**This is *fish*. The first sound in *fish* is /fff/.** Place the *f* and *m* Letter Cards under the picture. **My turn. I'm going to choose the letter that matches this picture's first sound.** Point to the correct letter: **f is the letter for /fff/ like the /fff/ in *fish*.**
Test knowledge of initial /f/	Place the *fan* Picture Card on the table.	Test	**This is *fan*. What is this? The first sound in *fan* is /fff/. What is the first sound in *fan*? That's right; /fff/ is the first sound in *fan*.** Place two letter cards under the picture. Vary the choice and order. **Your turn. Choose the letter that matches this picture's first sound. Everyone, think of which letter has the same sound as the /fff/ in *fan*. Does everyone know?** Call on a child to point to the correct letter. **What's the <u>name</u> of the letter you pointed to? What's the <u>sound</u> for that letter? That's right; f is the letter for /fff/ like the /fff/ in *fan*.** Reinforce the letter name and sound with the group: **Everyone, what's the <u>name</u> of the letter? What's the <u>sound</u> for that letter?** Continue with the remaining cards.

Ongoing Assessment

If... children make an error,	then... model the answer, have them repeat it, and return to the picture card a second time.

Writing/Spelling

Activity 7 Connect Sound to Letter

Letter Tag: p, m

Objective: Children connect sound to letter:
p/p/, m/m/.

Time: 6–8 minutes

	To Do	**To Say**
Introduce the game Letter Tag	Distribute a Letter Tag to each child.	We're going to play Letter Tag. I'm going to tell you the sound of a letter. You're going to tag the letter with your pencil.
Model the game	Display a Letter Tag.	**Model** I'll show you how to play Letter Tag. The first sound is /p/. I'm going to start at the arrow and tag the letter for /p/. Use a pencil to draw a line from the arrow to the correct letter.
		Lead Now it's your turn to tag the letter for /p/. Put your pencil on the first arrow and tag the letter for /p/. That's right; *p* is the letter for the sound /p/.
Play the game to test knowledge of /p/ and /m/		Say /p/ or /mmm/ and have children "tag" the correct letter. Use the sequence of letter sounds below.
		Put your pencil on the next arrow. When I say the sound, you tag the letter for that sound. Ready, /mmm/. Reinforce the group on the letter name and sound: **Everyone, what's the <u>name</u> of the letter you tagged? What's the <u>sound</u> for that letter?**
		Continue in the following order: **3. /mmm/, 4. /p/, 5. /mmm/, 6. /p/.** If time permits, start over from the top of the page with this sequence: **7. /p/, 8. /p/, 9. /mmm/, 10. /mmm/, 11. /mmm/, 12. /p/.**

Ongoing Assessment

If . . . children make an error, **then** . . . model the letter name and sound and have children repeat them. Have children tag the correct letter.

New Sound /f/
Review Sounds /p/, /m/
Key Phonologic Skill Isolate Initial Sound

Phonological Awareness and Alphabetic Understanding

Activity	Materials		Time
1. Alphabetic Introduce *f*/f/	Alphabet Card: *f*	Letter Card: *f* (one per child)	1–2 minutes
2. Phonologic Which Picture Begins with /f/?	Picture Choices: 8-1, 8-2, 8-3 *Teacher Resource Package 1*		4–5 minutes
3. Integrated Phonologic/Alphabetic Picture Scene Search: /p/	Alphabet Card: *p* Picture Scene /p/ *Teacher Resource Package 1*		4–5 minutes
4. Alphabetic Reintroduce *f*/f/; Discriminate *m, p,* and *f*	Alphabet Card: *f* Discrimination *Teacher Resource Package 1*		2–3 minutes

Writing and Spelling

Activity	Materials		Time
5. Writer's Warm-Up Introduce *f*	Writer's Warm-Up (one per child) *Student Activity Book 1, p. 19* Tracing Cards: *f, m, p*		2–3 minutes
6. Integrated Phonologic/Alphabetic Match a Picture's Initial Sound; Introduce *f*	Picture Cards: all *f* cards	Letter Cards: *f, p, m*	2–3 minutes
New **7. Phonologic/Spelling** Letter Writing Game: *f, p, m*	Letter Writing Game (one per child) *Student Activity Book 1, p. 20* Game Board 3	number cube (not provided) game markers (not provided)	6–8 minutes

Activity **1** Introduce Letter Name and Sound

Introduce *f/f/*

Objective: Children learn and trace *f/f/*.

Time: 1–2 minutes

	To Do	**To Say**	
Introduce letter name	Hold up the *f* Alphabet Card.	Model	**The name of this letter is *f*.**
		Lead	**Say the name with me: *f*.**
		Test	**What is the name of this letter?**
Introduce letter sound	Continue holding up the *f* Alphabet Card.	Model	**The sound for this letter is /fff/. When you say /fff/, your top teeth touch your bottom lip. Say /fff/ and feel your top teeth touch your bottom lip.**
		Lead	**Say the sound with me: /fff/.**
		Test	**What is the sound for this letter?**
Test knowledge of letter name and sound	Continue holding up the *f* Alphabet Card.	Test	**What is the name of this letter? What is the sound for this letter?**

Ongoing Assessment

If . . . children make an error,

then . . . tell them the name or sound and have them repeat it. Return to the letter a second time.

	Give individual turns on letter name and sound.		
Model tracing *f*	Distribute the *f* Letter Cards. Hold up the *f* Alphabet Card.	Model	**Everyone, watch. I'll trace the letter *f*.**
			Have children trace the *f* on their letter cards three times. Tell them to say /fff/ each time they trace the letter.

Ongoing Assessment

If . . . children make an error,

then . . . put your hand over their hand and guide them to trace the letter. Then have children try to trace the letter on their own. Repeat as necessary.

Phonological Awareness/Alphabetic Understanding

Activity 2 Isolate Initial Sound

Which Picture Begins with /f/?

Objective: Children isolate initial /f/.

Time: 4–5 minutes

	To Do		**To Say**
Model names of pictures	Gather the picture choices. Display Picture Choice 8-1. Point to *can*.	Model	**This is *can*. What is this?** Continue with the remaining pictures: *food, pin; mouse, pan, fox.* Test children on the picture names by pointing to the pictures one at a time and asking: **What is this?**
Introduce the game Which Picture Begins with /f/?			**We're going to play a game. I'll show you three pictures. You'll find the picture that has the first sound /fff/.** **Let's say /fff/. Remember, when you say /fff/, your top teeth touch your bottom lip. Say /fff/ and feel your top teeth touch your bottom lip.**
Model the game	Hold up Picture Choice 8-1. Display the pictures *can, food,* and *pin*. Cover the others.	Model	**My turn. I'll show you how to play the game. This is *can, food, pin*. I'll find the picture that has the first sound /fff/:** *food* (exaggerate the first sound). ***Food* has the first sound /fff/.** Exaggerate the first sound and say the word: **/fff/, *food*.** Model another example using *mouse, pan,* and *fox*.
Play the game to test knowledge of /f/	Hold up Picture Choice 8-2. Display the pictures *mow, pool,* and *fish*. Cover the others. Give individual turns.	Test	Have children name each picture. **Which picture has the first sound /fff/?** Confirm correct responses and prompt sound production: **Yes, *fish* begins with /fff/. Let's say /fff/. Remember, when you say /fff/, your top teeth touch your bottom lip. Say /fff/ and feel your top teeth touch your bottom lip, *fish*.** Continue with the bottom row of pictures (*fin, mitt, cup*) and Picture Choice 8-3 (*foot, maze, cat; cone, fan, peas*).

Ongoing Assessment

If . . . children make incorrect responses,

then . . . model the correct answer. Review the sound production cue. Have children repeat the correct answer. Go back to the example a second time.

59

Phonological Awareness/Alphabetic Understanding

Activity 3 · Isolate Initial Sound

Picture Scene Search: /p/

Objective: Children isolate initial /p/.

Time: 4–5 minutes

	To Do	To Say
Introduce the game	Hold up the *p* Alphabet Card.	We're going to play a new game. I'll show you a picture. You'll find the things in the picture that begin with **/p/**.
		Test · **The <u>name</u> of this letter is *p*. What is the <u>sound</u> for this letter?** Confirm correct responses. **Yes, /p/ is the sound for *p*. Remember, when you say /p/, your lips start out together. Then they open and a puff of air comes out of your mouth. Put your lips together and say /p/. Feel the puff of air that comes out of your mouth.**

Ongoing Assessment

If... children make incorrect responses,	**then**... model the correct sound and have children repeat it. Review the sound production cue. Repeat the test.

	To Do	To Say
Model the game	Hold up the picture scene.	**Model** · **My turn. I'll find something in the picture that begins with /p/.** Point to and name something that begins with /p/: **_____ begins with /p/.**
Play the game to test knowledge of /p/	Continue holding up the picture scene. Give individual turns.	**Test** · **Your turn to find something that begins with /p/.** Call on a child to point to and name something that begins with /p/. Confirm correct responses and have the group repeat it: **Yes, _____ begins with /p/. Everyone, say /p/, _____ .**
		Target words: *penguin, purse, pool, popcorn, pie, pizza, pretzels, pink (cotton candy), pear, peach, pineapple*

Phonological Awareness/Alphabetic Understanding

Activity 4 — Reintroduce Letter Name and Sound

Reintroduce f/f/; Discriminate m, p, and f

Objective: Children practice letter name and sound: f/f/.   Time: 2–3 minutes

	To Do	To Say	
Introduce letter name	Hold up the *f* Alphabet Card.	**Model**	**The <u>name</u> of this letter is *f*.**
		Lead	**Say the <u>name</u> with me: *f*.**
		Test	**What is the <u>name</u> of this letter?**
Introduce letter sound	Continue holding up the *f* Alphabet Card.	**Model**	**The <u>sound</u> for this letter is /fff/. When you say /fff/, your top teeth touch your bottom lip. Say /fff/ and feel your top teeth touch your bottom lip.**
		Lead	**Say the <u>sound</u> with me: /fff/.**
		Test	**What is the <u>sound</u> for this letter?**
Test knowledge of letter name and sound	Continue holding up the *f* Alphabet Card.	**Test**	**What is the <u>name</u> of this letter? What is the <u>sound</u> for this letter?**

Ongoing Assessment

	Give individual turns on letter name and sound.	If... children make incorrect responses,	then... tell them the name or sound and have them repeat it. Return to the letter a second time.

| **Discriminate *m*, *p*, and *f*** | Hold up the Discrimination sheet. Point to the first letter or symbol. | **Test** | **What is the <u>name</u> of this?** If it is a letter, also ask for the sound: **What is the <u>sound</u> for this letter?** Continue with the remaining letters and symbols. |

Ongoing Assessment

		If... children make incorrect responses,	then... tell them the name or sound and have them repeat it. Return to the beginning of the row for that letter or symbol. If children make no errors on the row, move on to the next row.

 **Writer's Warm-Up**

Introduce f

Objective: Children trace and write *f* and review writing *m* and *p*.

Time: 2–3 minutes

	To Do	To Say	
Review letter name and sound	Hold up the *f* Tracing Card		**What is the <u>name</u> of this letter? What is the <u>sound</u> for this letter?**
Model tracing f	Distribute a Writer's Warm-Up to each child. Hold up the *f* Tracing Card.	Model	**Everyone, watch as I trace the letter *f* with my finger.**
		Lead	**Now you trace the first two *f*'s on your warm-up sheet with your finger.**
	Model tracing *f* again.	Model	**Everyone, watch as I trace *f* again.**
		Lead	**Now use your pencil to trace the next two *f*'s on your warm-up sheet.**
Model writing f	Hold up the lined side of the *f* Tracing Card.	Model	**Everyone, watch as I write the letter *f*. I start at the dot and write the letter.**

Have children write the letter *f* two times on their warm-up sheets. Remind them to write their letters carefully.

Ongoing Assessment

If... children make an error,	**then...** have them write the letter again. If needed, put your hand over their hand and guide them to write the letter. Then have them write the letter on their own. Repeat as necessary.

Test children on writing f	Model writing *f* again.	Have children cover the letters they traced and wrote. Have them write the letter *f* two times from memory. Then have them uncover their papers and compare the letters.
		Do your letters look the same? Circle your best *f*.

Review

m and p

Have children trace and write each review letter on their warm-up sheets.

Ongoing Assessment

If... children make an error,	**then...** model tracing the letter with the tracing card and have them write the letter again. If needed, put your hand over their hand and guide them to write the letter. Then have them write the letter on their own. Repeat as necessary.

Writing/Spelling

Activity 6 Connect Sound to Letter

Match a Picture's Initial Sound; Introduce f

Objective: Children connect sound to letter: f/f/.

Time: 2–3 minutes

	To Do		**To Say**
Introduce the activity	Gather the picture cards and the letter cards.		Tell children that they are going to choose the letter that matches the first sound of some pictures.
Model the activity	Place the *fork* Picture Card on the table.	Model	**This is *fork*. The first sound in *fork* is /fff/.** Place the *p* and *f* Letter Cards under the picture. **My turn. I'm going to choose the letter that matches this picture's first sound.** Point to the correct letter: *f* **is the letter for /fff/ like the /fff/ in *fork*.**
Test knowledge of initial /f/	Display the *fox* Picture Card.	Test	**This is *fox*. What is this? The first sound in *fox* is /fff/. What is the first sound in *fox*? That's right; /fff/ is the first sound in *fox*.** Place two letter cards under the picture. Vary the choice and order. **Your turn. Choose the letter that matches this picture's first sound. Everyone, think of which letter has the same sound as the /fff/ in *fox*. Does everyone know?** Call on a child to point to the correct letter. **What's the <u>name</u> of the letter you pointed to? What's the <u>sound</u> for that letter? That's right; *f* is the letter for /fff/ like the /fff/ in *fox*.** Reinforce the letter name and sound with the group: **Everyone, what's the <u>name</u> of the letter? What is the <u>sound</u> for this letter?** Continue with the remaining cards.

Ongoing Assessment

If... children make an error,	then... model the correct answer, have them repeat it, and return to the picture card a second time.

Activity 7 — Connect Sound to Letter

New

Letter Writing Game: *f, p, m*

Objective: Children connect sound to letter: f/f/, p/p/, m/m/.   Time: 6–8 minutes

	To Do	**To Say**
Introduce the Letter Writing Game	Distribute a Letter Writing Game to each child.	Review the letter names and sounds. **We're going to play a letter writing game. I'm going to say the sound of a letter and you're going to write the letter for that sound. Every time we write a letter, someone will roll the number cube and move a marker on the game board.**
Model the game	Display a Letter Writing Game.	**Model** **Let's do one together. The first sound is /mmm/. I'm going to write the letter for that sound under the letter that stands for /mmm/.** Write the letter *m* in the *m* column on your sheet. **Lead** **Now you write the letter for the sound /mmm/. Start at the dot and write the letter. That's right; m is the letter for the sound /mmm/.**
Play the game to test knowledge of /f/, /p/, and /m/		**Test** **The next sound is /_/.** Vary the order of letter sounds. **Write the letter for that sound. Start at the dot and write the letter.** Reinforce the group on the letter name and sound: **Everyone, what's the <u>name</u> of the letter you wrote? What's the <u>sound</u> for that letter?** After children have written the letter, have one child roll the number cube and advance his or her marker on the game board. Continue playing the game until all of the columns have been filled in.

Ongoing Assessment

If . . . children make an error,	**then** . . . model the letter name and sound and have children repeat them. Have children write the correct letter.

LESSON 9

New Sound /f/
Review Sounds /p/, /m/
Key Phonologic Skill Isolate Initial Sound

Phonological Awareness and Alphabetic Understanding

Activity	Materials		Time
1. Alphabetic Introduce *f* /f/	Alphabet Card: *f*	Letter Card: *f* (one per child)	1–2 minutes
2. Integrated Phonologic/Alphabetic Which Picture Begins with /f/?	Alphabet Card: *f* Picture Choices: 9-1, 9-2, 9-3 Teacher Resource Package 1		4–5 minutes
New 3. Integrated Phonologic/Alphabetic Sound Match with /p/	Alphabet Card: *p* Sound Match Cards: a–f (one set per child) Teacher Resource Package 1 game markers (not provided) Sound Production Cue Card		4–5 minutes
4. Alphabetic Reintroduce *f* /f/; Discriminate *m, p,* and *f*	Alphabet Card: *f*	Discrimination Teacher Resource Package 1	2–3 minutes

Writing and Spelling

Activity	Materials		Time
New 5. Writer's Warm-Up Letter Mission; Review *f, m, p*	Letter Mission (one per child) Student Activity Book 1, p. 21 Tracing Cards: *f, m, p*		2–3 minutes
6. Integrated Phonologic/Alphabetic Match a Picture's Initial Sound; Introduce *f*	Picture Cards: all *f* cards	Letter Cards: *f, p, m*	2–3 minutes
New 7. Phonologic/Spelling Letter Matching: Review *f, p, m*	Picture Cards: *f, p, m* (three for each letter)	Letter Cards: *f, p, m* (three of each letter)	6–8 minutes

Activity 1 — Introduce Letter Name and Sound

Introduce f/f/

Objective: Children learn and trace f/f/.

Time: 1–2 minutes

	To Do	To Say	
Introduce letter name	Hold up the *f* Alphabet Card.	**Model**	The <u>name</u> of this letter is *f*.
		Lead	Say the <u>name</u> with me: *f*.
		Test	What is the <u>name</u> of this letter?
Introduce letter sound	Continue holding up the *f* Alphabet Card.	**Model**	The <u>sound</u> for this letter is /fff/. When you say /fff/, your top teeth touch your bottom lip. Say /fff/ and feel your top teeth touch your bottom lip.
		Lead	Say the <u>sound</u> with me: /fff/.
		Test	What is the <u>sound</u> for this letter?
Test knowledge of letter name and sound	Continue holding up the *f* Alphabet Card. Give individual turns on letter name and sound	**Test**	What is the <u>name</u> of this letter? What is the <u>sound</u> for this letter?

Ongoing Assessment

If... children make an error,	then... tell them the name or sound and have them repeat it. Return to the letter a second time.

Model tracing *f*	Distribute the *f* Letter Cards. Hold up the *f* Alphabet Card.	**Model**	Everyone, watch. I'll trace the letter *f*.
			Have children trace the *f* on their letter cards three times. Tell them to say /fff/ each time they trace the letter.

Ongoing Assessment

If... children make an error,	then... put your hand over their hand and guide them to trace the letter. Then have them try to trace the letter on their own. Repeat as necessary.

Phonological Awareness/Alphabetic Understanding

Which Picture Begins with /f/?

Objective: Children isolate initial /f/ and connect sound to letter.

Time: 4–5 minutes

	To Do	**To Say**
Model names of pictures	Gather the picture choices. Display Picture Choice 9-1. Point to *fork*.	**Model** **This is *fork*. What is this?** Continue with the remaining pictures *(cut, pig; moon, fire, peas)*. Test children on the picture names by pointing to the pictures one at a time and asking: **What is this?**
Introduce the game Which Picture Begins with /f/?	Hold up the *f* Alphabet Card.	**We're going to play a game. I'll show you a letter and three pictures. You'll find the picture that begins with the sound for the letter.** **The <u>name</u> of this letter is *f*. The <u>sound</u> for this letter is /fff/. Remember, when you say /fff/, your top teeth touch your bottom lip. Say /fff/ and feel your top teeth touch your bottom lip.** **Test** **What is the <u>sound</u> for this letter?**
Model the game	Hold up Picture Choice 9-1. Display the pictures *fork, cut,* and *pig*. Cover the others.	**Model** **My turn. I'll show you how to play the game. This is *fork, cut, pig*. I'll find the picture that has the first sound /fff/.** Point to the *f* Alphabet Card. **Fork** (exaggerate the first sound). **Fork has the first sound /fff/.** Exaggerate the first sound and say the word: **/fff/, fork.** Model another example: *moon, fire, peas.*
Play the game to test knowledge of initial /f/	Hold up the *f* Alphabet Card. Hold up Picture Choice 9-2. Display the pictures *cap, paw,* and *fan*. Cover the others. Give individual turns.	**Test** **What is the <u>sound</u> for this letter?** Have children name each picture. **Which picture has the first sound /fff/?** Confirm correct responses and prompt sound production: **Yes, *fan* has the first sound /fff/. Let's say /fff/. Remember, when you say /fff/, your top teeth touch your bottom lip. Say /fff/ and feel your top teeth touch your bottom lip: *fan*.** Continue with the bottom row of pictures *(foot, mop, coat)* and Picture Choice 9-3 *(man, fin, pool; cane, mitt, fox)*. **Ongoing Assessment** **If...** children make incorrect responses, **then...** model the correct answer. Review the sound production cue. Have children repeat the correct answer. Go back to the example a second time.

 **Activity**  **Isolate Initial Sound**

Sound Match with /p/

Objective: Children isolate picture's initial sound and connect to letter.

Time: 4–5 minutes

	To Do	**To Say**
Introduce the game Sound Match	Gather a game marker and one copy of Sound Match Cards a–f for each child.	**I'm going to teach you to play Sound Match. I'll give you a card. Then I'll show you a letter. You'll find the picture on the card that begins with the sound for the letter and put a marker on it.**
Model the game	Hold up the *p* Alphabet Card.	**Test** **The <u>name</u> of this letter is *p*. What is the <u>sound</u> for this letter?**
	Place Sound Match Card a on the table.	**Model** **My turn. I'll show you how to play the game. This is *mitt, pig, fan*. I'll find the picture that has the first sound /p/: *pig*** (exaggerate the first sound). ***Pig* begins with /p/.** Exaggerate the first sound and say the word: **/p/, *pig*. I'll put a marker on *pig* because *pig* has the first sound /p/.**
		Repeat with Sound Match Card b: *(foot, mouse, pie)*.
Play the game to test knowledge of initial /p/	Hold up the *p* Alphabet Card. Give each child a marker and a copy of Sound Match Card c.	**Test** **What is the <u>sound</u> for this letter?** Have children name each picture on the card *(pen, fox, moon)*. **Which picture has the first sound /p/?** Confirm correct responses: **Yes, *pen* has the first sound /p/. Everyone, put a marker on *pen* because *pen* has the first sound /p/.** Play the game again with Sound Match Cards d *(man, feather, pin)*, e *(fire, paw, mow)*, and f *(maze, fish, peas)*.

Ongoing Assessment

If...children give an incorrect picture name,	**then**...tell them the picture name and have them repeat it. Return to the picture and review it a second time.
If...children make incorrect responses,	**then**...model the correct answer. Review the sound production cue. Have children repeat the correct answer. Go back to the example a second time.

| | Give individual turns on Sound Match Cards a–f. | Have everyone name each picture on the card. Then call on an individual to tell which picture begins with /p/. |

Phonological Awareness/Alphabetic Understanding

Activity 4 — Reintroduce Letter Name and Sound

*Reintroduce f/f/;
Discriminate m, p, and f*

Objective: Children practice letter name and sound: f/f/.   Time: 2–3 minutes

	To Do		**To Say**
Introduce letter name	Hold up the *f* Alphabet Card.	Model	The <u>name</u> of this letter is *f*.
		Lead	Say the <u>name</u> with me: *f*.
		Test	What is the <u>name</u> of this letter?
Introduce letter sound	Continue holding up the *f* Alphabet Card.	Model	The <u>sound</u> for this letter is /fff/. When you say /fff/, your top teeth touch your bottom lip. Say /fff/ and feel your top teeth touch your bottom lip.
		Lead	Say the <u>sound</u> with me: /fff/.
		Test	What is the <u>sound</u> for this letter?
Test knowledge of letter name and sound	Continue holding up the *f* Alphabet Card.	Test	What is the <u>name</u> of this letter? What is the <u>sound</u> for this letter?

Ongoing Assessment

If... children make incorrect responses, **then...** tell them the name or sound and have them repeat it. Return to the letter a second time.

	Give individual turns on letter name and sound.		
Discriminate m, p, and f	Hold up the Discrimination sheet. Point to the first letter or symbol.	Test	What is the <u>name</u> of this? If it is a letter, also ask for the sound: What is the <u>sound</u> for this letter?

Continue with the remaining letters and symbols.

Ongoing Assessment

If... children make an error, **then...** tell them the name or sound and have them repeat it. Return to the beginning of the row for that letter or symbol. If children make no errors on the row, move on to the next row.

Activity 5 Writer's Warm-Up

Letter Mission: Review *f, m, p*

Objective: Children practice writing *f, m,* and *p*.

Time: 2–3 minutes

	To Do	**To Say**
Introduce the activity	Distribute a Letter Mission to each child.	**We're going to go on a letter mission. I'm going to tell you the name of a letter. You're going to write it. Let's see if we can help the dog get the bone!**
Model the activity	Hold up a Letter Mission.	**Model** **Let's do one together. The first letter is *f*. Everyone, watch as I start at the dot and write the letter *f*.** Write an *f* on your sheet.
		Lead **Now you write the letter *f*. Start at the dot and write the letter.**
Test knowledge of *f, m,* and *p*		Tell children the next letter is *m* and have them write it. Reinforce the group on the letter name: **Everyone, what's the <u>name</u> of the letter you wrote?** Continue with *m, p, f, p, f, f, m.*

Ongoing Assessment

If...children write the wrong letter or don't remember a letter,	**then**...show them the tracing card for the correct letter and model tracing the letter. Have children write the correct letter.

Activity **6** Connect Sound to Letter

Match a Picture's Initial Sound; Introduce f

Objective: Children connect /f/ to f.

Time: 2–3 minutes

	To Do		**To Say**
Introduce the activity	Gather the picture cards and the letter cards.		Tell children that they are going to choose the letter that matches the first sound of some pictures.
Model the activity	Place the *fin* Picture Card on the table.	Model	**This is *fin*. The first sound in *fin* is /fff/.** Place the *f* and *m* Letter Cards under the picture. **My turn. I'm going to choose the letter that matches this picture's first sound.** Point to the correct letter: ***f* is the letter for /fff/ like the /fff/ in *fin*.**
Test knowledge of initial /f/	Place the *fork* Picture Card on the table.	Test	**This is *fork*. What is this? The first sound in *fork* is /fff/. What is the first sound in *fork*? That's right; /fff/ is the first sound in *fork*.** Place two letter cards under the picture. Vary the choice and order.
			Your turn. Choose the letter that matches this picture's first sound. Everyone, think of which letter has the same sound as the /fff/ in *fork*. Does everyone know?
			Call on a child to point to the correct letter. **What's the <u>name</u> of the letter you pointed to? What's the <u>sound</u> for that letter? That's right; *f* is the letter for /fff/ like the /fff/ in *fork*.**
			Reinforce the letter name and sound with the group: **Everyone, what's the <u>name</u> of the letter? What's the <u>sound</u> for the letter?** Continue with the remaining cards.

Ongoing Assessment

If... children make an error,	then... model the answer, have them repeat it, and return to the picture card a second time.

Activity 7 Connect Sound to Letter

New

Letter Matching: Review f, p, m

Objective: Children connect sound to letter: f/f/, p/p/, m/m/.

Time: 6–8 minutes

	To Do	**To Say**
Introduce the activity	Place the f, p, and m Letter Cards in a pile. Spread the f, p, and m Picture Cards on the table.	**We're going to play a letter matching game. You're going to pick a letter and put it next to a picture that begins with the sound for that letter. Let's see if we can match all of the pictures!**
Model the activity		**Model** Let's do one together. I'll pick the first letter. Pick an f Letter Card from the pile.
		The sound for this letter is /fff/. Now I'll place the letter next to a picture that starts with the sound /fff/. The picture fan starts with the sound /fff/.
Test knowledge of f, p, and m		Have children take turns selecting a letter, telling its sound, and placing the letter next to a picture that begins with the sound.
		Reinforce the group on the first sound of each selected picture: **Everyone, what's the first sound in _____? What's the <u>name</u> of the letter for the sound /_/ like the /_/ in _____?**

Ongoing Assessment

If ... children make an error,	**then** ... model the letter sound and the picture's name and first sound.

New Sound /k/
Review Sounds /m/, /p/, /f/
Key Phonologic Skill Isolate Initial Sound

Phonological Awareness and Alphabetic Understanding

Activity	Materials		Time
1. Alphabetic Introduce *c*/k/	Alphabet Card: *c*	Letter Card: *c* (one per child)	1–2 minutes
2. Phonologic Does It Begin with /k/?	Picture Cards: *cat, five, can, cap, cup, pail*	Alphabet Card: *c*	4–5 minutes
3. Integrated Phonologic/Alphabetic Sound Match with /f/	Alphabet Card: *f* Sound Match Cards: a–f (one set per child) Teacher Resource Package 1 game markers (not provided)		4–5 minutes
4. Alphabetic Reintroduce *c*/k/; Discriminate *m, p,* and *f*	Alphabet Card: *c* Discrimination Teacher Resource Package 1		2–3 minutes

Writing and Spelling

Activity	Materials		Time
5. Writer's Warm-Up Introduce *c*	Tracing Cards: *c, m, p, f* Writer's Warm-Up (one per child) Student Activity Book 1, p. 22		2–3 minutes
6. Integrated Phonologic/Alphabetic Match a Picture's Initial Sound; Introduce *c*	Picture Cards: all *c* cards	Letter Cards: *c, f, p, m*	2–3 minutes
New **7. Phonologic/Spelling** Sound Dictation: Review *f, p, m*	Tracing Cards: *f, p, m* Write-On/Wipe-Off Cards (one per child)	markers (not provided)	6–8 minutes

Activity 1 Introduce Letter Name and Sound

Introduce c/k/

Objective: Children learn and trace c/k/.

Time: 1–2 minutes

	To Do	To Say	
Introduce letter name	Hold up the *c* Alphabet Card.	Model	The <u>name</u> of this letter is *c*.
		Lead	Say the <u>name</u> with me: *c*.
		Test	What is the <u>name</u> of this letter?
Introduce letter sound	Continue holding up the *c* Alphabet Card.	Model	The <u>sound</u> for this letter is /k/. When you say /k/, the back of your tongue is humped in the back of your mouth. Say /k/ and feel that the back of your tongue is humped in the back of your mouth.
		Lead	Say the <u>sound</u> with me: /k/.
		Test	What is the <u>sound</u> for this letter?
Test knowledge of letter name and sound	Continue holding up the *c* Alphabet Card.	Test	What is the <u>name</u> of this letter? What is the <u>sound</u> for this letter?

Ongoing Assessment

If . . . children make an error,	**then** . . . tell them the name or sound and have them repeat it. Return to the letter a second time.

Give individual turns on letter name and sound.

Model tracing c	Distribute a *c* Letter Card to each child. Hold up the *c* Alphabet Card.	Model	**Everyone, watch. I'll trace the letter c.**

Have children trace the *c* on their letter cards three times. Tell them to say /k/ each time they trace the letter.

Ongoing Assessment

If . . . children make an error,	**then** . . . put your hand over their hand and guide them to trace the letter. Then have children try to trace the letter on their own. Repeat as necessary.

Activity 2 — Isolate Initial Sound

Does It Begin with /k/?

Objective: Children isolate initial /k/.

Time: 4–5 minutes

	To Do	To Say	
Model names of pictures	Gather the picture cards. Place *cat* on the table.	**Model**	**This is *cat*. What is this?** Continue with *five, can, cap, cup,* and *pail*. Test children on the picture names by placing the cards on the table one at a time and asking: **What is this?**
Introduce the game Does It Begin with /k/?	Hold up the *c* Alphabet Card.		**We're going to play a game. I'll show you a picture. You'll tell whether it begins with /k/.** **Let's say /k/. When you say /k/, the back of your tongue is humped in the back of your mouth. Say /k/ and feel that the back of your tongue is humped in the back of your mouth.**
Model the game	Place the *cat* Picture Card on the table.	**Model**	**My turn. I'll say the name of the picture and then tell whether it begins with /k/: *cat*** (exaggerate the first sound). ***Cat* begins with /k/. The back of my tongue is humped in the back of my mouth when I say /k/, *cat*. Next picture: *five*** (exaggerate the first sound). ***Five* does not begin with /k/.**
Test knowledge of /k/	Place the *can* Picture Card on the table.	**Test**	**This is *can*. What is this? Does *can* begin with /k/?** Confirm correct responses and prompt sound production: **Yes, *can* begins with /k/.** **Let's say /k/. When you say /k/, the back of your tongue is humped in the back of your mouth. Say /k/ and feel that the back of your tongue is humped in the back of your mouth: *can*.** Continue with the remaining cards.
	Give individual turns.		

Ongoing Assessment

If... children make incorrect responses,	then... model the correct answer. Review the sound production cue. Have children repeat the correct answer. Go back to the example a second time.

 **Activity 3** Isolate Initial Sound

Sound Match with /f/

Objective: Children isolate picture's initial sound and connect to letter.

Time: 4–5 minutes

	To Do	**To Say**
Introduce the game Sound Match	Gather a marker and one copy of Sound Match Cards a–f for each child.	**I'm going to teach you how to play Sound Match. I'll give you a small card. Then I'll show you a letter. You'll find the picture on the card that begins with the sound for the letter and put a marker on it.**
Model the game	Hold up the *f* Alphabet Card. Place Sound Match Card a on the table.	**Test** **The <u>name</u> of this letter is *f*. What is the <u>sound</u> for this letter?** **Model** **My turn. I'll show you how to play the game. This is *mitt, pig, fan*. I'll find the picture that begins with /fff/.** Point to the *f* Alphabet Card. **Fan** (exaggerate the first sound). **Fan begins with /fff/.** Exaggerate the first sound and say the word: **/fff/, *fan*. I'll put a marker on *fan* because *fan* begins with /fff/.** Model again with Sound Match Card b *(foot, mouse, pie)*.
Play the game to test knowledge of initial /f/	Hold up the *f* Alphabet Card. Give each child a marker and a copy of Sound Match Card c *(pen, fox, moon)*. Give individual turns on Sound Match Cards a–f.	**Test** **What is the <u>sound</u> for this letter?** Have children name each picture. **Which picture begins with /fff/?** Point to the *f* Alphabet Card. Confirm correct responses: **Yes, *fox* begins with /fff/. Everyone, put a marker on *fox* because *fox* begins with /fff/.** Play the game again with Sound Match Cards d *(man, feather, pin)*, e *(fire, paw, mow)*, and f *(maze, fish, peas)*.

Ongoing Assessment

If... children make incorrect responses,	then... model the correct answer. Review the sound production cue. Have children repeat the correct answer. Go back to the example a second time.

Phonological Awareness/Alphabetic Understanding

Activity 4 Reintroduce Letter Name and Sound

Reintroduce c/k/;
Discriminate m, p, and f

Objective: Children practice letter name and sound: c/k/.   Time: 2–3 minutes

	To Do	To Say	
Introduce letter name	Hold up the *c* Alphabet Card.	Model	The <u>name</u> of this letter is *c*.
		Lead	Say the <u>name</u> with me: *c*.
		Test	What is the <u>name</u> of this letter?
Introduce letter sound	Continue holding up the *c* Alphabet Card.	Model	The <u>sound</u> for this letter is /k/. When you say /k/, the back of your tongue is humped in the back of your mouth. Say /k/ and feel that the back of your tongue is humped in the back of your mouth.
		Lead	Say the <u>sound</u> with me: /k/.
		Test	What is the <u>sound</u> for this letter?
Test knowledge of letter name and sound	Continue holding up the *c* Alphabet Card.	Test	What is the <u>name</u> of this letter? What is the <u>sound</u> for this letter?
	Give individual turns on letter name and sound.		**Ongoing Assessment**
			If...children make an error, **then**...tell them the name or sound, have them repeat the name or sound, and return to the letter a second time.
Discriminate *m*, *p*, and *f*	Hold up the Discrimination sheet. Point to the first letter or symbol.	Test	**What is the <u>name</u> of this?** If it is a letter, also ask for the sound: **What is the <u>sound</u> for this letter?**
			Continue with the remaining letters and symbols.
			Ongoing Assessment
			If...children make an error, **then**...tell them the name or sound and have them repeat it. Return to the beginning of the row for that letter or symbol. If children make no errors on the row, move on to the next row.

Activity **5** Writer's Warm-Up

Introduce c

Objective: Children trace and write *c* and review writing *m*, *p*, and *f*.   Time: 2–3 minutes

	To Do	**To Say**	
Review letter name and sound	Hold up the *c* Tracing Card.	**What is the <u>name</u> of this letter? What is the <u>sound</u> for this letter?**	
Model tracing c	Distribute a Writer's Warm-Up to each child. Hold up the *c* Tracing Card. Model tracing c again.	**Model** **Lead** **Model** **Lead**	**Everyone, watch as I trace the letter c with my finger.** **Now you trace the first two c's on your warm-up sheet with your finger.** **Everyone, watch as I trace c again.** **Now use your pencil to trace the next two c's on your warm-up sheet.**
Model writing c	Hold up the lined side of the *c* Tracing Card.	**Model**	**Everyone, watch as I write the letter c. I start at the dot and write the letter.** Have children write the letter *c* two times on their warm-up sheets. Remind them to write their letters carefully.

Ongoing Assessment

If... children make an error,	**then...** have them write the letter again. If needed, put your hand over their hand and guide them to write the letter. Then have them write the letter on their own. Repeat as necessary.

Test children on writing c	Continue to hold up the lined side of the *c* Tracing Card. Model writing *c* again.	Have children cover the letters they traced and wrote. Have them write the letter *c* two times from memory. Then have them uncover their papers and compare the letters. **Do your letters look the same? Circle the letter that is your best work.**

Review m, p, f		Have children trace and write each review letter on their warm-up sheets.

Ongoing Assessment

If... children make an error,	**then...** model writing the letter on the tracing card and have them write the letter again. If needed, put your hand over their hand and guide them to write the letter. Then have them write the letter on their own. Repeat as necessary.

Writing/Spelling

Activity 6 — Connect Sound to Letter

Match a Picture's Initial Sound; Introduce c

Objective: Children connect /k/ to c.

Time: 2–3 minutes

	To Do	To Say	
Introduce the activity	Gather the picture cards and the letter cards.		Tell children that they are going to choose the letter that matches the first sound of some pictures.
Model the activity	Place the *cat* Picture Card on the table.	**Model**	**This is cat. The first sound in cat is /k/.** Place the *c* and *m* Letter Cards under the picture. **My turn. I'm going to choose the letter that matches this picture's first sound.** Point to the correct letter: **c is the letter for /k/ like the /k/ in cat.**
Test knowledge of initial /k/	Place the *cup* Picture Card on the table.	**Test**	**This is cup. What is this? The first sound in cup is /k/. What is the first sound in cup? That's right; /k/ is the first sound in cup.** Place two letter cards under the picture. Vary the choice and order. **Your turn. Choose the letter that matches this picture's first sound. Everyone, think of which letter has the same sound as the /k/ in cup. Does everyone know?** Call on a child to point to the correct letter. **What's the <u>name</u> of the letter you pointed to? What's the <u>sound</u> for that letter? That's right; c is the letter for /k/ like the /k/ in cup.** Reinforce the letter name and sound with the group: **Everyone, what's the <u>name</u> of the letter? What's the <u>sound</u> for the letter?** Continue with the remaining cards.

Ongoing Assessment

If... children make an error,	then... model the answer, have them repeat it, and return to the picture card a second time.

Activity **7** Connect Sound to Letter

Sound Dictation: Review f, p, m

Objective: Children connect sound to letter:
f/f/, p/p/, m/m/.

Time: 6–8 minutes

	To Do	**To Say**
Introduce the activity	Gather the *f, p,* and *m* Tracing Cards. Distribute a Write-On/Wipe-Off Card and a marker to each child.	**Today we're going to review the letters *f, p,* and *m*. I'm going to tell you the sound of a letter. You're going to write the letter for that sound on your card.** Review the letter names and sounds using the tracing cards.
Model the activity	Hold up a Write-On/Wipe-Off Card.	**Model** **My turn. I'll show you how this activity works. The first sound is /p/. Now I'll write the letter for the sound /p/.** Write the letter *p* on your card. **The letter *p* is the letter for the sound /p/.** **Lead** **Your turn. Now you write the letter for the sound /p/.**
Test knowledge of *f, p,* and *m*		Dictate a sound and have children write the corresponding letter. Reinforce the group on the letter name and sound: **Everyone, what's the <u>name</u> of the letter you wrote? What is the <u>sound</u> for this letter?** Dictate each sound twice or as time allows. Erase the cards between sounds.

Ongoing Assessment

If... children write the wrong letter or don't remember a letter,	then... show them the tracing card for the correct letter. Trace the letter and say the letter sound.

New Sound /k/
Review Sounds /m/, /p/, /f/
Key Phonologic Skill Isolate Initial Sound

Phonological Awareness and Alphabetic Understanding

Activity	Materials	Time
1. Alphabetic Introduce *c*/k/	Alphabet Card: *c* Letter Card: *c* (one per child)	1–2 minutes
2. Phonologic Which Picture Begins with /k/?	Picture Choices: 11-1, 11-2, 11-3 Teacher Resource Package 1	4–5 minutes
3. Integrated Phonologic/Alphabetic Sound Match with /p/ and /f/	Alphabet Cards: *p, f* Sound Match Cards: a–f (one set per child) Teacher Resource Package 1 game markers (not provided)	4–5 minutes
4. Alphabetic Reintroduce *c*/k/; Discriminate *m, p, f,* and *c*	Alphabet Cards: *c, m, p, f* Discrimination Teacher Resource Package 1	2–3 minutes

Writing and Spelling

Activity	Materials	Time
5. Writer's Warm-Up Introduce *c*	Writer's Warm-Up (one per child) Student Activity Book 1, p. 23 Tracing Cards: *c, m, p, f*	2–3 minutes
6. Integrated Phonologic/Alphabetic Match a Picture's Initial Sound; Introduce *c*	Picture Cards: all *c* cards Letter Cards: *f, c, m, p*	2–3 minutes
7. Phonologic/Spelling First Sounds: Review *m, p, c, f*	First Sounds (one per child) Student Activity Book 1, p. 24	6–8 minutes

Activity **1** Introduce Letter Name and Sound

Introduce c/k/

Objective: Children learn and trace c/k/.

Time: 1–2 minutes

	To Do	**To Say**	
Introduce letter name	Hold up the *c* Alphabet Card.	Model	**The <u>name</u> of this letter is *c*.**
		Lead	**Say the <u>name</u> with me: *c*.**
		Test	**What is the <u>name</u> of this letter?**
Introduce letter sound	Continue holding up the *c* Alphabet Card.	Model	**The <u>sound</u> for this letter is /k/. When you say /k/, the back of your tongue is humped in the back of your mouth. Say /k/ and feel that the back of your tongue is humped in the back of your mouth.**
		Lead	**Say the <u>sound</u> with me: /k/.**
		Test	**What is the <u>sound</u> for this letter?**
Test knowledge of letter name and sound	Continue holding up the *c* Alphabet Card.	Test	**What is the <u>name</u> of this letter? What is the <u>sound</u> for this letter?**
	Give individual turns on letter name and sound.		**Ongoing Assessment** **If...** children make an error, **then...** tell them the name or sound and have them repeat it. Return to the letter a second time.
Model tracing *c*	Distribute the *c* Letter Cards. Hold up the *c* Alphabet Card.	Model	**Everyone, watch. I'll trace the letter *c*.** Have children trace the *c* on their letter cards three times. Tell them to say /k/ each time they trace the letter.
			Ongoing Assessment **If...** children make an error, **then...** put your hand over their hand and guide them to trace the letter. Then have them try to trace the letter on their own. Repeat as necessary.

Activity 2 Isolate Initial Sound

Which Picture Begins with /k/?

Objective: Children isolate initial /k/.

Time: 4–5 minutes

	To Do	To Say	
Model names of pictures	Gather the picture choices. Display Picture Choice 11-1. Point to *mop.*	**Model**	**This is *mop*. What is this?** Continue with the remaining pictures *(fork, coat; pie, cap, foot).* Test children on the picture names by pointing to the pictures one at a time and asking: **What is this?**
Introduce the game Which Picture Begins with /k/?			**We're going to play a game. I'll show you three pictures. You'll find the picture with the first sound /k/.** **Let's say /k/. Remember, when you say /k/, the back of your tongue is humped in the back of your mouth. Say /k/ and feel that the back of your tongue is humped in the back of your mouth.**
Model the game	Hold up Picture Choice 11-1. Display the pictures *mop, fork,* and *coat.* Cover the others.	**Model**	**My turn. I'll show you how to play the game. This is *mop, fork, coat*. I'll find the picture that has the first sound /k/: *coat*** (exaggerate the first sound). ***Coat* has the first sound /k/.** Exaggerate the first sound and say the word: **/k/, *coat*.** Model another example: *pie, cap, foot.*
Play the game to test knowledge of /k/	Hold up Picture Choice 11-2. Display the pictures *cut, fan,* and *pig.* Cover the others.		Have children name each picture. **Which picture has the first sound /k/?** Confirm correct responses and prompt sound production: **Yes, *cut* has the first sound /k/. Let's say /k/. Remember, when you say /k/, the back of your tongue is humped in the back of your mouth. Say /k/ and feel that the back of your tongue is humped in the back of your mouth: *cut*.** Continue with the bottom row of pictures *(pool, cup, maze)* and Picture Choice 11-3 *(fish, pan, cane; can, map, moon).*
	Give individual turns.		

Ongoing Assessment

If... children make incorrect responses,	then... model the correct answer. Review the sound production cue. Have children repeat the correct answer. Go back to the example a second time.

Activity **3** Isolate Initial Sound

Sound Match with /p/ and /f/

Objective: Children isolate pictures' initial sounds and connect to letter.

Time: 4–5 minutes

	To Do	**To Say**	
Introduce the game Sound Match with /p/ and /f/	Gather a marker and one copy of Sound Match Cards a–f for each child.		**I'm going to teach you to play Sound Match. First, I'll give you a small card. Then I'll show you a letter. You'll find the picture on the card that begins with the sound for the letter and put a marker on it. You'll need to be careful, though, because I'm going to show you two different letters.**
Model the game	Hold up the *p* Alphabet Card.	Test	**The <u>name</u> of this letter is *p*. What is the <u>sound</u> for the letter *p*?**
	Place Sound Match Card a on the table.	Model	**My turn. I'll show you how to play the game. This is *mitt, pig, fan*. I'll find the picture that begins with /p/.** Point to the *p* Alphabet Card. **Pig** (exaggerate the first sound). **Pig begins with /p/.** Exaggerate the first sound and say the word: **/p/, pig. I'll put a marker on *pig* because *pig* begins with /p/.**
			Model again with Sound Match Card b *(foot, mouse, pie)* and target sound /fff/.
Play the game to test knowledge of initial /p/ and /f/	Hold up the *p* Alphabet Card.	Test	**What is the <u>sound</u> for this letter?**
	Give each child a marker and a copy of Sound Match Card c *(pen, fox, moon)*.		Have children name each picture on the card. **Which picture begins with /p/?** Point to the *p* Alphabet Card. Confirm correct responses: **Yes, *pen* begins with /p/. Everyone, put a marker on *pen* because *pen* begins with /p/.**
			Repeat with Sound Match Cards d (target sound /fff/; pictures: *man, feather, pin*), e (target sound /fff/; pictures: *fire, paw, mow*), and f (target sound /p/; pictures: *maze, fish, peas*).
	Give individual turns on Sound Match Cards a–f, using /p/ or /fff/ as the target sound.		

Ongoing Assessment

If . . . children make incorrect responses,	**then** . . . model the correct answer. Review the sound production cue. Have children repeat the correct answer. Go back to the example a second time.

Phonological Awareness/Alphabetic Understanding

Activity 4 Reintroduce Letter Name and Sound

Reintroduce c/k/;
Discriminate m, p, f, and c

Objective: Children practice letter name and sound: c/k/.   Time: 2–3 minutes

	To Do	To Say	
Introduce letter name	Hold up the *c* Alphabet Card.	Model	The <u>name</u> of this letter is *c*.
		Lead	Say the <u>name</u> with me: *c*.
		Test	What is the <u>name</u> of this letter?
Introduce letter sound	Continue holding up the *c* Alphabet Card.	Model	The <u>sound</u> for this letter is /k/. When you say /k/, the back of your tongue is humped in the back of your mouth. Say /k/ and feel that the back of your tongue is humped in the back of your mouth.
		Lead	Say the <u>sound</u> with me: /k/.
		Test	What is the <u>sound</u> for this letter?
Test knowledge of letter name and sound	Continue holding up the *c* Alphabet Card.	Test	What is the <u>name</u> of this letter? What is the <u>sound</u> for this letter?
	Give individual turns on letter name and sound.		**Ongoing Assessment** **If...** children make incorrect responses, **then...** tell them the name or sound, have them repeat the name or sound, and return to the letter a second time.
Discriminate *m, p, f,* and *c*	Hold up the Discrimination sheet. Point to the first letter.	Test	What is the <u>name</u> of this letter? What is the <u>sound</u> for this letter? Continue with the remaining letters. **Ongoing Assessment** **If...** children make an error, **then...** tell them the name or sound and have them repeat it. Return to the beginning of the row for that letter. If children make no errors on the row, move on to the next row.

Phonological Awareness/Alphabetic Understanding

 **Activity** 5 **Writer's Warm-Up**

Introduce c

Objective: Children trace and write *c* and review writing *m, p,* and *f.*

Time: 2–3 minutes

	To Do	**To Say**	
Review letter name and sound	Hold up the *c* Tracing Card.	**What is the <u>name</u> of this letter? What is the <u>sound</u> for this letter?**	
Model tracing c	Distribute a Writer's Warm-Up to each child. Hold up the *c* Tracing Card. Model tracing *c* again.	Model	**Everyone, watch as I trace the letter c with my finger.**
		Lead	**Now you trace the first two c's on your warm-up sheet with your finger.**
		Model	**Everyone, watch as I trace c again.**
		Lead	**Now use your pencil to trace the next two c's on your warm-up sheet.**
Model writing c	Hold up the lined side of the *c* Tracing Card.	Model	**Everyone, watch as I write the letter c. I start at the dot and write the letter.**

Have children write the letter *c* two times on their warm-up sheets. Remind them to write their letters carefully.

Ongoing Assessment

If... children make an error,	then... have them write the letter again. If needed, put your hand over their hand and guide them to write the letter. Then have them write the letter on their own. Repeat as necessary.

Test children on writing c	Continue to hold up the lined side of the *c* Tracing Card. Model writing *c* again.	Have children cover the letters they traced and wrote. Have them write the letter *c* two times from memory. Then have them uncover their papers and compare the letters. **Do your letters look the same? Circle the letter that is your best work.**

Review **m, p, f**		Have children trace and write each review letter on their warm-up sheets.

Ongoing Assessment

If... children make an error,	then... use the tracing card to model writing the letter and have them write the letter again. If needed, put your hand over their hand and guide them to write the letter. Then have them write the letter on their own. Repeat as necessary.

Writing/Spelling

Activity 6 Connect Sound to Letter

Match a Picture's Initial Sound; Introduce c

Objective: Children connect /k/ to c.

Time: 2–3 minutes

	To Do		**To Say**
Introduce the activity	Gather the picture cards and the letter cards.		Tell children that they are going to choose the letter that matches the first sound of some pictures.
Model the activity	Place the *cup* Picture Card on the table.	Model	**This is cup. The first sound in cup is /k/.** Place the *f* and *c* Letter Cards under the picture. **My turn. I'm going to choose the letter that matches this picture's first sound.** Point to the correct letter: **c is the letter for /k/ like the /k/ in cup.**
Test knowledge of initial /k/	Place the *can* Picture Card on the table.	Test	**This is can. What is this? The first sound in can is /k/. What is the first sound in can? That's right; /k/ is the first sound in can.** Place two letter cards under the picture. Vary the choice and order. **Your turn. Choose the letter that matches this picture's first sound. Everyone, think of which letter has the same sound as the /k/ in can. Does everyone know?** Call on a child to point to the correct letter. **What's the <u>name</u> of the letter you pointed to? What's the <u>sound</u> for that letter? That's right; c is the letter for /k/ like the /k/ in can.** Reinforce the letter name and sound with the group: **Everyone, what's the <u>name</u> of the letter? What's the <u>sound</u> for that letter?** Continue with *cap, cat, cow, coat, cookie,* and *carrot.*

Ongoing Assessment

If... children make an error,	then... model the answer, have them repeat it, and return to the picture card a second time.

Activity **7** Connect Sound to Letter

First Sounds: Review m, p, c, f

Objective: Children connect initial sound to letter: m/m/, p/p/, c/k/, f/f/.

Time: 6–8 minutes

	To Do	**To Say**	
Introduce the activity	Distribute a First Sounds page to each child.		Tell children that they are going to write the letter that matches the first sound of some pictures.
Model the activity	Hold up a First Sounds page. Point to the picture of *moon*.	**Model**	**This is *moon*. The first sound in *moon* is /mmm/. I'm going to write the letter for the sound /mmm/ like the /mmm/ in *moon*.** Write the letter *m* under the picture.
		Lead	**Now you write the letter for the sound /mmm/ like the /mmm/ in *moon*. Start at the dot and write the letter. That's right; *m* is the letter for /mmm/ like the /mmm/ in *moon*.**
Test knowledge of *p, c, f,* and *m*	Point to the picture of *pin* on the First Sounds page.	**Test**	**This is *pin*. What is the first sound in *pin*? That's right; /p/ is the first sound in *pin*.**
			Your turn. Write the letter that matches this picture's first sound. Everyone, write the letter for the same sound as the /p/ in *pin*. Start at the dot and write the letter.
			Reinforce the group on the letter name and sound: **Everyone, what's the <u>name</u> of the letter you wrote? What's the <u>sound</u> for that letter?**
			Continue with the remaining pictures.

Ongoing Assessment

If... children make an error,	then... model the letter name and sound and have children repeat them. Have children write the correct letter.

Writing/Spelling

LESSON 12

New Sound /k/
Review Sounds /m/, /p/, /f/
Key Phonologic Skill Isolate Initial Sound

Phonological Awareness and Alphabetic Understanding

Activity	Materials		Time
1. Alphabetic Introduce *c*/k/	Alphabet Card: *c*	Letter Card: *c* (one per child)	1–2 minutes
2. Integrated Phonologic/Alphabetic Which Picture Begins with /k/?	Alphabet Card: *c* Picture Choices: 12-1, 12-2, 12-3 Teacher Resource Package 1		4–5 minutes
3. Integrated Phonologic/Alphabetic First Sound Mix-Up Game with /f/ and /k/	Picture Cards: all *f* and *c* cards	Letter Cards: *f, c*	4–5 minutes
4. Alphabetic Reintroduce *c*/k/; Discriminate *m, p, f,* and *c*	Alphabet Card: *c* Discrimination Teacher Resource Package 1		2–3 minutes

Writing and Spelling

Activity	Materials		Time
New **5. Writer's Warm-Up** Memory Review: *m, p, f, c*	Write-On/Wipe-Off Cards (one per child) markers (not provided)	Tracing Cards: *m, p, f, c*	2–3 minutes
6. Integrated Phonologic/Alphabetic Match a Picture's Initial Sound; Introduce *c*	Picture Cards: all *c* cards	Letter Cards: *c, p, f, m*	2–3 minutes
7. Phonologic/Spelling Letter Cross-Out Game: *c, f, p, m*	Picture Cards: *can, coat, cat, fan, fish, fox, man, mop, pail, pig* Letter Cross-Out (one per child) Student Activity Book 1, p. 25		6–8 minutes

Activity 1 Introduce Letter Name and Sound

Introduce c /k/

Objective: Children learn and trace c/k/.

Time: 1–2 minutes

	To Do	**To Say**	
Introduce letter name	Hold up the *c* Alphabet Card.	Model	The <u>name</u> of this letter is *c*.
		Lead	Say the <u>name</u> with me: *c*.
		Test	What is the <u>name</u> of this letter?
Introduce letter sound	Continue holding up the *c* Alphabet Card.	Model	The <u>sound</u> for this letter is /k/. When you say /k/, the back of your tongue is humped in the back of your mouth. Say /k/ and feel that the back of your tongue is humped in the back of your mouth.
		Lead	Say the <u>sound</u> with me: /k/.
		Test	What is the <u>sound</u> for this letter?
Test knowledge of letter name and sound	Continue holding up the *c* Alphabet Card. Give individual turns on letter name and sound.	Test	What is the <u>name</u> of this letter? What is the <u>sound</u> for this letter?

Ongoing Assessment

If... children make an error,	then... tell them the name or sound and have them repeat it. Return to the letter a second time.

Model tracing *c*	Distribute the *c* Letter Cards. Hold up the *c* Alphabet Card.	Model	Everyone, watch. I'll trace the letter *c*. Have children trace the *c* on their letter cards three times. Tell them to say /k/ each time they trace the letter.

Ongoing Assessment

If... children make an error,	then... put your hand over their hand and guide them to trace the letter. Then have them try to trace the letter on their own. Repeat as necessary.

Activity 2 Isolate Initial Sound

Which Picture Begins with /k/?

Objective: Children isolate initial /k/ and connect sound to letter.

Time: 4–5 minutes

	To Do	To Say	
Model names of pictures	Gather the picture choices. Display Picture Choice 12-1. Point to *cone*.	Model	**This is *cone*. What is this?** Continue with the remaining pictures: *pig, maze; dog, cup,* and *mouse*. Test children on the picture names by pointing to the pictures one at a time and asking: **What is this?**
Introduce the game Which Picture Begins with /k/?			**We're going to play a game. I'll show you a letter. Then I'll show you three pictures. You'll find the picture that begins with the sound for the letter.**
	Hold up the *c* Alphabet Card.	Model	**The <u>name</u> of this letter is *c*. The <u>sound</u> for this letter is /k/. Remember, when you say /k/, the back of your tongue is humped in the back of your mouth. Say /k/ and feel that the back of your tongue is humped in the back of your mouth.**
		Test	**What is the <u>sound</u> for this letter?**
Model the game	Hold up Picture Choice 12-1. Display the pictures *cone, pig,* and *maze*. Cover the others.	Model	**My turn. I'll show you how to play the game. This is *cone, pig, maze*. I'll find the picture that has the first sound /k/.** Point to the *c* Alphabet Card. **Cone** (exaggerate the first sound). **Cone has the first sound /k/.** Exaggerate the first sound and say the word: **/k/, cone.** Model again with *dog, cup,* and *mouse*.
Play the game to test knowledge of initial /k/	Hold up the *c* Alphabet Card. Hold up Picture Choice 12-2. Display the pictures *fin, coat,* and *mow*. Cover the others *(pen, foot, can)*.	Test	**What is the <u>sound</u> for this letter?** Have children name each picture. **Which picture has the first sound /k/?** Confirm correct responses and prompt sound production: **Yes, *coat* has the first sound /k/. Let's say /k/. Remember, when you say /k/, the back of your tongue is humped in the back of your mouth. Say /k/ and feel that the back of your tongue is humped in the back of your mouth: *coat*.** Continue with the bottom row of pictures and Picture Choice 12-3 *(peas, mitt, cat; cap, pin, food)*.
	Give individual turns.		

Ongoing Assessment

If... children make incorrect responses,	then... model the correct answer. Review the sound production cue. Have children repeat the correct answer. Go back to the example a second time.

Activity **3** Isolate Initial Sound

*First Sound Mix-Up Game
with /f/ and /k/*

Objective: Children isolate initial /f/ and /k/.　　　　Time: 4–5 minutes

	To Do	**To Say**
Review names of pictures	Gather the *c* and *f* Picture Cards.	For each picture, ask: **What is this?**
Introduce the game First Sound Mix-Up	Mix the picture cards and place them in a pile on the table. Place the *c* and *f* Letter Cards on the table.	**Today we're going to play First Sound Mix-Up. I'll hold up a picture. You'll tell me the name of the picture and its first sound. You'll need to be careful, though, because the pictures are all mixed up. Some of the pictures begin with /fff/ and some begin with /k/.**
Model the game	Choose a picture card from the pile.	**Model** **My turn. I'll show you how to play the game. This is *fin*. I'll say the first sound in *fin*: /fff/. Now I'll place *fin* next to the letter for the sound /fff/.** Place *fin* next to the *f* Letter Card. **Remember, the <u>name</u> of this letter is *f*. The <u>sound</u> for *f* is /fff/.**
	Display the next picture card.	**I'll do one more. This is *can*. I'll say the first sound in *can*: /k/. Now I'll place *can* next to the letter for the sound /k/.** Place *can* next to the *c* Letter Card. **Remember, the <u>name</u> of this letter is *c*. The <u>sound</u> for *c* is /k/.**
Play the game to test knowledge of /f/ and /k/	Display the next picture card.	**Test** **This is *cup*. What is this? What is the first sound in *cup*?** Confirm correct responses and prompt sound production: **Yes, /k/ is the first sound in *cup*. Remember, when you say /k/, the back of your tongue is humped in the back of your mouth. Say /k/ and feel that the back of your tongue is humped in the back of your mouth: *cup*. Now place *cup* next to the letter for the sound /k/.** Call on a child to place *cup* next to the letter for the sound /k/. **What's the name of the letter for the sound /k/? That's right; *c* is the letter for /k/ like the /k/ in *cup*.** Continue with three to five more examples.
	Give individual turns.	**Ongoing Assessment**
		If...children make incorrect responses, **then**...tell them the answer and have them repeat it. Place the picture back in the pile so that you can return to it a second time.

Phonological Awareness/Alphabetic Understanding

Activity 4 Reintroduce Letter Name and Sound

Reintroduce c/k/;
Discriminate m, p, f, and c

Objective: Children practice letter name and sound: c/k/.   Time: 2–3 minutes

	To Do	**To Say**	
Introduce letter name	Hold up the *c* Alphabet Card.	Model	The <u>name</u> of this letter is *c*.
		Lead	Say the <u>name</u> with me: *c*.
		Test	What is the <u>name</u> of this letter?
Introduce letter sound	Continue holding up the *c* Alphabet Card.	Model	The <u>sound</u> for this letter is /k/. When you say /k/, the back of your tongue is humped in the back of your mouth. Say /k/ and feel that the back of your tongue is humped in the back of your mouth.
		Lead	Say the <u>sound</u> with me: /k/.
		Test	What is the <u>sound</u> for this letter?
Test knowledge of letter name and sound	Continue holding up the *c* Alphabet Card.	Test	What is the <u>name</u> of this letter? What is the <u>sound</u> for this letter?
	Give individual turns on letter name and sound.	**Ongoing Assessment**	
		If...children make incorrect responses,	then...tell them the name or sound, have them repeat the name or sound, and return to the letter a second time.
Discriminate m, p, f, and c	Hold up the Discrimination sheet. Point to the first letter.	Test	What is the <u>name</u> of this letter? What is the <u>sound</u> for this letter?
		Continue with the remaining letters.	
		Ongoing Assessment	
		If...children make an error,	then...tell them the name or sound and have them repeat it. Return to the beginning of the row for that letter. If children make no errors on the row, move on to the next row.

Memory Review: m, p, f, c

Objective: Children write review letters: *m, p, f, c.*

Time: 2–3 minutes

	To Do	**To Say**
Introduce the activity	Gather the tracing cards. Distribute a Write-On/Wipe-Off Card and a marker to each child.	**Today we're going to review the letters *m, p, f,* and *c.* I'm going to name a letter. You're going to write the letter on your Write-On/Wipe-Off Card.** Review the letter names using the tracing cards.
Model the activity	Hold up a Write-On/ Wipe-Off Card.	**Model** **My turn. I'll show you how this activity works. The first letter is *c.* Now I'll write the letter *c* on my card.** Write a *c* on your card. **Lead** **Your turn. Now you write the letter *c* on your card.**
Test knowledge of *m, p, f,* and *c*		Name a letter and have children write the letter on their cards. Reinforce the group on the letter name: **Everyone, what's the <u>name</u> of the letter you wrote?** Dictate each letter twice or as time allows. Erase the cards between letters.

Ongoing Assessment

If... children write the wrong letter or don't remember a letter,	**then**... show them the tracing card for the letter. Trace the letter and say the letter name.

Activity 6 — Connect Sound to Letter

Match a Picture's Initial Sound; Introduce c

Objective: Children connect /k/ to c.

Time: 2–3 minutes

	To Do	To Say	
Introduce the activity	Gather the picture cards and the letter cards.		Tell children that they are going to choose the letter that matches the first sound of some pictures.
Model the activity	Place the *coat* Picture Card on the table.	Model	**This is coat. The first sound in coat is /k/.** Place the *c* and *p* Letter Cards under the picture. **My turn. I'm going to choose the letter that matches this picture's first sound.** Point to the correct letter: **c is the letter for /k/ like the /k/ in coat.**
Test knowledge of initial /k/	Place the *cap* Picture Card on the table.	Test	**This is cap. What is this? The first sound in cap is /k/. What is the first sound in cap? That's right; /k/ is the first sound in cap.** Place two letter cards under the picture. Vary the choice and order. **Your turn. Choose the letter that matches this picture's first sound. Everyone, think of which letter has the same sound as the /k/ in cap. Does everyone know?** Call on a child to point to the correct letter. **What's the name of the letter you pointed to? What's the sound for that letter? That's right; c is the letter for /k/ like the /k/ in cap.** Reinforce the letter name and sound with the group: **Everyone, what's the <u>name</u> of the letter? What is the <u>sound</u> for this letter?** Continue with the remaining cards.
	Give individual turns.		

Ongoing Assessment

If... children make an error,	then... model the answer, have them repeat it, and return to the picture card a second time.

Activity 7 Connect Sound to Letter

Letter Cross-Out Game: c, f, p, m

Objective: Children connect sound to letter:
c/k/, f/f/, p/p/, m/m/.

Time: 6–8 minutes

	To Do	**To Say**
Introduce the game Letter Cross-Out	Gather the picture cards. Distribute a Letter Cross-Out to each child.	Tell children that they are going to cross out the letters that go with the first sound of some pictures. **Let's see if we can cross out all of the letters on the sheet!**
Model the game	Place the *can* Picture Card on the table.	**Model** **This is *can*. The first sound in *can* is /k/.** Hold up a Letter Cross-Out. **I'm going to cross out a letter for the same sound as the /k/ in *can*.** Cross out one of the *c*'s.
		Lead **Now you cross out a letter for the same sound as the /k/ in *can*. That's right; *c* is the letter for /k/ like the /k/ in *can*.**
Play the game to test knowledge of *c, f, p,* and *m*	Display the *man* Picture Card.	**Test** **This is *man*. What is this? The first sound in *man* is /mmm/. What is the first sound in *man*? That's right; /mmm/ is the first sound in *man*. Now cross out the letter for the same sound as the /mmm/ in *man*.**
		Reinforce the group on the letter name and sound: **Everyone, what's the <u>name</u> of the letter you crossed out? What is the <u>sound</u> for this letter?**
		Continue with the remaining cards until all of the letters have been crossed out.

Ongoing Assessment

If... children make an error,	**then...** point to the correct letter and say its sound. Have children repeat the sound and cross out the correct letter.

New Sound /t/
Review Sounds /m/, /p/, /f/, /k/
Key Phonologic Skill Isolate Initial Sound

Phonological Awareness and Alphabetic Understanding

Activity	Materials		Time
1. Alphabetic Introduce *t*/t/	Alphabet Card: *t*	Letter Card: *t* (one per child)	1–2 minutes
2. Phonologic Does It Begin with /t/?	Picture Cards: *tag, ten, tire, tape, fan, mop*		4–5 minutes
3. Integrated Phonologic/Alphabetic Sound Match with /k/, /f/, and /p/	Sound Match Cards: 13a–13b (one each per child) Teacher Resource Package 1 game markers (not provided)	Alphabet Cards: *c, f, p* Sound Production Cue Card	4–5 minutes
New **4. Alphabetic** Reintroduce *t*/t/; Grab Bag Game	Alphabet Card: *t* Letter Cards: *m, p, f, c*	paper bag (not provided)	4–5 minutes

Writing and Spelling

Activity	Materials		Time
5. Writer's Warm-Up Introduce *t*	Writer's Warm-Up (one per child) Student Activity Book 1, p. 26 Tracing Cards: *t, c, f, p, m*	marker (not provided)	2–3 minutes
6. Integrated Phonologic/Alphabetic Match a Picture's Initial Sound; Introduce *t*	Picture Cards: all *t* cards	Letter Cards: *t, c, f, p, m*	2–3 minutes
7. Phonologic/Spelling Letter Race: *c, f, p, m*	Letter Race (one per child) Student Activity Book 1, p. 27	Picture Cards: *can, cow, carrot; fin, fork, fish; pig, pail, puzzle; man, mop, monkey*	6–8 minutes

Activity 1 Introduce Letter Name and Sound

Introduce t/t/

Objective: Children learn and trace t/t/.

Time: 1–2 minutes

	To Do	To Say	
Introduce letter name	Hold up the *t* Alphabet Card.	Model	**The <u>name</u> of this letter is *t*.**
		Lead	**Say the <u>name</u> of the letter with me: *t*.**
		Test	**What is the <u>name</u> of this letter?**
Introduce letter sound	Continue holding up the *t* Alphabet Card.	Model	**The <u>sound</u> for this letter is /t/. When you say /t/, the tip of your tongue touches above your top teeth. Say /t/ and feel the tip of your tongue touch above your top teeth.**
		Lead	**Say the <u>sound</u> with me: /t/.**
		Test	**What is the <u>sound</u> for this letter?**
Test knowledge of letter name and sound	Continue holding up the *t* Alphabet Card.	Test	**What is the <u>name</u> of this letter? What is the <u>sound</u> for this letter?**
	Give individual turns on letter name and sound.		**Ongoing Assessment** **If**...children make an error, **then**...tell them the name or sound and have them repeat it. Return to the letter a second time.
Model tracing *t*	Distribute the *t* Letter Cards. Hold up the *t* Alphabet Card.	Model	**Watch. I'll trace the letter *t*.** Have children trace the *t* on their letter cards three times. Tell them to say /t/ each time they trace the letter.
			Ongoing Assessment **If**...children make an error, **then**...put your hand over their hand and guide them to trace the letter. Then have children try to trace the letter on their own. Repeat as necessary.

Activity 2 Isolate Initial Sound

Does It Begin with /t/?

Objective: Children isolate initial /t/.

Time: 4–5 minutes

	To Do	To Say	
Model names of pictures	Gather the picture cards. Place the *tag* Picture Card on the table.	**Model**	**This is *tag*. What is this?** Have children repeat. Continue with *ten, tire, tape, fan,* and *mop.* Test children on the picture names by placing the cards on the table one at a time and asking: **What is this?**
Introduce the game Does It Begin with /t/?	Practice production of the target sound.		Tell children they will play a game. They will find the pictures that begin with /t/. **Let's say /t/. When you say /t/, the tip of your tongue touches above your top teeth. Say /t/ and feel the tip of your tongue touch above your top teeth.**
Model the game	Gather the *tag* and *fan* Picture Cards. Place *tag* on the table.	**Model**	**My turn. I'll say the name of the picture and then tell if it begins with /t/: *tag*** (exaggerate the first sound). ***Tag* begins with /t/. The tip of my tongue touches above my top teeth when I say /t/, *tag*. Next picture: *fan*** (exaggerate the first sound). ***Fan* does not begin with /t/.**
Play the game to test knowledge of /t/	Place the *ten* Picture Card on the table.	**Test**	**Your turn. What is this? Does *ten* begin with /t/?** Confirm correct responses and prompt sound production: **Yes, *ten* begins with /t/. Let's say /t/. When you say /t/, the tip of your tongue touches above your top teeth. Say /t/ and feel the tip of your tongue touch above your top teeth: *ten*.** Continue with three other examples: *tire, tape, mop.*
	Give individual turns.		

Ongoing Assessment

If... children make incorrect responses,	then... model the correct answer. Review the sound production cue. Have children repeat the correct answer. Go back to the example a second time.

Activity **3** Isolate Initial Sound

Sound Match with /k/, /f/, and /p/

Objective: Children isolate initial /k/, /f/, and /p/.   Time: 4–5 minutes

	To Do	**To Say**	
Introduce the game Sound Match	Give each child a copy of Sound Match Card 13a and three game markers.		**We're going to play Sound Match, and we're going to use bigger game cards than last time. Here's how to play. I'll show you a letter. You'll find the picture on your Sound Match card that begins with the sound for that letter and put a marker on it. I'm going to show you three different letters, so be careful.**
Model the game	Place your Sound Match card in front of you, facing the children.	Model	**My turn. Here's how to play Sound Match.**
	Hold up the *p* Alphabet Card.	Test	**What is the <u>sound</u> for this letter?**
	Point to and name the pictures on your Sound Match card.	Model	**This is *fox, pig, tent, tire, cut, tag.* My turn. I'll find the picture that begins with /p/.** Point to the *p* Alphabet Card. **Pig** (exaggerate the first sound). **Pig begins with /p/.** Exaggerate the first sound and say the word: **/p/, pig. Let's all place a marker on *pig*.** Model one more example using target sound /fff/ to match *fox*.
Play the game to test knowledge of initial /k/, /f/, and /p/	Continue using Sound Match Card 13a with markers on *pig* and *fox*.	For each picture, ask: **What is this?**
		Ongoing Assessment
		If . . . children make incorrect responses,	then . . . tell them the name of the picture and have them repeat it. Come back to the picture the children named incorrectly and review it a second time.
	Continue playing. Hold up the *c* Alphabet Card.	Test	**What is the <u>sound</u> for this letter? Which picture begins with /k/? Yes,** *cut* **begins with /k/. Place a marker on** *cut* **because** *cut* **begins with /k/.**
		Ongoing Assessment
		If . . . children make incorrect responses,	then . . . model the correct answer. Review the sound production cue. Have children repeat the correct answer. Go back to the example a second time.
		After everyone places a marker on *cut*, say: **Look! We filled in a whole column.** Run your finger up and down the middle column. **Clear off your cards. Let's start a new game!**

Phonological Awareness/Alphabetic Understanding

To Do	To Say
Distribute Sound Match Card 13b.	Point to and name each picture: **This is *tie, tub, toe, cane, pool, fin.*** Point to each picture again and ask: **What is this?** Play the game for target sounds /p/, /k/, and /f/. Use the same procedure as in the first game. Play until the group wins. Then have children clear off their cards.
Give individual turns.	Point to each picture on Sound Match Card 13a, and have children name the picture. Then say: **Look at your Sound Match card. Who can name the picture that begins with /fff/?** Give each child up to three turns, one for each target sound. Then repeat the same procedure using Sound Match Card 13b.

Activity 4 Review Letter Name and Sound

Reintroduce t/t/; Grab Bag Game
Objective: Children practice letter name and sound: t/t/. Time: 4–5 minutes

	To Do	**To Say**	
Introduce letter name	Hold up the *t* Alphabet Card.	Model	The <u>name</u> of this letter is *t*.
		Lead	Say the <u>name</u> of this letter with me: *t*.
		Test	What is the <u>name</u> of this letter?
Introduce letter sound	Continue holding up the *t* Alphabet Card.	Model	The <u>sound</u> for this letter is /t/. When you say /t/, the tip of your tongue touches above your top teeth. Say /t/ and feel the tip of your tongue touch above your top teeth.
		Lead	Say the <u>sound</u> with me: /t/.
		Test	What is the <u>sound</u> for this letter?
Test knowledge of letter name and sound	Continue holding up the *t* Alphabet Card.	Test	What is the <u>name</u> of this letter? What is the <u>sound</u> for this letter?
	Give individual turns.		**Ongoing Assessment** If...children make incorrect responses, then...tell them the name or sound, have them repeat the name or sound, and return to the letter a second time.
Introduce the game Grab Bag	Place the *m, p, f,* and *c* Letter Cards into a brown paper bag.	Have a child pull out a letter from the bag and hand it to you. Hold up the letter. Test the group: **What is the <u>name</u> of this letter? What is the <u>sound</u> for this letter?** If the group answers correctly, place the letter card in a pile on the table. **Ongoing Assessment** If...children make incorrect responses, then...tell them the name or sound of the letter and have them repeat it. Place the letter card back in the bag. Continue playing until all the cards have been removed from the bag. If time permits, provide individual turns.	

Phonological Awareness/Alphabetic Understanding

Activity 5 Writer's Warm-Up

Introduce t

Objective: Children trace and write *t* and review writing *p*, *c*, *f*, and *m*.

Time: 2–3 minutes

	To Do	To Say	
Review letter name and sound	Hold up the *t* Tracing Card.	**What is the <u>name</u> of this letter? What is the <u>sound</u> for this letter?**	
Model tracing t	Distribute a Writer's Warm-Up to each child. Hold up the *t* Tracing Card.	Model	**Watch as I trace the letter *t* with my finger.**
		Lead	**Now you trace the first two *t*'s on your warm-up sheet with your finger.**
	Model tracing *t* again	Model	**Watch as I trace *t* again.**
		Lead	**Now use your pencil to trace the next two *t*'s.**
Model writing t	Hold up the lined side of the *t* Tracing Card.	Model	**Watch as I write the letter *t*. I start at the dot and write the letter.**
		Lead	**Now you write two *t*'s. Start at the dot like I did. Write carefully.**

Ongoing Assessment

If...children make incorrect responses,	then...have them write the letter again. If needed, put your hand over their hand and guide them to write the letter. Then have them write the letter on their own. Repeat as necessary.

Test children on writing t	Model writing *t* again.	Have children cover the letters they traced and wrote. Have them write the letter *t* twice from memory. Then have them uncover their papers and compare the letters. **Do your letters look the same? Circle your best letter.**
Review ***p, c, f, m***	Gather the tracing cards. Review how to trace and write each review letter.	Have children trace and write each review letter on their warm-up sheets.

Ongoing Assessment

If...children make an error,	then...model writing the letter using the tracing card and have them write the letter again. If needed, put your hand over their hand and guide them to write the letter. Then have them write the letter on their own. Repeat as necessary.

Activity **6** Connect Sound to Letter

Match a Picture's Initial Sound; Introduce t

Objective: Children connect /t/ to t.

Time: 2–3 minutes

	To Do	**To Say**	
Introduce the activity	Gather the picture cards and the letter cards.		**You're going to choose the letter that goes with the first sound of some pictures.**
Model the activity	Place the *tape* Picture Card on the table.	**Model**	**This is *tape*. The first sound in *tape* is /t/.** Place the *t* and *m* Letter Cards under the picture. **I'm going to choose the letter that matches this picture's first sound.** Point to the correct letter: ***t* is the letter for /t/ like the /t/ in *tape*.**
Test knowledge of initial sound	Place the *tire* Picture Card on the table.	**Test**	**This is *tire*. What is this? The first sound in *tire* is /t/. What is the first sound in tire? That's right, /t/ is the first sound in tire.** Place the *t* and *p* Letter Cards under the picture. **Your turn. Choose the letter that matches this picture's first sound. Which letter is the letter for the /t/ in *tire*? Do you think you know?** Call on a child to point to the correct letter. **What's the <u>name</u> of the letter you pointed to? What's the <u>sound</u> for this letter? That's right; t is the letter for /t/ like the /t/ in *tire*.** Reinforce the letter name and sound with the group: **Everyone, what's the <u>name</u> of the letter? What's the <u>sound</u> for the letter?** Continue with the remaining cards.

Ongoing Assessment

If...children make an error,	**then**...model the answer, have them repeat it, and return to the picture card a second time.

Activity 7 Connect Sound to Letter

Letter Race: c, f, p, m

Objective: Children isolate initial sound and write the corresponding letter.

Time: 6–8 minutes

	To Do	To Say	
Review letter names and sounds	Gather the picture cards. Hold up a Letter Race.	Review the names and sounds of letters on the sheet.	
Introduce the game Letter Race	Distribute a Letter Race to each child.	**We're going to have a letter race. I'm going to show you a picture and you're going to write the letter for its first sound on one of the racetracks. Which letter do you think will win?**	
Model the game	Place the *pig* Picture Card on the table. Hold up a Letter Race.	Model	**Let's do one together. This is *pig*. The first sound in *pig* is /p/. I'm going to write the letter for the sound /p/ on the racetrack of the letter for the same sound as the /p/ in *pig*.**
		Lead	**Now you write the letter for the sound /p/ on the racetrack. Start at the dot and write the letter. That's right; *p* is the letter for /p/ like the /p/ in *pig*.**
Play the game to test children on /k/, /f/, /p/, and /m/	Place the *man* Picture Card on the table.	Test	**This is *man*. What is this? What is the first sound in *man*? That's right; /mmm/ is the first sound in *man*. Now write the letter on the racetrack of the letter for the sound /mmm/ in *man*. Start at the dot and write the letter.**
			Reinforce the group on the letter name and sound: **Everyone, what's the <u>name</u> of the letter you just wrote? What's the <u>sound</u> for the letter?**
			Continue the game with the remaining picture cards until one letter wins. Vary the order of the pictures.

Ongoing Assessment

If...children make an error,	then...model the letter name and sound and have children repeat them. Have children write the correct letter.

New Sound /t/
Review Sounds /m/, /p/, /f/, /k/
Key Phonologic Skill Isolate Initial Sound

Phonological Awareness and Alphabetic Understanding

Activity	Materials		Time
1. Alphabetic Introduce *t*/t/	Alphabet Card: *t*	Letter Card: *t* (one per child)	1–2 minutes
2. Phonologic Which Picture Begins with /t/?	Picture Choices: 14-1, 14-2, 14-3 Teacher Resource Package 1		4–5 minutes
3. Integrated Phonologic/Alphabetic Sound Match with /k/, /f/, /p/, and /m/	Sound Match Cards: 14a–14b (one per child) Teacher Resource Package 1 Sound Production Cue Card	game markers (four per child/not provided) Alphabet Cards: *p, c, m, f*	4–5 minutes
New **4. Alphabetic** Reintroduce *t*/t/; Partners Game	Alphabet Card: *t*	Letter Cards: *m, p, f, c, t* (one per pair of children)	4–5 minutes

Writing and Spelling

Activity	Materials		Time
5. Writer's Warm-Up Introduce *t*	Tracing Cards: *t, p, m, c, f* Writer's Warm-Up (one per child) Student Activity Book 1, p. 28		2–3 minutes
6. Integrated Phonologic/Alphabetic Match a Picture's Initial Sound; Introduce *t*	Picture Cards: all *t* cards	Letter Cards: *t, m, f, c, p*	2–3 minutes
7. Phonologic/Spelling Letter Tag: *t, c, f, p, m*	Letter Tag (one per child) Student Activity Book 1, p. 29		6–8 minutes

Activity 1 Introduce Letter Name and Sound

Introduce t/t/

Objective: Children learn and trace *t*/t/.

Time: 1–2 minutes

	To Do	**To Say**	
Introduce letter name	Hold up the *t* Alphabet Card.	Model	The <u>name</u> of this letter is *t*.
		Lead	Say the <u>name</u> of the letter with me: *t*.
		Test	What is the <u>name</u> of this letter?
Introduce letter sound	Continue holding up the *t* Alphabet Card.	Model	The <u>sound</u> for this letter is /t/. When you say /t/, the tip of your tongue touches above your top teeth. Say /t/ and feel the tip of your tongue touch above your top teeth.
		Lead	Say the <u>sound</u> with me: /t/.
		Test	What is the <u>sound</u> for this letter?
Test knowledge of letter name and sound	Continue holding up the *t* Alphabet Card.	Test	What is the <u>name</u> of this letter? What is the <u>sound</u> for this letter?

Ongoing Assessment

If...children make an error,   then...tell them the letter name or sound and have them repeat it. Return to the letter a second time.

	Give individual turns on letter name and sound.		
Model tracing *t*	Distribute the *t* Letter Cards. Hold up the *t* Alphabet Card.	Model	Watch. I'll trace the letter *t*.
		Lead	Now you trace the letter *t* three times with your finger. Say /t/ each time you trace the letter.

Ongoing Assessment

If...children make an error,   then...put your hand over their hand and guide them to trace the letter. Then have children try to trace the letter on their own. Repeat as necessary.

Phonological Awareness/Alphabetic Understanding

Activity 2 Isolate Initial Sound

Which Picture Begins with /t/?

Objective: Children isolate initial /t/.

Time: 4–5 minutes

	To Do	**To Say**	
Model picture names	Gather the picture choices. Display Picture Choice 14-1. Point to *fan*.	Model	**This is *fan*. What is this?** Continue with *tag, cup; tape, mouse,* and *fire*. Test children on the picture names. Point to each picture and ask: **What is this?**
Introduce the game Which Picture Begins with /t/?	Practice production of the target sound.		**We're going to play a game. I'll show you three pictures. You'll find the one with the first sound /t/.**
		Lead	**Let's say /t/. Remember, when you say /t/, the tip of your tongue touches above your top teeth. Say /t/ and feel the tip of your tongue touch above your top teeth.**
Model the game	Display Picture Choice 14-1. Cover the bottom row.	Model	**My turn. I'll show you how to play the game. This is *fan, tag, cup*. I'll find the picture with the first sound /t/: *tag. Tag* has the first sound /t/.** Exaggerate the first sound and say the word: **/t/, *tag*.** Model another example with *tape, mouse,* and *fire*.
Play the game to test knowledge of /t/	Display Picture Choice 14-2. Cover the bottom row.		Point to each picture and ask: **What is this?** *(tie, cone, maze; cap, fox, toe)* **Which picture has the first sound /t/?** Confirm correct responses and prompt sound production: **Yes, *tie* has the first sound /t/. Let's say /t/. Remember, when you say /t/, the tip of your tongue touches above your top teeth. Say /t/ and feel the tip of your tongue touch above your top teeth: *tie*.** Continue with the bottom row of pictures and Picture Choice 14-3 *(can, mop, teeth; man, tail, fish)*.
	Give individual turns.		**Ongoing Assessment** **If...** children make incorrect responses, **then...** model the correct answer. Review the sound production cue. Have children repeat the correct answer. Go back to the example a second time.

Activity **3** Isolate Initial Sound

Sound Match with /k/, /f/, /p/, and /m/

Objective: Children isolate pictures' initial sounds and connect to letter.

Time: 4–5 minutes

	To Do	**To Say**
Introduce the game Sound Match	Give each child four game markers and a copy of Sound Match Card 14a.	**We're going to play the Sound Match Game again. Here's how to play. I'll show you a letter. You'll find the picture on your Sound Match card that begins with the sound for that letter and put a marker on it. Listen carefully because I'm going to show you four different letters.**

	To Do	**To Say**
Model the game	Place your Sound Match card on the table, facing the children.	**Model** **My turn. Here's how to play Sound Match.**
	Hold up the *p* Alphabet Card.	**Test** **What is the <u>sound</u> for this letter?**
	Point to and name the pictures on your card.	**Model** **This is *tail, mouse, fan, toe, pen, tag, tub, cone, tie*. I'll find the picture that begins with /p/.** Point to the *p* Alphabet Card. **Pen** (exaggerate the first sound). **Pen begins with /p/.** Exaggerate the first sound and say the word: **/p/, pen. Let's all place a marker on *pen* because *pen* begins with /p/.** Model one more example using target sound /fff/ to match *fan*.

	To Do	**To Say**
Play the game to test knowledge of initial /k/, /f/, /p/, and /m/	Review the pictures on Sound Match Card 14a. Keep markers on *pen* and *fan*.	Point to each picture and ask: **What is this?**

Ongoing Assessment

If...children make incorrect responses, | **then**...tell them the name of the picture and have them repeat it. Come back to the picture the children named incorrectly and review it a second time.

Continue playing. Hold up the *c* Alphabet Card.

Test   **What is the <u>sound</u> for this letter? Which picture begins with /k/? Yes, *cone* begins with /k/. Put your marker on *cone* because *cone* begins with /k/.**

Ongoing Assessment

If...children make incorrect responses, | **then**...model the correct answer. Use the Sound Production Cue Card to review the sound production cue. Have children repeat the correct answer. Go back to the example a second time.

Phonological Awareness/Alphabetic Understanding

To Do	To Say
	Repeat the procedure for target sound /mmm/. After everyone places a marker on *mouse* say: **Look! We just filled in a whole column.** Run your finger up and down the middle column. **Clear off your Sound Match cards. It's time to start another game.**
Distribute Sound Match Card 14b.	Point to and name each picture: **This is *tag, maze, tire, tent, toe, tie, fish, pool, can.*** Then point to each picture again and ask: **What is this?** Play the game for target sounds /p/, /k/, /f/, and /m/. Use the same procedure you used in the first game. Play until the group wins. Then have children clear off their cards.
Give individual turns.	Point to each picture on Sound Match Card 14a, and have children name each picture in unison. Then say: **Look at your Sound Match card. Who can name the picture that begins with /fff/?** Give each child up to three turns, one for each target sound. Then repeat the same procedure using Sound Match Card 14b.

Activity 4 Review Letter Name and Sound

New

Reintroduce t/t/; Partners Game
Objective: Children practice letter name and sound: *t/t/*.   Time: 4–5 minutes

	To Do	**To Say**	
Introduce letter name	Hold up the *t* Alphabet Card.	Model	The <u>name</u> of this letter is *t*.
		Lead	Say the <u>name</u> of this letter with me: *t*.
		Test	What is the <u>name</u> of this letter?
Introduce letter sound	Continue holding up the *t* Alphabet Card.	Model	The <u>sound</u> for this letter is /t/. When you say /t/, the tip of your tongue touches above your top teeth. Say /t/ and feel the tip of your tongue touch above your top teeth.
		Lead	Say the <u>sound</u> with me: /t/.
		Test	What is the <u>sound</u> for this letter?
Test knowledge of letter name and sound	Continue holding up the *t* Alphabet Card.	Test	What is the <u>name</u> of this letter? What is the <u>sound</u> for this letter?

Ongoing Assessment

Give individual turns.	If...children make an error,	then...tell them the letter name or sound, have them repeat the name or sound, and return to the letter a second time.

Introduce the Partners Game	Assign each child a partner. Give each pair a letter card for *m, p, f, c,* and *t*.	Explain the game: **We're going to play the Partners Game. You will show a letter card to your partner. Your partner will tell you the name and sound of that letter. If your partner says the correct letter name and sound, you will give him or her the letter card. If your partner makes a mistake, you will tell him or her the correct letter name and sound and then place the card on the bottom of your pile. You will continue playing until your partner has all of the cards. Then you will switch.**

Activity 5 Writer's Warm-Up

Introduce *t*

Objective: Children trace and write and review writing *p, c, f,* and *m*.

Time: 2–3 minutes

	To Do	**To Say**	
Review letter name and sound	Hold up the *t* Tracing Card.		**What is the <u>name</u> of this letter? What is the <u>sound</u> for this letter?**
Model tracing *t*	Distribute a Writer's Warm-Up to each child. Hold up the *t* Tracing Card.	Model	**Watch as I trace the letter *t* with my finger.**
		Lead	**Now you trace the first two *t*'s on your Writer's Warm-Up with your finger.**
	Model tracing *t* again.	Model	**Watch as I trace *t* again.**
		Lead	**Now use your pencil to trace the next two *t*'s.**
Model writing *t*	Hold up the lined side of the *t* Tracing Card.	Model	**Watch as I write the letter *t*. I start at the dot and write the letter.**
		Lead	**Now you write two letter *t*'s. Start at the dot like I did. Write carefully.**

Ongoing Assessment

If...children make an error,	then... have them write the letter again. If needed, put your hand over their hand and guide them to write the letter. Then have them write the letter on their own. Repeat as necessary.

| **Test children on writing *t*** | Hold up the lined side of the *t* Tracing Card. Model writing *t* again. | Model | **Watch as I write the letter *t* again. I start at the dot and write the letter.** |
| | | | Have children cover the letters they traced and wrote. Have them write the letter *t* two times from memory. Then have them uncover their papers and compare the letters. **Do your letters look the same? Circle your best letter.** |

Review

p, c, f, m

Have children trace and write each review letter on their warm-up sheets.

Ongoing Assessment

If...children make an error,	then... model writing the letter using the tracing card and have them write the letter again. If needed, put your hand over their hand and guide them to write the letter. Then have them write the letter on their own. Repeat as necessary.

 **Activity** **6** **Connect Sound to Letter**

Match a Picture's Initial Sound; Introduce t

Objective: Children connect initial sound to letter.   Time: 2–3 minutes

	To Do	**To Say**	
Introduce the activity	Gather the picture cards and the letter cards.		**You're going to choose the letter that goes with the first sound of some pictures.**
Model the activity	Place the *tag* Picture Card on the table.	Model	**This is *tag*. The first sound in *tag* is /t/.** Place the *t* and *m* Letter Cards under the picture.
			I'm going to choose the letter that matches this picture's first sound. Point to the correct letter: ***t* is the letter for /t/ like the /t/ in *tag*.**
Test knowledge of initial sound	Place the *tape* Picture Card on the table.	Test	**This is *tape*. What is this? The first sound in *tape* is /t/. What is the first sound in *tape*? That's right, /t/ is the first sound in *tape*.** Place the *t* and *f* Letter Cards under the picture.
			Your turn. Choose the letter that matches this picture's first sound. Think. Which letter is the letter for the /t/ in *tape*? Do you think you know?
			Call on a child to point to the correct letter. **What's the <u>name</u> of the letter you pointed to? What's the <u>sound</u> for that letter? That's right; *t* is the letter for /t/ like the /t/ in *tape*.** Reinforce the letter name and sound with the group: **Everyone, what's the <u>name</u> of the letter? What's the <u>sound</u> for the letter?** Continue with the remaining cards.

Ongoing Assessment

If...children make an error,	then...model the answer, have them repeat it, and return to the picture card a second time.

Writing/Spelling

Activity 7 **Connect Sound to Letter**

Letter Tag: t, c, f, p, m

Objective: Children connect sound to letter.

Time: 6–8 minutes

	To Do	**To Say**	
Introduce the game Letter Tag	Distribute a Letter Tag to each child.	**We are going to play Letter Tag. I'm going to tell you the sound for a letter and you're going to tag the letter with your pencil.**	
Model the game	Hold up a Letter Tag.	Model	**My turn. I'll show you how to play Letter Tag. The first sound is /t/. I'm going to start at the arrow and tag the letter for the sound /t/.** Draw a line from the arrow to the letter *t*.
		Lead	**Your turn. Put your pencil on the first arrow and tag the letter for the sound /t/. That's right; the letter *t* is the letter for the sound /t/.**
Play the game to test children on *c*/k/, *f*/f/, *p*/p/, and *m*/m/	Say a letter sound and have children tag the correct letter.	Test	**Place your pencil on the next arrow.** (Have children move across the page.) **When I say the sound, you tag the letter for that sound. Ready? The next sound is /p/.**
			Reinforce the letter name and sound: **Everyone, what's the <u>name</u> of the letter you just tagged? What's the <u>sound</u> for the letter?** Continue playing in this sequence: /k/, /k/, /m/, /f/. If time allows, start again from the top of the page with the following sequence: /f/, /p/, /k/, /p/, /t/, /m/.

Ongoing Assessment

If...children make an error,   then...model the letter name and sound and have children repeat them. Have children tag the correct letter.

New Sound /t/
Review Sounds /m/, /p/, /f/, /k/
Key Phonologic Skill Isolate Initial Sound

Phonological Awareness and Alphabetic Understanding

Activity	Materials	Time
1. Alphabetic Introduce *t*/t/	Alphabet Card: *t* Letter Card: *t* (one per child)	1–2 minutes
2. Integrated Phonologic/Alphabetic Which Picture Begins with /t/?	Picture Choices: 15-1, 15-2, 15-3 Alphabet Card: *t* Teacher Resource Package 1	4–5 minutes
3. Integrated Phonologic/Alphabetic Sound Match with /k/, /f/, /p/, and /m/	Sound Match Cards: 15a–15e (one card per child) Teacher Resource Package 1 game markers (four per child/not provided) Alphabet Cards: *c, p, m, f*	4–5 minutes
New **4. Alphabetic** Reintroduce *t*/t/; Be the Teacher Game	Alphabet Cards: *t, m, p, f, c*	4–5 minutes

Writing and Spelling

Activity	Materials	Time
5. Writer's Warm-Up Letter Mission: Review *t, c, f, p, m*	Letter Mission (one per child) Tracing Cards: Student Activity Book 1, p. 30 *t, c, p, m, f*	2–3 minutes
6. Integrated Phonologic/Alphabetic Match a Picture's Initial Sound; Introduce *t*	Picture Cards: all *t* cards Letter Cards: *t, f, m, c, p*	2–3 minutes
7. Phonologic/Spelling Letter Writing Game: Review *t, c, f, p, m*	Letter Writing Game (one per child) Student Activity Book 1, p. 31 game markers (one per child/not provided) Game Board 3 number cube (not provided)	6–8 minutes

Activity 1 Introduce Letter Name and Sound

Introduce t /t/

Objective: Children learn and trace t /t/.

Time: 1–2 minutes

	To Do	**To Say**	
Introduce letter name	Hold up the *t* Alphabet Card.	Model	**The <u>name</u> of this letter is *t*.**
		Lead	**Say the <u>name</u> with me.**
		Test	**What is the <u>name</u> of this letter?**
Introduce letter sound	Continue holding up the *t* Alphabet Card.	Model	**The <u>sound</u> for this letter is /t/. When you say /t/, the tip of your tongue touches above your top teeth. Say /t/ and feel the tip of your tongue touch above your top teeth.**
		Lead	**Say the <u>sound</u> with me: /t/.**
		Test	**What is the <u>sound</u> for this letter?**
Test knowledge of letter name and sound	Continue holding up the *t* Alphabet Card.	Test	**What is the <u>name</u> of this letter? What is the <u>sound</u> for this letter?**
	Give individual turns on letter name and sound.	**Ongoing Assessment** If...children make an error,	then...tell them the letter name or sound and have them repeat it. Repeat the test.
Model tracing *t*	Distribute the *t* Letter Cards. Hold up the *t* Alphabet Card.	Model	**Watch. I'll trace the letter *t*.**
		Lead	**Now you trace the letter *t* three times with your finger. Say /t/ each time you trace the letter.**
		Ongoing Assessment If...children make an error,	then...put your hand over their hand and guide them to trace the letter. Then have children try to trace the letter on their own. Repeat as necessary.

Phonological Awareness/Alphabetic Understanding

Activity 2 — Isolate Initial Sound

Which Picture Begins with /t/?

Objective: Children isolate initial /t/ and connect sound to letter.

Time: 4–5 minutes

	To Do		**To Say**
Model names of pictures	Gather the picture choices. Place Picture Choice 15-1 on the table. Point to *fork*.	**Model**	**This is *fork*. What is this?** Continue with the remaining pictures: *map, teeth, cup, toe, fin*. Then test children on all the picture names. For each picture, ask: **What is this?**
Introduce the game Which Picture Begins with /t/?			**Now we're going to play a game. I'll show you a letter. You'll find the picture that begins with the <u>sound</u> for that letter.**
Model the game	Hold up the *t* Alphabet Card.	**Model**	**The <u>name</u> of this letter is *t*. The <u>sound</u> for this letter is /t/. Remember, when you say /t/, the tip of your tongue touches above your top teeth. Say /t/ and feel the tip of your tongue touch above your top teeth.**
		Test	**What is the <u>sound</u> for this letter?**
	Display Picture Choice 15-1. Cover the pictures in the bottom row.	**Model**	**My turn. I'll show you how to play.** Point to each picture in the top row and say: **This is *fork, map, teeth*. I'll find the picture that has the first sound /t/.** Point to the *t* Alphabet Card. ***Teeth* begins with /t/.** Exaggerate the /t/ in *teeth*. Exaggerate the first sound and say the word: **/t/, *teeth*.** Model one more example with the bottom row: *cup, toe, fin*.
Play the game to test knowledge of /t/	Hold up the *t* Alphabet Card.	**Test**	**What is the <u>sound</u> for this letter?**
	Display Picture Choice 15-2 *(tire, moon, can; maze, fish, tail)*. Cover up the bottom row.		Point to each picture and ask: **What is this? Which picture has the first sound /t/?** Point to the *t* Alphabet Card. Confirm correct responses and prompt sound production: **Yes, *tire* has the first sound /t/. Let's say /t/. When you say /t/, the tip of your tongue touches above your top teeth. Say /t/ and feel the tip of your tongue touch above your top teeth: *tire*.** Continue with the bottom row of pictures and Picture Choice 15-3 *(cap, tag, fire; tub, cane, mow)*.
	Give individual turns.		

Ongoing Assessment

If . . . children make incorrect responses,	**then** . . . model the correct answer. Review the sound production cue. Have children repeat the correct answer. Go back to the example a second time. If this activity is very difficult, use two pictures.

 **Activity** **3** **Isolate Initial Sound**

Sound Match with /k/, /f/, /p/, and /m/

Objective: Children isolate picture's initial sounds and connect to letter.

Time: 4–5 minutes

	To Do	**To Say**
Introduce the game Sound Match	Gather Sound Match Cards 15a–15e and the game markers.	**Today we're going to play Sound Match. I'll show you a letter. Then you'll find the picture on your Sound Match card that begins with the <u>sound</u> for that letter and place a marker on it. Watch carefully because I'm going to show you four different letters. Each person has a different Sound Match card, so we won't know who's going to win.**
Test children on how to play the game	Distribute the Sound Match cards and game markers to children. Hold up the *c* Alphabet Card and point to it.	Have children review the picture names: **Before we start, whisper to yourself the name of each picture to be sure you know each one. Raise your hand if you don't know one and I'll tell it to you.** The picture names are listed below. **Test** **What is the <u>sound</u> for this letter? Find the picture on your Sound Match card that begins with /k/ and put a marker on it.** Have each child name the picture he or she put the marker on. Confirm correct responses and have the whole group repeat the word: **Yes, *coat* begins with /k/. Everybody, say /k/, *coat*.**

> ## Ongoing Assessment
>
> **If…** children make an incorrect response,   **then…** model the correct answer. Review the sound production cue. Have children repeat the correct answer.

	To Do	**To Say**
Play the game to test knowledge of initial sounds	Repeat the game procedure for /m/, /p/, and /f/.	**Let's continue playing. If you fill up a whole row or column, call out "Sound Match!"** When a child wins, have everyone clear off their Sound Match cards. Collect the cards, mix them up, and redistribute them. Play a second round, testing the sounds in the following order: /f/, /k/, /m/, /p/.

Sound Match Picture Names

15a: *tub, tent, coat/tape, tie, mitt/paw, toe, fish*
15b: *tie, tag, pin/toe, tub, tail/fork, cap, mouse*
15c: *fire, mop, pan/tag, tape, tent/tie, cat, toe*
15d: *cut, tape, tail/man, tag, tub/fan, tie, pie*
15e: *moon, cup, tub/tent, foot, tag/tail, pig, toe*

Phonological Awareness/Alphabetic Understanding

Activity 4 Review Letter Name and Sound

Reintroduce t/t/; Be the Teacher Game
Objective: Children practice letter name and sound: *t/t/*.   Time: 4–5 minutes

	To Do	To Say	
Introduce letter name	Hold up the *t* Alphabet Card.	Model	**The name of this letter is *t*.**
		Lead	**Say the name of this letter with me: *t*.**
		Test	**What is the name of this letter?**
Introduce letter sound	Continue holding up the *t* Alphabet Card.	Model	**The sound for this letter is /t/. When you say /t/, the tip of your tongue touches above your top teeth. Say /t/ and feel the tip of your tongue touch above your top teeth.**
		Lead	**Say the sound with me: /t/.**
		Test	**What is the sound for this letter?**
Test knowledge of letter name and sound	Continue holding up the *t* Alphabet Card.	Test	**What is the name of this letter? What is the sound for this letter?**

Ongoing Assessment

If... children make an error,	then... tell them the letter name or sound, have them repeat the name or sound, and return to the letter a second time.

Ask individuals: **What is the name of this letter? What is the sound for this letter?**

Introduce the game Be the Teacher	Choose a child to be the "teacher." Give him or her the *m, p, f, c,* and *t* Alphabet Cards.	Tell the "teacher" to hold up the first Alphabet Card. Have the "teacher" ask: **What is the name of this letter? What is the sound for this letter?** Allow the group to respond to each question. If the group answers correctly, have the "teacher" place the Alphabet Card on the table.

Ongoing Assessment

If... the group makes an error,	then... prompt the "teacher" to tell the letter name or sound and place the Alphabet Card at the bottom of the pile.

Continue until all of the letters and sounds have been identified correctly. Then have the "teacher" give individual turns.

Activity 5 — Writer's Warm-Up

Letter Mission: Review *t, c, f, p, m*

Objective: Children practice writing letters.

Time: 2–3 minutes

	To Do	To Say	
Introduce the activity	Distribute a Letter Mission to each child.		**We're going on a letter mission. I'm going to tell you the <u>name</u> of a letter and you're going to write it. Let's see if we can help the dog get the bone!**
Model the activity	Hold up a Letter Mission.	Model	**Let's do one together. The first letter is *t*. Watch as I start at the dot and write the letter *t*.** Write a *t* on your sheet.
		Lead	**Now you write the letter *t*. Start at the dot and write the letter.**
Lead the activity to test writing *t, c, f, p,* and *m*	Continue naming letters for children to write.	Test	**Now write the letter *c*.** Reinforce the group on the letter name: **What is the <u>name</u> of the letter you just wrote?** Continue with the following: *p, m, t, p, f, f, c.*

Ongoing Assessment

If...children write the wrong letter or don't remember a letter,

then...show them the tracing card of the correct letter and model tracing the letter. Have them write the letter.

Activity 6 Connect Sound to Letter

Match a Picture's Initial Sound; Introduce t

Objective: Children connect initial sound to letter.

Time: 2–3 minutes

	To Do	**To Say**	
Introduce the activity	Gather the picture cards and the letter cards.		**You're going to choose the letter that goes with the first sound of some pictures.**
Model the activity	Place the *tire* Picture Card on the table.	Model	**This is *tire*. The first sound in *tire* is /t/.** Place the *t* and *f* Letter Cards under the picture. **I'm going to choose the letter that matches this picture's first sound.** Point to the correct letter and say: ***t* is the letter for the sound /t/ like the /t/ in *tire*.**
Test knowledge of initial sound /t/	Display the *top* Picture Card.	Test	**This is *top*. What is this? The first sound in *top* is /t/. What is the first sound in *top*? That's right, /t/ is the first sound in *top*.** Place the *t* and *m* Letter Cards on the table. **Your turn. Choose the letter that matches this picture's first sound. Think. Which letter stands for the /t/ in *top*? Do you think you know?** Call on a child to point to the correct letter. **What's the <u>name</u> of the letter you pointed to? What is the <u>sound</u> for that letter? That's right; *t* is the letter for /t/ like the /t/ in *top*.** Reinforce the letter name and sound with the group: **Everyone, what's the <u>name</u> of the letter? What's the <u>sound</u> for the letter?** Continue with the remaining cards.

Ongoing Assessment

If... children make an error,	**then...** model the answer, have them repeat it, and return to the picture card a second time.

Activity 7 Connect Sound to Letter

Letter Writing Game:
Review *t, c, f, p, m*

Objective: Children connect initial sound to letter.

Time: 6–8 minutes

	To Do	To Say
Review letter names and sounds	Hold up a Letter Writing Game.	Point to each letter and ask: **What is the <u>name</u> of this letter? What is the <u>sound</u> for this letter?**
Introduce the Letter Writing Game	Distribute a Letter Writing Game to each child.	**We're going to play a letter writing game. I'll say a word and you'll write the letter that goes with the word's first sound. Then someone will roll the number cube and move his or her marker on the game board.**
Model the game	Place a Letter Writing Game on the table.	**Model** **Let's do one together. The first word is *tape*. The first sound in *tape* is /t/. I'm going to write the letter for the same sound as the /t/ in *tape*.** Write a *t* in the *t* column. **Now you write the letter for the sound /t/. Start at the dot and write the letter. That's right, *t* is the letter for /t/ like the /t/ in *tape*.**
Play the game to test children on *t, c, f, p,* and *m*	Dictate words from the Word Bank below. Vary the order.	**Test** **The next word is *carrot*. What is the first sound in *carrot*? That's right, /k/ is the first sound in *carrot*. Now write the letter for the sound /k/ like the /k/ in *carrot*. Start at the dot and write the letter. Everyone, what's the <u>name</u> of the letter you wrote? What's the <u>sound</u> for that letter?**
		After everyone has written the letter, have one child roll the number cube and advance his or her marker on the game board. Continue the game until all of the letters have been written.

Word Bank

tie	cap	feather	paw	moon
tire	cup	fork	popcorn	mug
	carrot	fox	pool	mountain

Ongoing Assessment

If... children make an error,	then... model the letter name and sound, have children repeat them, and have children write the correct letter.

Writing/Spelling

New Sound /s/
Review Sounds /m/, /p/, /f/, /k/, /t/
Key Phonologic Skill Isolate Initial Sound

Phonological Awareness and Alphabetic Understanding

Activity	Materials		Time
1. Alphabetic Introduce s/s/	Alphabet Card: s	Letter Card: s (one per child)	1–2 minutes
2. Phonologic Does It Begin with /s/?	Picture Cards: sock, can, saw, soup, tape, sunglasses		4–5 minutes
3. Phonologic First Sound Song with /t/	Picture Cards: turkey, turtle, top		4–5 minutes
New **4. Alphabetic** Reintroduce s/s/; Find the Sound Game	Alphabet Card: s Letter Cards: m, p, f, c, t (one each per child)		4–5 minutes

Writing and Spelling

Activity	Materials		Time
5. Writer's Warm-Up Introduce s	Tracing Cards: s, f, m, c, t, p Writer's Warm-Up (one per child) Student Activity Book 1, p. 32		2–3 minutes
6. Integrated Phonologic/Alphabetic Match a Picture's Initial Sound; Introduce s	Picture Cards: all s cards	Letter Cards: t, c, f, p, m, s	2–3 minutes
7. Phonologic/Spelling Letter Matching: t, c, f, p	Alphabet Cards: t, c, f, p Letter Cards: t, c, f, p (three of each)	Picture Cards: t, c, f, p (three to four for each letter)	6–8 minutes

Activity 1 Introduce Letter Name and Sound

Introduce s/s/

Objective: Children learn and trace s/s/.

Time: 1–2 minutes

	To Do	To Say	
Introduce letter name	Hold up the *s* Alphabet Card.	Model	**The <u>name</u> of this letter is *s*.**
		Lead	**Say the <u>name</u> with me: *s*.**
		Test	**What is the <u>name</u> of this letter?**
Introduce letter sound	Continue holding up the *s* Alphabet Card.	Model	**The <u>sound</u> for this letter is /sss/. When you say /sss/, the tip of your tongue touches above your top teeth. It makes a snake sound. Say /sss/ and hear the snake sound.**
		Lead	**Say the <u>sound</u> with me: /sss/.**
		Test	**What is the <u>sound</u> for this letter?**
Test knowledge of letter name and sound	Continue holding up the *s* Alphabet Card. Give individual turns on letter name and sound.	Test	**What is the <u>name</u> of this letter? What is the <u>sound</u> for this letter?**

Ongoing Assessment

If... children make an error,   then... tell them the letter name or sound and have them repeat it. Repeat the test.

	To Do	To Say	
Model tracing *s*	Distribute the *s* Letter Cards. Hold up the *s* Alphabet Card.	Model	**Watch. I'll trace the letter *s*.**
		Lead	**Now you trace the letter *s* three times with your finger. Say /sss/ each time you trace the letter.**

Ongoing Assessment

If... children make an error,   then... put your hand over their hand and guide them to trace the letter. Then have the children try to trace the letter on their own. Repeat as necessary.

Phonological Awareness/Alphabetic Understanding

Activity 2 Isolate Initial Sound

Does It Begin with /s/?

Objective: Children isolate initial /s/.

Time: 4–5 minutes

	To Do	To Say	
Model names of pictures	Gather the picture cards. Place the *sock* Picture Card on the table.	Model	**This is *sock*. What is this?** Have children repeat. Continue with *can, saw, soup, tape,* and *sunglasses.*
	Hold up each picture card.	Test	**What is this?** Have children identify each picture again.
Introduce the game Does It Begin with /s/?	Practice production of the target sound.		Tell children they will play a game. They will find the pictures that begin with /s/. **Let's say /sss/. When you say /sss/, the tip of your tongue touches above your top teeth. It makes a snake sound. Say /sss/ and hear the snake sound.**
Model the game	Place the *sock* Picture Card on the table.	Model	**My turn. I'll say the name of the picture and then tell if it begins with /sss/: *sock*** (exaggerate the first sound). ***Sock* begins with /sss/. My voice makes a snake sound when I say /sss/, *sock*. Next picture: *can*** (exaggerate the first sound). ***Can* does not begin with /sss/.**
Play the game to test knowledge of /s/	Place the *saw* Picture Card on the table.	Test	**Your turn. What is this? Does *saw* begin with /sss/?** Confirm correct responses and prompt sound production: **Yes, *saw* begins with /sss/. Let's say /sss/. When you say /sss/, the tip of your tongue touches above your top teeth. It makes a snake sound. Say /sss/ and hear the snake sound: *saw*.** Continue the test with three other examples: *soup, tape, sunglasses.*
	Give individual turns.		

Ongoing Assessment

If... children make incorrect responses, **then...** model the correct answer. Review the sound production cue. Have children repeat the correct answer. Go back to the example a second time.

Phonological Awareness/Alphabetic Understanding

Activity 3 — Isolate Initial Sound

First Sound Song with /t/

Objective: Children isolate initial /t/ in a song.

Time: 4–5 minutes

	To Do	**To Say**
Introduce the song	Place the *turkey, turtle,* and *top* Picture Cards on the table.	Tell children they are going to learn a song. You will show them three pictures that begin with /t/. These pictures will be in the song. **Model** — **This is *turkey, turtle, top.*** Point to the pictures as you say the words. **Lead** — **Say the names of the pictures with me: *turkey, turtle, top.***
Review /t/	Practice /t/ sound production.	Point to the pictures as you name them: ***turkey, turtle,* and *top* all begin with /t/. Say the sound /t/ with me. Remember, when you say /t/, the tip of your tongue touches above your top teeth. Say /t/ and feel the tip of your tongue touch above your top teeth.**
Model the song	Sing the lyrics to the tune of "Old McDonald Had a Farm." Point to each picture as you sing its name.	**Model** — **Listen as I sing. What is the sound that begins these words: *turkey, turtle, top*? /t/ is the sound that begins these words: *turkey, turtle, top.* With a /t/ /t/ here and a /t/ /t/ there, here a /t/, there a /t/, everywhere a /t/ /t/. /t/ is the sound that begins these words: *turkey, turtle, top.*** Lead children through the song several times, pointing to the pictures as they sing: **Sing it with me.**
Test knowledge of initial sound /t/	Test children on the first sound of each picture from the song. Give individual turns.	**Test** — **Your turn. Say the first sound in *turkey.*** Confirm correct responses and prompt the sound production cue. Repeat for *turtle* and *top.*

Ongoing Assessment

If...children make an error,	then...model the answer, have children repeat it, and return to the example a second time.

Phonological Awareness/Alphabetic Understanding

Activity 4 Review Letter Name and Sound

Reintroduce s/s/; Find the Sound Game

Objective: Children practice letter name and sound: s/s/.   Time: 4–5 minutes

	To Do	To Say	
Introduce letter name	Hold up the *s* Alphabet Card.	Model	**The name of this letter is *s*.**
		Lead	**Say the name of this letter with me: *s*.**
		Test	**What is the name of this letter?**
Introduce letter sound	Continue holding up the *s* Alphabet Card.	Model	**The sound for this letter is /sss/. When you say /sss/, the tip of your tongue touches above your top teeth. It makes a snake sound. Say /sss/ and hear the snake sound.**
		Lead	**Say the sound with me: /sss/.**
		Test	**What is the sound for this letter?**
Test knowledge of letter name and sound	Continue holding up the *s* Alphabet Card.	Test	**What is the name of this letter? What is the sound for this letter?**

Ongoing Assessment

If...children make an error, | then...tell them the letter name or sound, have them repeat the name or sound, and return to the letter a second time.

	To Do	To Say	
	Continue holding up the *s* Alphabet Card.		Ask individuals: **What is the name of this letter? What is the sound for this letter?**
Play the game Find the Sound	Have each child line up letter cards for *m*, *p*, *f*, *c*, and *t*.		Explain the game: **I'll say a sound and then I'll count to three. When I get to three, you hold up the letter for the sound.**
		Model	**Let me show you: /fff/. One, two, three.** Hold up the f Letter Card.
		Lead	**Let's play: /t/. One, two, three.**
		Test	**What sound are you holding up? Yes, /t/.** Have children return their letter cards to the table. Continue, calling each sound at least once. Then give individual turns.

Ongoing Assessment

If...children make an error, | then...tell them the sound and have them repeat it. Return to the sound a second time.

Activity **5** Writer's Warm-Up

Introduce s

Objective: Children trace and write *s* and write review letters *f, m, c, t,* and *p*.

Time: 2–3 minutes

	To Do	To Say	
Review letter name and sound	Hold up the *s* Tracing Card.		**What is the <u>name</u> of this letter? What is the <u>sound</u> for this letter?**
Model tracing *s*	Distribute a Writer's Warm-Up to each child. Continue holding up the *s* Tracing Card.	Model	**Watch as I trace the letter *s* with my finger.**
		Lead	**Now you trace the first two letter *s*'s on your warm-up sheet with your finger.**
	Model tracing *s* again.	Model	**Watch as I trace *s* again.**
		Lead	**Now use your pencil to trace the next two *s*'s.**
Model writing *s*	Hold up the lined side of the *s* Tracing Card.	Model	**Watch as I write the letter *s*. I start at the dot and write the letter.**
		Lead	**Now you write two letter *s*'s. Start at the dot like I did. Write carefully.**

Ongoing Assessment

If... children make an error,	**then...** have them write the letter again. If needed, put your hand over their hand and guide them to write the letter. Then have them write the letter on their own. Repeat as necessary.

Test children on writing *s*	Hold up the lined side of the *s* Tracing Card. Model writing *s* again.	Have children cover the letters they traced and wrote. Have them write the letter *s* two times from memory. Then have them uncover their papers and compare the letters. **Do your letters look the same? Circle your best letter.**

Review *f, m, c, t, p*		**Trace *f* with your pencil. Now write *f*.** Continue this procedure for *m, c, t,* and *p*.

Ongoing Assessment

If... children make an error,	**then...** model writing the letter using the tracing card and have them write the letter again. If needed, put your hand over their hand and guide them to write the letter. Then have them write the letter on their own. Repeat as necessary.

Activity 6 Connect Sound to Letter

Match a Picture's Initial Sound; Introduce s

Objective: Children connect initial sound to letter.

Time: 2–3 minutes

	To Do	**To Say**	
Introduce the activity	Gather the picture cards and the letter cards.		**You're going to choose the letter that goes with the first sound of some pictures.**
Model the activity	Place the *sun* Picture Card on the table.	Model	**This is *sun*. The first sound in *sun* is /sss/.** Place the *p* and *s* Letter Cards under the picture.
			I'm going to choose the letter that matches this picture's first sound. Point to the correct letter: ***s* is the letter for /sss/ like the /sss/ in *sun*.**
Test knowledge of initial sound /s/	Display the *sock* Picture Card.	Test	**This is *sock*. What is this? The first sound in *sock* is /sss/. What is the first sound in *sock*? That's right, /sss/ is the first sound in *sock*.** Place the *s* and *f* Letter Cards under the picture.
			Your turn. Choose the letter that matches this picture's first sound. Which letter is the letter for the /sss/ in *sock*? Do you know?
			Call on a child to point to the correct letter. **What's the <u>name</u> of the letter you pointed to? What is the <u>sound</u> for that letter? That's right; *s* is the letter for /sss/ like the /sss/ in *sock*.** Reinforce the letter name and sound with the group: **Everyone, what's the <u>name</u> of the letter? What's the <u>sound</u> for the letter?** Continue with at least three more examples.

Ongoing Assessment

If...children make an error,	then...model the answer, have them repeat it, and return to the picture card a second time.

Activity 7 Connect Sound to Letter

Letter Matching: *t, c, f, p*

Objective: Children connect initial sound to letter.

Time: 6–8 minutes

	To Do	**To Say**
Review letter names and sounds	Gather the alphabet cards. Hold up the *t* Alphabet Card.	**What is the <u>name</u> of this letter? What is the <u>sound</u> for this letter?** Continue this procedure for *c, f,* and *p*.
Introduce the activity	Mix up the letter cards and place them in a pile on the table. Spread out the picture cards face up on the table.	**We're going to play a game. You'll pick a letter and place it next to a picture that begins with the sound for that letter. Let's see if we can match all of the pictures!**
Model the activity		**Model** **Let's do one together. I'll pick the first letter.** Choose a letter from the pile. **This is the letter for the sound /_/. Now I'll place the letter next to a picture that starts with the sound /_/. The picture _____ starts with /_/.**
Play the game to test *f*/f/, *t*/t/, *c*/k/, and *p*/p/		Have children take turns selecting a letter, saying the letter's sound, and placing the letter next to a picture with the same initial sound. Reinforce the group on the first sound of each chosen picture: **Everyone, what's the first sound you hear in _____? What's the name of the letter for the /_/ sound in _____?**

Ongoing Assessment

If...children make an error,	then...model the letter sound and picture's name and first sound.

LESSON 17

New Sound /s/
Review Sounds /m/, /p/, /f/, /k/, /t/
Key Phonologic Skill Isolate Initial Sound

Phonological Awareness and Alphabetic Understanding

Activity	Materials		Time
1. **Alphabetic** Introduce *s/s/*	Alphabet Card: *s*	Letter Card: *s* (one per child)	1–2 minutes
2. **Phonologic** Which Picture Begins with /s/?	Picture Choices: 17-1, 17-2, 17-3 Teacher Resource Package 1		4–5 minutes
3. **Integrated Phonologic/Alphabetic** Picture Scene Search: /t/	Alphabet Card: *t* Picture Scene /t/ Teacher Resource Package 1		4–5 minutes
New 4. **Alphabetic** Reintroduce *s/s/*; Letters Board Game	Alphabet Card: *s* Game Cards: *m, p, f, c, t, s* (two of each) Game Board 3	game markers (one per child/ not provided) number cubes (two/not provided)	4–5 minutes

Writing and Spelling

Activity	Materials		Time
5. **Writer's Warm-Up** Introduce *s*	Tracing Card: *s* Writer's Warm Up (one per child) Student Activity Book 1, p. 33		2–3 minutes
6. **Integrated Phonologic/Alphabetic** Match a Picture's Initial Sound; Introduce *s*	Picture Cards: all *s* cards	Letter Cards: *s, t, c, f, p, m*	2–3 minutes
7. **Phonologic/Spelling** First Sounds Dictation: *s, t, c, f, p, m*	Tracing Cards: *s, t, c, f, p, m* Write-On/Wipe-Off Cards (one per child)	markers and erasers (not provided)	6–8 minutes

Activity 1 Introduce Letter Name and Sound

Introduce s/s/

Objective: Children learn and trace s/s/.

Time: 1–2 minutes

	To Do		**To Say**
Introduce letter name	Hold up the *s* Alphabet Card.	Model	The <u>name</u> of this letter is *s*.
		Lead	Say the <u>name</u> with me: *s*.
		Test	What is the <u>name</u> of this letter?
Introduce letter sound	Continue holding up the *s* Alphabet Card.	Model	The <u>sound</u> for this letter is /sss/. When you say /sss/, the tip of your tongue touches above your top teeth. It makes a snake sound. Say /sss/ and hear the snake sound.
		Lead	Say the <u>sound</u> with me: /sss/.
		Test	What is the <u>sound</u> for this letter?
Test knowledge of letter name and sound	Continue holding up the *s* Alphabet Card.	Test	What is the <u>name</u> of this letter? What is the <u>sound</u> for this letter?
	Give individual turns on letter name and sound.		**Ongoing Assessment**
			If...children make an error, then...tell them the letter name or sound and have them repeat it. Repeat the test.
Model tracing *s*	Distribute the *s* Letter Cards. Hold up the *s* Alphabet Card. Model how to trace *s* with your finger.	Model	Watch. I'll trace the letter *s*.
		Lead	Now you trace the letter *s* three times with your finger. Say /sss/ each time you trace the letter.
			Ongoing Assessment
			If...children make an error, then...put your hand over their hand and guide them to trace the letter. Then have them try to trace the letter on their own. Repeat as necessary.

Activity **2** Isolate Initial Sound

Which Picture Begins with /s/?

Objective: Children isolate initial /s/.

Time: 4–5 minutes

	To Do		**To Say**
Model picture names	Gather the picture choices. Place Picture Choice 17-1 on the table. Point to *sun*.	**Model**	**This is *sun*. What is this?** Continue with *mop, cat; food, sit, paw.* Then point to each picture and test children on the picture name: **What is this?**
Introduce the game Which Picture Begins with /s/?	Practice production of the target sound.		We're going to play a game. I'll show you three pictures. You'll need to find the one that has the first sound /sss/. Let's say /sss/. Remember, when you say /sss/, the tip of your tongue touches above your top teeth. It makes a snake sound. Say /sss/ and hear the snake sound.
Model the game	Model two examples.	**Model**	**My turn. I'll show you how to play the game.** Display Picture Choice 17-1. Cover the bottom picture row. Point to each picture in the top row and say: **This is *sun, mop, cat*. I'll find the picture that has the first sound /sss/: *sun*. *Sun* has the first sound /sss/.** Exaggerate the first sound and say the word: **/sss/, *sun*.** Cover the top picture row and model another example with *food, sit,* and *paw*.
Play the game to test knowledge of initial /s/	Display Picture Choice 17-2. Cover the bottom row.	**Test**	**What is this?** Point to each picture in the row: *cone, soap, pin*. **Which picture has the first sound /sss/?** Confirm correct responses and prompt sound production: **Yes, *soap* has the first sound /sss/. Let's say /sss/. Remember, when you say /sss/, the tip of your tongue touches above your top teeth. It makes a snake sound. Say /sss/ and hear the snake sound: *soap*.** Continue with the bottom row of pictures (*fire, man, sandwich*) and Picture Choice 17-3 (*fan, pool, sock; saw, can, mitt*).
	Give individual turns.		**Ongoing Assessment** **If...**children make incorrect responses, **then...**model the correct answer. Review the sound production cue. Have children repeat the correct answer. Go back to the example a second time.

135

Phonological Awareness/Alphabetic Understanding

 **Activity 3** **Isolate Initial Sound**

Picture Scene Search: /t/

Objective: Children isolate initial /t/ in a picture.

Time: 4–5 minutes

	To Do		**To Say**
Introduce the game Picture Scene Search: /t/			**We're going to play a game. I'm going to show you a picture. You're going to find things in it that have the first sound /t/.**
Test knowledge of /t/	Hold up the *t* Alphabet Card.	**Test**	**The <u>name</u> of this letter is t. What is the <u>sound</u> for this letter?** Confirm correct responses: **Yes, /t/. When you say /t/, the tip of your tongue touches above your top teeth. Say /t/ and feel the tip of your tongue touch above your top teeth.**

Ongoing Assessment

If...children make incorrect responses,	then...model the correct sound and have children repeat it. Review the sound production cue. Repeat a second time.

Model and play the game	Hold up the picture scene.	**Model**	**My turn. I'll find something in the picture that has the first sound /t/.** Point to and name something that begins with /t/: *table. **Table** has the first sound /t/.*
	Give individual turns.	**Lead**	**Your turn to find something that has the first sound /t/.** If children point to an object that begins with /t/, confirm their selection and ask them to name the object. Confirm correct responses and have the group repeat it: **Yes, teapot has the first sound /t/. Everybody, say /t/, teapot.**

Target pictures: *table, turkey, teapot, tie, tomato, teeth, towel, telephone, toast, tail, tiger, turtle, tape*

Phonological Awareness/Alphabetic Understanding

Activity 4 Review Letter Name and Sound

Reintroduce s/s/; Letters Board Game

Objective: Children practice letter name and sound: *s/s/*.   Time: 4–5 minutes

	To Do	**To Say**	
Introduce letter name	Hold up the *s* Alphabet Card.	Model	**The <u>name</u> of this letter is *s*.**
		Lead	**Say the <u>name</u> with me: *s*.**
		Test	**What is the <u>name</u> of this letter?**
Introduce letter sound	Continue holding up the *s* Alphabet Card.	Model	**The <u>sound</u> for this letter is /sss/. When you say /sss/, the tip of your tongue touches above your top teeth. It makes a snake sound. Say /sss/ and hear the snake sound.**
		Lead	**Say the <u>sound</u> with me: /sss/.**
		Test	**What is the <u>sound</u> for this letter?**
Test knowledge of letter name and sound	Hold up the *s* Alphabet Card.	Test	**What is the <u>name</u> of this letter? What is the <u>sound</u> for this letter?**
	Give individual turns.		

> ### Ongoing Assessment
> **If...** children make incorrect responses, **then...** tell them the letter name or sound, have them repeat it, and return to the letter a second time.

Introduce the Letters Board Game	Mix the game cards. Place the cards in a pile, face down. Gather the game board, a marker for each child, and two number cubes.	**We're going to play a game. When it's your turn, you'll roll the number cubes. Then you'll pick the top card from the pile of game cards. Then you'll name the letter and tell what the sound for that letter is. If you're right, you'll get to move your marker the number of spaces showing on the number cubes.**
Play the game to test knowledge of *m/m/*, *p/p/*, *f/f/*, *c/k/*, *t/t/*, and *s/s/*	Give individual turns.	Call on a child to roll the number cubes and choose a card from the pile. **What is the <u>name</u> of the letter? What is the <u>sound</u> for this letter?** If the child answers correctly, he or she places the game card at the bottom of the pile and moves the marker the number of spaces showing on the number cubes. Play the game until one child reaches the finish line or until time runs out. Play another round if time permits.

> ### Ongoing Assessment
> **If...** a child makes an error, **then...** tell the letter name or sound, have everyone repeat it, and place the card at the bottom of the pile. The child does not move his or her marker.

Activity **5** Writer's Warm-Up

Introduce s

Objective: Children trace and write *s* and review writing *f, m, c, t,* and *p*.   Time: 2–3 minutes

	To Do	**To Say**	
Review letter name and sound	Hold up the *s* Tracing Card.	**What is the <u>name</u> of this letter? What is the <u>sound</u> for this letter?**	
Model tracing *s*	Distribute a Writer's Warm-Up to each child. Model tracing *s* with your finger on the tracing card. Model tracing *s* again.	Model Lead Model Lead	**Watch as I trace the letter *s*.** **Now you trace the first two letter *s*'s on your warm-up sheet with your finger.** **Watch as I trace the letter *s* again.** **Now use your pencil to trace the next two *s*'s.**
Model writing *s*	Hold up the lined side of the *s* Tracing Card.	Model Lead	**Watch as I write the letter *s*. I start at the dot.** **Now you write two letter *s*'s. Start at the dot.**

Ongoing Assessment

If...children make an error,	then...have them write the letter again. If needed, put your hand over their hand and guide them to write the letter. Then have them write the letter on their own. Repeat as necessary.

Test children on writing *s*	Hold up the lined side of the *s* Tracing Card. Model writing *s* again.	Have children cover the letters they wrote and have them write the letter twice from memory. Then have them uncover their letters and compare the letters. **Do your letters look the same? Circle your best letter.**
Review *f, m, c, t, p*		**Watch as I trace the letter *f*. Now you trace *f*. Now write *f* with your pencil.** Continue this procedure for *m, c, t,* and *p*.

Ongoing Assessment

If...children make an error,	then...use the tracing card to model writing the letter, and have them write the letter again. If needed, put your hand over their hand and guide them to write the letter. Then have them write the letter on their own. Repeat as necessary.

Activity **6** **Connect Sound to Letter**

Match a Picture's Initial Sound;
Introduce s

Objective: Children connect sound to letter: s/s/.

Time: 2–3 minutes

	To Do	**To Say**	
Introduce the activity	Gather the picture cards and the letter cards.	**You're going to choose the letter that goes with the first sound of some pictures.**	
Model the activity	Place the *soap* Picture Card on the table.	Model	**This is soap. The first sound in soap is /sss/.** Place the *t* and *s* Letter Cards under the picture.
			I'm going to choose the letter for this picture's first sound. Point to the correct letter and say: **s is the letter for /sss/ like the /sss/ in soap.**
Test knowledge of initial sound	Display the *seal* Picture Card.	Test	**This is seal. What is this? The first sound in seal is /sss/. What is the first sound in seal? That's right; /sss/ is the first sound in seal.** Place the *s* and *p* Letter Cards under the picture.
			Your turn. Choose the letter that matches this picture's first sound. Which letter is the letter for the /sss/ in seal? Do you know?
			Call on a child to point to the correct letter. **What's the <u>name</u> of the letter you pointed to? What is the <u>sound</u> for that letter? That's right; s is the letter for /sss/ like the /sss/ in seal.** Reinforce the letter name and sound with the group: **Everyone, what's the <u>name</u> of the letter? What's the <u>sound</u> for the letter?** Continue with the remaining cards.

Ongoing Assessment

If... children make an error,	**then...** model the answer, have them repeat it, and return to the picture card a second time.

Activity 7 Connect Sound to Letter

First Sounds Dictation:
s, t, c, f, p, m

Objective: Children isolate and write initial sounds of words.   Time: 6–8 minutes

	To Do	**To Say**	
Review letter names and sounds	Gather the tracing cards. Hold up each tracing card.	**Test**	**What's the <u>name</u> of this letter? What's the <u>sound</u> for this letter?**
Introduce the activity	Distribute a Write-On/Wipe-Off Card and a marker to each child.		**I'm going to tell you a word. On your Write-On/Wipe-Off Card, you're going to write the letter for the first sound in the word.**
Model the activity	Use a Write-On/Wipe-Off Card and a marker.	**Model**	**My turn. The first word is *sit*. The first sound in *sit* is /sss/. I'll write the letter for the sound /sss/ in *sit*.** Write the letter *s* on your Write-On/Wipe-Off Card. **The letter *s* is the letter for the sound /sss/. Your turn. Write the letter for the sound /sss/. That's right, *s* is the letter for the sound /sss/ like the /sss/ in *sit*.**
Test children on *s, t, c, f, p,* and *m*	For each initial sound, dictate at least two words from the Word Bank. Vary the order.	**Test**	**The next word is *coat*. What's the first sound in *coat*? That's right, /k/ is the first sound in *coat*. Now write the letter for the same sound as the /k/ in *coat*.** Reinforce the group on the letter name and sound: **Everyone, what's the <u>name</u> of the letter you wrote? What's the <u>sound</u> for the letter?**

Word Bank

soap	tiger	coat	football	pizza	monkey
seal	turtle	car	fizz	pen	mop
sit	teeth	candle	fire	pie	mail
sun	tag	cup	fun	pumpkin	mouse

Ongoing Assessment

If...children write the wrong letter or don't remember a letter,	**then**...show them the correct tracing card. Model tracing the letter and say the letter sound.

New Sound /s/
Review Sounds /m/, /p/, /f/, /k/, /t/
Key Phonologic Skill Isolate Initial Sound

Phonological Awareness and Alphabetic Understanding

Activity	Materials		Time
1. Alphabetic Introduce *s*/s/	Alphabet Card: *s*	Letter Card: *s* (one per child)	1–2 minutes
2. Integrated Phonologic/Alphabetic Which Picture Begins with /s/?	Picture Choices: 18-1, 18-2, 18-3 Teacher Resource Package 1	Alphabet Card: *s*	4–5 minutes
3. Integrated Phonologic/Alphabetic First Sound Mix-Up Game with /t/ and /s/	Picture Cards: *top, tire, tent, turkey, sun, soap, seal, sandwich*	Letter Cards: *t, s* Sound Production Cue Card	4–5 minutes
New **4. Integrated Phonologic/Alphabetic** Reintroduce *s*/s/; Pictures to Letters Game	Alphabet Card: *s* Picture Cards: *man, pig, fork, coat, top, soap*	Letter Cards: *m, p, f, c, t, s* (one per child) paper bag (not provided) Sound Production Cue Card	4–5 minutes

Writing and Spelling

Activity	Materials		Time
5. Writer's Warm-Up Memory Review: *s, t, c, f, p, m*	Tracing Cards: *s, t, c, f, p, m* Write-On/Wipe-Off Cards (one per child)	markers and erasers (not provided)	2–3 minutes
6. Integrated Phonologic/Alphabetic Match a Picture's Initial Sound; Introduce *s*	Picture Cards: *sun, soap, saw, seal, sock, soup, sandwich*	Letter Cards: *s, t, f, c, p, m*	2–3 minutes
7. Phonologic/Spelling First Sounds: *m, t, s, c, f*	First Sounds (one per child) Student Activity Book 1, p. 34		6–8 minutes

Activity 1 Introduce Letter Name and Sound

Introduce s/s/

Objective: Children learn and trace s/s/.

Time: 1–2 minutes

	To Do	**To Say**	
Introduce letter name	Hold up the *s* Alphabet Card.	Model	The <u>name</u> of this letter is *s*.
		Lead	Say the <u>name</u> with me: *s*.
		Test	What is the <u>name</u> of this letter?
Introduce letter sound	Continue holding up the *s* Alphabet Card.	Model	The <u>sound</u> for this letter is /sss/. When you say /sss/, the tip of your tongue touches above your top teeth. It makes a snake sound. Say /sss/ and hear the snake sound.
		Lead	Say the <u>sound</u> with me: /sss/.
		Test	What is the <u>sound</u> for this letter?
Test knowledge of letter name and sound	Continue holding up the *s* Alphabet Card.	Test	What is the <u>name</u> of this letter? What is the <u>sound</u> for this letter?
	Give individual turns on letter name and sound.		**Ongoing Assessment** If... children make an error, then... tell them the letter name or sound and have them repeat it. Repeat the test.
Model tracing *s*	Distribute the *s* Letter Cards. Hold up the *s* Alphabet Card.	Model	Watch. I'll trace the letter *s*.
		Lead	Now you trace the letter *s* three times with your finger. Say /sss/ each time you trace the letter.
			Ongoing Assessment If... children make an error, then... put your hand over their hand and guide them to trace the letter. Then have the children try to trace the letter on their own. Repeat as necessary.

Activity 2 Isolate Initial Sound

Which Picture Begins with /s/?

Objective: Children isolate initial /s/ and connect to letter.   Time: 4–5 minutes

	To Do		**To Say**
Model names of pictures	Gather the picture choices. Place Picture Choice 18-1 on the table. Point to the first picture.	Model	**This is *seal*. What is this?** Continue with the remaining pictures: *pan, coat; map, fin, sick.* Then test children on all of the picture names. For each picture, ask: **What is this?**
Introduce the game Which Picture Begins with /s/?			Now we're going to play a game. I'll show you a letter and three pictures. You'll find the picture that begins with the sound for that letter.
Model the game	Hold up the *s* Alphabet Card.	Model	**The <u>name</u> of this letter is *s*. The <u>sound</u> for this letter is /sss/. Remember, when you say /sss/, the tip of your tongue touches above your top teeth. It makes a snake sound. Say /sss/ and hear the snake sound.**
		Test	**What is the <u>sound</u> for this letter?**
	Cover the pictures in the bottom row of Picture Choice 18-1.	Model	**This is how to play.** Point to each picture and say: **This is *seal, pan, coat*. I'll find the picture that has the first sound /sss/.** Point to the *s* Alphabet Card. **Seal has the first sound /sss/.** Exaggerate the /sss/. Exaggerate the first sound again and say the word: **/sss/, *seal*.** Model the next row.
Play the game to test knowledge of /s/	Hold up the *s* Alphabet Card. Display Picture Choice 18-2 *(moon, soap, fork; sun, paw, cap).* Cover up the bottom row of pictures.	Test	**What is the <u>sound</u> for this letter?** Point to each picture in the top row and ask: **What is this?** Have children tell the name of each picture. **Which picture has the first sound /sss/?** Point to the *s* Alphabet Card. Confirm correct responses and prompt sound production: **Yes, *soap* has the first sound /sss/. Let's say /sss/. Remember, when you say /sss/, the tip of your tongue touches above your top teeth. It makes a snake sound. Say /sss/ and hear the snake sound: *soap*.** Continue with the bottom row of pictures and Picture Choice 18-3 *(cane, pig, sock; mitt, saw, foot).*
	Give individual turns.		

Ongoing Assessment

If... children make incorrect responses,   **then...** model the correct answer. Review the sound production cue. Have children repeat the correct answer. Go back to the example a second time. If this activity is very difficult, use two pictures instead of three.

Activity 3 Connect Sound to Letter

First Sound Mix-Up Game with /t/ and /s/

Objective: Children connect initial sound to letter: *t/t/, s/s/*.   Time: 4–5 minutes

	To Do	**To Say**
Review names of pictures	Gather the picture cards.	Hold up each picture card and ask: **What is this?**
Introduce the game First Sound Mix-Up	Mix up the picture cards. Place the *t* and *s* Letter Cards on the table.	**We're going to play a game called First Sound Mix-Up. I'll hold up a picture. You'll say the name of the picture and tell me its first sound. You'll have to be careful because the pictures are all mixed up. Some of the pictures begin with /t/ and some begin with /sss/.**
Model the game	Display *top*.	**Model** **I'll show you how to play. This is *top*. I'll say the first sound in *top*: /t/. Now I'll put *top* next to the letter for the sound /t/.** Place the picture next to the *t* Letter Card. **Remember, the <u>name</u> of this letter is *t*. The <u>sound</u> for *t* is /t/.**
	Display *sun*.	**I'll do one more. This is *sun*. I'll say the first sound in *sun*: /sss/. Now I'll place *sun* next to the letter for the sound /sss/.** Place the picture next to the *s* Letter Card. **Remember, the <u>name</u> of this letter is *s*. The <u>sound</u> for the letter *s* is /sss/.**
Play the game to test knowledge of initial sounds	Test children with the next four to six pictures.	**Test** **What is this? Say the first sound in _____.** Confirm correct responses and prompt sound production for /t/ or /sss/ (use the Sound Production Cue Card). Have children place each picture next to the letter for its first sound.
	Give individual turns.	**Ongoing Assessment** **If**...children make incorrect responses, **then**...tell them the answer and have them repeat it. Place the picture back in the pile so that you can return to it a second time.

Phonological Awareness/Alphabetic Understanding

Activity 4 Review Letter Name and Sound

 **New**

Reintroduce s/s/; Pictures to Letters Game

Objective: Children practice letter name and sound: *s/s/*.   Time: 4–5 minutes

	To Do	**To Say**	
Introduce letter name	Hold up the *s* Alphabet Card.	Model	The <u>name</u> of this letter is *s*.
		Lead	Say the <u>name</u> with me.
		Test	What is the <u>name</u> of this letter?
Introduce letter sound	Continue holding up the *s* Alphabet Card.	Model	The <u>sound</u> for this letter is /sss/. When you say /sss/, the tip of your tongue touches above your top teeth. It makes a snake sound. Say /sss/ and hear the snake sound.
		Lead	Say the <u>sound</u> with me: /sss/.
		Test	What is the <u>sound</u> for this letter?
Test knowledge of letter name and sound	Continue holding up the *s* Alphabet Card.

Give individual turns. | Test | What is the <u>name</u> of this letter? What is the <u>sound</u> for this letter? |

Ongoing Assessment

If...children make incorrect responses,	then...tell them the letter name or sound, have them repeat it, and return to the letter a second time.

Introduce the game Pictures to Letters	Place the picture cards in the paper bag. Distribute the letter cards. Have children line up the cards in front of them on the table. (If you think six letters will be too difficult, you can have them use sets of only three or four letters at a time.)	We're going to play a game with your letters. I'll pull a picture from the bag, and we'll name the picture and its first sound. Then I'll say "One, two, three, go!" When you hear me say "go," you'll find the letter for the picture's first sound and hold it up. Remember, don't hold up your letter until I say "go."

Phonological Awareness/Alphabetic Understanding

	To Do		**To Say**
Model the game	Line up a set of letter cards in front of you.	Model	**My turn. I'll show you how to play.** Pull a picture from the bag. Use the following procedure for the picture you pulled. *Moon* is used as an example. **This is *moon*. What is this? I'll say the first sound in *moon*: /mmm/. Say the first sound in *moon*. Yes, /mmm/. Remember, when you say /mmm/, your lips come together. Put your lips together and say /mmm/, *moon*.** (Use the Sound Production Cue Card for other sounds.) **Now, when I hear "go," I'll hold up the *m* Letter Card. One, two, three, go!** Hold up the *m* Letter Card. **See, I'm holding up the *m* Letter Card because *m* is the letter for the sound /mmm/ like the /mmm/ in *moon*.** Return the letter card to the table. Set *moon* next to the *m* Letter Card.
Play the game to test knowledge of initial sounds /m/, /p/, /f/, /k/, /t/, and /s/	Play the game with children.	Test	**Your turn to play.** Pull a picture from the bag. **This is _____. What is this? Say the first sound in _____. Yes, /_/. Remember, when you say /_/,** (give sound production cue using Sound Production Cue Card). **Repeat the picture word: _____. When you hear "go," hold up the letter for the /_/ in _____. One, two, three, go! Everybody, what letter are you holding? Yes, _____. You found the letter _____ because _____ is the letter for /_/ like the /_/ in _____. Say /_/, _____. Now place your letter card on the table.** Place the picture next to the appropriate letter card.

Ongoing Assessment

If... children cannot correctly identify the first sound of the picture,	**then...** tell them the first sound and have them repeat it. Prompt children on sound production using the Sound Production Cue Card.
If... children hold up the wrong letter card,	**then...** repeat the sound and hold up the correct letter card. Have children find the correct letter card, hold it up, and say the sound with you.

Activity 5 Writer's Warm-Up

Memory Review: s, t, c, f, p, m

Objective: Children write *s, t, c, f, p,* and *m*.

Time: 2–3 minutes

	To Do	**To Say**	
Review letter names	Gather the tracing cards. Hold up each tracing card.	Test	**What's the <u>name</u> of this letter?**
Model the activity	Distribute the Write-On/ Wipe-Off Cards, markers, and erasers.	Model	**I'll show you how this activity works. The first letter is *s*. Now I'll write the letter *s* on my Write-On/Wipe-Off Card.**
Test children on *s, t, c, f, p,* and *m*		Test	**The first letter is *s*. Write *s* on your card. Everyone, what's the name of the letter you wrote? Good. Now erase your cards and let's do the next letter.** Continue with *t, c, f, p,* and *m*. Dictate each letter at least twice or as time allows.

Ongoing Assessment

If... children write the wrong letter or don't remember a letter,	then... show them the correct tracing card. Model tracing the letter with your finger and say the letter name.

Activity 6 Connect Sound to Letter

Match a Picture's Initial Sound; Introduce s

Objective: Children connect initial sound to letter.

Time: 2–3 minutes

	To Do		To Say
Introduce the activity	Gather the picture cards and the letter cards.		**You're going to choose the letter that goes with the first sound of some pictures.**
Model the activity	Place the *sun* Picture Card on the table.	Model	**This is *sun*. The first sound in *sun* is /sss/.** Place the *s* and *t* Letter Cards under the picture. **I'm going to choose the letter that matches this picture's first sound.** Point to the correct letter: ***s* is the letter for /sss/ like the /sss/ in *sun*.**
Test knowledge of initial sound	Display the *soap* Picture Card.	Test	**This is *soap*. What is this? The first sound in *soap* is /sss/. What is the first sound in *soap*? That's right; /sss/ is the first sound in *soap*.** Place the *f* and *s* Letter Cards under the picture. **Your turn. Choose the letter that matches this picture's first sound. Which letter is the letter for the sound /sss/ in *soap*? Do you know?** Call on a child to point to the correct letter. **What's the <u>name</u> of the letter you pointed to? What is the <u>sound</u> for that letter? That's right; *s* is the letter for /sss/ like the /sss/ in *soap*.** Reinforce the letter name and sound with the group: **Everyone, what's the <u>name</u> of the letter? What's the <u>sound</u> for the letter?** Continue with the remaining cards.

Ongoing Assessment

If...children make an error,	**then**...model the answer, have them repeat it, and return to the picture card a second time.

Writing/Spelling

Activity 7 Connect Sound to Letter

First Sounds: m, t, s, c, f

Objective: Children write *m, t, s, c,* and *f*.

Time: 6–8 minutes

	To Do	**To Say**	
Introduce the activity	Distribute a First Sounds page to each child.	**You're going to write the letter for the first sound of some pictures.**	
Model the activity	Point to the first picture on the First Sounds page.	Model	**This picture is *maze*. The first sound in *maze* is /mmm/. I'm going to write the letter for /mmm/ like the /mmm/ in *maze*.** Write *m* under the picture. **Now you write the letter for /mmm/ like the /mmm/ in *maze*. Start at the dot and write the letter. That's right, *m* is the letter for the sound /mmm/ like the /mmm/ in *maze*.**
Test children on *t, s, c,* and *f*	Point to the next picture on the First Sounds Page.	Test	**This picture is *tire*. What is the first sound in *tire*? That's right, /t/ is the first sound in *tire*. Your turn. Write the letter for the same sound as the /t/ in *tire*. Start at the dot and write the letter.** Reinforce the group on the letter name and sound: **Everyone, what's the __name__ of the letter you wrote? What is the __sound__ for the letter?**

Ongoing Assessment

If...children make an error,	**then**...model the letter name and sound. Have children repeat the letter name and sound and write the correct letter.

New Sound /d/
Review Sounds /m/, /f/, /k/, /t/, /s/
Key Phonologic Skill Isolate Initial Sound

Phonological Awareness and Alphabetic Understanding

Activity	Materials	Time
1. Alphabetic Introduce *d*/d/	Alphabet Card: *d* Letter Card: *d* (one per child)	1–2 minutes
2. Phonologic Does It Begin with /d/?	Picture Cards: *dog, man, doll, pig, dime, deer*	4–5 minutes
3. Phonologic First Sound Song with /s/	Picture Cards: *sandwich, sock, seal*	4–5 minutes
4. Alphabetic Reintroduce *d*/d/; Grab Bag Game: *m, f, c, t, s*	Alphabet Card: *d* paper bag Letter Cards: *m, f, c, t, s*	4–5 minutes

Writing and Spelling

Activity	Materials		Time
5. Writer's Warm-Up Introduce *d*	Tracing Cards: *d, s, t, c, f, p, m* Writer's Warm-Up (one per child) Student Activity Book 1, p. 35		2–3 minutes
6. Integrated Phonologic/Alphabetic Match a Picture's Initial Sound; Introduce *d*	Picture Cards: *dog, door, deer, dish, duck, dime, doll*	Letter Cards: *d, s, t, c, f, p, m*	2–3 minutes
7. Phonologic/Spelling Letter Cross-Out: *s, t, c, f, p*	Letter Cross-Out (one per child) Student Activity Book 1, p. 36	Picture Cards: *sun, saw; ten, turtle; coat, cookie; fish, fox; pen, puzzle*	6–8 minutes

Activity 1 Introduce Letter Name and Sound

Introduce d /d/

Objective: Children learn and trace d/d/.

Time: 1–2 minutes

	To Do	**To Say**	
Introduce letter name	Hold up the *d* Alphabet Card.	Model	The <u>name</u> of this letter is *d*.
		Lead	Say the <u>name</u> with me.
		Test	What is the <u>name</u> of this letter?
Introduce letter sound	Continue holding up the *d* Alphabet Card.	Model	This is the letter for the <u>sound</u> /d/. When you say /d/, the tip of your tongue touches above your top teeth. Say /d/ and feel the tip of your tongue touch above your top teeth. Place your hand on your throat to see if your voice box is on when you say /d/. Yes, your throat moves when you say /d/ because your voice box is on.
		Lead	Say the <u>sound</u> with me: /d/.
		Test	What is the <u>sound</u> for this letter?
Test letter name and sound	Continue holding up the *d* Alphabet Card.	Test	What is the <u>name</u> of this letter? What is the <u>sound</u> for this letter?
	Give individual turns on letter name and sound.	**Ongoing Assessment**	
		If...children make an error,	then...tell them the name or sound, have them repeat the name or sound, and return to the letter a second time.
Model tracing *d*	Distribute a letter card to each child. Model how to trace *d* using your alphabet card.	Model	Watch. I'll trace the letter *d*. Now you trace the letter *d* on your letter card three times. Say /d/ each time you trace the letter.
		Ongoing Assessment	
		If...children make an error,	then...place your hand over their hand and guide the tracing of the letter. Then have children try to trace the letter on their own. Repeat as necessary.

Phonological Awareness/Alphabetic Understanding

Activity 2 Isolate Initial Sound

Does It Begin with /d/?

Objective: Children isolate initial /d/.

Time: 4–5 minutes

	To Do	**To Say**	
Model names of pictures	Gather the picture cards. Place the *dog* Picture Card on the table.	Model	**This is *dog*. What is this?** Continue with *man, doll, pig, dime,* and *deer*. Then test children on the picture names by placing the cards on the table one at a time and asking: **What is this?**
Introduce the game Does It Begin with /d/?	Practice production of the target sound.		Tell children they will play a game. They need to find the pictures with the first sound /d/. **Let's say /d/. When you say /d/, the tip of your tongue touches above your top teeth. Say /d/ and feel the tip of your tongue touch above your top teeth. Place your hand on your throat to see if your voice box is on when you say /d/. Yes, your throat moves when you say /d/ because your voice box is on.**
Model the game	Model two examples.	Model	**My turn. I'll say the name of the picture and then tell whether the first sound is /d/: dog** (exaggerate the first sound). ***Dog* begins with /d/. The tip of my tongue touches above my top teeth and my voice box is on when I say /d/, *dog*. The next picture is *man*** (exaggerate the first sound). ***Man* does not begin with /d/.**
Play the game to test knowledge of /d/	Test children with four other examples: *doll, pig, dime, deer*.	Test	**What is this? Does *doll* begin with /d/?** Confirm correct responses and prompt sound production: **Yes, *doll* begins with /d/. Let's say /d/. When you say /d/, the tip of your tongue touches above your top teeth. Say /d/ and feel the tip of your tongue touch above your top teeth. Place your hand on your throat to see whether your voice box is on when you say /d/. Yes, your throat moves when you say /d/ because your voice box is on: *doll*.**
	Give individual turns.		

Ongoing Assessment

If...children make incorrect responses,	then...model the correct answer. Review the sound production cue. Have children repeat the correct answer. Go back to the example a second time.

153

Activity **3** Isolate Initial Sound

First Sound Song with /s/
Objective: Children isolate initial sound /s/.

Time: 4–5 minutes

	To Do		**To Say**
Introduce the First Sound Song	Display the picture cards for *sandwich, sock,* and *seal.*		**You are going to learn a song. Look at the three pictures that begin with /sss/. These pictures will be in the song.**
Model the song	Point to the pictures as you say the names.	Model	**This is *sandwich, sock, seal.* The first sound in *sandwich, sock,* and *seal* is /sss/. Say the sound /sss/ with me. Remember, when you say /sss/, the tip of your tongue touches above your top teeth. It makes a snake sound. Say /sss/ and hear the snake sound.**
	Sing the song.		Point to each picture as you sing its name. Sing the following words to the tune of "Old MacDonald Had a Farm": **What is the first sound in these words: *sandwich, sock, seal*? /sss/ is the first sound in these words: *sandwich, sock, seal.* With a /sss/, /sss/ here and a /sss/, /sss/ there, here a /sss/, there a /sss/, everywhere a /sss/, /sss/. /sss/ is the first sound in these words: *sandwich, sock, seal.*** Lead children through the song several times, pointing to the pictures as they sing.
Test knowledge of initial sound	Test children on the first sound of each picture from the song.	Test	**It's your turn. What is this? Say the first sound of the picture name.** Confirm correct responses and prompt sound production.
	Give individual turns on identifying the first sound of a picture.		

Ongoing Assessment

If... children make an error,	then... model the answer, have children repeat it, and return to the example a second time.

Phonological Awareness/Alphabetic Understanding

Activity 4 — Review Letter Name and Sound

Reintroduce d/d/;
Grab Bag Game: m, f, c, t, s

Objective: Children identify letter name and sound: d/d/.

Time: 4–5 minutes

	To Do	To Say	
Introduce letter name	Hold up the *d* Alphabet Card.	Model	The <u>name</u> of this letter is *d*.
		Lead	Say the <u>name</u> with me.
		Test	What is the <u>name</u> of this letter?
Introduce letter sound	Continue holding up the *d* Alphabet Card.	Model	This is the letter for the <u>sound</u> /d/. When you say /d/, the tip of your tongue touches above your top teeth. Say /d/ and feel the tip of your tongue touch above your top teeth. Place your hand on your throat to see if your voice box is on when you say /d/. Yes, your throat moves when you say /d/ because your voice box is on.
		Lead	Say the <u>sound</u> with me: /d/.
		Test	What is the <u>sound</u> for this letter?
Test letter name and sound	Continue holding up the *d* Alphabet Card.	Test	What is the <u>name</u> of this letter? What is the <u>sound</u> for this letter?

Ongoing Assessment

If...children make an error,   then...tell them the name or sound, have them repeat the name or sound, and return to the letter a second time.

Play the Grab Bag Game	Place letter cards for *m, f, c, t,* and *s* in a paper bag.	Have children take turns pulling a letter out of the bag. Hold up the letter and test the group on the letter name and sound: **What is the <u>name</u> of this letter? What is the <u>sound</u> for this letter?** If the group correctly states the name and sound of the letter, place the letter card in a pile on the table. Continue playing the game until all cards have been removed from the bag. If time permits, provide individual turns.

Give individual turns on letter name and sound.

Ongoing Assessment

If...children make an error,   then...tell them the name or sound, have them repeat the name or sound, and place the letter card back in the bag.

155

Phonological Awareness/Alphabetic Understanding

Activity 5 Writer's Warm-Up

Introduce d

Objective: Children trace and write *d* and review writing *f, p, m, c, s,* and *t*.

Time: 2–3 minutes

	To Do	**To Say**	
Review letter name and sound	Hold up the *d* Tracing Card.	**What is the <u>name</u> of this letter? What is the <u>sound</u> for this letter?**	
Model tracing d	Distribute a Writer's Warm-Up to each child. Continue holding up the *d* Tracing Card. Model tracing *d* again.	**Model**	**Watch as I trace the letter *d* with my finger.**
		Lead	**Now you trace the first two *d*'s with your finger on your Writer's Warm-Up.**
		Model	**Watch as I trace *d* again.**
		Lead	**Now use your pencil to trace the next two *d*'s.**
Model writing d	Hold up the lined side of the *d* Tracing Card.	**Model**	**Watch as I write the letter *d*. I start at the dot and write the letter.** Have children write the letter twice on their warm-up sheets. Remind children to write carefully.

Ongoing Assessment

If...children make an error,	**then**...ask them to write the letter again. If needed, place your hand over their hand and guide them in writing the letter. Then have children write the letter on their own. Repeat as necessary.

Test writing d	Model writing *d* again.	Have children cover the letters they wrote and write the letter twice from memory. Then have them uncover their letters and compare them. **Do your letters look the same? Circle the letter that is your best work.**

Review *f, p, m, c, s, t*		Have children trace and write each review letter.

Ongoing Assessment

If...children make an error,	**then**...use the tracing card to model writing the letter and ask them to write the letter again. If needed, place your hand over their hand and guide them in writing the letter. Then have children write the letter on their own. Repeat as necessary.

Writing/Spelling

Match a Picture's Initial Sound; Introduce d

Objective: Children match a picture's initial sound to letter.   Time: 2–3 minutes

	To Do	**To Say**
Introduce the activity	Gather the *d* Picture Cards and the *d, s, t, c, f, p,* and *m* Letter Cards.	**You're going to choose the letter that goes with the first sound of some pictures.**
Model the activity	Place the *dog* Picture Card on the table, facing children.	**Model** **This is *dog*. The first sound in *dog* is /d/.** Place the *m* and *d* Letter Cards below the picture. **I'm going to choose the letter that matches this picture's first sound.** Point to the correct letter: ***d* is the letter for /d/ like the /d/ in *dog*.**
Test knowledge of initial sound	Display the *door* Picture Card. Place the *d* Letter Card and one other on the table. Vary the choice and order of letters.	**Test** **This is *door*. What is this? The first sound in *door* is /d/. What is the first sound in *door*? That's right, /d/ is the first sound in *door*.** **It's your turn to choose the letter that matches this picture's first sound. Everyone, think of which letter has the same sound as the /d/ in *door*. Does everyone know?** Call on an individual child to point to the correct letter. **What's the <u>name</u> of the letter you pointed to? What is the <u>sound</u> for that letter? That's right; *d* is the letter for /d/ like the /d/ in *door*.** Reinforce the letter name and sound with the group: **Everyone, what's the <u>name</u> of the letter? What's the <u>sound</u> for the letter?** Continue with the remaining cards.

Ongoing Assessment

If... children make an error,	**then...** model the answer, have them repeat it, and return to the picture card a second time.

157

Writing/Spelling

Activity 7 Connect Sound to Letter

Letter Cross-Out: s, t, c, f, p

Objective: Children connect sound to letter.

Time: 6–8 minutes

	To Do	To Say
Introduce the activity	Gather the picture cards. Distribute a Letter Cross-Out to each child.	**You're going to cross out letters that go with the first sound of some pictures. Let's see if we can cross out all the letters on the sheet!**
Model the activity	Place the *sun* Picture Card on the table.	**Model** — **This is *sun*. The first sound in *sun* is /sss/. I'm going to cross out a letter for the sound /sss/ in *sun*.** Cross out an *s* on your cross-out sheet. **Now you cross out a letter for the sound /sss/ in *sun*. That's right, *s* is the letter for /sss/ like the /sss/ in *sun*.**
Test children on *s, t, c, f,* and *p*	Place the *fish* Picture Card on the table.	**Test** — **This is *fish*. What is this? What is the first sound in *fish*? That's right, /fff/ is the first sound in *fish*. Now cross out the letter for the same sound as the /fff/ in *fish*. Everyone, what's the <u>name</u> of the letter you crossed out? And what is the <u>sound</u> for this letter?** Continue to test children with other pictures until all other letters are crossed out. Vary the order in which you test the pictures.

Ongoing Assessment

If... children make an error,	then... point to the correct letter and model the letter sound. Have children repeat the sound and cross out the correct letter.

New Sound /d/
Review Sounds /m/, /f/, /k/, /t/, /s/
Key Phonologic Skill Isolate Initial Sound

Phonological Awareness and Alphabetic Understanding

Activity	Materials		Time
1. Alphabetic Introduce *d*/d/	Alphabet Card: *d*	Letter Card: *d* (one per child)	1–2 minutes
2. Phonologic Which Picture Begins with /d/?	Picture Choices: 20-1, 20-2, 20-3 Teacher Resource Package 1		4–5 minutes
3. Integrated Phonologic/Alphabetic Sound Match with /s/, /t/, /k/, and /f/	Letter Cards: *s, t, c, f* game markers (four per child/not provided) Sound Production Cue Card	Sound Match Cards: 20a–20e (one card per child) Teacher Resource Package 1	4–5 minutes
4. Alphabetic Reintroduce *d*/d/; Partners Game	Alphabet Card: *d* Letter Cards: *m, f, c, t, s, d* (one each per pair of children)		4–5 minutes

Writing and Spelling

Activity	Materials		Time
5. Writer's Warm-Up Introduce *d*	Tracing Cards: *d, s, t, c, f, p, m* Writer's Warm-Up (one per child) Student Activity Book 1, p. 37		2–3 minutes
6. Integrated Phonologic/Alphabetic Match a Picture's Initial Sound; Introduce *d*	Picture Cards: *deer, dish, dime, door, duck, dog, doll*	Letter Cards: *d, f, s, p, t, m, c*	2–3 minutes
7. Phonologic/Spelling Letter Race: *d, s, t, c*	Letter Race (one per child) Student Activity Book 1, p. 38 Picture Cards: *deer, dish, dime; cat, coat, cookie; tag, tape, ten; saw, soap, seal*		6–8 minutes

Activity 1 Introduce Letter Name and Sound

Introduce d/d/

Objective: Children learn and trace d/d/.

Time: 1–2 minutes

	To Do	**To Say**	
Introduce letter name	Hold up the *d* Alphabet Card.	Model	The <u>name</u> of this letter is *d*.
		Lead	Say the <u>name</u> with me.
		Test	What is the <u>name</u> of this letter?
Introduce letter sound	Continue holding up the *d* Alphabet Card.	Model	This letter is for the <u>sound</u> /d/. When you say /d/, the tip of your tongue touches above your top teeth. Say /d/ and feel the tip of your tongue touch above your top teeth. Place your hand on your throat to see if your voice box is on when you say /d/. Yes, your throat moves when you say /d/ because your voice box is on.
		Lead	Say the <u>sound</u> with me: /d/.
		Test	What is the <u>sound</u> for this letter?
Test letter name and sound	Continue holding up the *d* Alphabet Card.	Test	What is the <u>name</u> of this letter? What is the <u>sound</u> for this letter?

Ongoing Assessment

If...children make an error,	**then**... tell them the name or sound, have them repeat the name or sound, and return to the letter a second time.

Give individual turns on letter name and sound.

Model tracing d	Model how to trace *d* using your alphabet card.	Model	Watch. I'll trace the letter *d*.
	Distribute a *d* Letter Card to each child.		Now, you trace the letter *d* on your letter card three times. Say /d/ each time you trace the letter.

Ongoing Assessment

If...children make an error,	**then**... place your hand over their hand and guide the tracing of the letter. Then have children try to trace the letter on their own. Repeat as necessary.

Phonological Awareness/Alphabetic Understanding

Activity 2 Isolate Initial Sound

Which Picture Begins with /d/?

Objective: Children isolate initial /d/.

Time: 4–5 minutes

	To Do	To Say	
Model names of pictures	Gather the picture choices. Place Picture Choice 20-1 on the table. Point to and name each picture: *moon, deer, cup; fire, seal, dot.*	**Model**	**This is *moon*. What is this?** Continue this procedure for each picture. Test children on the picture names by pointing to the pictures one at a time and asking: **What is this?** Repeat for Picture Choices 20-2 and 20-3.
Introduce the game Which Picture Begins with /d/?	Practice production of the target sound.		**I'll show you three pictures and you'll find the one that has the first sound /d/.** **Let's say /d/. Remember, when you say /d/, the tip of your tongue touches above your top teeth. Say /d/ and feel the tip of your tongue touch above your top teeth. Place your hand on your throat to see if your voice box is on when you say /d/. Yes, your throat moves when you say /d/ because your voice box is on.**
Model the game	Model two examples.	**Model**	**I'll show you how to play the game.** Display Picture Choice 20-1. Cover the bottom row of pictures. **This is *moon, deer, cup*. *Deer* has the first sound /d/.** Exaggerate the first sound of the correct picture and then say the word: **/d/, *deer*.** Model one more example with the bottom row of pictures: *fire, seal, dot.* Cover the top row of pictures.
Play the game to test knowledge of /d/	Test with examples from Picture Choice 20-2 (*dog, soap, mouse; cone, fan, doll*) and 20-3 (*dive, can, foot; sandwich, dock, map*).	**Test**	Cover the pictures not in use. Ask children to tell the name of each picture: **What is this? Which picture has the first sound /d/?** Confirm correct responses and prompt sound production: **Yes, *dog* has the first sound /d/. Let's say /d/. Remember, when you say /d/, the tip of your tongue touches above your top teeth. Say /d/ and feel the tip of your tongue touch above your top teeth. Place your hand on your throat to see if your voice box is on when you say /d/. Yes, your throat moves when you say /d/ because your voice box is on: *dog*.**
	Give individual turns.		

Ongoing Assessment

If...children make an error,	then... model the correct answer. Review the sound production cue. Have children repeat the correct answer. Go back to the example a second time.

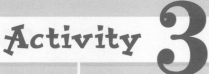

Activity **3** Isolate Initial Sound

Sound Match with /s/, /t/, /k/, and /f/

Objective: Children isolate picture's initial sounds and connect to letter.

Time: 4–5 minutes

	To Do	**To Say**
Introduce the game Sound Match	Gather the Sound Match cards.	**You are going to play Sound Match. I will show you a letter. You must find a picture that begins with the sound for the letter and place a marker on it. When you have a marker on each picture in a row, say "Sound Match!" That means you've won.**
Model the game	Hold up the *s* Letter Card and point to the letter. Distribute a Sound Match Card and four markers to each child.	**Test** **What is the <u>sound</u> for this letter?** **Model** Ask children to whisper the name of each picture on their cards and to raise their hand if they don't know one. The picture names are listed below. **Find a picture on your card that begins with /sss/ and place a marker on it.** Go around the table and have each child tell the picture he or she placed the marker on. Confirm correct responses and have the whole group repeat the word: **Yes, sun begins with /sss/. Everybody, say /sss/, sun.** Repeat for target sounds /f/, /k/, and /t/. When a child wins, have all children clear off their cards.
Play the game to test knowledge of initial sounds	Repeat with /t/, /s/, /f/, and /k/.	Collect the cards, mix them, and redistribute them to children. Play a second round of the game with the target sounds /t/, /s/, /f/, and /k/.

Ongoing Assessment

If...children make incorrect responses,	then...model the correct answer. Review the sound production cue using the Sound Production Cue Card. Have children repeat the correct answer.

Sound Match Picture Names

20a: *dive, deer, desk/sun, can, tag/donut, fire, dog*

20b: *dime, fish, dog/saw, tent, donut/doll, cat, deer*

20c: *donut, doll, fan/dime, dive, saw/deer, tie, coat*

20d: *foot, sick, tail/dog, dime, dive/cane, doll, donut*

20e: *deer, dime, fin/desk, donut, dive/seal, tire, cap*

Phonological Awareness/Alphabetic Understanding

Activity 4 Review Letter Name and Sound

Reintroduce d/d/; Partners Game

Objective: Children practice letter name and sound: /d/d.   Time: 4–5 minutes

	To Do	**To Say**	
Introduce letter name	Hold up the *d* Alphabet Card.	Model	The <u>name</u> of this letter is *d*.
		Lead	Say the <u>name</u> with me.
		Test	What is the <u>name</u> of this letter?
Introduce letter sound	Continue holding up the *d* Alphabet Card.	Model	The <u>sound</u> for this letter is /d/. When you say /d/, the tip of your tongue touches above your top teeth. Say /d/ and feel the tip of your tongue touch above your top teeth. Place your hand on your throat to see whether your voice box is on when you say /d/. Yes, your throat moves when you say /d/ because your voice box is on.
		Lead	Say the <u>sound</u> with me: /d/.
		Test	What is the <u>sound</u> for this letter?
Test letter name and sound	Continue holding up the *d* Alphabet Card. Give individual turns on letter name and sound.	Test	What is the <u>name</u> of this letter? What is the <u>sound</u> for this letter?

Ongoing Assessment

If...children make an error,	**then**...tell them the letter name or sound, have them repeat the name or sound, and return to the letter a second time.

Play the Partners Game	Give each pair of children a set of letter cards.	**Today you are going to practice the names and sounds of letters with a partner.** Place your cards in a pile on the table. The first player shows the top card and asks for the letter name and sound. If the second player answers correctly, the first player gives the card to him or her. If the second player makes a mistake, the first player should give the correct name or sound and place the letter card on the bottom of the pile. Play until the second player has all the cards. Then switch roles.

163

Phonological Awareness/Alphabetic Understanding

Activity 5 Writer's Warm-Up

Introduce d

Objective: Children trace and write *d* and review writing *f*, *p*, *m*, *c*, *s*, and *t*.
Time: 2–3 minutes

	To Do	**To Say**	
Review letter name and sound	Hold up the *d* Tracing Card.	**What is the <u>name</u> of this letter? What is the <u>sound</u> for this letter?**	
Model tracing *d*	Distribute a Writer's Warm-Up to each child. Continue holding up the *d* Tracing Card. Model tracing *d* again.	Model	**Watch as I trace the letter *d* with my finger.**
		Lead	**Now you trace the first two *d*'s on your warm-up sheet with your finger.**
		Model	**Watch as I trace *d* again.**
		Lead	**Now use your pencil to trace the next two *d*'s.**
Model writing *d*	Use the lined side of the tracing card.	Model	**Watch as I write the letter *d*. I start at the dot and write the letter.** Have children write the letter twice on their warm-up sheets. Remind children to write their letters carefully and correctly.

Ongoing Assessment

If...children make an error,	then... ask them to write the letter again. If they need assistance, place your hand over their hand and guide the writing of the letter. Then have children write the letter independently. Repeat as necessary.

Test writing *d*	Model writing *d* again.	Have children cover the letters they wrote and write the letter twice from memory. Then have them uncover their letters and compare them. **Do your letters look the same? Circle the letter that is your best work.**

Review *f, p, m c, s, t*		Have children trace and write each review letter.

Ongoing Assessment

If...children make an error,	then... use the tracing card to model writing the letter and ask them to write the letter again. If necessary, place your hand over their hand and guide the writing of the letter. Then have children write the letter on their own. Repeat as necessary.

Writing/Spelling

Activity **6** Connect Sound to Letter

Match a Picture's Initial Sound; Introduce d

Objective: Children match a picture's initial sound to letter.   Time: 2–3 minutes

	To Do		**To Say**
Introduce the activity	Gather the *d* Picture Cards and the *d, s, t, c, f, p,* and *m* Letter Cards.		Tell children that they are going to choose the letter that goes with the first sound of some pictures.
Model the activity	Place the *deer* Picture Card on the table, facing children.	Model	**This is *deer*. The first sound in *deer* is /d/.** Place the *d* and *s* Letter Cards under the picture, facing children. **I'm going to choose the letter that matches this picture's first sound.** Point to the correct letter: ***d* is the letter for /d/ like the /d/ in *deer*.**
Test children with other examples	Display the *dish* Picture Card. Place two letter cards on the table. Vary the choice and order of letters.	Test	**This is *dish*. What is this? What is the first sound in *dish*? That's right, /d/ is the first sound in *dish*.** **It's your turn to choose the letter that matches this picture's first sound. Everyone, think of which letter has the same sound as the /d/ in *dish*. Does everyone know?** Call on an individual child to point to the correct letter. **What's the <u>name</u> of the letter you pointed to? What's the <u>sound</u> for the letter? That's right; *d* is the letter for /d/ like the /d/ in *dish*.** Continue this procedure for the remaining pictures.

Ongoing Assessment

If... children make an error,	then... model the answer, have them repeat it, and return to the picture card a second time.

Reinforce letter name and sound	Show the *d* Letter Card.	**Everyone, what's the <u>name</u> of this letter? What's the <u>sound</u> for this letter?**

 **Connect Sound to Letter**

Activity 7

Letter Race: d, s, t, c

Objective: Children isolate initial sound and write the corresponding letter.

Time: 6–8 minutes

	To Do	**To Say**	
Introduce the activity	Distribute a Letter Race to each child. Gather the picture cards.	**We are going to have a letter race. I will show you a picture and then you will write the letter that goes with the picture's first sound on the right racetrack. Which letter do you think will win?**	
Model the activity	Place the *deer* Picture Card on the table, facing children.	Model	**Let's do one together. This is *deer*. The first sound in *deer* is /d/. I'm going to write the letter on the racetrack next to the letter for the /d/ in *deer*.** Write the letter on the *d* racetrack. **Now you write the letter for /d/. Start at the dot and write the letter. That's right, *d* is the letter for /d/, like the /d/ in *deer*.**
Test children on *d, s, t,* and *c*	Place the *cat* Picture Card on the table.	Test	**This is *cat*. What is this? What is the first sound in *cat*? That's right, /k/ is the first sound in *cat*. Now write the letter on the racetrack next to the letter for the /k/ in *cat*. Start at the dot and write the letter.**
			Reinforce the letter name and sound: **Everyone, what's the name of the letter you wrote? And what is the sound for the letter?** Continue this procedure for the remaining pictures, until one letter wins.

Ongoing Assessment

If...children make an error,	**then**...model the letter name and sound. Have children repeat the letter name and sound and write the correct letter.

Writing/Spelling

Phonological Awareness and Alphabetic Understanding

Activity	Materials	Time
1. Alphabetic Introduce *d*/d/	Alphabet Card: *d* Letter Card: *d* (one per child)	1–2 minutes
2. Integrated Phonologic/Alphabetic Which Picture Begins with /d/?	Alphabet Card: *d* Picture Choices: 21-1, 21-2, 21-3 Teacher Resource Package 1	4–5 minutes
3. Integrated Phonologic/Alphabetic Picture Scene Search: /s/	Alphabet Card: *s* Picture Scene /s/	4–5 minutes
4. Alphabetic Reintroduce *d*/d/; Be the Teacher Game	Alphabet Card: *d* Letter Cards: *d, s, t, c, f, m*	4–5 minutes

Writing and Spelling

Activity	Materials	Time
5. Writer's Warm-Up Letter Mission: Review *d, s, t, c, f, p, m*	Letter Mission (one per child) Student Activity Book 1, p. 39 Tracing Cards: *d, s, t, c, f, p, m*	2–3 minutes
6. Integrated Phonologic/Alphabetic Match a Picture's Initial Sound; Introduce *d*	Picture Cards: *deer, door, dish,* *duck, dime, dog, doll* Letter Cards: *d, s,* *t, c, f, p, m*	2–3 minutes
7. Phonologic/Spelling Letter Tag: *d, s, t, c, f, m*	Letter Tag (one per child) Student Activity Book 1, p. 40	6–8 minutes

Activity 1 Introduce Letter Name and Sound

Introduce d/d/

Objective: Children learn and trace d/d/.

Time: 1–2 minutes

	To Do	**To Say**	
Introduce letter name	Hold up the *d* Alphabet Card.	Model	**The <u>name</u> of this letter is d.**
		Lead	**Say the <u>name</u> with me.**
		Test	**What is the <u>name</u> of this letter?**
Introduce letter sound	Continue holding up the *d* Alphabet Card.	Model	**This is the letter for the <u>sound</u> /d/. When you say /d/, the tip of your tongue touches above your top teeth. Say /d/ and feel the tip of your tongue touch above your top teeth. Place your hand on your throat to see if your voice box is on when you say /d/. Yes, your throat moves when you say /d/ because your voice box is on.**
		Lead	**Say the <u>sound</u> with me: /d/.**
		Test	**What is the <u>sound</u> for this letter?**
Test letter name and sound	Continue holding up the *d* Alphabet Card.	Test	**What is the <u>name</u> of this letter? What is the <u>sound</u> for this letter?**
	Give individual turns on letter name and sound.	**Ongoing Assessment**	
		If... children make an error,	then... tell them the letter name or sound, have them repeat the name or sound, and return to the letter a second time.
Model tracing d	Model how to trace *d* using your *d* Alphabet Card.	Model	**Watch. I'll trace the letter d.**
	Distribute a *d* Letter Card to each child.		**Trace the letter d on your letter card three times. Say /d/ each time you trace the letter.**
		Ongoing Assessment	
		If... children make an error,	then... place your hand over their hand and guide the tracing of the letter. Then have children try to trace the letter on their own. Repeat as necessary.

Phonological Awareness/Alphabetic Understanding

Activity 2 Isolate Initial Sound

Which Picture Begins with /d/?

Objective: Children isolate initial /d/ and connect sound to letter.

Time: 4–5 minutes

	To Do	**To Say**	
Model names of pictures	Gather the picture choices. Place Picture Choice 21-1 on the table. Point to *fish*.	Model	**This is *fish*. What is this?** Point to and name each picture: *fish, cane, dog; dock, sun, fin.* Repeat for Picture Choices 21-2 and 21-3
Introduce the game Which Picture Begins with /d/?	Hold up the *d* Alphabet Card. Practice production of the target sound.		**I'll show you three pictures. You'll need to find the picture that has the first sound /d/.**
		Model	**The <u>name</u> of this letter is *d*. This is the letter for the <u>sound</u> /d/. Remember, when you say /d/, the tip of your tongue touches above your top teeth. Say /d/ and feel the tip of your tongue touch above your top teeth. Place your hand on your throat to see if your voice box is on when you say /d/. Yes, your throat moves when you say /d/ because your voice box is on.**
		Test	**What is the <u>sound</u> for this letter?**
Model the game	Display Picture Choice 21-1. Cover the bottom row of pictures. Point to each picture as you name it.	Model	**This is *fish, cane, dog*. My turn. I'll find the picture with the first sound /d/.** Point to the letter *d*. **Dog** (exaggerate the first sound). **The first sound in *dog* is /d/; /d/, *dog*.** Cover the top row of pictures and repeat the procedure.
Play the game to test knowledge of /d/	Hold up the *d* Alphabet Card and test the sound.	Test	**What is the <u>sound</u> for this letter?**
	Display Picture Choice 21-2 (*cap, deer, mop; dot, man, soap*) and 21-3 (*saw, fork, dime; mow, doll, can*) one at a time. Cover the pictures not in use.		Ask children to tell the name of each picture: **What is this?** Point to the letter *d*. **Which picture has the first sound /d/?** Confirm correct responses and prompt sound production: **Yes, *deer* has the first sound /d/. Let's say /d/. Remember, when you say /d/, the tip of your tongue touches above your top teeth. Say /d/ and feel the tip of your tongue touch above your top teeth. Place your hand on your throat to see if your voice box is on when you say /d/. Yes, your throat moves when you say /d/ because your voice box is on: *deer*.**
	Give individual turns.		

Ongoing Assessment

If...children make incorrect responses,	**then**...model the correct answer. Review the sound production cue and have children repeat the correct answer. Go back to the example a second time.

Activity 3 — Isolate Initial Sound

Picture Scene Search: /s/

Objective: Children connect initial sound to picture.

Time: 4–5 minutes

	To Do	**To Say**	
Review letter name and sound	Hold up the *s* Alphabet Card.	Model	**The <u>name</u> of this letter is *s*. What is the <u>sound</u> for this letter? Yes, /sss/. When you say /sss/, the tip of your tongue touches above your top teeth. It makes a snake sound. Say /sss/ and hear the snake sound.**
Introduce the Picture Scene Search	Hold up the picture scene.		**Let's play a game. I'll show you a picture, and you will find things in the picture that have the first sound /sss/.**
	Hold up the *s* Alphabet Card and test the sound.	Test	**What is the <u>sound</u> for this letter?**

Ongoing Assessment

If... children make incorrect responses,	**then...** model the correct sound and have children repeat it. Review the sound production cue. Repeat the test.

	To Do	**To Say**	
Model the game	Hold up the picture scene.	Model	**My turn. I'll find something in the picture that has the first sound /sss/.** Name and point to something in the picture scene that has the first sound /s/: **sun has the first sound /sss/.**
Play the game to test knowledge of initial /s/	Give individual turns. Target pictures: *string, sun, sky, sailboat, sandcastle, spoon, salad, swimming, sandwich, seashell, strawberry*	Test	**It's your turn to find something that has the first sound /sss/.** Confirm each correct response and have the group repeat it: **Yes, *string* has the first sound /sss/. Everybody, say /sss/, *string*.**

Activity 4 Review Letter Name and Sound

Reintroduce d/d/;
Be the Teacher Game

Objective: Children practice letter name and sound: d/d/.   Time: 4–5 minutes

	To Do	**To Say**	
Introduce letter name	Hold up the *d* Alphabet Card.	Model	The <u>name</u> of this letter is *d*.
		Lead	Say the <u>name</u> of the letter with me.
		Test	What is the <u>name</u> of this letter?
Introduce letter sound	Continue holding up the *d* Alphabet Card.	Model	This is the letter for the <u>sound</u> /d/. When you say /d/, the tip of your tongue touches above your top teeth. Say /d/ and feel the tip of your tongue touch above your top teeth. Place your hand on your throat to see if your voice box is on when you say /d/. Yes, your throat moves when you say /d/ because your voice box is on.
		Lead	Say the <u>sound</u> with me: /d/.
		Test	What is the <u>sound</u> for this letter?
Test letter name and sound	Continue holding up the *d* Alphabet Card. Give individual turns on letter name and sound.	Test	What is the <u>name</u> of this letter? What is the <u>sound</u> for this letter?

Ongoing Assessment

If...children make an error,   then...tell them the letter name or sound, have them repeat the name or sound, and return to the letter a second time.

Play the Be the Teacher Game	Gather the *m, f, c, t, s,* and *d* Letter Cards.	**Now one of you is going to be the teacher. The teacher will ask the group the name and sound of some letters.**

Choose a child to hold up each letter card and test the group on the letter name and sound: **What is the <u>name</u> of this letter? What is the <u>sound</u> for this letter?** If the group answers correctly, have the "teacher" place the letter card in a pile on the table. Have the "teacher" continue to play the game until the name and sound for each letter have been correctly identified. Then place all the cards back in a pile and ask the "teacher" to give individual turns.

Ongoing Assessment

If...children make an error,   then...prompt the child playing the teacher to tell the letter name or sound and to place the letter card at the back of the pile.

 **Writer's Warm-Up**

Letter Mission:
Review *d, s, t, c, f, p, m*
Objective: Children practice writing letters.

Time: 2–3 minutes

	To Do	**To Say**	
Introduce the activity	Distribute a Letter Mission to each child.		**We are going on a letter mission. I'm going to tell you the name of a letter and you are going to write it. Let's see if we can help the dog get the bone!**
Model the activity	Hold up a Letter Mission. Point to the first letter space.	Model	**Let's do one together. The first letter is *d*. Watch as I start at the dot and write the letter *d*.** Write the letter on the activity sheet. **Now you write the letter *d*. Start at the dot and write the letter.**
Lead the activity	Continue to hold up a Letter Mission. Point to the next letter space.	Lead	**Now write the letter *p*. Start at the dot and write the letter. Everyone, what's the name of the letter you wrote?** Continue this procedure for *m, s, f, t, c, d,* and *p*.

Ongoing Assessment

If...children write the wrong letter or don't remember a letter,	**then**... show them the tracing card of the correct letter and model tracing the letter.

Writing/Spelling

 # Activity 6 Connect Sound to Letter

Match a Picture's Initial Sound; Introduce d

Objective: Children connect initial sound to letter.

Time: 2–3 minutes

	To Do	**To Say**	
Introduce the activity	Gather the *d* Picture Cards and the *d, s, t, c, f, p,* and *m* Letter Cards.		**You are going to choose the letter that goes with the first sound of some pictures.**
Model the activity	Place the *doll* Picture Card on the table, facing children.	**Model**	**This is *doll*. The first sound in *doll* is /d/.** Place the *m* and *d* Letter Cards under the picture, facing children. **I'm going to choose the letter that matches this picture's first sound.** Point to the correct letter: ***d* is the letter for /d/ like the /d/ in *doll*.**
Test knowledge of initial sound	Display the *deer* Picture Card. Place the *d* and *t* Letter Cards under the picture.	**Test**	**This is *deer*. What is this? What is the first sound in *deer*? That's right, /d/ is the first sound in *deer*.** **It's your turn to choose the letter that matches this picture's first sound. Everyone, think of which letter is the letter for the sound /d/ in *deer*. Does everyone know?** Call on an individual child to point to the correct letter. **What's the <u>name</u> of the letter you pointed to? What is the <u>sound</u> for the letter? That's right; *d* is the letter for /d/ like the /d/ in *deer*.** Continue this procedure for the remaining pictures. Vary the choice and order of letters.

Ongoing Assessment

If... children make an error,	**then...** model the answer, have children repeat it, and return to the picture a second time.

Activity **7** Connect Sound to Letter

Letter Tag: d, s, t, c, f, m
Objective: Children connect sound to letter.

Time: 6–8 minutes

	To Do	**To Say**	
Introduce the activity	Distribute a Letter Tag to each child.		**We are going to play Letter Tag. I'm going to tell you the sound of a letter and you are going to tag the letter with your pencil.**
Model the activity	Place a Letter Tag sheet on the table, facing children.	Model	**I'll show you how to play Letter Tag. The first sound is /t/. I'm going to start at the arrow and tag the letter for the sound /t/.** Draw a line from the arrow to the correct letter with a pencil. **Now it's your turn to tag the letter for the sound /t/. Place your pencil on the first arrow and tag the letter for the sound /t/. That's right, *t* is the letter for the sound /t/.**
Test children on *f, s, d, c,* and *m*	Say a letter sound and have children tag the correct letter. Follow the boxes left to right across the page.	Test	**Place your pencil on the next arrow. When I say the sound, you tag the letter for that sound. Ready? Here's the sound: /fff/.** Reinforce the letter name and sound: **Everyone, what's the <u>name</u> of the letter you tagged? What is the <u>sound</u> for the letter?** Continue with this sequence: /s/, /d/, /k/, /m/. If time allows, do a second sequence starting again from the top of the page: /s/, /f/, /k/, /m/, /s/, /t/.

Ongoing Assessment

If… children make an error,	**then…** model the letter name and sound and have children repeat them. Have children tag the correct letter.

New Sound /l/
Review Sounds /m/, /p/, /f/, /k/, /t/, /s/, /d/
Key Phonologic Skill Isolate Initial Sound

Phonological Awareness and Alphabetic Understanding

Activity	Materials	Time
1. Alphabetic Introduce *l*/l/	Alphabet Card: *l* Letter Card: *l* (one per child)	1–2 minutes
2. Phonologic Does It Begin with /l/?	Picture Cards: *lip, cat, lock, leaf, leg, map*	4–5 minutes
3. Phonologic First Sound Song with /d/	Picture Cards: *deer, doll, dime*	4–5 minutes
4. Alphabetic Reintroduce *l*/l/; Letters Board Game	Alphabet Card: *l* Game Cards: *m, p, f, c, t, s, d* (two of each) Game Board 3	number cube (not provided) game markers (one per child/not provided)	4–5 minutes

Writing and Spelling

Activity	Materials	Time
5. Writer's Warm-Up Introduce *l*	Tracing Cards: *l, f, s, p, t, d, m, c* Writer's Warm-Up (one per child) Student Activity Book 1, p. 41	2–3 minutes
6. Integrated Phonologic/Alphabetic Match a Picture's Initial Sound; Introduce *l*	Picture Cards: *leg, leaf, lamb, lip(s), lock, log, lollipop, ladybug, loaf*	Letter Cards: *l, c, d, s, t, f, p, m*	2–3 minutes
7. Phonologic/Spelling Letter Writing Game: *d, s, t, c, p, m*	Letter Writing Game (one per child) Student Activity Book 1, p. 42	Game Board 3 game markers (not provided)	6–8 minutes

Activity 1 — Introduce Letter Name and Sound

Introduce l/\l/

Objective: Children learn and trace /l/.

Time: 1–2 minutes

	To Do	To Say	
Introduce letter name	Hold up the *l* Alphabet Card.	**Model**	The <u>name</u> of this letter is *l*.
		Lead	Say the <u>name</u> with me.
		Test	What is the <u>name</u> of this letter?
Introduce letter sound	Continue holding up the *l* Alphabet Card.	**Model**	This is the letter for the <u>sound</u> /lll/. When you say /lll/, the tip of your tongue touches above your top teeth and stays there. Say /lll/ and feel the tip of your tongue touch above your top teeth and stay there.
		Lead	Say the <u>sound</u> with me: /lll/.
		Test	What is the <u>sound</u> for this letter?
Test letter name and sound	Continue holding up the *l* Alphabet Card. Give individual turns on letter name and sound.	**Test**	What is the <u>name</u> of this letter? What is the <u>sound</u> for this letter?

Ongoing Assessment

If... children make an error,	then... tell them the letter name or sound, have them repeat the name or sound, and return to the letter a second time.

Model tracing *l*	Model how to trace *l* using your *l* Alphabet Card. Distribute an *l* Letter Card to each child.	**Model**	Watch. I'll trace the letter *l*. Trace the letter *l* on your letter card three times. Say /lll/ each time you trace the letter.

Ongoing Assessment

If... children make an error,	then... place your hand over their hand and guide the tracing of the letter. Then have children try to trace the letter on their own. Repeat as necessary.

Activity 2 — Isolate Initial Sound

Does It Begin with /l/?

Objective: Children isolate initial /l/.

Time: 4–5 minutes

	To Do		**To Say**
Model names of pictures	Gather the picture cards. Place the *lip* Picture Card on the table.	**Model**	**This is *lip*. What is this?** Have children repeat. Continue with *cat, lock, leaf, leg,* and *map*. Then test children on the picture names by placing the cards on the table one at a time and asking: **What is this?**
Introduce the game Does It Begin with /l/?	Practice production of the target sound.		To play this game you need to find pictures that begin with /lll/. Let's say /lll/. When you say /lll/, the tip of your tongue touches above your top teeth and stays there. Say /lll/ and feel the tip of your tongue touch above your top teeth and stay there.
Model the game	Hold up the *lip* Picture Card.	**Model**	**My turn. I'll say the name of the picture and then tell if it begins with /lll/: *lip*** (exaggerate the first sound). ***Lip* begins with /lll/. The tip of my tongue touches above my top teeth when I say /lll/, *lip*. Look at the next picture: *cat*** (exaggerate the first sound). ***Cat* does not begin with /lll/.**
Play the game to test knowledge of /l/	Hold up the *lock* Picture Card.

Give individual turns. | **Test** | **What is this? Does *lock*** (exaggerate the first sound) **begin with /lll/?** Confirm correct responses and prompt sound production: **Yes, *lock* begins with /lll/. Let's say /lll/. When you say /lll/, the tip of your tongue touches above your top teeth and stays there. Say /lll/ and feel the tip of your tongue touch above your top teeth and stay there: *lock*.** Continue with *leaf, leg,* and *map*. |

Ongoing Assessment

If... children make an error,	**then...** model the correct answer. Review the sound production cue. Have children repeat the correct answer. Go back to the example a second time.

Activity **3** **Isolate Initial Sound**

First Sound Song with /d/

Objective: Children isolate initial sound /d/.

Time: 4–5 minutes

	To Do	**To Say**
Introduce the First Sound Song	Gather the Picture Cards *deer, doll,* and *dime.*	**You are going to learn a song. I will show you three pictures that begin with /d/. These pictures will be in the song.**
	Model the names of the pictures. Point to each picture as you say its name.	**This is *deer, doll, dime.* Say the names of the pictures with me: *deer, doll, dime.* *Deer, doll,* and *dime* all begin with /d/. Say the sound /d/ with me.**
	Practice production of the target sound.	**Remember, when you say /d/, the tip of your tongue touches above your top teeth. Say /d/ and feel the tip of your tongue touch above your top teeth. Place your hand on your throat to see whether your voice box is on when you say /d/. Yes, your throat moves when you say /d/ because your voice box is on.**
Model the song		**Model** Sing the following words to the tune of "Old MacDonald Had a Farm." Point to each picture as you sing its name: **What is the sound that begins these words: *deer, doll, dime*? Yes, /d/ is the sound that begins these words: *deer, doll, dime.* With a /d/, /d/ here and a /d/, /d/ there, here a /d/, there a /d/, everywhere a /d/, /d/. /d/ is the sound that begins these words: *deer, doll, dime.***
	Lead children through the song several times.	**Lead** **Sing it with me.** Point to each picture as children sing its name.
Test initial sound knowledge	Hold up the *deer* Picture Card.	**Test** **Your turn. Say the first sound in *deer*.** Confirm correct responses and prompt sound production. Continue with the other pictures in the song.
	Give individual turns.	

Ongoing Assessment

If... children make an incorrect response,	then... model the answer. Have children repeat the answer. Return to the example a second time.

Activity 4 Review Letter Name and Sound

Reintroduce l/l/;
Letters Board Game

Objective: Children practice letter name and sound: l/l/.   Time: 4–5 minutes

	To Do	**To Say**	
Introduce letter name	Hold up the *l* Alphabet Card.	Model	**The <u>name</u> of this letter is *l*.**
		Lead	**Say the <u>name</u> with me.**
		Test	**What is the <u>name</u> of this letter?**
Introduce letter sound	Continue holding up the *l* Alphabet Card.	Model	**This is the letter for the <u>sound</u> /lll/. When you say /lll/, the tip of your tongue touches above your top teeth and stays there. Say /lll/ and feel the tip of your tongue touch above your top teeth and stay there.**
		Lead	**Say the <u>sound</u> with me: /lll/.**
		Test	**What is the <u>sound</u> for this letter?**
Test letter name and sound	Continue holding up the *l* Alphabet Card.	Test	**What is the <u>name</u> of this letter? What is the <u>sound</u> for this letter?** Then give individual turns on the letter name and sound.

Ongoing Assessment

If... children make an error,   then... tell them the letter name or sound, have them repeat the name or sound, and return to the letter a second time.

Play the Letters Board Game	Gather the game board, game cards, markers, and number cube.	Place the game cards face down in a pile on the table. Tell children that they are going to play the Letters Board Game. **Each of you will get a turn to roll the number cube, pick the top card from the pile of game cards, and tell the letter name and sound. If you give the correct name and sound, you will move your marker the number of spaces rolled on the number cube.**

Ongoing Assessment

If... a child makes an error,   then... tell the child the letter name or sound, have everyone repeat it, and place the card at the bottom of the pile. The child does not get to move the marker.

Play the game until one child makes it to the finish line or time runs out. If time permits, play another round of the game.

Activity **5** Writer's Warm-Up

Introduce *l*

Objective: Children trace and write and review writing *f*, *s*, *p*, *t*, *d*, *m*, and *c*.

Time: 2–3 minutes

	To Do	**To Say**	
Review letter name and sound	Hold up the *l* Tracing Card.	**What is the <u>name</u> of this letter? What is the <u>sound</u> for this letter?**	
Model tracing *l*	Distribute a Writer's Warm-Up to each child. Continue holding up the *l* Tracing Card.	Model	**Watch as I trace the letter *l* with my finger.**
		Lead	**Now you trace the first two *l*'s on your warm-up sheet with your finger.**
	Model tracing *l* again.	Model	**Watch as I trace *l* again.**
		Lead	**Now use your pencil to trace the next two *l*'s.**
Model writing *l*	Use the lined side of the *l* Tracing Card.	Model	**Watch as I write the letter *l*. I start at the dot and write the letter.** Have children write the letter twice on their warm-up sheets. Remind them to write their letters carefully.

Ongoing Assessment

If... children make an error,	then... ask them to write the letter again. If necessary, place your hand over their hand and guide the writing of the letter. Then have children write the letter on their own. Repeat as necessary.

| **Test writing *l*** | Model writing *l* again. | Have children cover the letters they wrote and write the letter twice from memory. Then have them uncover their letters and compare them.
Do your letters look the same? Circle the letter that is your best work. |
|---|---|---|

| **Review**
f, s, p, t, d, m, c		Have children trace and write each review letter one time.

Ongoing Assessment

If... children make an error,	then... use the tracing card to model writing the letter and ask them to write the letter again. If necessary, place your hand over their hand and guide the writing of the letter. Then have children write the letter on their own. Repeat as necessary.

Writing/Spelling

Activity **6** Connect Sound to Letter

Match a Picture's Initial Sound; Introduce l

Objective: Children match /l/ to *l*.

Time: 2–3 minutes

	To Do	**To Say**
Introduce the activity	Gather the *l* Picture Cards and the *l, d, s, t, c, f, p,* and *m* Letter Cards.	**You're going to choose the letter that goes with the first sound of some pictures.**
Model the activity	Place the *leg* Picture Card on the table, facing children.	**Model** **This is *leg*. The first <u>sound</u> in *leg* is /lll/.** Place the *l* and *c* Letter Cards below the picture. **I'm going to choose the letter that matches this picture's first sound.** Point to the correct letter: *l* **is the letter for /lll/, like the /lll/ in *leg*.**
Test knowledge of initial sound	Display the *leaf* Picture Card. Place the *l* and *f* Letter Cards under the picture.	**Test** **This is *leaf*. What is this? The first sound in *leaf* is /lll/. What is the first sound in *leaf*? That's right, /lll/ is the first sound in *leaf*.** **It's your turn to choose the letter that matches this picture's first sound. Everyone, think of which letter is the letter for the sound /lll/ in *leaf*. Does everyone know?** Call on an individual child to point to the correct letter. **What's the <u>name</u> of the letter you pointed to? What is the <u>sound</u> for this letter? That's right; *l* is the letter for /lll/ like the /lll/ in *leaf*. Everyone, what's the <u>name</u> of the letter? What's the <u>sound</u> for the letter?** Continue with the remaining cards.

Ongoing Assessment

If... children make an error,	**then...** model the answer, have them repeat it, and return to the picture card a second time.

Activity 7 Connect Sound to Letter

Letter Writing Game:
d, s, t, c, p, m

Objective: Children connect initial sound to letter.

Time: 6–8 minutes

	To Do	**To Say**	
Introduce the activity	Distribute a Letter Writing Game to each child.	Review the letter names and sounds on the activity sheet. **We are going to play a letter writing game. I'll say a word, and you will write the letter that goes with the word's first sound. Every time we write a letter, someone will roll the number cube and move his or her marker on the game board.**	
Model the activity	Hold up a Letter Writing Game.	Model	**Let's do one together. The first word is** *tape*. **The first sound in** *tape* **is /t/. I'll write the letter for /t/ in the right place.**
		Lead	**Now you write the letter for /t/. Start at the dot and write the letter. That's right;** *t* **is the letter for /t/, like the /t/ in** *tape*.
Test children on *d, s, t, c, p,* **and** *m*		Test	**The next word is** *duck*. **What is the first sound in** *duck*? **That's right, /d/ is the first sound in** *duck*. **Now write the letter for the /d/ in** *duck*. **Start at the dot and write the letter.** Reinforce the letter name and sound: **Everyone, what's the name of the letter you wrote? And what's the sound for this letter?** Dictate a word from the Word Bank and have children write the letter that goes with the word's first sound in the correct column. Vary the order of words. After each letter is written, choose one child to roll the number cube and advance his or her marker on the game board.

Word Bank

teeth	coat	map	pin	dime	soap
tub	cane	mouse	pumpkin	dog	sick
table	candle	monkey	pie	donut	sun
turtle	crayon	milk shake	pizza	dinosaur	sew

Ongoing Assessment°

If... children make an error,	then... model the letter name and sound and have children repeat them. Have children write the correct letter.

LESSON 23

New Sound /l/
Review Sounds /m/, /p/, /f/, /k/, /t/, /s/, /d/
Key Phonologic Skill Isolate Initial Sound

Phonological Awareness and Alphabetic Understanding

Activity	Materials	Time
1. Alphabetic Introduce *l*/l/	Alphabet Card: *l* Letter Card: *l* (one per child)	1–2 minutes
2. Phonologic Which Picture Begins with /l/?	Picture Choices: 23-1, 23-2, 23-3 Teacher Resource Package 1	4–5 minutes
3. Integrated Phonologic/Alphabetic Sound Match with /d/, /s/, /p/, and /m/	Alphabet Cards: *d, s, p, m* game markers (four per child/ not provided) Sound Match Cards: 23a–23e Teacher Resource Package 1	4–5 minutes
4. Alphabetic Reintroduce *l*/l/; Find the Sound Game	Alphabet Card: *l* Letter Cards: *m, p, f, c, t, s, d, l* (one of each per child)	4–5 minutes

Writing and Spelling

Activity	Materials	Time
5. Writer's Warm-Up Introduce *l*	Tracing Cards: *l, f, s, p, t, d, c* Writer's Warm-Up (one per child) Student Activity Book 1, p. 43	2–3 minutes
6. Integrated Phonologic/Alphabetic Match a Picture's Initial Sound; Introduce *l*	Picture Cards: all *l* cards Letter Cards: *l, d, s, t, c, f, p, m*	2–3 minutes
7. Phonologic/Spelling Letter Matching: Review *l, d, s, t*	Picture Cards: *dog, dish, door, ladybug, leaf, lock, sock, soup, sunglasses, ten, top, turtle* Letter Cards: *l, d, s, t* (three of each)	6–8 minutes

Activity **1** Introduce Letter Name and Sound

Introduce l/l/

Objective: Children learn and trace /l/.

Time: 1–2 minutes

	To Do	To Say	
Introduce letter name	Hold up the *l* Alphabet Card.	Model	**The <u>name</u> of this letter is *l*.**
		Lead	**Say the <u>name</u> with me.**
		Test	**What is the <u>name</u> of this letter?**
Introduce letter sound	Continue holding up the *l* Alphabet Card.	Model	**This is the letter for the <u>sound</u> /lll/. When you say /lll/, the tip of your tongue touches above your top teeth and stays there. Say /lll/ and feel the tip of your tongue touch above your top teeth and stay there.**
		Lead	**Say the <u>sound</u> with me: /lll/.**
		Test	**What is the <u>sound</u> for this letter?**
Test letter name and sound	Continue holding up the *l* Alphabet Card. Give individual turns on letter name and sound.	Test	**What is the <u>name</u> of this letter? What is the <u>sound</u> for this letter?**

Ongoing Assessment

If... children make an error,

then... tell them the letter name or sound, have them repeat the name or sound, and return to the letter a second time.

	To Do	To Say	
Model tracing *l*	Model how to trace *l* using your alphabet card.	Model	**Watch. I'll trace the letter *l*.** Distribute an *l* Letter Card to each child. Ask children to trace the letter *l* on their letter cards three times. Tell them to say /lll/ each time they trace the letter.

Ongoing Assessment

If... children make an error,

then... place your hand over their hand and guide the tracing of the letter. Then have children try to trace the letter on their own. Repeat as necessary.

Phonological Awareness/Alphabetic Understanding

Activity 2 Isolate Initial Sound

Which Picture Begins with /l/?

Objective: Children isolate initial sound /l/.

Time: 4–5 minutes

	To Do		**To Say**
Model names of pictures	Gather the picture choices. Display Picture Choice 23-1. Point to *lamb*.	**Model**	**This is *lamb*. What is this?** Model the names of pictures selected for the game: *lamb, tag, sandwich, cap, leg, cat.* Have children repeat them. Test children on the names of the pictures by pointing to each picture and asking: **What is this?** Repeat for Picture Choices 23-2 and 23-3.
Introduce the game Which Picture Begins with /l/?	Practice production of the target sound.		Tell children that they will play a game with /lll/. Tell them that you will show them three pictures and they should find the one with the first sound /lll/. **Let's say /lll/. When you say /lll/, the tip of your tongue touches above your top teeth and stays there. Say /lll/ and feel the tip of your tongue touch above your top teeth and stay there.**
Model the game	Display Picture Choice 23-1. Model two examples.	**Model**	**I'll show you how to play the game.** Display the pictures *lamb, tag,* and *sandwich.* Cover the other pictures. Name the pictures: **This is *lamb, tag, sandwich.* I'll find the picture that has the first sound /lll/: *lamb. Lamb* has the first sound /lll/.** Exaggerate the first sound and then say the word: **/lll/, *lamb.*** Model one more example with *cap, leg,* and *cat.*
Play the game to test knowledge of /l/	Test the group with four other examples.	**Test**	Display Picture Choice 23-2 (*tub, can, leaf; light, dime, sick*), covering the pictures not in use. Ask children to tell the name of each picture: **What is this? Which picture has the first sound /lll/?** Confirm correct responses and prompt sound production: **Yes, *leaf* has the first sound /lll/. Let's say /lll/. When you say /lll/, the tip of your tongue touches above your top teeth and stays there. Say /lll/ and feel the tip of your tongue touch above your top teeth and stay there: *leaf.*** Repeat for the bottom row of pictures and Picture Choice 23-3 (*dog, log, sock; cane, teeth, lid*).

Ongoing Assessment

If... children make an error,	**then...** model the correct answer. Review the sound production cue. Have children repeat the correct answer. Go back to the example a second time.

Give individual turns.

185

Phonological Awareness/Alphabetic Understanding

Activity **3** Isolate Initial Sound

Sound Match with /d/, /s/, /p/, and /m/

Objective: Children isolate a picture's initial sound and connect sound to letter.

Time: 4–5 minutes

	To Do		**To Say**
Introduce the game Sound Match	Gather the Sound Match cards and the game markers.		Tell children that they are going to play Sound Match. You will show them a letter. They will find a picture on the card with the first sound for the letter and place a marker on it.

Model the game

Distribute a Sound Match card and four markers to each child. Hold up the *d* Alphabet Card and point to the letter.

Test

What is the <u>sound</u> for this letter?

Ask children to whisper the name of each picture on their cards to themselves and to raise their hands if they don't know one. (The picture names are given below.) **Find the picture on your card that has the first sound /d/ and place a marker on it.**

Go around the table and have each child state the picture he or she put the marker on. Confirm correct responses and have the whole group repeat the word: **Yes, *deer* has the first sound /d/. Everybody, say /d/, *deer*.**

Ongoing Assessment

If... children make incorrect responses,

then... model the correct answer. Review the sound production cue and have children repeat the correct answer.

Play the game to test initial sound knowledge

Repeat with target sounds /m/, /p/, and /s/.

When a child wins by completing a row or a column, have the group clear off their cards. Collect the cards and mix and redistribute them. Play a second round of the game, this time with target sounds /sss/, /d/, /mmm/, and /p/, in that order.

Sound Match Picture Names
23a: *deer, sick, pool; lock, lamb, light; lips, leg, man*
23b: *doughnut, leaf, log; lock, lid, lamb; saw, peas, mitt*
23c: *leg, pan, lips; leaf, mouse, soap; light, desk, log*
23d: *saw, doughnut, map; lid, leg, lock; lamb, pie, lips*
23e: *log, light, sun; dive, leaf, mow; leg, lid, paw*

Activity 4 Review Letter Name and Sound

Reintroduce l/\/; Find the Sound Game

Objective: Children practice letter name and sound: l/\/.   Time: 4–5 minutes

	To Do	To Say	
Introduce letter name	Hold up the *l* Alphabet Card.	**Model**	**The <u>name</u> of this letter is *l*.**
		Lead	**Say the <u>name</u> with me.**
		Test	**What's the <u>name</u> of this letter?**
Introduce letter sound	Continue holding up the *l* Alphabet Card.	**Model**	**This is the letter for the <u>sound</u> /lll/. When you say /lll/, the tip of your tongue touches above your top teeth and stays there. Say /lll/ and feel the tip of your tongue touch above your top teeth and stay there.**
		Lead	**Say the <u>sound</u> with me: /lll/.**
		Test	**What is the <u>sound</u> for this letter?**
Test letter name and sound	Continue holding up the *l* Alphabet Card and address the group. Then give individual turns on the letter name and sound.	**Test**	**What is the <u>name</u> of this letter? What is the <u>sound</u> for this letter?**

Ongoing Assessment

If... children make an error,   then... tell them the letter name or sound, have them repeat the name or sound, and return to the letter a second time.

Play the game Find the Sound	Give each child a set of letter cards for *m, p, f, c, t, s, d*, and *l*.	Have children line up the letter cards in front of them. Explain that you will say a sound and they will have to find the letter for the sound and hold it up as you count to three. **Here's your first sound: /d/. One, two, three. Go! Everybody, what letter are you holding? Yes, *d*; *d* is the letter for /d/.** Have children place their letters back on the table. Then continue calling out sounds.
	Provide the opportunity for individual turns.	

Ongoing Assessment

If... children make an error,   then... tell them the letter, have them repeat it, and return to the sound a second time.

 **Activity 5 Writer's Warm-Up**

Introduce l

Objective: Children trace and write *l* and review writing *f, s, p, t, d,* and *c*.   Time: 2–3 minutes

	To Do	**To Say**
Review letter name and sound	Hold up the *l* Tracing Card.	**What is the <u>name</u> of this letter? What is the <u>sound</u> for this letter?**
Model tracing *l*	Distribute a Writer's Warm-Up to each child. Continue holding up the *l* Tracing Card.	**Model** **Watch as I trace the letter *l* with my finger.** **Lead** **Now you trace the first two *l*'s on your warm-up sheet.** Have children trace with their fingers. Then model tracing *l* again and have children trace the next two letters with their pencils.
Model writing *l*	Use the lined side of the *l* Tracing Card.	**Model** **Watch as I write the letter *l*. I start at the dot and write the letter.** Have children write the letter twice on their sheets. Remind children to write their letters carefully.

Ongoing Assessment

If... children make an error,	**then...** ask them to write the letter again. If necessary, place your hand over their hand and guide the writing of the letter. Then have children write the letter on their own. Repeat as necessary.

Test writing *l*	Model writing *l* again.	Have children cover the letters they wrote and write the letter twice from memory. Then have them uncover their papers and compare the letters. **Do your letters look the same? Circle the letter that is your best work.**

Review *f, s, p, t, d, c*		Have children trace and write each review letter one time.

Ongoing Assessment

If... children make an error,	**then...** use the tracing card to model tracing the letter. Ask them to write the letter again. If necessary, place your hand over their hand and guide the writing of the letter. Then have children write the letter on their own. Repeat as necessary.

Writing/Spelling

Activity 6 Connect Sound to Letter

Match a Picture's Initial Sound; Introduce l

Objective: Children match a picture's initial sound to letter.   Time: 2–3 minutes

	To Do	**To Say**	
Introduce the activity	Gather the *l* Picture Cards and the *l, d, s, t, c, f, p,* and *m* Letter Cards.		Tell children that they are going to choose the letter that goes with the first sound of some pictures.
Model the activity	Place the *leaf* Picture Card on the table, facing children.	**Model**	**This is *leaf*. The first sound in *leaf* is /lll/.** Place the *l* and *c* Letter Cards below the picture. **I'm going to choose the letter that matches this picture's first sound.** Point to the correct letter: ***l* is the letter for /lll/ like the /lll/ in *leaf*.**
Test knowledge of initial sound	Display the *leg* Picture Card. Place two letter cards under the picture. Vary the choice and order of letters.	**Test**	**This is *leg*. What is this? What is the first sound in *leg*? That's right, /lll/ is the first sound in *leg*.** **It's your turn to choose the letter that matches this picture's first sound. Everyone, think of which letter is the letter for the sound /lll/ in *leg*. Does everyone know?** Call on an individual child to point to the correct letter. **What's the <u>name</u> of the letter you pointed to? What is the <u>sound</u> for that letter? That's right; *l* is the letter for /lll/ like the /lll/ in *leg*.** Reinforce the letter name and sound with the group: **Everyone, what's the <u>name</u> of the letter? What's the <u>sound</u> for the letter?** Continue the testing procedure for the remaining picture cards.

Ongoing Assessment

If... children make an error,	then... model the answer, have them repeat it, and return to the picture card a second time.

Activity 7 — Connect Sound to Letter

Letter Matching: Review l, d, s, t

Objective: Children connect initial sound to letter.

Time: 6–8 minutes

	To Do	To Say
Review letter names and sounds	Hold up the *l, d, s,* and *t* Letter Cards, one at a time.	**What's the <u>name</u> of this letter? What's the <u>sound</u> for this letter?**
Introduce the activity	Place the letter cards in a pile. Spread the picture cards on the table, facing children.	**We are going to play a letter matching game. You will pick a letter and place it next to a picture that begins with the sound for that letter. Let's see if we can match all the pictures!**
Model the activity		**Model** **Let's do one together. I'll pick the first letter.** Pick an *l* Letter Card from the pile. **This is the letter for /lll/. Now I'll place the letter next to a picture that has the first sound /lll/. The picture** *lock* **starts with /lll/.**
Test children on *l, d, s,* and *t*		**Test** Have children take turns selecting a letter, saying the letter's sound, and placing the letter next to a picture that begins with the sound. Reinforce the group on identifying the first sound of each picture: **Everyone, what's the first sound in _____? What's the name of the letter for /_/ like the /_/ in _____?**

Ongoing Assessment

If... children make an error,	then... model the letter sound and the picture's name and initial sound.

New Sound /l/
Review Sounds /m/, /p/, /f/, /k/, /t/, /s/, /d/
Key Phonologic Skill Isolate Initial Sound

Phonological Awareness and Alphabetic Understanding

Activity	Materials	Time
1. Alphabetic Introduce *l*/l/	Alphabet Card: *l* Letter Card: *l* (one per child)	1–2 minutes
2. Integrated Phonologic/Alphabetic Which Picture Begins with *l*?	Alphabet Card: *l* Picture Choices: 24-1, 24-2, 24-3 Teacher Resource Package 1	4–5 minutes
3. Integrated Phonologic/Alphabetic First Sound Mix-Up Game with /d/ and /l/	Letter Cards: *d, l* Sound Production Cue Card · Picture Cards: all *d* and *l* cards	4–5 minutes
4. Integrated Phonologic/Alphabetic Reintroduce *l*/l/; Pictures to Letters Game	Alphabet Card: *l* Picture Cards: *man, pig, fan, cat, ten, sun, duck, lock* · Letter Cards: *m, p, f, c, t, s, d, l* (one per child) paper bag	4–5 minutes

Writing and Spelling

Activity	Materials	Time
5. Writer's Warm-Up Memory Review: *l, d, s, t, c, f, p, m*	Write-On/Wipe-Off Cards (one per child) Tracing Cards: *l, d, s, t, c, f, p, m* markers (not provided)	2–3 minutes
6. Integrated Phonologic/Alphabetic Match a Picture's Initial Sound; Introduce *l*	Picture Cards: all *l* cards · Letter Cards: *l, d, s, t, c, f, p, m*	2–3 minutes
7. Phonologic/Spelling First Sounds Dictation: Review *l, d, s, t, c, f*	Write-On/Wipe-Off Cards (one per child) markers (not provided) · erasers (not provided) Tracing Cards: *l, d, s, t, c, f*	6–8 minutes

Activity 1 Introduce Letter Name and Sound

Introduce l/\/

Objective: Children learn and trace l/\/.

Time: 1–2 minutes

	To Do	To Say	
Introduce letter name	Hold up the *l* Alphabet Card.	Model	The <u>name</u> of this letter is *l*.
		Lead	Say the <u>name</u> with me.
		Test	What is the <u>name</u> of this letter?
Introduce letter sound	Continue holding up the *l* Alphabet Card.	Model	This is the letter for the <u>sound</u> /lll/. When you say /lll/, the tip of your tongue touches above your top teeth and stays there. Say /lll/ and feel the tip of your tongue touch above your top teeth and stay there.
		Lead	Say the <u>sound</u> with me: /lll/.
		Test	What is the <u>sound</u> for this letter?
Test letter name and sound	Continue holding up the *l* Alphabet Card.	Test	What is the <u>name</u> of this letter? What is the <u>sound</u> for this letter?
	Give individual turns on letter name and sound.	**Ongoing Assessment**	
		If... children make an error,	**then...** tell them the name or sound, have them repeat the name or sound, and return to the letter a second time.
Model tracing *l*	Model how to trace *l* using your Alphabet Card.	Model	Watch. I'll trace the letter *l*.
	Distribute an *l* Letter Card to each child.		Ask children to trace the letter *l* on their letter cards three times. Tell them to say /lll/ each time they trace the letter.
		Ongoing Assessment	
		If... children make an error,	**then...** place your hand over their hand and guide the tracing of the letter. Then have children try to trace the letter on their own. Repeat as necessary.

Phonological Awareness/Alphabetic Understanding

Activity **2** Isolate Initial Sound

Which Picture Begins with l?

Objective: Children isolate initial /l/.

Time: 4–5 minutes

	To Do		**To Say**
Model names of pictures	Gather the picture choices. Place Picture Choice 24-1 on the table. Point to *sun.*	Model	**This is *sun.* What is this?** Model the names of the pictures: *sun, lock, toe; dot, cup, log.* Have children repeat them. Then test children on the names of the pictures by pointing to each picture and asking: **What is this?** Repeat for Picture Choices 24-2 and 24-3.
Introduce the game Which Picture Begins with *l*?			**I will show you a letter and three pictures. You'll find the picture that has the same first sound as the sound for the letter.**
Model the game	Hold up the *l* Alphabet Card.	Model	**It's my turn to show you how to play the game. The <u>name</u> of this letter is *l.* This is the letter for the <u>sound</u> /lll/. Remember, when you say /lll/, the tip of your tongue touches above your top teeth and stays there. Say /lll/ and feel the tip of your tongue touch above your top teeth and stay there.**
		Test	**What's the <u>sound</u> for this letter?**
	Display Picture Choice 24-1. Cover the bottom row.	Model	**This is *sun, lock, toe.* I'll find the picture that begins with /lll/.** Point to the letter *l.* **Lock** (exaggerate the first sound). **The first sound in *lock* is /lll/; /lll/, *lock.*** Model another example with *dot, cup,* and *log.*
Play the game to test knowledge of /l/	Hold up the *l* Alphabet Card and test the sound.	Test	**What is the <u>sound</u> for this letter?** Display Picture Choice 24-2 (*tire, dive, lips; lamb, sit, cut*). Ask children to name each picture: **What is this?** Point to the letter *l.* **Which picture begins with /lll/?** Confirm correct responses and prompt sound production: **Yes, *lips* begins with /lll/. Let's say /lll/. Remember, when you say /lll/, the tip of your tongue touches above your top teeth and stays there. Say /lll/ and feel the tip of your tongue touch above your top teeth and stay there: *lips.*** Repeat this procedure for Picture Choice 24-3: *leaf, soap, coat; dock, leg, tape.*
	Give individual turns.		

Ongoing Assessment

If... children make an error,	**then...** model the correct answer. Then review the sound production cue. Have children repeat the correct answer. Go back to the example a second time.

Phonological Awareness/Alphabetic Understanding

Activity **3** Isolate Initial Sound

First Sound Mix-Up Game with /d/ and /l/

Objective: Children isolate initial /d/ and /l/.

Time: 4–5 minutes

	To Do	**To Say**
Introduce the First Sound Mix-Up Game	Gather the letter cards and the picture cards. Mix the picture cards and place them in a pile. Place the letter cards on the table, facing the children.	Review the picture names by holding up each picture card and asking: **What is this?** Tell children that you will hold up a picture. They will say the name of the picture and then tell the first sound. Explain that the pictures are mixed up. Some of the pictures begin with /d/ and some begin with /lll/.
Model the game	Model two examples.	**Model** I'll show you how to play the game. Display the first picture in the pile. **This is *deer*. I'll say the first sound in *deer*: /d/. Now I'll place *deer* next to the letter for the sound /d/.** Place the picture of *deer* next to the *d* Letter Card. **Remember, the <u>name</u> of this letter is *d*; *d* is the letter for the sound /d/. I'll do one more.** Model again with an *l* picture, such as *lock*.
Play the game to test initial sound knowledge	Display the next picture in the pile. Give individual turns.	**Test** **What is this? Say the first sound in *log*.** Confirm correct responses and prompt sound production: **Yes, the first sound in *log* is /lll/. Remember, when you say /lll/, the tip of your tongue touches above your top teeth and stays there. Say /lll/ and feel the tip of your tongue touch above your top teeth and stay there: *log*. Place *log* next to the letter for the sound /lll/.** Repeat with four to five more examples. Use the Sound Production Cue Card to prompt sound production.

Ongoing Assessment

If... children make an error,	**then...** tell them the answer and have them repeat it. Place the picture back in the pile so you can return to it a second time.

Phonological Awareness/Alphabetic Understanding

 **Review Letter Name and Sound**

Reintroduce l/l/;
Pictures to Letters Game

Objective: Children practice letter name and sound: /l/.

Time: 4–5 minutes

	To Do	**To Say**	
Introduce letter name	Hold up the *l* Alphabet Card.	Model	**The <u>name</u> of this letter is *l*.**
		Lead	**Say the <u>name</u> with me: *l*.**
		Test	**What is the <u>name</u> of this letter?**
Introduce letter sound	Continue holding up the *l* Alphabet Card.	Model	**The <u>sound</u> for this letter is /lll/. When you say /lll/, the tip of your tongue touches above your top teeth and stays there. Say /lll/ and feel the tip of your tongue touch above your top teeth and stay there.**
		Lead	**Say the <u>sound</u> with me: /lll/.**
		Test	**What is the <u>sound</u> for this letter?**
Test letter name and sound	Continue holding up the *l* Alphabet Card. Test the group and then give individual turns.	Test	**What is the <u>name</u> of this letter? What is the <u>sound</u> for this letter?**

> ### Ongoing Assessment
>
> | **If...** children make an error, | **then...** tell them the letter name or sound, have them repeat the name or sound, and return to the letter a second time. |
> |---|---|

| **Introduce and model the Pictures to Letters Game** | Gather the picture cards and place them in a paper bag. Give each child a letter card for *m, p, f, c, t, s, d,* and *l*. | Model | **We're going to play the Pictures to Letters Game. I'll show you how to play the game.** Pull a picture from the bag. **This is *lock*** (for example). **What is this? I'll say the first sound in *lock*: /lll/. Say the first sound in *lock*. Yes, /lll/. When you say /lll/, the tip of your tongue touches above your top teeth and stays there. Say /lll/ and feel the tip of your tongue touch above your top teeth and stay there: *lock*. I'll hold up *l*.** Look at your letter cards. **One, two, three, go!** Hold up your *l* Letter Card after you say "go." **See, I found *l* for the /lll/ in *lock*.** Return the letter card to the table. Set the picture of *lock* next to the *l* Letter Card. |

Phonological Awareness/Alphabetic Understanding

To Do

Play the game to
test knowledge of
/m/, /p/, /f/, /k/, /t/,
/s/, /d/, and /l/

Give individual turns.

To Say

Test

It's your turn to play the game. Pull a picture from the bag. **This is** *ten* (for example)**. What is this? Say the first sound in** *ten***. Yes, /t/. Say /t/. Remember, when you say /t/, the tip of your tongue touches above your top teeth. Say /t/ and feel the tip of your tongue touch above your top teeth:** *ten***. Hold up the letter for /t/. One, two, three, go! Everybody, what letter are you holding? Yes,** *t* **is the letter for /t/. You found the letter** *t* **for** *ten***. Say /t/,** *ten***.** Set the picture of *ten* next to the *t* Letter Card. Continue until all pictures have been pulled from the bag.

Ongoing Assessment

If... children cannot correctly identify the first sound of a picture,	then... tell them the first sound and have them repeat it. Prompt children on sound production using the Sound Production Cue Card.
If... children hold up the wrong letter card,	then... repeat the sound and hold up the correct letter card. Have children find the correct letter card, hold it up, and say the sound with you.

Phonological Awareness/Alphabetic Understanding

Activity 5 Writer's Warm-Up

Memory Review:
l, d, s, t, c, f, p, m

Objective: Children write letters from memory.

Time: 2–3 minutes

	To Do	**To Say**
Review letter names and sounds	Gather the *l, d, s, t, c, f, p,* and *m* Tracing Cards.	Hold up a tracing card and review the letter name and sound: **What's the <u>name</u> of this letter? What's the <u>sound</u> for this letter?**
Model the activity	Give each child a Write-On/Wipe-Off Card and a marker.	**Model** **I'll show you how this activity works. The first letter is *l*. Now I'll write the letter *l* on my card.**
Test children on writing *l, d, s, t, c, f, p,* and *m*		**Test** Dictate a letter name and have children write the letter on their cards. Dictate each letter at least twice or as often as time allows. After children write a letter, reinforce the letter name: **Everyone, what's the <u>name</u> of the letter you wrote?** After each letter, have children erase their cards.

Ongoing Assessment

If... children write the wrong letter or don't remember a letter,

then... show them the tracing card of the correct letter. Model tracing the letter and say the letter name.

Activity **6** Connect Sound to Letter

Match a Picture's Initial Sound;
Introduce l

Objective: Children connect /l/ to *l*.

Time: 2–3 minutes

	To Do	**To Say**	
Introduce the activity	Gather the *l* Picture Cards and the *l, d, s, t, c, f, p,* and *m* Letter Cards.		Tell children that they are going to choose the letter that goes with the first sound of some pictures.
Model the activity	Place the *lock* Picture Card on the table, facing children.	Model	**This is *lock*. The first sound in *lock* is /lll/.** Place the *l* and *c* Letter Cards below the picture, facing children. **I'm going to choose the letter that matches this picture's first sound.** Point to the correct letter: *l* **is the letter for /lll/ like the /lll/ in *lock*.**
Test knowledge of initial sound	Display the *lamb* Picture Card. Place the *l* and *d* Letter Cards under the picture.	Test	**This is *lamb*. What is this? What is the first sound in *lamb*? That's right, /lll/ is the first sound in *lamb*.** **It's your turn to choose the letter that matches this picture's first sound. Everyone, think of which letter is the letter for the same sound as the /lll/ in *lamb*. Does everyone know?** Call on an individual child to point to the correct letter. **What's the <u>name</u> of the letter you pointed to? What is the <u>sound</u> for that letter? That's right; *l* is the letter for /lll/ like the /lll/ in *lamb*.** Reinforce the letter name and sound with the group: **Everyone, what's the <u>name</u> of the letter? What is the <u>sound</u> for this letter?** Continue the test procedure for the remaining pictures.

Ongoing Assessment

If... children make an error,	**then...** model the answer, have them repeat it, and return to the picture card a second time.

Activity 7 — Connect Sound to Letter

First Sounds Dictation:
Review *l, d, s, t, c, f*

Objective: Children connect initial sound to written letter.

Time: 6–8 minutes

	To Do	**To Say**
Review letter names and sounds	Gather the tracing cards. Hold up the *l* Tracing Card.	Review the letter name and sound: **The <u>name</u> of this letter is *l*. The <u>sound</u> for this letter is /lll/. What is the <u>name</u> of this letter? What is the <u>sound</u> for this letter?** Repeat this procedure for *d, s, t, c,* and *f*.
Introduce the activity	Give each child a Write-On/Wipe-Off Card and a marker.	**I will say a word and you will write the letter for the word's first sound.**
Model the activity	Hold up a Write-On/ Wipe-Off Card.	**Model** **I'll show you how this activity works. The first word is *sit*. The first sound in *sit* is /sss/. Now I'll write the letter for the same sound as the /sss/ in *sit*.** Write the letter on your card. **The letter *s* is the letter for the sound /sss/. Now it's your turn to write the letter for the sound /sss/. That's right, the letter *s* is the letter for the sound /sss/ like the /sss/ in *sit*.**
Test children on writing *l, d, t, c,* and *f*		**Test** Dictate words from the Word Bank and have children write the letter for each word's first sound. **The next word is *car*. What is the first sound in *car*? That's right, /k/ is the first sound in *car*. Now write the letter for the same sound as the /k/ in *car*.** Reinforce the letter name and sound: **Everyone, what's the <u>name</u> of the letter you wrote? What is the <u>sound</u> for that letter?** Have children erase their cards after they write each letter.

Word Bank

sandwich	table	cut	feather	dot	lock
soap	tail	car	fizz	donkey	lighthouse
sad	teeth	carrot	fire	dock	lid
strawberry	tire	cup	fox	doll	ladybug

Ongoing Assessment

If... children write the wrong letter or don't remember a letter,	**then**... show the tracing card for the correct letter. Model tracing the letter and say the letter sound.

New Sound /a/

Review Sounds /m/, /p/, /f/, /k/, /t/, /s/, /d/, /l/

Key Phonologic Skill Isolate Initial Sound

Phonological Awareness and Alphabetic Understanding

Activity	Materials	Time
1. Alphabetic Introduce a/a/	Alphabet Card: *a* Letter Card: *a* (one per child)	1–2 minutes
2. Phonologic Does It Begin with /a/?	Picture Cards: *ant, soap, alligator, dime, antler, astronaut*	4–5 minutes
3. Phonologic First Sound Song with /l/	Picture Cards: *ladybug, lollipop, leaf*	4–5 minutes
4. Alphabetic Reintroduce a/a/; Letter Game: *m, p, f, c, t, s, d, l*	Alphabet Card: *a* Game Cards: *m, p, f, c, t, s, d, l* Game Board 3 marker for each child (not provided) number cube (not provided)	4–5 minutes

Writing and Spelling

Activity	Materials	Time
5. Writer's Warm-Up Introduce *a*	Writer's Warm-Up (one per child) Student Activity Book 1, p. 44 Tracing Cards: *a, l, d, s, t, f, c*	2–3 minutes
6. Integrated Phonologic/Alphabetic Match a Picture's Initial Sound: *a*	Picture Cards: all *a* cards Letter Cards: *a, l, d, s, t, f, c*	2–3 minutes
7. Phonologic/Spelling First Sounds: Review *l, d, s, t, p*	First Sounds (one per child) Student Activity Book 1, p. 45	6–8 minutes

Activity **1** Introduce Letter Name and Sound

Introduce a/a/

Objective: Children learn and trace a/a/.

Time: 1–2 minutes

	To Do	**To Say**	
Introduce letter name	Hold up the *a* Alphabet Card.	Model	**The <u>name</u> of this letter is *a*.**
		Lead	**Say the <u>name</u> with me: *a*.**
		Test	**What is the <u>name</u> of this letter?**
Introduce letter sound	Continue holding up the *a* Alphabet Card.	Model	**The <u>sound</u> for this letter is /aaa/. When you say /aaa/, your jaw and tongue are down. Say /aaa/ and feel your jaw and tongue go down.**
		Lead	**Say the <u>sound</u> with me: /aaa/.**
		Test	**What is the <u>sound</u> for this letter?**
Test knowledge of letter name and sound	Continue holding up the *a* Alphabet Card. Test the group. Then give individual turns.	Test	**What is the <u>name</u> of this letter? What is the <u>sound</u> for this letter?**

Ongoing Assessment

If... children make an error,	then... tell them the name or sound, have them repeat the name or sound, and return to the letter a second time.

Model tracing *a*	Distribute an *a* Letter Card to each child. Hold up the *a* Alphabet Card.	Model	**Watch. I'll trace the letter *a*.**
			Ask children to trace the letter *a* on their letter cards three times. Have them say /aaa/ each time they trace the letter.

Ongoing Assessment

If... children make an error,	then... put your hand over the children's hands and guide the tracing of the letter. Then have the children try to trace the letter on their own. Repeat as necessary.

Phonological Awareness/Alphabetic Understanding

 **Activity** **2** **Isolate Initial Sound**

Does It Begin with /a/?

Objective: Children isolate initial /a/.

Time: 4–5 minutes

	To Do	**To Say**	
Model names of pictures	Gather the picture cards. Place the *ant* Picture Card on the table.	Model	**This is *ant*. What is this?** Have children repeat. Continue with *antler, astronaut, alligator, dime,* and *soap*. Then test children on the picture names by placing the cards on the table again, one at a time, and asking: **What is this?**
Introduce the game Does It Begin with /a/?	Practice production of the target sound.		Tell children they will play a game. They will find the pictures that have the first sound /aaa/. **Let's say /aaa/. When you say /aaa/, your jaw and tongue are down. Say /aaa/ and feel your jaw and tongue go down.**
Model the game	Place the *ant* and *soap* Picture Cards on the table.	Model	**My turn. I'll say the name of the picture and then tell if it has the first sound /aaa/: *ant*** (exaggerate the first sound). ***Ant* has the first sound /aaa/. My jaw and tongue go down when I say /aaa/, *ant*. Look at the next picture: *soap*** (exaggerate the first sound). ***Soap* does not have the first sound /aaa/.**
Play the game to test knowledge of initial /a/	Test with four other examples: *alligator, dime, antler, astronaut.*	Test	**What is this? Does *alligator*** (exaggerate the first sound) **have the first sound /aaa/?** Confirm correct responses and prompt sound production: **Yes, *alligator* has the first sound /aaa/. Let's say /aaa/. Remember, when you say /aaa/, your jaw and tongue are down. Say /aaa/ and feel your jaw and tongue go down: *alligator*.** Continue with *dime, antler,* and *astronaut.*
	Give individual turns.		

Ongoing Assessment

If...children make an error,	then...model the correct answer. Review the sound production cue. Have children repeat the correct answer. Go back to the example a second time.

Activity **3** Isolate Initial Sound

First Sound Song with /l/

Objective: Children isolate initial /l/ in a song.

Time: 4–5 minutes

	To Do		**To Say**
Introduce the First Sound Song	Gather and display the *ladybug, lollipop,* and *leaf* Picture Cards.		Tell children that they are going to learn a song. You will show three pictures that begin with /l/. The pictures will be in the song.
	Model the names of the pictures.	Model	**This is *ladybug, lollipop, leaf.* Say the names of the pictures with me: *ladybug, lollipop, leaf. Ladybug, lollipop,* and *leaf* all begin with /lll/.**
	Practice production of /l/.		**Say the sound /lll/ with me. Remember, when you say /lll/, the tip of your tongue touches above your top teeth and stays there. Say /lll/ and feel the tip of your tongue touch above your top teeth and stay there.**
Model the song	Continue to display the picture cards.	Model	Sing the following words to the tune of "Old MacDonald Had a Farm." Point to each picture as you sing its name. **What is the sound that begins these words: *ladybug, lollipop, leaf?* /lll/ is the sound that begins these words: *ladybug, lollipop, leaf.* With a /lll/, /lll/ here and a /lll/, /lll/ there, here a /lll/, there a /lll/, everywhere a /lll/, /lll/. /lll/ is the sound that begins these words: *ladybug, lollipop, leaf.***
Lead the song	Sing the song with children several times.	Lead	**Sing the song with me.** Point to each picture as children sing its name.
Test knowledge of initial /l/	Continue to display the picture cards. Point to *ladybug.*	Test	**It's your turn. Say the first sound in *ladybug.*** Confirm correct responses and prompt sound production. Continue with names of other pictures in the song.

Ongoing Assessment

| | Give individual turns. | **If…**children make incorrect responses, | **then…**model the answer. Have children repeat the answer. Return to the example a second time. |

Phonological Awareness/Alphabetic Understanding

Activity 4 Review Letter Name and Sound

Reintroduce a/a/;
Letter Game: m, p, f, c, t, s, d, l

Objective: Children practice letter name and sound: a/a/.   Time: 4–5 minutes

	To Do	**To Say**	
Introduce letter name	Hold up the *a* Alphabet Card.	Model	**The <u>name</u> of this letter is *a*.**
		Lead	**Say the <u>name</u> with me: *a*.**
		Test	**What is the <u>name</u> of this letter?**
Introduce letter sound	Continue holding up the *a* Alphabet Card.	Model	**The <u>sound</u> for this letter is /aaa/. When you say /aaa/, your jaw and tongue are down. Say /aaa/ and feel your jaw and tongue go down.**
		Lead	**Say the <u>sound</u> with me: /aaa/.**
		Test	**What is the <u>sound</u> for this letter?**
Test knowledge of letter name and sound	Continue holding up the *a* Alphabet Card.	Test	**What is the <u>name</u> of this letter? What is the <u>sound</u> for this letter?**

Give individual turns on letter name and sound.

Ongoing Assessment

If...children make an error,	**then**...tell them the name or sound, have them repeat the name or sound, and return to the letter a second time.

Play the Letter Game

Gather Game Board 3, a marker for each child, a number cube, and the game cards. Place the game cards face down in a pile on the table.

We are going to play the Letter Game. Explain that each child will get a turn to roll the number cube, pick the top card from the pile of game cards, and name the letter and sound on the card.

Ask each child who chooses a letter: **What is the <u>name</u> of this letter? What is the <u>sound</u> for this letter?** After correctly stating the name and sound of the letter, the child moves the marker on the game board. Play the game until one child makes it to the finish line or time runs out. If time permits, play another round.

Ongoing Assessment

If...a child makes an error,	**then**...tell the child the name or sound, have everyone repeat it, and place the card at the bottom of the pile. The child does not get to move the marker.

 **Activity 5** 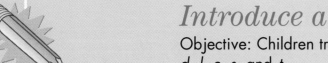 **Writer's Warm-Up**

Introduce *a*

Objective: Children trace and write *a* and review writing *f, d, l, c, s,* and *t.*   Time: 2–3 minutes

	To Do	**To Say**	
Review letter name and sound	Hold up the *a* Tracing Card.	**What is the <u>name</u> of this letter? What is the <u>sound</u> for this letter?**	
Model tracing *a*	Distribute a Writer's Warm-Up to each child. Continue holding up the *a* Tracing Card.	Model	**Watch as I trace the letter *a* with my finger.**
		Lead	**Now trace the first two *a*'s on your warm-up sheet with your finger.**
	Model tracing *a* again.	Model	**Everyone, watch as I trace the letter *a* again.**
		Lead	**Now use your pencil to trace the two *a*'s on the next line.**
Model writing *a*	Hold up the lined side of the *a* Tracing Card.	Model	**Watch as I write the letter *a*. I start at the dot and write the letter.**
	Have children write the letter *a* two times on their warm-up sheets.	Lead	**Now you write two *a*'s. Start at the dot like I did. Write carefully.**

Ongoing Assessment

If... children make an error,	**then...** ask them to write the letter again. If necessary, put your hand over the children's hands and guide the writing of the letter. Then have the children write the letter on their own. Repeat as necessary.

Test writing *a*

Have children cover the letters they have written. Have them write *a* two times from memory. Then have them uncover their papers and compare the letters.

Do your letters look the same? Circle your best *a*.

Review *f, d, l, c, s, t*

Have children trace and write each review letter one time.

Ongoing Assessment

If... children make an error,	**then...** use the tracing card to model tracing the letter. Ask them to write the letter again. If necessary, put your hand over their hand and guide them to write the letter. Then have them write the letter on their own. Repeat as necessary.

 **Connect Sound to Letter**

Match a Picture's Initial Sound: a

Objective: Children connect initial sound to letter: a/a/.   Time: 2–3 minutes

	To Do	**To Say**	
Introduce the activity	Gather the picture cards and letter cards.	Tell children that they are going to choose the letter that matches the first sound of some pictures.	
Model the activity	Place the *apple* Picture Card on the table.	Model	**This is apple. The first sound in apple is /aaa/.** Place the *a* and *l* Letter Cards below the picture. **I'm going to choose the letter that matches this picture's first sound.** Point to the correct letter: **a is the letter for /aaa/ like the /aaa/ in apple.**
Test knowledge of initial sound	Place the *ant* Picture Card on the table.	Test	**This is ant. What is this? The first sound in ant is /aaa/. What is the first sound in ant? That's right; /aaa/ is the first sound in ant.** Place two letter cards under the picture. Vary the choice and order. **It's your turn to choose the letter that matches this picture's first sound. Everyone, think of which letter has the same sound as the /aaa/ in ant.** Call on an individual child to point to the correct letter. **What's the <u>name</u> of the letter you pointed to? What is the <u>sound</u> for this letter? That's right; a is the letter for /aaa/ like the /aaa/ in ant.** Continue with the remaining picture cards.

Ongoing Assessment

If...children make an error,	then...model the answer, have them repeat it, and return to the picture card a second time.

Reinforce letter name and sound	Show the *a* Letter Card.	**Everyone, what's the <u>name</u> of this letter? What's the <u>sound</u> for this letter?**

Activity **7** Connect Sound to Letter

First Sounds:
Review *l, d, s, t, p*

Objective: Children connect sound to written letter.

Time: 6–8 minutes

	To Do		**To Say**
Introduce the activity	Distribute a First Sounds page to each child.		Tell children that they are going to write the letter that goes with the first sound of some pictures.
Model the activity	Hold up a First Sounds page. Point to *dog*.	**Model**	**This is *dog*. The first sound in *dog* is /d/. I'm going to write the letter for the sound /d/ like the /d/ in *dog*.** Write the letter *d* under the picture.
		Lead	**Now you write the letter for the sound /d/ like the /d/ in *dog*. Start at the dot and write the letter. That's right, *d* is the letter for the sound /d/ like the /d/ in *dog*.**
Test children on *l, d, s, t,* and *p*	Continue to hold up a First Sounds page. Point to *tape*.	**Test**	**This is *tape*. What is the first sound in *tape*? That's right, /t/ is the first sound in *tape*. It's your turn to write the letter that goes with this picture's first sound. Everyone, write the letter for the sound /t/ in *tape*. Start at the dot and write the letter.** Reinforce the group on the letter name and sound: **Everyone, what's the <u>name</u> of the letter you wrote? What is the <u>sound</u> for this letter?**

Ongoing Assessment

If... children make an error,	then... model the letter name and sound. Have children repeat them and write the correct letter.

New Sound /a/
Review Sounds /p/, /f/, /k/, /t/, /s/, /d/, /l/
Key Phonologic Skill Isolate Initial Sound

Phonological Awareness and Alphabetic Understanding

Activity	Materials	Time
1. Alphabetic Introduce *a*/a/	Alphabet Card: *a* Letter Card: *a* (one per child)	1–2 minutes
2. Phonologic Which Picture Has the First Sound /a/?	Picture Choices: 26-1, 26-2, 26-3 Teacher Resource Package 1	4–5 minutes
3. Alphabetic Picture Scene Search: /l/	Alphabet Card: *l* Picture Scene: /l/ Teacher Resource Package 1	4–5 minutes
4. Alphabetic Reintroduce *a*/a/; Partners Game	Alphabet Card: *a* Game Cards: *p, f, c, t, s, d, l, a* (one set per pair of children)	4–5 minutes

Writing and Spelling

Activity	Materials	Time
5. Writer's Warm-Up Introduce *a*	Writer's Warm-Up (one per child) Student Activity Book 1, p. 46 Tracing Cards: *a, l, d, s, t, f, c*	2–3 minutes
6. Integrated Phonologic/Alphabetic Match a Picture's Initial Sound: *a*	Picture Cards: all *a* cards Letter Cards: *a, l, d, s, t, f, c*	2–3 minutes
7. Phonologic/Spelling Letter Cross-Out: *a, l, d, s, c*	Letter Cross-Out (one per child) Student Activity Book 1, p. 47	6–8 minutes

Activity 1 Introduce Letter Name and Sound

Introduce a/a/

Objective: Children learn and trace a/a/.

Time: 1–2 minutes

	To Do	**To Say**	
Introduce letter name	Hold up the *a* Alphabet Card.	Model	**The <u>name</u> of this letter is *a*.**
		Lead	**Say the <u>name</u> with me: *a*.**
		Test	**What is the <u>name</u> of this letter?**
Introduce letter sound	Continue holding up the *a* Alphabet Card.	Model	**The <u>sound</u> for this letter is /aaa/. When you say /aaa/, your jaw and tongue are down. Say /aaa/ and feel your jaw and tongue go down.**
		Lead	**Say the <u>sound</u> with me: /aaa/.**
		Test	**What is the <u>sound</u> for this letter?**
Test knowledge of letter name and sound	Continue holding up the *a* Alphabet Card. Give individual turns on letter name and sound.	Test	**What is the <u>name</u> of this letter? What is the <u>sound</u> for this letter?**

Ongoing Assessment

If...children make an error,	then...tell them the name or sound, have them repeat the name or sound, and return to the letter a second time.

| **Model tracing *a*** | Distribute the *a* Letter Cards. Model tracing *a* on your alphabet card. | Model | **Watch. I'll trace the letter *a*.**

Ask children to trace the letter *a* on their letter cards three times. Tell them to say /aaa/ each time they trace the letter. |

Ongoing Assessment

If...children make an error,	then...put your hand over the children's hands and guide the tracing of the letter. Then have children try to trace the letter on their own. Repeat as necessary.

Phonological Awareness/Alphabetic Understanding

Activity **2** Isolate Initial Sound

Which Picture Has the First Sound /a/?

Objective: Children isolate initial /a/.

Time: 4–5 minutes

	To Do		**To Say**
Model names of pictures	Gather the picture choices. Place Picture Choice 26-1 on the table. Point to *ant*.	Model	**This is *ant*. What is this?** Continue with the remaining pictures *(sun, deer; toe, lock, astronaut)*. Test children on the picture names by pointing to the pictures one at a time and asking: **What is this?** Repeat for Picture Choices 26-2 *(tub, alligator, lips; antlers, doll, sit)* and 26-3 *(dog, seal, apple; leg, alligator, tire)*.
Introduce the game Which Picture Has the First Sound /a/?			Tell children they will play a game with their new sound /aaa/. Tell them that you will show them three pictures. They will find the one that has the first sound /aaa/.
Model the game	Display Picture Choice 26-1. Cover the bottom row.	Model	**This is *ant, sun, deer*. I'll find the picture that has the first sound /aaa/: *ant*** (exaggerate the first sound). ***Ant* has the first sound /aaa/.** Exaggerate the first sound and then say the word: **/aaa/, *ant*.** Model another example with *toe, lock, astronaut*.
Play the game to test knowledge of initial /a/	Display Picture Choice 26-2. Cover the bottom row. Give individual turns.		Ask children to name each picture: **What is this? Which picture has the first sound /aaa/?** Confirm correct responses and prompt sound production: **Yes, *alligator* has the first sound /aaa/. Say /aaa/ and feel your jaw and tongue go down: *alligator*.** Continue with the bottom row of pictures and Picture Choice 26-3.

Ongoing Assessment

If... children make incorrect responses,	**then**... model the correct answer. Review the sound production cue. Have children repeat the correct answer. Go back to the example a second time.

Phonological Awareness/Alphabetic Understanding

Activity 3 Isolate Initial Sound

Picture Scene Search: /l/

Objective: Children identify initial /l/ pictures.

Time: 4–5 minutes

	To Do	**To Say**
Introduce the game Picture Scene Search: /l/	Hold up the picture scene.	Tell children that they will play a game. You will show them a picture. They will find things in the picture that have the first sound /lll/.
Test letter sound	Hold up the *l* Alphabet Card.	**The <u>name</u> of this letter is *l*. What is the <u>sound</u> for this letter? Yes, /lll/. When you say /lll/, the tip of your tongue touches above your top teeth and stays there. Say /lll/ and feel the tip of your tongue touch above your top teeth and stay there.**

Ongoing Assessment

If...children make incorrect responses, **then**...model the correct sound and have children repeat it. Review the sound production cue. Repeat a second time.

Model the game	Hold up the picture scene.	**Model** **It's my turn. I'll find something in the picture that has the first sound /lll/.** Point to and name something in the picture scene that begins with /lll/: *lake* **begins with /lll/. Everybody, say /lll/,** *lake.*
Play the game to test knowledge of initial /l/	Give individual turns. Target words: *ladder, ladybug, leaf, log, lawnmower, lollipop, lunch box, lake, lemonade, lick, lady*	**Test** **It's your turn to find something that has the first sound /lll/.** Confirm each correct response and have the group repeat it: **Yes, _____ has the first sound /lll/. Everybody, say /lll/, _____.**

Ongoing Assessment

If...children select a picture that does not begin with /l/, **then**...model a correct answer. Review the sound production cue. Have children repeat the correct answer and try again.

Phonological Awareness/Alphabetic Understanding

Activity 4 Review Letter Name and Sound

Reintroduce a/a/; Partners Game

Objective: Children connect sound to letter: a/a/.

Time: 4–5 minutes

	To Do	**To Say**	
Reintroduce letter name	Hold up the *a* Alphabet Card.	Model	The <u>name</u> of this letter is *a*.
		Lead	Say the <u>name</u> with me.
		Test	What is the <u>name</u> of this letter?
Reintroduce letter sound	Continue holding up the *a* Alphabet Card.	Model	The <u>sound</u> for this letter is /aaa/. When you say /aaa/, your jaw and tongue are down. Say /aaa/ and feel your jaw and tongue go down.
		Lead	Say the <u>sound</u> with me: /aaa/.
		Test	What is the <u>sound</u> for this letter?
Test knowledge of letter name and sound	Continue holding up the *a* Alphabet Card.	Test	What is the <u>name</u> of this letter? What is the <u>sound</u> for this letter?

Ongoing Assessment

If... children make an error,

then... tell them the name or sound, have them repeat the name or sound, and return to the letter a second time.

	Give individual turns on letter name and sound.		
Introduce the Partners Game	Gather the game cards.		We are going to practice letter names and sounds with a partner. Watch as _____ and I play. I will show_____ a card. _____ will tell me the name of the letter and the sound for the letter. If _____ is correct, I will give _____ the card. If _____ is wrong, I will tell the name and sound of the letter and place the card back in the pile. When _____ has all of the cards, we will switch roles.
Play the game			Give each pair of children a set of game cards. Have children play the game. Listen to assess who may need more help.

213

Phonological Awareness/Alphabetic Understanding

Activity 5 Writer's Warm-Up

Introduce a

Objective: Children trace and write *a* and review writing *f*, *d*, *l*, *c*, *s*, and *t*.

Time: 2–3 minutes

	To Do	**To Say**
Review letter name and sound	Hold up the *a* Tracing Card.	**What is the <u>name</u> of this letter? What is the <u>sound</u> for this letter?**
Model tracing *a*	Distribute a Writer's Warm-Up to each child. Continue holding up the *a* Tracing Card. Model tracing *a* again.	Model **Watch as I trace the letter *a* with my finger.** Lead **Now you trace the first two *a*'s on your warm-up sheet.** Have children use their pencils to trace the next two *a*'s on their warm-up sheets.
Model writing *a*	Hold up the lined side of the *a* Tracing Card.	Model **Watch as I write the letter *a*. I start at the dot and write the letter.** Have children write the letter two times on their warm-up sheets. Remind children to write their letters carefully.

Ongoing Assessment

If...children make an error, then...put your hand over the children's hands and guide the writing of the letter. Then have children try to write the letter on their own. Repeat as necessary.

Test knowledge of writing *a*	Model writing *a* again.	Have children cover the letters they traced and wrote. Have them write the letter two times from memory. Then have them uncover their papers and compare the letters. **Do your letters look the same? Circle the letter that is your best work.**

Review

f, d, l, c, s, t

Have children trace and write each review letter one time.

Ongoing Assessment

If...children make an error, then...use the tracing card to model tracing the letter. Ask them to write the letter again. If needed, put your hand over the children's hands and guide the writing of the letter. Then have children try to write the letter on their own. Repeat as necessary.

Activity 6 Connect Sound to Letter

Match a Picture's Initial Sound: a

Objective: Children connect sound to letter: a/a/.

Time: 2–3 minutes

	To Do	**To Say**	
Introduce the activity	Gather the picture cards and the letter cards.	Tell children that they are going to choose the letter that goes with the first sound of some pictures.	
Model the activity	Place the *ant* Picture Card on the table.	**Model**	**This is ant. The first sound in ant is /aaa/.** Place the *f* and *a* Letter Cards under the picture. **I'm going to choose the letter that matches this picture's first sound.** Point to the correct letter: **a is the letter for /aaa/ like the /aaa/ in ant.**
Test knowledge of initial sound	Place the *alligator* Picture Card on the table.	**Test**	**This is alligator. What is this? The first sound in alligator is /aaa/. What is the first sound in alligator? That's right, /aaa/ is the first sound in alligator.** Place two letter cards under the picture. Vary the choice and order of letters. **It's your turn to choose the letter that matches this picture's first sound. Everyone, think of which letter has the same sound as the /aaa/ in alligator.** Call on an individual to point to the correct letter. **What's the <u>name</u> of the letter you pointed to? What is the <u>sound</u> for this letter? That's right, a is the letter for /aaa/ like the /aaa/ in alligator.** Reinforce the letter name and sound with the group: **Everyone, what's the <u>name</u> of the letter? What is the <u>sound</u> for this letter?**
Reinforce letter name and sound	Show the *a* Letter Card.		**What's the <u>name</u> of this letter? What is the <u>sound</u> for this letter?**

Ongoing Assessment

If...children make an error,	then...model the answer, have them repeat it, and return to the picture card a second time.

Activity 7 Connect Sound to Letter

Letter Cross-Out: a, l, d, s, c

Objective: Children connect initial sound to letter: a/a/, l/l/, d/d/, s/s/, and c/k/.

Time: 6–8 minutes

	To Do	**To Say**
Introduce the Letter Cross-Out Game	Distribute a Letter Cross-Out to each child.	Tell children that they are going to cross out letters that go with the first sound of some words. **Let's see if we can cross out all of the letters on the sheet!**
Model the game	Hold up a Letter Cross-Out.	**Model** **Let's do one together. The first word is *sandwich*. The first sound in *sandwich* is /sss/. I'm going to cross out a letter for the sound /sss/ in *sandwich*.** Cross out one of the *s*'s on your cross-out sheet. **Lead** **Now you cross out a letter for the same sound as the /sss/ in *sandwich*. That's right; *s* is the letter for the sound /sss/ like the /sss/ in *sandwich*.**
Play the game to test children on *a, l, d, s,* and *c*		**Test** **The next word is *lock*. What is the first sound in *lock*? That's right; /lll/ is the first sound in *lock*. Now cross out the letter for the same sound as the /lll/ in *lock*.** Reinforce the group on the letter name and sound: **Everyone, what's the name of the letter you crossed out? What is the sound for this letter?** Dictate words in random order from the Word Bank until all of the letters have been crossed out. **Word Bank** **astronaut** **leaf** **dog** **soap** **castle** **alligator** **doll** **carrot**

Ongoing Assessment

If...children make an error,	**then**...point to the correct letter and model the letter sound. Have children repeat the sound and cross out the correct letter.

New Sound /a/
Review Sounds /m/, /p/, /k/, /t/, /s/, /d/, /l/
Key Phonologic Skill Isolate Initial Sound

Phonological Awareness and Alphabetic Understanding

Activity	Materials	Time
1. Alphabetic Introduce *a*/a/	Alphabet Card: *a* Letter Card: *a* (one per child)	1–2 minutes
2. Integrated Phonologic/Alphabetic Which Picture Has the First Sound /a/?	Alphabet Card: *a* Picture Choices: 27-1, 27-2, 27-3 Teacher Resource Package 1	4–5 minutes
3. Integrated Phonologic/Alphabetic Sound Match with Letter Tiles: /l/, /d/, /s/, /t/	Letter Tiles: *l, d, s, t* (one per child) Sound Match Cards: 27a–27e Teacher Resource Package 1	4–5 minutes
4. Alphabetic Reintroduce *a*/a/; Be the Teacher Game	Alphabet Cards: *m, p, c, t, s, d, l, a*	4–5 minutes

Writing and Spelling

Activity	Materials		Time
5. Writer's Warm-Up Letter Mission: Review *a, l, d, s, t, c, f, p, m*	Letter Mission (one per child) Student Activity Book 1, p. 48	Tracing Cards: *a, l, d, s, t, c, f, p, m*	2–3 minutes
6. Integrated Phonologic/Alphabetic Match a Picture's Initial Sound: *a*	Picture Cards: all *a* cards Letter Cards: *a, l, d, s, t, f, c*		2–3 minutes
7. Phonologic/Spelling Letter Race: *a, l, d, s*	Letter Race (one per child) Student Activity Book 1, p. 49		6–8 minutes

Activity 1 Introduce Letter Name and Sound

Introduce a/a/

Objective: Children learn and trace a/a/.

Time: 1–2 minutes

	To Do	**To Say**	
Introduce letter name	Hold up the *a* Alphabet Card.	Model	The <u>name</u> of this letter is *a*.
		Lead	Say the <u>name</u> with me: *a*.
		Test	What is the <u>name</u> of this letter?
Introduce letter sound	Continue holding up the *a* Alphabet Card.	Model	The <u>sound</u> for this letter is /aaa/. When you say /aaa/, your jaw and tongue are down. Say /aaa/ and feel your jaw and tongue go down.
		Lead	Say the <u>sound</u> with me: /aaa/.
		Test	What is the <u>sound</u> for this letter?
Test knowledge of letter name and sound	Continue holding up the *a* Alphabet Card. Give individual turns on letter name and sound.	Test	What is the <u>name</u> of this letter? What is the <u>sound</u> for this letter?

Ongoing Assessment

If...children make an error,	then...tell them the name or sound, have them repeat the name or sound, and return to the letter a second time.

Model tracing *a*	Distribute the *a* Letter Cards. Hold up the *a* Alphabet Card.	Model	Watch. I'll trace the letter *a*.
			Ask children to trace the letter *a* on their letter cards three times. Tell them to say /aaa/ each time they trace the letter.

Ongoing Assessment

If...children make an error,	then...put your hand over the children's hands and guide the tracing of the letter. Then have children try to trace the letter on their own. Repeat as necessary.

Phonological Awareness/Alphabetic Understanding

Activity 2 Isolate Initial Sound

Which Picture Has the First Sound /a/?

Objective: Children isolate initial /a/ and connect to letter.　　Time: 4–5 minutes

	To Do	To Say	
Model names of pictures	Gather the picture choices. Place Picture Choice 27-1 on the table. Point to *leaf*.	Model	**This is *leaf*. What is this?** Continue with the remaining pictures *(astronaut, dime; alligator, tub, cone)*. Test children on the picture names by pointing to the pictures one at a time and asking: **What is this?** Repeat for Picture Choices 27-2 *(cut, light, ant; tire, antlers, dot)* and 27-3 *(astronaut, dive, teeth; lid, cup, apple)*.
Introduce the game Which Picture Has the First Sound /a/?			Tell children that you will show them a letter and three pictures. They will find the picture that begins with the sound for the letter.
	Hold up the *a* Alphabet Card. Practice production of the target sound.	Model	**The name of this letter is *a*. The sound for this letter is /aaa/. Remember, when you say /aaa/, your jaw and tongue are down. Say /aaa/ and feel your jaw and tongue go down.**
		Test	**What is the sound for this letter?**
Model the game	Display Picture Choice 27-1. Cover the bottom row.	Model	**This is *leaf, astronaut, dime*. I'll find the picture that has the first sound /aaa/: *astronaut*** (exaggerate the first sound). ***Astronaut* has the first sound /aaa/.** Exaggerate the first sound of the picture and then say the word: **/aaa/, *astronaut*.**
			Model another example with *alligator, tub*, and *cone*.
Test knowledge of initial /a/	Hold up the *a* Alphabet Card.	Test	**What is the sound for this letter?**
	Display Picture Choice 27-2. Cover the bottom row.		Ask children to tell the name of each picture: **What is this? Which picture has the first sound /aaa/?** Confirm correct responses and prompt sound production: **Yes, *ant* has the first sound /aaa/. Let's say /aaa/. Remember, when you say /aaa/, your jaw and tongue are down. Say /aaa/ and feel your jaw and tongue go down: *ant*.**
			Continue with the bottom row of pictures and Picture Choice 27-3.
	Give individual turns.		

Ongoing Assessment

If...children make incorrect responses,	then...model the correct answer. Review the sound production cue. Have children repeat the correct answer. Go back to the example a second time.

Activity 3 Isolate Initial Sound

Sound Match with Letter Tiles: l/l/, d/d/, s/s/, and t/t/

Objective: Children connect initial sound to letter.

Time: 4–5 minutes

	To Do		To Say
Introduce Sound Match with Letter Tiles	Gather Sound Match Cards 27a–27e and the letter tiles.		Tell children that they are going to play Sound Match, but today they will use letter tiles instead of markers.
Model the game	Place Sound Match Card 27a and the letter tiles *l, d, s,* and *t* on the table, facing children.	**Model**	**My turn. I'll show you how to play Sound Match with Letter Tiles. Listen: /lll/. I'll find the letter for the sound /lll/.** Hold up the *l* Letter Tile. **L is the letter for the sound /lll/. Everybody, what is the sound for the letter *l*? Now I'll find a picture with the first sound /lll/ on my Sound Match card.** Have children name the pictures on your Sound Match card. Point to the letter tile for *l*. **Which picture has the first sound /lll/?** *Log* **has the first sound /lll/.** Say the first sound of the correct picture and then say the word: **/lll/,** *log.* **I'll place my *l* Letter Tile on *log* because *log* begins with *l*.**
Lead the game	Give each child a Sound Match card and the letter tiles *l, d, s,* and *t*.	**Lead**	**Let's try one together. Listen: /d/. Find the letter for the sound /d/.** Hold up the *d* Letter Tile. **D is the letter for the sound /d/. Everybody, what is the sound for the letter *d*? Now find a picture with the first sound /d/ on your Sound Match card.** (See p. 221 for the picture names.) **Place the *d* Letter Tile on the picture.** Have children name the picture on which they placed the letter tile. Confirm correct responses. **Clear off your Sound Match card and we will begin.**

Phonological Awareness/Alphabetic Understanding

To Do	To Say

Play the game to test knowledge of initial sounds

Test with /s/, /t/, /l/, and /d/.

Test

Listen: /sss/. Find the letter for the sound /sss/ and hold it up. Confirm correct responses: **Yes, _s_ is the letter for the sound /sss/. What is the sound for the letter _s_?**

Ongoing Assessment

If . . . children hold up the wrong letter tile,	**then . . .** model the correct answer. Have children hold up the correct letter tile. Then review the sound production cue.

Now find a picture with the first sound /sss/ on your Sound Match card and place your _s_ Letter Tile on it. Have children name the picture on which they placed the letter tile. Confirm correct responses.

Ongoing Assessment

If . . . children make incorrect responses,	**then . . .** model the correct answer. Review the sound production cue. Have children repeat the correct answer.

Remind children to say "Sound Match" as soon as they fill up a whole row or column. When a child wins, have the group clear off their cards. Then collect, mix, and redistribute the cards. Play a second round of the game with the target sounds /t/, /lll/, /d/, and /sss/.

Sound Match Picture Names

27a: *cane, ant, fish; sandwich, log, tie; pie, dive, man*
27b: *tub, moon, fin; soap, cat, pool; doughnut, leaf, apple*
27c: *lid, tape, sit; fire, pan, alligator; cone, mow, dog*
27d: *lock, deer, tail; ant, map, cut; sandwich, pig, fire*
27e: *maze, tag, pie; apple, doughnut, sun; foot, lamb, cup*

Phonological Awareness/Alphabetic Understanding

Activity 4 Review Letter Name and Sound

Reintroduce a/a/; Be the Teacher Game

Objective: Children connect sound to letter: m/m/, p/p/,
c/k/, t/t/, s/s/, d/d/, l/l/, a/a/.

Time: 4–5 minutes

	To Do	To Say	
Introduce letter name	Hold up the *a* Alphabet Card.	Model	The <u>name</u> of this letter is *a*.
		Lead	Say the <u>name</u> with me.
		Test	What is the <u>name</u> of this letter?
Introduce letter sound	Continue holding up the *a* Alphabet Card.	Model	The <u>sound</u> for this letter is /aaa/. When you say /aaa/, your jaw and tongue are down. Say /aaa/ and feel your jaw and tongue go down.
		Lead	Say the <u>sound</u> with me: /aaa/.
		Test	What is the <u>sound</u> for this letter?
Test knowledge of letter name and sound	Continue holding up the *a* Alphabet Card.	Test	What is the <u>name</u> of this letter? What is the <u>sound</u> for this letter?

Ongoing Assessment

Give individual turns on letter name and sound.

If...children make an error,	then...tell them the name or sound, have them repeat the name or sound, and return to the letter a second time.

Play the game Be the Teacher	Select a child to be the teacher. Give the "teacher" the alphabet cards.	Have the child hold up each alphabet card and test the group on the letter name and sound: **What is the <u>name</u> of this letter? What is the <u>sound</u> for this letter?** If the group correctly states the letter name and sound, the "teacher" places the alphabet card in a pile on the table. The "teacher" continues to play the game with the group until the correct letter name and sound for each alphabet card have been identified. Then the "teacher" gives individual turns.

Ongoing Assessment

If...children make an error,	then...prompt the child who is playing the teacher to tell the name or sound and to place the card at the bottom of the pile.

222

Phonological Awareness/Alphabetic Understanding

Activity 5 Writer's Warm-Up

Letter Mission: Review *a, l, d, s, t, c, f, p, m*

Objective: Children connect letter name to written letter.

Time: 2–3 minutes

	To Do	To Say	
Introduce the activity	Display a Letter Mission.	**We are going on a letter mission. I'm going to tell you the name of a letter and you are going to write it. Let's see if we can help the dog get the bone!**	
Model the activity	Distribute a Letter Mission to each child. Hold up a Letter Mission.	Model	**Let's do one together. The first letter is *a*. Watch as I start at the dot and write the letter *a*.** Write an *a* on your sheet.
		Lead	**Now you write the letter *a*. Start at the dot and write the letter.**
Lead the activity			Say the name of each letter: *l, d, s, t, c, f, p, m.* Have children write the letter. Reinforce the group on the letter name: **Everyone, what's the <u>name</u> of the letter you wrote?**

Ongoing Assessment

If...children write the wrong letter or don't remember a letter,	then...show them the tracing card of the correct letter and model tracing the letter.

Activity 6 Connect Sound to Letter

Match a Picture's Initial Sound: a

Objective: Children connect /a/ to a.

Time: 2–3 minutes

	To Do	**To Say**
Introduce the activity	Gather the picture cards and the Letter Cards.	Tell children that they are going to choose the letter that goes with the first sound of some pictures.
Model the activity	Place the *apple* Picture Card on the table.	**Model** **This is *apple*. The first sound in *apple* is /aaa/.** Place the *a* and *c* Letter Cards under the picture. **I'm going to choose the letter that matches this picture's first sound.** Point to the correct letter: ***a* is the letter for /aaa/ like the /aaa/ in *apple*.**
Test knowledge of initial sound	Place the *ant* Picture Card on the table.	**Test** **This is *ant*. What is this? What is the first sound in *ant*? That's right, /aaa/ is the first sound in *ant*.** Place two letter cards under the picture. Vary the choice and order. **It's your turn to choose the letter that matches this picture's first sound. Everyone, think of which letter has the same sound as the /aaa/ in *ant*. Does everyone know?** Call on an individual child to point to the correct letter. **What's the <u>name</u> of the letter you pointed to? What's the <u>sound</u> for that letter? That's right; *a* is the letter for /aaa/ like the /aaa/ in *ant*.** Reinforce the letter name and sound with the group: **Everyone, what's the <u>name</u> of the letter? What's the <u>sound</u> for this letter?**
Reinforce letter name and sound	Show the *a* Letter Card.	**Everyone, what's the <u>name</u> of this letter? What's the <u>sound</u> for this letter?**

Ongoing Assessment

If...children make an error,	then...model the answer, have them repeat it, and return to the picture card a second time.

Activity 7 Connect Sound to Letter

Letter Race: *a, l, d, s*

Objective: Children isolate initial sound and connect sound to written letter.

Time: 6–8 minutes

	To Do	To Say	
Introduce the activity	Distribute a Letter Race to each child.		**We are going to have a letter race. I will tell you a word. You will write the letter that goes with the word's first sound. Which letter do you think will win?**
Model the activity	Place a Letter Race on the table, facing children.	Model	**Let's do one together. The first word is *alligator*. The first sound in *alligator* is /aaa/. I'm going to write the letter for the /aaa/ in *alligator* on the racetrack of the letter for the /aaa/ in *alligator*.** Write an *a* on the *a* racetrack. **Now you write the letter for the sound /aaa/. Start at the dot and write the letter. That's right; *a* is the letter for the sound /aaa/ like the /aaa/ in *alligator*.**
Test children on *a, l, d,* and *s*		Test	**The next word is *sick*. What is the first sound in *sick*? That's right; /sss/ is the first sound in *sick*. Now write the letter for the /sss/ in *sick* on the racetrack of the letter for the /sss/ in *sick*.**

Reinforce the group on the letter name and sound: **What's the <u>name</u> of the letter you wrote? What's the <u>sound</u> for this letter?**

Dictate words from the Word Bank. Vary the order in which you test the words until one letter wins.

Word Bank

apple	lace	dog	sunshine
astronaut	lemon	dance	soap
	leaf	dinosaur	

Ongoing Assessment

If...children make an error,	**then**...model the letter name and sound and have children repeat them. Have children write the correct letter.

LESSON 28

New Sound /a/
Review Sounds /m/, /p/, /f/, /k/, /t/, /s/, /d/, /l/
Key Phonologic Skill Isolate Initial Sound

Phonological Awareness and Alphabetic Understanding

Activity	Materials	Time
New **1. Alphabetic** Review *a*/a/	Alphabet Card: *a*	1–2 minutes
2. Integrated Phonologic/Alphabetic Picture Scene Search: /a/	Alphabet Card: *a* Picture Scene /a/ Teacher Resource Package 1	4–5 minutes
New **3. Phonologic** Identify Initial Sound with a 3-Square Strip	3-Square Strip (one per child) Picture Cards: *lip, sun, mop, tag, cup*	4–5 minutes
4. Alphabetic Review *a*/a/; Find the Sound Game	Alphabet Card: *a* Letter Cards: *m, p, f, t, s, d, l, a* (one of each per child)	4–5 minutes

Writing and Spelling

Activity	Materials	Time
5. Writer's Warm-Up Review *a, l, d, s, t, c, f, p, m*	Writer's Warm-Up (one per child) Student Activity Book 1, p. 50 Tracing Cards: *a, l, d, s, t, c, f, p, m*	2–3 minutes
6. Integrated Phonologic/Alphabetic Match a Picture's Initial Sound: /a/	Picture Cards: all *a* cards Letter Cards: *a, l, d, s, t, f, c*	2–3 minutes
7. Phonologic/Spelling Letter Tag: *a, l, d, s, f, m*	Letter Tag (one per child) Student Activity Book 1, p. 51	6–8 minutes

Activity 1 — Review Letter Name and Sound

Review a/a/

Objective: Children review letter name and sound: a/a/.

Time: 1–2 minutes

	To Do	**To Say**	
Test knowledge of letter name and sound	Hold up the *a* Alphabet Card.	Test	**What is the <u>name</u> of this letter? What is the <u>sound</u> for this letter?**
	Give individual turns on letter name and sound.		

Ongoing Assessment

If... children make an error,

then... tell them the name or sound, have them repeat the name or sound, and return to the letter a second time.

Activity 2 Isolate Initial Sound

Picture Scene Search: /a/

Objective: Children identify pictures with initial sound /a/.　　Time: 4–5 minutes

	To Do	**To Say**
Review letter name and sound	Hold up the *a* Alphabet Card.	**The <u>name</u> of this letter is *a*. What is the <u>sound</u> for this letter?** Confirm correct responses: **Yes, /aaa/. When you say /aaa/, your jaw and tongue are down. Say /aaa/ and feel your jaw and tongue go down.**

Ongoing Assessment

If...children make incorrect responses,	**then**...model the correct sound and have them repeat it. Review the sound production cue. Review a second time.

	To Do	**To Say**
Introduce the game Picture Scene Search: /a/	Hold up the picture scene.	Tell children you will show them a picture. They will find things in the picture that begin with /aaa/.
Model the game	Continue holding up the picture scene.	**Model** **My turn. I'll find something in the picture that begins with /aaa/.** Point to and name something that begins with /aaa/: *ant*. *Ant* begins with /aaa/. Everyone, say /aaa/, *ant*.
Play the game to test knowledge of initial /a/	Give individual turns. Target words: *ant, apple, alligator, antlers, astronaut, animals*	**Test** **It's your turn to find something that begins with /aaa/.** Confirm each correct response and have the group repeat it: **Yes, *apple* begins with /aaa/. Everybody, say /aaa/, *apple*.**

Ongoing Assessment

If...children select a picture that does not begin with /a/,	**then**...model a correct answer. Review the sound production cue. Have children repeat the correct answer and try again.

229

Phonological Awareness/Alphabetic Understanding

Activity **3** Isolate Initial Sound

Identify Initial Sound with a 3-Square Strip

Objective: Children isolate initial sound.

Time: 4–5 minutes

	To Do	**To Say**	
Introduce the activity		Today we're going to listen for the first sound of some pictures.	
Model the activity	Gather the picture cards and place them face down in a pile on the table. Place a 3-Square Strip on the table, facing children.	Model	**My turn to play the game.** Choose a picture from the pile. **This is *lip*. Watch. I will say the sounds slowly and point to a square as I say each sound: /lll/ /iii/ /p/.** Point to a square as you say each sound. **Now I'll say the first sound in *lip* and point to the first square: /lll/.** Point to the first square on your strip. **This is the first sound.**
Lead the activity	Give each child a 3-Square Strip.	Lead	**Now let's do it together.** Call on a child to choose a picture from the pile. **What is this? Listen. I will say the sounds slowly. We will all point to a square as I say each sound: /sss/ /uuu/ /nnn/.** Have children point to the squares in turn with you as you say each sound. **Now let's say the first sound in *sun* and point to the first square: /sss/.** Point to the first square on your strip. Have children point to the first square on their strips. **We're touching the first sound.** Repeat with the remaining pictures.

Phonological Awareness/Alphabetic Understanding

Activity 4 Review Letter Name and Sound

Review a/a/; Find the Sound Game

Objective: Children review letter name and sound: a/a/.   Time: 4–5 minutes

	To Do	To Say
Review letter name and sound	Hold up the *a* Alphabet Card.	**What is the <u>name</u> of this letter? What is the <u>sound</u> for this letter?**

Ongoing Assessment

If…children make an error,	then…tell them the name or sound, have them repeat the name or sound, and return to the letter a second time.

Give individual turns on letter name and sound.

	To Do	To Say
Introduce the game Find the Sound	Gather the letter cards.	Give each child a set of letter cards. Tell children to place the cards face up on the table in front of them. **Now we're going to play Find the Sound. I'll say a sound. You'll find the card with the letter for the sound. Then after I count to three, you'll hold up the card.**
Model the game	Place the letter cards on the table, facing children.	Model **My turn. The sound is /t/. One, two, three, go! I am looking for the letter for the sound /t/.** Hold up the *t* Letter Card. **The letter *t* is the letter for the sound /t/.**
Play the game		**Your turn. The next sound is /d/. One, two, three, go! Everybody, look for the letter for the sound /d/. Yes, *d* is the letter for the sound /d/.** Have children return the card to the table. Then call the next sound. Call out each sound at least once, though sounds may be called several times. After the group plays the game, provide the opportunity for individual turns.

Ongoing Assessment

If…children make an error,	then…tell them the letter name, have them repeat the letter name, and return to the sound a second time.

Activity 5 — Writer's Warm-Up

Review *p, c, f, m, l, s, t, a, d*

Objective: Children trace and write review letters:
p, c, f, m, l, s, t, a, d.

Time: 2–3 minutes

	To Do	**To Say**
Review letter names	Distribute a Writer's Warm-Up to each child. Hold up a Writer's Warm-Up. Point to *p*.	**What is the <u>name</u> of this letter?** Continue with the remaining letters.
Test children on writing *p, c, f, m, l, s, t, a,* and *d*		Have children trace and write each review letter one time. After they have completed the review, ask them to circle their best letters.

Ongoing Assessment

If . . . children make an error,	**then** . . . use the tracing card to model tracing the letter. Ask them to write the letter again. If needed, put your hand over the children's hands and guide the writing of the letter. Then have children try to write the letter on their own. Repeat as necessary.

Activity 6 Connect Sound to Letter

Match a Picture's Initial Sound: a

Objective: Children connect initial /a/ to a.

Time: 2–3 minutes

	To Do		**To Say**
Introduce the activity	Gather the picture cards and the letter cards.		Tell children that they are going to choose the letter that goes with the first sound of some pictures.
Model the activity	Place the *antler* Picture Card on the table.	Model	**My turn. I'll show you how this activity works. This is antler. The first sound in antler is /aaa/.** Place the *a* and *d* Letter Cards below the picture. **I'm going to choose the letter that matches this picture's first sound.** Point to the correct letter: **a is the letter for /aaa/ like the /aaa/ in antler.**
Test knowledge of initial sound	Place the *ant* Picture Card on the table.	Test	**This is ant. What is this? The first sound in ant is /aaa/. What is the first sound in ant? That's right; /aaa/ is the first sound in ant.** Place two letter cards under the picture. Vary the choice and order. **It's your turn to choose the letter that matches this picture's first sound. Everyone, think of which letter has the same sound as the /aaa/ in ant. Does everyone know?** Call on an individual to point to the correct letter. **What's the <u>name</u> of the letter you pointed to? What is the <u>sound</u> for this letter? That's right; a is the letter for /aaa/ like the /aaa/ in ant.** Continue with the remaining cards.

Ongoing Assessment

If...children make an error,	then...model the answer, have them repeat it, and return to the picture card a second time.

Reinforce letter name and sound	Display the *a* Letter Card.	**What's the <u>name</u> of this letter? What is the <u>sound</u> for this letter?**

Activity **7** Connect Sound to Letter

Letter Tag: Review a, l, d, s, f, m

Objective: Children connect sound to letter.

Time: 6–8 minutes

	To Do		**To Say**
Introduce the activity	Display a Letter Tag.		**We are going to play Letter Tag. I will tell you the sound of a letter, and you will tag the letter with your pencil.**
Model the activity	Distribute a Letter Tag to each child. Place a Letter Tag on the table, facing children.	**Model**	**I'll show you how to play Letter Tag. The first sound is /d/. I'm going to start at the arrow and tag the letter for the sound /d/.** Draw a line from the arrow to the correct letter with a pencil.
		Lead	**Now it's your turn to tag the letter for the sound /d/. Put your pencil on the first arrow and tag the letter for the sound /d/. That's right; *d* is the letter for the sound /d/.**
Test children on /a/, /l/, /d/, /s/, /f/, and /m/	Say a letter sound and have children tag the correct letter. Follow the boxes left to right across the page.	**Test**	**Put your pencil on the next arrow. When I say the sound, you tag the letter for that sound. Ready? The next sound is /sss/.** Reinforce the group on the letter name and sound: **Everyone, what's the <u>name</u> of the letter you tagged? What is the <u>sound</u> for this letter?**
			Continue with this sequence: /lll/, /d/, /mmm/, /fff/. If time allows, do a second sequence starting again from the top of the page: /lll/, /sss/, /lll/, /d/, /sss/, /aaa/.

Ongoing Assessment

If...children make an error,	then...model the letter name and sound and have children repeat them. Have children tag the correct letter.

Writing/Spelling

New Sound /a/
Review Sounds /m/, /p/, /f/, /k/, /t/, /s/, /d/, /l/
Key Phonologic Skill Isolate Initial Sound

Phonological Awareness and Alphabetic Understanding

Activity	Materials	Time
1. Alphabetic Review *a*/a/	Alphabet Card: *a* Letter Card: *a* (one per child)	1–2 minutes
2. Phonologic First Sound Song with /a/	Picture Cards: *alligator, apple, ant*	4–5 minutes
3. Phonologic Identify Initial Sound with a 3-Square Strip	3-Square Strip (one per child) Picture Cards: *sun, fan, top, dog, leg, can, man, pan*	4–5 minutes
4. Alphabetic Review *a*/a/; Grab Bag Game	Alphabet Card: *a* paper bag Game Cards: *m, p, f,* (not provided) *c, s, d, l, a*	4–5 minutes

Writing and Spelling

Activity	Materials	Time
5. Writer's Warm-Up Memory Review: *a, l, d, s, t, c, f, p, m*	Write-On/Wipe-Off Card Tracing Cards: *a, l, d,* (one per child) *s, t, c, f, p, m* markers and eraser (not provided)	2–3 minutes
6. Integrated Phonologic/Alphabetic Match a Picture's Initial Sound: /a/	Picture Cards: all *a* cards Letter Cards: *a, l, d, s, t, c, f, p, m*	2–3 minutes
7. Phonologic/Spelling Letter Writing Game: Review *l, s, c, a, t, d*	Letter Writing Game Game Board 3 (one per child) Student Activity Book 1, p. 52 game markers (one per child/not provided)	6–8 minutes

Activity **1** Review Letter Name and Sound

Review a/a/

Objective: Children review letter name and sound: a/a/.

Time: 1–2 minutes

	To Do	**To Say**
Review letter name and sound	Hold up the *a* Alphabet Card.	**What is the <u>name</u> of this letter? What is the <u>sound</u> for this letter?**
	Give individual turns on letter name and sound.	**Ongoing Assessment**

Ongoing Assessment	
If...children make an error,	**then**...tell them the name or sound, have them repeat the name or sound, and return to the letter a second time.

Activity 2 Isolate Initial Sound

First Sound Song with /a/

Objective: Children isolate initial /a/ in a song.

Time: 4–5 minutes

	To Do	**To Say**	
Introduce the First Sound Song	Display the *alligator, apple,* and *ant* Picture Cards.	**Today we're going to sing a song. I'll show you three pictures that begin with /aaa/. These pictures will be in the song.**	
		Model	**This is *alligator, apple, ant.* Say the names of the pictures with me: *alligator, apple, ant. Alligator, apple,* and *ant* all begin with /aaa/. Say the sound /aaa/ with me. Remember, when you say /aaa/, your jaw and tongue are down. Say /aaa/ and feel your jaw and tongue go down.**
Model the song	Continue to display the picture cards.	Model	Sing the following words to the tune of "Old MacDonald Had a Farm." Point to each picture as you sing its name. **What is the sound that begins these words: *alligator, apple, ant?* /aaa/ is the sound that begins these words: *alligator, apple, ant.* With an /aaa/, /aaa/ here and an /aaa/, /aaa/ there, here an /aaa/, there an /aaa/, everywhere an /aaa/, /aaa/. /aaa/ is the sound that begins these words: *alligator, apple, ant.***
			Sing it with me. Point to each picture as children sing its name.
Lead the song	Lead children through the song several times, pointing to the pictures as they sing.	Lead	**Now sing the song with me.**
Test knowledge of initial /a/	Continue to display the picture cards. Point to *alligator*.	Test	**It's your turn. Say the first sound in *alligator*.** Confirm correct responses and prompt sound production. Then continue with *apple* and *ant*.
	Give individual turns.		

Ongoing Assessment

If...children make an error,	then...model the answer. Have children repeat the answer. Return to the example a second time.

Phonological Awareness/Alphabetic Understanding

Activity 3 — Isolate Initial Sound

Identify Initial Sound with a 3-Square Strip

Objective: Children locate sound on a 3-Square Strip.

Time: 4–5 minutes

	To Do		To Say
Introduce the activity			**Today we're going to listen for the first sound of some pictures.**
Model the activity	Place a 3-Square Strip on the table. Place the picture cards face down in a pile on the table.	Model	**My turn to play the game.** Choose a picture from the pile. **This is *sun*. Watch, I will say the sounds in *sun* and point to a square as I say each sound: /sss/ /uuu/ /nnn/.** Point to a square as you say each sound. **Now I'll say the first sound in *sun* and point to the first square: /sss/.** Point to the first square on your strip. **This is the first sound.**
Lead the activity	Give each child a 3-Square Strip. Use the *fan* and *top* Picture Cards.	Lead	**Now let's do it together.** Call on a child to choose a picture from the pile. **Everybody, what is this? I will say the sounds in *fan*. We will all point to a square as I say each sound: /fff/ /aaa/ /nnn/.** Have children point to squares in turn with you as you say each sound. **Now let's say the first sound in *fan* and point to the first square: /fff/.** Point to the first square on your strip. Have children point to the first square on their strips. **We're touching the first sound.** Repeat with *top*.
Test the activity		Test	**Your turn.** Call on a child to choose a picture from the pile. **Everybody, what is this? I will say the sounds in *dog*. You point to a square as I say each sound: /d/ /ooo/ /g/.** Have children point to a square as you say each sound. **Now say the first sound in *dog* and point to the first square. Good. You're touching the first sound: /d/.** Continue with the remaining cards. Then give individual turns.

Phonological Awareness/Alphabetic Understanding

Activity 4 Review Letter Name and Sound

Review a/a/; Grab Bag Game

Objective: Children review letter name and sound: a/a/.   Time: 4–5 minutes

	To Do	**To Say**	
Test knowledge of letter name and sound	Hold up the *a* Alphabet Card. Give individual turns on letter name and sound.	**Test**	**What is the <u>name</u> of this letter? What is the <u>sound</u> for this letter?**

Ongoing Assessment

If…children make an error,	**then**…tell them the name or sound, have them repeat the name or sound, and return to the letter a second time.

	To Do	**To Say**
Play the Grab Bag Game	Gather the game cards and place them in a brown paper bag.	Have children take turns pulling a letter out of the bag. Hold up the card and test the group on the letter name and sound: **What is the <u>name</u> of this letter? What is the <u>sound</u> for this letter?** If children correctly state the name and sound of the letter, place the card in a pile on the table. Play the game until all the cards have been removed from the bag. If time permits, provide individual turns.

Ongoing Assessment

If…children make an error,	**then**…tell them the name or sound, have them repeat the name or sound, and place the card back in the bag.

Phonological Awareness/Alphabetic Understanding

Activity 5 — Writer's Warm-Up

Memory Review: a, l, d, s, t, c, f, p, m

Objective: Children write letters from memory.

Time: 2–3 minutes

	To Do	**To Say**
Review letter names	Gather the tracing cards.	Use the tracing cards to review the letter names.
Introduce the activity	Distribute a Write-On/Wipe-Off Card and a marker to each child.	**I'm going to tell you the name of a letter. You're going to write the letter on your card.**
Model the activity	Hold up a Write-On/Wipe-Off Card.	**Model** **I'll show you what to do. The first letter is *a*. I will write the letter *a* on my Write-On/Wipe-Off Card.** Write an *a* on the card and show children.
Test children on writing *a, l, d, s, t, c, f, p,* and *m*		**Test** Dictate each letter name and have children write the correct letter on their Write-On/Wipe-Off Cards. Reinforce the group on the letter name. **Everyone, what is the name of the letter you wrote?** After each letter, have children erase their Write-On/Wipe-Off Cards. Dictate each letter at least twice, or as time allows.

Ongoing Assessment

If...children write the wrong letter or don't remember a letter,   **then**...show them the tracing card of the correct letter. Model tracing the letter and say the letter name.

Activity **6** Connect Sound to Letter

Match a Picture's Initial Sound: /a/
Objective: Children connect sound to letter: a/a/.   Time: 2–3 minutes

	To Do	**To Say**	
Introduce the activity	Gather the picture cards and the *a, l, d, s, t, f, c, p,* and *m* Letter Cards.	Tell children that they are going to choose the letter that goes with the first sound of some pictures.	
Model the activity	Place the *alligator* Picture Card on the table, facing children.	**Model**	**This is *alligator*. The first sound in *alligator* is /aaa/.** Place the *m* and *a* Letter Cards under the picture. **I'm going to choose the letter that matches this picture's first sound.** Point to the correct letter: ***a* is the letter for /aaa/ like the /aaa/ in *alligator*.**
Test knowledge of initial sound	Place the *ant* Picture Card on the table.	**Test**	**This is *ant*. What is this? The first sound in *ant* is /aaa/. What is the first sound in *ant*? That's right; /aaa/ is the first sound in *ant*.** Place two letter cards under the picture. Vary the choice and order of letters. **It's your turn to choose the letter that matches this picture's first sound. Everyone, think of which letter makes the same sound as the /aaa/ in *ant*. Does everyone know?** Call on an individual child to point to the correct letter. **What's the name of the letter you pointed to? What's the sound for that letter? That's right; *a* is the letter for /aaa/ like the /aaa/ in *ant*.** Reinforce the letter name and sound with the group: **Everyone, what's the <u>name</u> of this letter? What is the <u>sound</u> for this letter?** Continue with at least three more examples.

Ongoing Assessment

If...children make an error,	then...model the answer, have them repeat it, and return to the picture card a second time.

Activity 7 Connect Sound to Letter

Letter Writing Game:
Review l, s, c, a, t, d

Objective: Children connect initial sound to letter.

Time: 6–8 minutes

	To Do	**To Say**
Review letter names and sounds	Hold up a Letter Writing Game. Point to each letter.	For each letter, ask: **What is the <u>name</u> of this letter? What is the <u>sound</u> for this letter?**
Introduce the Letter Writing Game	Distribute a Letter Writing Game to each child.	**We're going to play a letter writing game. I'll say a word and you'll write the letter that goes with the word's first sound. Then someone will roll the number cube and move his or her marker on the game board.**
Model the game	Place a Letter Writing Game on the table.	**Model** **Let's do one together. The first word is** *dog*. **The first sound in** *dog* **is /d/. I'm going to write the letter for the same sound as the /d/ in** *dog*. Write a *d* in the *d* column. **Now you write the letter for the sound /d/. Start at the dot and write the letter. That's right;** *d* **is the letter for the sound /d/ like the /d/ in** *dog*.
Play the game to test children on *l, s, c, a, t,* **and** *d*	Dictate words from the Word Bank. Vary the order.	**Test** **The next word is** *carrot*. **What is the first sound in** *carrot*? **That's right, /k/ is the first sound in** *carrot*. **Now write the letter for the same sound as the /k/ in** *carrot*. **Start at the dot and write the letter. Everyone, what's the <u>name</u> of the letter you wrote? What's the <u>sound</u> for that letter?**

After everyone has written the letter, have one child roll the number cube and advance his or her marker on the game board. Continue the game until all the letters have been written.

Word Bank

ladybug	soap	cat	apple	top	duck
lock	sun	cap	antler	ten	dime
leaf	seal		ant	turkey	

Ongoing Assessment

| **If...** children make an error, | **then...** model the letter name and sound and have children repeat them. Have children write the correct letter. |

Writing/Spelling

New Sound /a/
Review Sounds /m/, /p/, /f/, /k/, /t/, /s/, /d/, /l/
Key Phonologic Skill Isolate Initial Sound

Phonological Awareness and Alphabetic Understanding

Activity	Materials	Time
1. Alphabetic Review *a*/a/	Alphabet Card: *a*	1–2 minutes
2. Integrated Phonologic/Alphabetic Picture Scene Search: /a/, /m/, /l/, /p/	Alphabet Cards: *a, m, p, l* Picture Scene /a/, /m/, /l/, /p/ (review) Teacher Resource Package 1	4–5 minutes
3. Phonologic Identify Initial Sound with a 3-Square Strip	3-Square Strip (one per child) Picture Cards: *tag, ant, lip, dog, sun, cat, map, fin*	4–5 minutes
4. Integrated Phonologic/Alphabetic Reintroduce *l*/l/; Pictures to Letters Game	Alphabet Card: *l* Letter Cards: *m, p, f, c, t, d, l, a* (one of each per child) Picture Cards: *man, pan, fan, coat, deer, turtle, alligator, log*	4–5 minutes

Writing and Spelling

Activity	Materials	Time
5. Writer's Warm-Up Letter Mission: Review *a, l, d, s, t, c, f, p, m*	Letter Mission (one per child) Student Activity Book 1, p. 53 Tracing Cards: *a, l, d, s, t, c, f, p, m*	2–3 minutes
6. Integrated Phonologic/Alphabetic Match a Picture's Initial Sound: /a/	Picture Cards: all *a* cards Letter Cards: *a, l, d, s, t, f, c, p, m*	2–3 minutes
7. Phonologic/Spelling Letter Matching: Review *a, l, d, s*	Picture Cards: *a, l, d, s* (three of each letter) Letter Cards: *a, l, d, s* (three of each letter)	6–8 minutes

Activity 1 Review Letter Name and Sound

Review a/a/

Objective: Children review letter name and sound: a/a/.

Time: 1–2 minutes

	To Do	**To Say**
Review letter name and sound	Hold up the *a* Alphabet Card.	**What is the <u>name</u> of this letter? What is the <u>sound</u> for this letter?**

Ongoing Assessment

If...children make an error,   then...tell them the name or sound, have them repeat the name or sound, and return to the letter a second time.

Activity 2 Isolate Initial Sound

Picture Scene Search: /a/, /m/, /l/, /p/

Objective: Children identify pictures that
begin with /a/, /m/, /l/, /p/.

Time: 4–5 minutes

	To Do		**To Say**
Introduce the activity	Hold up the picture scene.		Tell children that you will show them a picture that has in it things that begin with /a/, /m/, /l/, and /p/. They will look for things in the picture that begin with each sound.
Test knowledge of letter sound	Hold up the *a* Alphabet Card.	**Test**	**The name of this letter is *a*. What is the sound for this letter?** Confirm correct responses. **Yes, /aaa/. Remember, when you say /aaa/, your jaw and tongue are down. Say /aaa/ and feel your jaw and tongue go down.**

Ongoing Assessment

If...children make incorrect responses,	**then**...model the correct sound and have them repeat it. Review the sound production cue. Repeat a second time.

	To Do		**To Say**
Model the activity	Hold up the picture scene.	**Model**	**My turn. I'll find something in the picture that begins with /aaa/.** Point to and name something in the picture scene that begins with /aaa/: ***Antlers* begins with /aaa/.**
Test knowledge of initial sound	Give individual turns. Target words: *antlers, apple, alligator, moon, merry-go-round, map, lamp, ladybug, lion, pillow, plate*	**Test**	**It's your turn to find something that begins with /aaa/.** Confirm each correct response and have the group repeat it: **Yes, _____ begins with /aaa/. Everybody say /aaa/, _____.** Next, focus on /m/: review the letter name, sound, and sound production cue. Model finding a picture that begins with /m/. Then have children find examples in the picture scene. Repeat for /l/ and /p/. Afterward, ask children to name the pictures that begin with /a/ with their eyes closed. **Close your eyes. Can you remember a picture that begins with /aaa/?** Repeat for /m/, /l/, and /p/.

Activity **3** Isolate Initial Sound

Identify Initial Sound with a 3-Square Strip

Objective: Children locate sound on a 3-Square Strip.   Time: 4–5 minutes

	To Do		**To Say**	
Introduce and model the activity	Place a 3-Square Strip on the table. Place the picture cards face down in a pile on the table.	**Model**	**We're going to listen for the first sound of some picures. I'll show you how to play the game.** Choose a picture from the pile. **This is *tag*. Watch. I will say the sounds in *tag* and point to a square as I say each sound: /t/ /aaa/ /g/.** Point to a square as you say each sound. **Now I'll say the first sound in *tag* and point to the first square: /t/.** Point to the first square on your strip. **This is the first sound.**	
Test knowledge of initial sound	Give each child a 3-Square Strip.	**Test**	**Your turn.** Call on a child to choose a picture from the pile. **Everybody, what is this? I will say the sounds in *ant*. You point to a square as I say each sound: /aaa/ /nnn/ /t/.** Have children point to a square as you say each sound. **Now say the first sound in *ant* and point to the first square. Good. You're touching the first sound: /aaa/.**	
			Continue with the remaining pictures. Then give individual turns.	

246

Phonological Awareness/Alphabetic Understanding

Activity 4 Review Letter Name and Sound

Reintroduce l/l/; Pictures to Letters Game

Objective: Children review letter name and sound: l/l/.   Time: 4–5 minutes

	To Do	**To Say**	
Introduce letter name	Hold up the *l* Alphabet Card.	Model	The <u>name</u> of this letter is *l*.
		Lead	Say the <u>name</u> with me.
		Test	What is the <u>name</u> of this letter?
Introduce letter sound	Continue holding up the *l* Alphabet Card.	Model	The <u>sound</u> for this letter is /lll/. When you say /lll/, the tip of your tongue goes up to touch the top of your mouth behind your teeth. Say /lll/ and feel the tip of your tongue go up to touch the top of your mouth behind your teeth.
		Lead	Say the <u>sound</u> with me: /lll/.
		Test	What is the <u>sound</u> for this letter?
Test knowledge of letter name and sound	Continue holding up the *l* Alphabet Card.	Test	What is the <u>name</u> of this letter? What is the <u>sound</u> for this letter?

Ongoing Assessment

If...children make an error,	**then**...tell them the name or sound, have them repeat the name or sound, and return to the letter a second time.

	Give individual turns on letter name and sound.	
Introduce the game Pictures to Letters	Gather the picture cards. Give each child letter cards for *m, p, f, c, t, d, l,* and *a*.	Place the picture cards in a paper bag and shake them up. Have children line up the letter cards in front of them on the table. Tell children that you will pull a picture from the bag. They will say the first sound of the picture and then find the letter for the sound. Then they'll hold up the letter when you give them the signal: "One, two, three, go!"

	To Do		**To Say**
Model the game		**Model**	**My turn. I'll show you how to play the game.** Pull the *alligator* Picture Card from the bag. **This is *alligator*. What is this? I'll say the first sound in *alligator*: /aaa/. Say the first sound in *alligator*. Yes, /aaa/. When you say /aaa/, your jaw and tongue are down. Say /aaa/ and feel your jaw and tongue go down: *alligator*. I'll hold up the letter for /aaa/.** Look down at your line of letter cards. **One, two, three, go!** Hold up your *a* Letter Card. **See, I found /aaa/ for *alligator*.** Return the *a* Letter Card to the table. Place the picture of *alligator* next to the *a* Letter Card.
Play the game to test knowledge of /m/, /p/, /f/, /k/, /t/, /d/, /l/, and /a/		**Test**	**It's your turn to play the game.** Pull a picture from the bag. **This is *fan*. What is this? Say the first sound in *fan*. Yes, /fff/. Remember, when you say /fff/, your top teeth touch your bottom lip. Say /fff/ and feel your top teeth touch your bottom lip: *fan*. Hold up the letter for /fff/. One, two, three, go! Everybody, what's the sound for the letter you are holding? Yes, /fff/; /fff/ for *fan*. Say /fff/, *fan*.** Have children return their *f* Letter Cards to the table. Place the picture of *fan* next to your *f* Letter Card. Continue the game until all pictures have been pulled from the bag.

Give individual turns.

Ongoing Assessment

If... children cannot correctly identify the first sound of the picture,

then... tell them the first sound and have them repeat it. Review the sound production cue.

If... children hold up the wrong letter card,

then... repeat the sound and hold up the correct letter card. Have children find the correct letter card, hold it up, and say the sound with you.

Phonological Awareness/Alphabetic Understanding

Activity 5 Writer's Warm-Up

Letter Mission: Review a, l, d, s, t, c, f, p, m

Objective: Children connect letter name to written letter.

Time: 2–3 minutes

	To Do	To Say
Introduce the activity	Display a Letter Mission.	**We are going on a letter mission. I'm going to tell you the name of a letter and you are going to write it. Let's see if we can help the dog get the bone!**
Model the activity	Distribute a Letter Mission to each child. Hold up a Letter Mission.	**Model** **Let's do one together. The first letter is *a*. Watch as I start at the dot and write the letter *a*.** Write an *a* on your sheet. **Lead** **Now you write the letter *a*. Start at the dot and write the letter.**
Lead the activity		Say the name of each remaining letter: *l, d, s, t, c, f, p,* and *m.* Have children write the letter. Reinforce the group on the letter name: **Everyone, what's the name of the letter you wrote?**

Ongoing Assessment

If...children write the wrong letter or don't remember a letter,

then...show them the tracing card of the correct letter and model tracing the letter.

Activity 6 Connect Sound to Letter

Match a Picture's First Sound: /a/

Objective: Children connect initial /a/ to *a*.

Time: 2–3 minutes

	To Do	**To Say**	
Introduce the activity	Gather the picture cards and the letter cards.		Tell children that they are going to choose the letter that matches a picture's first sound.
Model the activity	Place the *apple* Picture Card on the table, facing children.	**Model**	**This is *apple*. The first sound in *apple* is /aaa/.** Place the *a* and *l* Letter Cards below the picture. **I'm going to choose the letter that matches this picture's first sound.** Point to the correct letter: ***a* is the letter for /aaa/ like the /aaa/ in *apple*.**
Test knowledge of initial sound	Place the *astronaut* Picture Card on the table.	**Test**	**This is *astronaut*. What is this? The first sound in *astronaut* is /aaa/. What is the first sound in *astronaut*? That's right; /aaa/ is the first sound in *astronaut*.** Place two letter cards under the picture. Vary the choice and order of letters. **It's your turn to choose the letter that matches this picture's first sound. Everyone, which letter has the same sound as the /aaa/ in *astronaut*?** Call on an individual child to point to the correct letter. **What's the name of the letter you pointed to? What is the sound for this letter? That's right; *a* is the letter for /aaa/ like the /aaa/ in *astronaut*.** Reinforce the letter name and sound with the group: **Everyone, what's the <u>name</u> of this letter? What is the <u>sound</u> for this letter?** Continue with the remaining pictures, as time allows.

Ongoing Assessment

If...children make an error,	**then**...model the answer, have them repeat it, and return to the picture card a second time.

Activity **7** Connect Sound to Letter

Letter Matching: Review a, l, d, s

Objective: Children connect sound to
letter: /a/a/, /l/l/, /d/d/, /s/s/.

Time: 6–8 minutes

	To Do	**To Say**
Review letter names and sounds	Hold up Letter Cards *a, l, d,* and *s,* one at a time.	For each letter, ask: **What is the <u>name</u> of this letter? What is the <u>sound</u> for this letter?**
Introduce the activity	Place the letter cards face down in a pile on the table. Spread the picture cards on the table, facing students.	**We are going to play a letter matching game. You will pick a letter and put it next to a picture that begins with the sound for the letter. Let's see if we can match all of the pictures!**
Model the activity		**Model** **Let's do one together. I'll pick the first letter.** Pick an *a* Letter Card from the pile. **The sound for this letter is /aaa/. Now I'll put the letter next to a picture that starts with the sound /aaa/. The picture** *astronaut* **starts with /aaa/.**
Test children on ***l, d,*** **and** ***s***		**Test** Have children take turns selecting a letter, saying the letter's sound, and placing the letter next to a picture that begins with the sound. Reinforce the group on identifying the first sound of each picture: **Everyone, what's the first sound in _____? What's the name of the letter for the sound /_/ like the /_/ in _____?**

Ongoing Assessment

If...children make an error,	then...model the letter sound and the picture's name and first sound.

LESSON 31

New Sound /o/
Review Sounds /m/, /p/, /f/, /k/, /t/, /s/, /d/, /l/, /a/
Key Phonologic Skill Isolate Initial and Final Sounds

Phonological Awareness and Alphabetic Understanding

Activity	Materials		Time
1. Alphabetic Introduce o/o/	Alphabet Card: o	Letter Card: o (one per child)	1–2 minutes
2. Phonologic Does It Begin with /o/?	Picture Cards: ox, tire, otter, octopus, olive, sun		4–5 minutes
New **3. Phonologic** Last Sounds Freeze Game	Picture Cards: mud, cap, ant, pot, map	3-Square Strips (one per child)	4–5 minutes
4. Alphabetic Reintroduce o/o/; Find the Sound Game	Alphabet Card: o Letter Cards: d, m, p, f, c, t, s, l, a (one set per child)		4–5 minutes

Writing and Spelling

Activity	Materials		Time
5. Writer's Warm-Up Introduce o	Tracing Cards: o, a, s, d, t, l, c Writer's Warm-Up (one per child) Student Activity Book 1, p. 54		2–3 minutes
6. Integrated Phonologic/Alphabetic Match a Picture's Last Sound: /p/	Picture Cards: cap, soup, jeep, cup, map, tape, soap, mop, up	Letter Cards: p, l, c, s	2–3 minutes
7. Phonologic/Spelling Letter Cross-Out Game for Final Sounds: /l/, /d/, /s/, /t/	Letter Cross-Out (one per child) Student Activity Book 1, p. 55		6–8 minutes

Activity 1 Introduce Letter Name and Sound

Introduce o/o/

Objective: Children connect sound to letter o/o/.

Time: 1–2 minutes

	To Do	To Say	
Introduce letter name	Hold up the *o* Alphabet Card.	Model	**The name of this letter is *o*.**
		Lead	**Say the name with me.**
		Test	**What is the name of this letter?**
Introduce letter sound	Continue holding up the *o* Alphabet Card.	Model	**The sound for this letter is /ooo/. When you say /ooo/, your mouth is open and your jaw drops. Put your hand under your chin and say /ooo/. See, your mouth opened and your jaw dropped.**
		Lead	**Say the sound with me: /ooo/.**
		Test	**What is the sound for this letter?**
Test letter name and sound	Continue holding up the *o* Alphabet Card.	Test	**What is the name of this letter? What is the sound for this letter?**
	Give individual turns on letter name and sound.		**Ongoing Assessment** **If**…children make an error, **then**…tell them the letter name or sound, and repeat the test.
Model tracing *o*	Hold up the *o* Alphabet Card. Model how to trace *o*.	Model	**Watch. I'll trace the letter *o*.** Distribute *o* Letter Cards. **Now you trace the letter *o* three times with your finger. Say /ooo/ each time you trace the letter.**
			Ongoing Assessment **If**…children make an error, **then**…put your hand over their hand and guide them to trace the letter. Then have the children try to trace the letter on their own. Repeat as necessary.

Activity **2** Isolate Initial **Sound**

Does It Begin with /o/?
Objective: Children isolate initial /o/.

Time: 4–5 minutes

	To Do		**To Say**
Model names of pictures	Place the *ox* Picture Card on the table.	Model	**This is ox. What is this?** Have children repeat. Continue with *otter, octopus, olive, tire, sun*. Then test children on the picture names by placing the cards on the table one at a time and asking: **What is this?**
Introduce the game Does It Begin with /o/?	Practice production of the target sound.		Tell children they will play a game. They need to find the pictures that begin with /ooo/. **Let's say /ooo/. When you say /ooo/, your mouth is open and your jaw drops. Put your hand under your chin and say /ooo/. See, your mouth opened and your jaw dropped.**
Model the game	Gather the *ox* and *tire* Picture Cards. Place *ox* on the table.	Model	**My turn. I'll say the name of the picture and then tell if it begins with /ooo/: ox** (exaggerate the first sound). **Ox begins with /ooo/. My mouth is open and my jaw drops when I say /ooo/, ox. Look at the next picture: tire** (exaggerate the first sound). **Tire does not begin with /ooo/.**
Play the game to test knowledge of /o/	Place the *otter* Picture Card on the table.	Test	**Your turn. What is this? Does otter begin with /ooo/?** Confirm correct responses and prompt sound production: **Yes, otter begins with /ooo/. Let's say /ooo/. When you say /ooo/, your mouth is open and your jaw drops. Open your mouth and say /ooo/, otter.** Continue with three other examples: *octopus, olive, sun*.

Ongoing Assessment

	Give individual turns.	**If**...children make incorrect responses,	**then**...model the correct answer, review the sound production cue, and have children repeat the correct answer. Go back to the example a second time.

Activity **3** Identify Final Sound

New

Last Sounds Freeze Game

Objective: Children identify the final sound in words and locate position on a 3-Square Strip.

Time: 4–5 minutes

	To Do		**To Say**
Introduce and model the game Last Sounds Freeze	Arrange the picture cards in a pile. Give each child a 3-Square Strip. Place the *mud* Picture Card on the table.	**Model**	**This is *mud*. Watch. I'll say the sounds in *mud* and point to a square as I say each sound: /mmm/ /uuu/ /d/. Listen again. I'll say the sounds in *mud* and point to a square as I say each sound. When I say "freeze," I'll keep my finger on the box I'm touching.** Say the word: **/mmm/ /uuu/ /d/.** Freeze! Keep your finger on the last box on the card. **I'm touching the last sound in *mud*: /d/.**
Play the game to test knowledge of final sounds	Use Pictures Cards: *cap, ant, pot, map.*	**Test**	**Now let's do one together.** Place the *cap* Picture Card on the table. **I will say the sounds in *cap*. We will all point to a square as I say each sound.** When you say the sounds slowly in a word that begins with a stop sound, such as *cap*, pause briefly after the first sound and then move to the next two sounds: **/k/** (pause) **/aaa/ /p/. Listen again. I will say the sounds in *cap*, and we will all point to a square as I say each sound. When I say "freeze," we will keep our fingers on the box we are touching. Here we go: /k/ /aaa/ /p/. Freeze!** Children should follow your lead, keeping their fingers on the last box of the strip. **We're touching the last sound in *cap*: /p/. Everyone, say the last sound in *cap* with me: /p/.** Repeat with *ant, pot,* and *map.*

Activity 4 Reintroduce Letter Name and Sound

Reintroduce o/o/;
Find the Sound Game

Objective: Children practice letter name and sound: o/o/.   Time: 4–5 minutes

	To Do	**To Say**	
Introduce letter name	Hold up the *o* Alphabet Card.	Model	**The name of this letter is *o*.**
		Lead	**Say the name of this letter with me: *o*.**
		Test	**What is the name of this letter?**
Introduce letter sound	Continue holding up the *o* Alphabet Card.	Model	**The sound for this letter is /ooo/. When you say /ooo/, your mouth is open and your jaw drops. Open your mouth and say /ooo/.**
		Lead	**Say the sound with me: /ooo/.**
		Test	**What is the sound for this letter?**
Test letter name and sound	Continue holding up the *o* Alphabet Card.	Test	**What is the name of this letter? What is the sound for this letter?**

Ongoing Assessment

If...children make an error,	then...tell them the letter name or sound, have them repeat the name or sound, and return to the letter a second time.

	Continue holding up the *o* Alphabet Card.	Ask individuals: **What is the name of this letter? What is the sound for this letter?**

Play the game Find the Sound with *d, m, p, f, c, t, s, l, a*	Have children line up the letter cards in front of them.	Lead	**I'll say a sound. You'll find the letter for the sound and hold it up when I count to three. Let's try one: /d/. One, two, three! Everybody, what letter are you holding up? Yes, *d*; *d* is the letter for /d/.** Have children return their letter cards to the table. Continue with *m, p, f, c, t, s, l, a*. After the group plays the game, provide an opportunity for individual turns.

Ongoing Assessment

If...children make an error,	then...hold up the correct letter card. Have them repeat the sound and hold up the correct letter card. Return to the sound a second time.

Activity 5 — Writer's Warm-Up

Introduce o

Objective: Children trace and write *o* and review writing *a, s, d, t, l,* and *c.*

Time: 2–3 minutes

	To Do	To Say	
Review letter name and sound	Hold up the *o* Tracing Card.	**What is the <u>name</u> of this letter? What is the <u>sound</u> for this letter?**	
Model tracing o	Continue holding up the *o* Tracing Card. Model tracing *o* with your finger. Distribute a Writer's Warm-Up to each child.	Model	**Watch as I trace the letter o.**
		Lead	**Watch as I trace the letter o again. Now you trace the first two letter o's on your warm-up sheet with your finger. Use your pencil to trace the next two o's.**
Model writing o	Hold up the lined side of the *o* Tracing Card.	Model	**Watch as I write the letter o. I start at the dot and write the letter.**
		Lead	**Now you write two letter o's. Start at the dot like I did. Write carefully.**

Ongoing Assessment

If . . . children make an error,	**then** . . . have them write the letter again. If needed, put your hand over their hand and guide them to write the letter. Then have them write the letter on their own. Repeat as necessary.

Test writing o	Hold up the lined side of the *o* Tracing Card. Model writing *o* again.	Have children cover the letters they traced and wrote. Have them write the letter *o* two times from memory. Then have them uncover their papers and compare the letters. **Do your letters look the same? Circle your best letter.**

 Review

a, s, d, t, l, c

Trace *a*. Now write *a* with your pencil. Continue this procedure for *s, d, t, l, c.*

Ongoing Assessment

If . . . children make an error,	**then** . . . use the tracing card to model tracing the letter. Ask them to write the letter again. If needed, guide the writing of the letter. Then have children try to write the letter on their own.

Writing/Spelling

Connect Sound to Letter

Match a Picture's Last Sound: /p̲/
Objective: Children connect final sound to letter: p/p/.   Time: 2–3 minutes

	To Do	To Say	
Introduce the activity	Gather the picture cards and letter cards.		**You're going to choose the letter that goes with the last sound of some pictures.**
Model the activity	Place the *cap* Picture Card on the table. Place the *p* and *l* Letter Cards under the picture.	Model	**This is *cap*. The last sound in *cap* is /p/.** **I'm going to choose the letter that matches this picture's last sound.** Point to the correct letter: **p is the letter for /p/ like the /p/ in *cap*.**
Test knowledge of final sound	Display the *soup* Picture Card. Place the *c* and *p* Letter Cards on the table.	Test	**This is *soup*. What is this? The last sound in *soup* is /p/. What is the last sound in *soup*? That's right; /p/ is the last sound in *soup*. Your turn. Choose the letter that matches this picture's last sound. Which letter has the same sound as the /p/ in *soup*? Do you know?** Call on a child to point to the correct letter. **What's the <u>name</u> of the letter you pointed to? What is the <u>sound</u> for this letter? That's right; p is the letter for /p/ like the /p/ in *soup*. Everyone, what's the <u>name</u> of this letter? What's the <u>sound</u> for this letter?** Continue with at least three more examples.

Ongoing Assessment

If... children make an error,	then... model the answer, have them repeat it, and return to the picture card a second time.

Activity 7 Identify Final Sounds

Letter Cross-Out Game for Final Sounds: /l/, /d/, /s/, /t/

Objective: Children identify final sound and connect to letter.   Time: 6–8 minutes

	To Do	**To Say**	
Introduce the game	Distribute a Letter Cross-Out to each child.		**We're going to play Letter Cross-Out. I'll say a word. You'll cross out the letter for the last sound in the word. Let's see if we can cross out all the letters on the sheet!**
Model the game	Model one example.	**Model**	**Let's do one together. The first word is _miss_. The last sound in _miss_ is /sss/. I'm going to cross out a letter for the same sound as the /sss/ in _miss_.** Cross out one of the _s_'s on your Letter Cross-Out. **Now you cross out the letter for the same sound as the /sss/ in _miss_. That's right; _s_ is the letter for /sss/ like the /sss/ in _miss_.**
Play the game to test knowledge of final sounds	Test children with words from the Word Bank until all letters are crossed out. Vary the order in which you dictate words.	**Test**	**The next word is _mitt_. What is the last sound in _mitt_? That's right; /t/ is the last sound in _mitt_. Cross out the letter for the same sound as the /t/ in _mitt_. Everyone, what's the <u>name</u> of the letter you crossed out? What is the <u>sound</u> for this letter?**

Word Bank

mill	mad	mess	mat
mall	maid	moose	magnet
mail	mud	mouse	meat
meal	mood		

Ongoing Assessment

If . . . children make an error,	**then** . . . point to the correct letter and model the letter sound. Have children repeat the sound and cross out the letter.

Writing/Spelling

LESSON 32

New Sound /o/
Review Sounds /f/, /k/, /t/, /s/, /d/, /l/, /a/
Key Phonologic Skill Isolate Initial and Final Sounds

Phonological Awareness and Alphabetic Understanding

Activity	Materials		Time
1. Alphabetic Introduce o/o/	Alphabet Card: o	Letter Card: o (one per child)	1–2 minutes
2. Phonologic Does It Begin with /o/?	Picture Choices: 32-1, 32-2, 32-3 Teacher Resource Package 1		4–5 minutes
3. Phonologic Last Sounds Freeze Game	Picture Cards: *mop, cat, cup, bat, red*	3-Square Strip (one per child)	4–5 minutes
4. Alphabetic Reintroduce o/o/; Grab Bag Game	Alphabet Card: o Letter Cards: *a, c, d, f, l, o, s, t*	paper bag (not provided)	4–5 minutes

Writing and Spelling

Activity	Materials		Time
5. Writer's Warm-Up Introduce o	Tracing Cards: *o, a, s, d, t, l, c* Writer's Warm-Up (one per child) Student Activity Book 1, p. 56		2–3 minutes
6. Integrated Phonologic/Alphabetic Match a Picture's Last Sound: /l/, /p/	Picture Cards: *bell, mop, cap, jeep, soap, nail, well, bowl, tape, seal*	Letter Cards: *l, f, p, c, s*	2–3 minutes
7. Phonologic/Spelling Tic-Tac-Toe: Final Sounds /l/, /d/, /s/, /t/, /k/, /f/, /p/, /m/	Tic-Tac-Toe (one per child) Student Activity Book 1, p. 57		6–8 minutes

Activity 1 — Introduce Letter Name and Sound

Introduce o/o/
Objective: Children learn and trace o/o/.

Time: 1–2 minutes

	To Do	**To Say**	
Introduce letter name	Hold up the *o* Alphabet Card.	Model	The <u>name</u> of this letter is *o*.
		Lead	Say the <u>name</u> with me.
		Test	What is the <u>name</u> of this letter?
Introduce letter sound	Continue holding up *o* Alphabet Card.	Model	The <u>sound</u> for this letter is /ooo/. When you say /ooo/, your mouth is open and your jaw drops. Put your hand under your chin and say /ooo/. See, your mouth opened and your jaw dropped.
		Lead	Say the <u>sound</u> with me: /ooo/.
		Test	What is the <u>sound</u> for this letter?
Test letter name and sound	Continue holding up *o* Alphabet Card.	Test	What is the <u>name</u> of this letter? What is the <u>sound</u> for this letter?

Ongoing Assessment
If... children make an error, **then...** tell them the letter name or sound, and repeat the test.

	Give individual turns on letter name and sound.		
Model tracing o	Hold up the *o* Alphabet Card. Model how to trace *o*.	Model	Watch. I'll trace the letter *o*. Distribute *o* Letter Cards. **Now you trace the letter *o* three times with your finger. Say /ooo/ each time you trace the letter.**

Ongoing Assessment
If... children make an error, **then...** put your hand over their hand and guide them to trace the letter. Then have the children try to trace the letter on their own. Repeat as necessary.

Activity 2 Isolate Initial Sound

Does It Begin with /o/?

Objective: Children isolate initial /o/.

Time: 4–5 minutes

	To Do		**To Say**
Model picture names	Place Picture Choice 32-1 on the table. Point to *lips*.	Model	**This is *lips*. What is this?** Have children repeat. Continue with *otter, sock; foot, dime, octopus*. Test children on the picture names. Point to each picture again and ask: **What is this?**
Introduce the game Does It Begin with /o/?	Practice production of the target sound.		**We're going to play a game. I'll show you three pictures. You'll need to find the one that has the first sound /ooo/.** **Let's say /ooo/. Remember, when you say /ooo/, your mouth is open and your jaw drops. Put your hand under your chin and say /ooo/. See, your mouth opened and your jaw dropped.**
Model the game	Model two examples.	Model	**My turn. I'll show you how to play the game.** Display Picture Choice 32-1. Cover the bottom picture row. Point to each picture in the top row and say: **This is *lips, otter, sock*. Otter has the first sound /ooo/.** Exaggerate the first sound and then say: **/ooo/, *otter*.** Cover the top picture row and model another example with *foot, dime, octopus*.
Play the game to test knowledge of /o/	Complete the activity with Picture Choices 32-2 and 32-3, covering each picture row not in use. The pictures are *lamb, doll, olive; ox, seal, log; octopus, fish, sick; leg, soap, otter*.	Test	Point to each of the three pictures in a row and ask: **What is this? Which picture has the first sound /ooo/?** Confirm correct responses and prompt sound production. For example: **Yes, *olive* has the first sound /ooo/. Let's say /ooo/. Remember, when you say /ooo/, your mouth is open and your jaw drops. Put your hand under your chin and say /ooo/. See, your mouth opened and your jaw dropped: *olive*.**

Ongoing Assessment

If...children make incorrect responses,	**then...** model the correct answer, review the sound production cue, have children repeat the correct answer, and go back to the example a second time.

Activity **3** Identify Final Sound

Last Sounds Freeze Game

Objective: Children identify the final sound in words and locate position on a 3-Square Strip.

Time: 4–5 minutes

	To Do	To Say
Introduce and model the game Last Sounds Freeze	Arrange the picture cards in a pile. Give each child a 3-Square Strip. Place the *mop* Picture Card on the table.	**Model** **This is *mop*. Watch. I'll say the sounds in *mop* and point to a square as I say each sound: /mmm/ /ooo/ /p/. Listen again. I'll say the sounds in *mop* and point to a square as I say each sound. When I say "freeze," I'll keep my finger on the box I'm touching.** Say the word: **/mmm/ /ooo/ /p/. Freeze!** Keep your finger on the last box on the card. **I'm touching the last sound in *mop*: /p/.**
Play the game to test knowledge of final sounds	Display the *cat* Picture Card.	**Test** **Your turn. I will say the sounds in *cat*. You will point to a square as I say each sound. Listen carefully. When I say "freeze," keep your finger on the box you are touching. Here we go: /k/ /aaa/ /t/. Freeze!** Children should follow your lead, keeping their fingers on the last box of the strip. **You're touching the last sound in *cat*: /t/. Everyone, say the last sound in *cat* with me: /t/.** Repeat with *cup, bat, red*.

Reintroduce o/o/; Grab Bag Game
Objective: Children practice letter name and sound: o/o/.   Time: 4–5 minutes

	To Do	**To Say**	
Introduce letter name	Hold up the *o* Alphabet Card.	Model	**The <u>name</u> of this letter is o.**
		Lead	**Say the <u>name</u> of this letter with me: o.**
		Test	**What is the <u>name</u> of this letter?**
Introduce letter sound	Continue holding up the *o* Alphabet Card.	Model	**The <u>sound</u> for this letter is /ooo/. When you say /ooo/, your mouth is open and your jaw drops. Open your mouth and say /ooo/.**
		Lead	**Say the <u>sound</u> with me: /ooo/.**
		Test	**What is the <u>sound</u> for this letter?**
Test letter name and sound	Continue holding up the *o* Alphabet Card.	Test	**What is the <u>name</u> of this letter? What is the <u>sound</u> for this letter?**

Ongoing Assessment

If... children make an error,   **then...** tell them the letter name or sound, have them repeat the name or sound, and return to the letter a second time.

Continue holding up the *o* Alphabet Card.   Ask individuals: **What is the <u>name</u> of this letter? What is the <u>sound</u> for this letter?**

Play the game Grab Bag with *a, c, d, f, l, o, s, t*	Place the letter cards into a brown paper bag. Have a child pull out a letter from the bag and hand it to you. Hold up the letter.	Test the group: **What is the <u>name</u> of this letter? What is the <u>sound</u> for this letter?** If the group answers correctly, place the letter card in a pile on the table. Continue playing until all the cards have been removed from the bag. If time permits, provide individual turns.

Ongoing Assessment

If... children make an error,   **then...** tell them the name or sound of the letter and have them repeat it. Then place the letter card back in the bag.

Activity 5 Writer's Warm-Up

Introduce o

Objective: Children trace and write o and review writing
a, s, d, t, l, and *c.*

Time: 2–3 minutes

	To Do	**To Say**	
Review letter name and sound	Hold up the *o* Tracing Card.	**What is the <u>name</u> of this letter? What is the <u>sound</u> for this letter?**	
Model tracing *o*	Continue holding up the *o* Tracing Card. Model tracing *o* with your finger. Distribute a Writer's Warm-Up to each child.	Model	**Watch as I trace the letter *o*.**
		Lead	**Watch as I trace the letter *o* again. Now you trace the first two letter *o*'s on your warm-up sheet with your finger. Use your pencil to trace the next two *o*'s.**
Model writing *o*	Hold up the lined side of the *o* Tracing Card.	Model	**Watch as I write the letter *o*. I start at the dot and write the letter.**
		Lead	**Now you write two letter *o*'s. Start at the dot like I did. Write carefully.**

Ongoing Assessment

If...children make an error,	then... have them write the letter again. If needed, put your hand over their hand and guide them to write the letter. Then have them write the letter on their own. Repeat as necessary.

Test writing *o*	Hold up the lined side of the *o* Tracing Card. Model writing *o* again.	Have children cover the letters they traced and wrote. Have them write the letter *o* two times from memory. Then have them uncover their papers and compare the letters. **Do your letters look the same? Circle your best letter.**
Review *a, s, d, t, l, c*		**Trace *a*. Now write *a* with your pencil.** Continue this procedure for *s, d, t, l, c.*

Ongoing Assessment

If...children make an error,	then... use the tracing card to model tracing the letter. Ask them to write the letter again. If needed, guide the writing of the letter. Then have children try to write the letter on their own. Repeat as necessary.

Activity **6** Identify Final Sound

Match a Picture's Last Sound: /l/, /p/

Objective: Children connect final sound to letter: l/l/, p/p/.   Time: 2–3 minutes

	To Do		**To Say**
Introduce the activity	Gather the picture cards and letter cards.		**You're going to choose the letter that goes with the last sound of some pictures.**
Model the activity	Place the *bell* Picture Card on the table. Place the *l* and *f* Letter Cards under the picture.	Model	**This is *bell*. The last sound in *bell* is /lll/.** **I'm going to choose the letter that matches this picture's last sound.** Point to the correct letter: ***l* is the letter for /lll/ like the /lll/ in *bell*.**
Test knowledge of final sound	Display the *mop* Picture Card. Place the *c* and *p* Letter Cards on the table.	Test	**This is *mop*. What is this? The last sound in *mop* is /p/. What is the last sound in *mop*? That's right; /p/ is the last sound in *mop*. Your turn. Choose the letter that matches this picture's last sound. Think. Which letter has the same sound as the /p/ in *mop*? Do you think you know?** Call on a child to point to the correct letter. **What's the <u>name</u> of the letter you pointed to? What is the <u>sound</u> for this letter? That's right; *p* is for /p/ like the /p/ in *mop*. Everyone, what's the <u>name</u> of this letter? What's the <u>sound</u> for this letter?** Continue with at least three more examples.

Ongoing Assessment

If . . . children make an error,	**then** . . . model the answer, have them repeat it, and return to the picture card a second time.

Activity Identify Final Sound

Tic-Tac-Toe: Final Sounds /l/, /d/, /s/, /t/, /k/, /f/, /p/, /m/

Objective: Children connect final sound to letter.   Time: 6–8 minutes

	To Do		**To Say**
Introduce the game	Distribute a Tic-Tac-Toe to each child.		**We're going to play Tic-Tac-Toe. When I say a word, you will make an *x* over the letter that goes with the word's last sound. Let's see if we can cross out three letters in a row to get Tic-Tac-Toe!** Show children how they can get three letters in a row across and down.
Model the game	Model one example.	Model	**Let's do one together on the first Tic-Tac-Toe. The first word is *mess*. The last sound in *mess* is /sss/. I'm going to make an *x* over the letter for the same sound as the /sss/ in *mess*.** Make an *x* over one of the letter *s*'s on your Tic-Tac-Toe. **Now you cross out a letter for the same sound as the /sss/ in *mess*. That's right, *s* is for /sss/ like the /sss/ in *mess*.**
Play the game to test final /l/, /d/, /s/, /t/, /k/, /f/, /p/, /m/	Play three games. For each game, dictate words from the Word Bank in the order given.	Test	**The next word is *mad*. What is the last sound in *mad*? That's right, /d/ is the last sound in *mad*. Now make an *x* over the letter that has the same sound as the /d/ in *mad*. Everyone, what's the <u>name</u> of the letter you crossed out? What is the <u>sound</u> for that letter?** Continue playing until someone wins. Then play the second and third games.

Word Bank

Square 1: mess, mad, moss, mall, mop, mom

Square 2: pass, pet, pit, puff, pop, pull

Square 3: dot, dim, dad, doll, doughnut, dip, duck

Ongoing Assessment

If...children make an error,	then...point to the correct letter and model the letter sound. Have children repeat the sound and cross out the correct letter.

Writing/Spelling

New Sound /o/
Review Sounds /m/, /p/, /k/, /t/, /s/, /d/, /a/
Key Phonologic Skill Isolate Initial and Final Sounds

LESSON 33

Phonological Awareness and Alphabetic Understanding

Activity	Materials		Time
1. Alphabetic Introduce *o*/o/	Alphabet Card: *o*	Letter Card: *o* (one per child)	1–2 minutes
2. Integrated Phonologic/Alphabetic Does It Begin with /o/?	Picture Choices: 33-1, 33-2, 33-3 *Teacher Resource Package 1* Alphabet Card: *o*		4–5 minutes
3. Phonologic Last Sounds Freeze Game	Picture Cards: *mud, cap, cat, map, bed*	3-Square Strip (one per child)	4–5 minutes
4. Alphabetic Reintroduce *o*/o/; Letters Board Game	Alphabet Card: *o* Letter Cards: *m, p, c, t, s, d, a, o* Game Board 3	markers (one per child/ not provided) number cube (not provided)	4–5 minutes

Writing and Spelling

Activity	Materials		Time
5. Writer's Warm-Up Memory Review: *o, a, l, d, s, t*	Tracing Cards: *o, a, l, d, s, t* Write-On/Wipe-Off Cards	markers (one per child/ not provided)	2–3 minutes
6. Integrated Phonologic/Alphabetic Match a Picture's Last Sound: /t/, /s/	Picture Cards: *net, quilt, cat, goat, mouse, grapes, octopus, house*	Letter Cards: *a, t, s, p, c*	2–3 minutes
New 7. Phonologic/Spelling Letter Race: Final *l, d, t, p*	Letter Race (one per child) *Student Activity Book 1, p. 58*		6–8 minutes

Activity 1 Introduce Letter Name and Sound

Introduce o/o/

Objective: Children learn and trace o/o/.

Time: 1–2 minutes

	To Do	**To Say**	
Introduce letter name	Hold up the *o* Alphabet Card.	**Model**	**The <u>name</u> of this letter is o.**
		Lead	**Say the <u>name</u> with me.**
		Test	**What is the <u>name</u> of this letter?**
Introduce letter sound	Continue holding up the *o* Alphabet Card.	**Model**	**The <u>sound</u> for this letter is /ooo/. When you say /ooo/, your mouth is open and your jaw drops. Put your hand under your chin and say /ooo/. See, your mouth opened and your jaw dropped.**
		Lead	**Say the <u>sound</u> with me: /ooo/.**
		Test	**What is the <u>sound</u> for this letter?**
Test letter name and sound	Continue holding up the *o* Alphabet Card.	**Test**	**What is the <u>name</u> of this letter? What is the <u>sound</u> for this letter?**

Ongoing Assessment

If...children make an error,   then...tell them the letter name or sound, and repeat the test.

Model tracing o	Hold up the *o* Alphabet Card. Model how to trace *o*.	**Model**	**Watch. I'll trace the letter o.**
			Distribute *o* Letter Cards. **Now you trace the letter o three times with your finger. Say /ooo/ each time you trace the letter.**

Ongoing Assessment

If...children make an error,   then...put your hand over their hand and guide them to trace the letter. Then have the children try to trace the letter on their own. Repeat as necessary.

Phonological Awareness/Alphabetic Understanding

Does It Begin with /o/?

Objective: Children isolate initial /o/ and connect sound to letter.

Time: 4–5 minutes

	To Do		**To Say**	
Model picture names	Place Picture Choice 33-1 on the table. Point to *otter*.	**Model**	**This is *otter*. What is this?** Repeat for the remaining pictures (*leaf, sun; lid, teeth, olive*). Then test children on all the picture names. Point to each picture and ask: **What is this?**	
Introduce the game Does It Begin with /o/?			**We're going to play a game. I'll show you a letter and three pictures. You'll need to find the picture that has the same first sound as the letter.**	
Model the game	Hold up the *o* Alphabet Card.	**Model**	**The name of this letter is *o*. The sound for this letter is /ooo/. Remember, when you say /ooo/, your mouth is open and your jaw drops. Open your mouth and say /ooo/.**	
		Test	**What is the sound for this letter?**	
		Model	**My turn. I'll show you how to play the game.** Display Picture Choice 33-1. Cover the bottom picture row. Point to each picture in the top row and say: **This is otter, leaf, sun. Otter has the first sound /ooo/.** Exaggerate the first sound and then say: **/ooo/, otter.** Cover the top picture row and model another example with *lid, teeth, olive.*	
Play the game to test knowledge of /o/	Complete the activity with Picture Choices 33-2 and 33-3, covering each picture row not in use. The pictures are *dive, tag, ox; antlers, octopus, sit; alligator, olive, sandwich; ox, tape, light.*	**Test**	Point to each of the three pictures in a row and ask: **What is this? Which picture has the first sound /ooo/?** Confirm correct responses and prompt sound production. For example: **Yes, ox has the first sound /ooo/. Let's say /ooo/. Remember, when you say /ooo/, your mouth is open and your jaw drops. Put your hand under your chin and say /ooo/. See, your mouth opened and your jaw dropped: ox.**	

Ongoing Assessment

If...children make incorrect responses,	**then**...model the correct answer, review the sound production cue, have children repeat the correct answer, and go back to the example a second time.

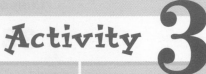

Last Sounds Freeze Game

Objective: Children identify the final sound in words and locate position on a 3-Square Strip.

Time: 4–5 minutes

	To Do	**To Say**	
Introduce and model the game Last Sounds Freeze	Arrange the picture cards in a pile. Give each child a 3-Square Strip. Place the *mud* Picture Card on the table.	**Model**	**This is *mud*. Watch. I'll say the sounds in *mud* and point to a square as I say each sound: /mmm/ /uuu/ /d/. Listen again. I'll say the sounds in *mud* and point to a square as I say each sound. When I say "freeze," I'll keep my finger on the box I'm touching.** Say the word: **/mmm/ /uuu/ /d/. Freeze!** Keep your finger on the last box on the card. **I'm touching the last sound in *mud*: /d/.**
Play the game to test final sounds	Use picture cards: *cap, cat, map, bed.*	**Test**	**Your turn.** Place the *cap* Picture Card on the table. **I will say the sounds in *cap*. You will point to a square as I say each sound. Listen carefully. When I say "freeze," keep your finger on the box you are touching. Here we go: /k/ /aaa/ /p/. Freeze!** Children should follow your lead, keeping their fingers on the last box of the strip. **You're touching the last sound in *cap*: /p/. Everyone, say the last sound in *cap* with me: /p/.** Repeat with *cat, map, bed.*

Activity 4 Reintroduce Letter Name and Sound

Reintroduce o/o/; Letters Board Game

Objective: Children practice letter name and
sound: o/o/.

Time: 4–5 minutes

	To Do	**To Say**	
Introduce letter name	Hold up the *o* Alphabet Card.	Model	**The <u>name</u> of this letter is o.**
		Lead	**Say the <u>name</u> of this letter with me: o.**
		Test	**What is the <u>name</u> of this letter?**
Introduce letter sound	Continue holding up the *o* Alphabet Card.	Model	**The <u>sound</u> for this letter is /ooo/. When you say /ooo/, your mouth is open and your jaw drops. Open your mouth and say /ooo/.**
		Lead	**Say the <u>sound</u> with me: /ooo/.**
		Test	**What is the <u>sound</u> for this letter?**
Test letter name and sound	Continue holding up the *o* Alphabet Card.	Test	**What is the <u>name</u> of this letter? What is the <u>sound</u> for this letter?** First test the group. Then give individual turns.

Ongoing Assessment

If...children make an error,	then...tell them the letter name or sound, have them repeat the name or sound, and return to the letter a second time.

Introduce the Letters Board Game	Mix up the letter cards. Place the cards in a pile. Gather the game board, a marker for each child, and a number cube.	Lead	**We're going to play a game. When it's your turn, you will pick the top card from the pile of letter cards and name the letter and the sound. If you're right, you will roll the number cube and move your marker that many spaces.**
Play the game to test m/m/, p/p/, c/k/, t/t/, s/s/, d/d/, a/a/, o/o/	Give individual turns. Ask each child about the letter he or she picked.		**What is the <u>name</u> of the letter? What is the <u>sound</u> for this letter?** If correct, the child moves the marker the number of spaces on the number cube. Play the game until one child reaches the finish line or until time runs out. Play another round if time permits.

Ongoing Assessment

If...a child makes an error,	then...tell the letter name or sound, have everyone repeat it, and place the card at the bottom of the pile. The child does not move his or her marker.

273

Phonological Awareness/Alphabetic Understanding

Activity 5 Writer's Warm-Up

Memory Review: o, a, l, d, s, t

Objective: Children write review letters from memory:
o, a, l, d, s, t.

Time: 2–3 minutes

	To Do	To Say	
Review letter names	Gather the *o, a, l, d, s,* and *t* Tracing Cards. Hold them up, one at a time. Review the letter names.		**What is the <u>name</u> of this letter?**
Model the activity	Distribute Write-On/Wipe-Off Cards and markers to children. Model one example.	Model	**My turn. I'll show you how this activity works. The first letter is *o*. I'll write the letter *o* on my card.**
Test review letters: *o, a, l, d, s, t*	Test children on the remaining letters.	Test	**Your turn. The next letter is *a*. Write the letter *a* on your card. Everyone, what's the <u>name</u> of the letter you wrote? Good. Now erase your card. Here's the next letter.** Continue with the remaining letters. Dictate each letter at least twice or as time allows.

Ongoing Assessment

If... children write the wrong letter or don't remember a letter,

then... show them the tracing card, model tracing the letter, and say the letter name.

Activity **6** Identify Final Sound

Match a Picture's Last Sound: /t/, /s/

Objective: Children connect final sound to letter: *t*/t/, *s*/s/.   Time: 2–3 minutes

	To Do		**To Say**
Introduce the activity	Gather the picture cards and letter cards.		**You're going to choose the letter that goes with the last sound of some pictures.**
Model the activity	Place the *net* Picture Card on the table. Place the *s* and *t* Letter Cards under the picture.	Model	**This is *net*. The last sound in *net* is /t/.** **I'm going to choose the letter that matches this picture's last sound.** Point to the correct letter: ***t* is the letter for /t/ like the /t/ in *net*.**
Test knowledge of final sound	Display the *quilt* Picture Card. Place the *t* and *s* Letter Cards on the table.	Test	**This is *quilt*. What is this? The last sound in *quilt* is /t/. What is the last sound in *quilt*? That's right; /t/ is the last sound in *quilt*. Your turn. Choose the letter that matches this picture's last sound. Think. Which letter has the same sound as the /t/ in *quilt*? Do you think you know?** Call on a child to point to the correct letter. **What's the <u>name</u> of the letter you pointed to? What is the <u>sound</u> for this letter? That's right; *t* is the letter for /t/ like the /t/ in *quilt*. Everyone, what's the <u>name</u> of this letter? What's the <u>sound</u> for this letter?** Continue with at least three more examples.

Ongoing Assessment

If . . . children make an error,	**then** . . . model the answer, have them repeat it, and return to the picture card a second time.

Activity 7 — Identify Final Sound

Letter Race: Final l, d, t, p

Objective: Children connect final sound to letter.

Time: 6–8 minutes

	To Do	**To Say**
Practice *l*/l/, *d*/d/, *t*/t/, and *p*/p/	Point to each letter on the Letter Race and review the letter name and sound.	**What is the <u>name</u> of this letter? What is the <u>sound</u> for this letter?**
Introduce the game Letter Race	Distribute a Letter Race to each child.	**We're going to have a letter race. I'm going to tell you a word and you're going to write the letter for its last sound on the racetrack. Which letter do you think will win?**
Model the game	Model the activity.	**Model** **Let's do one together. The first word is *seal*. The last sound in *seal* is /lll/. I'm going to write the letter for the same sound as the /lll/ in *seal* on the racetrack. Watch where I write it. Now you write the letter for /lll/ on the racetrack. Start at the dot and write the letter. That's right; *l* is for /lll/ like the /lll/ in *seal*.**
Play the game to test knowledge of /l/, /d/, /t/, /p/	Continue the game with the words in the Word Bank until one letter wins. Vary the order of the words.	**Test** **The next word is *soap*. What is the last sound in *soap*? That's right, /p/ is the last sound in *soap*. Now find the /p/ racetrack and write the letter for the same sound as the /p/ in *soap*. Everyone, what's the <u>name</u> of the letter you wrote? What is the <u>sound</u> for that letter?**

Word Bank

seed	sit	spill	sad
shout	sleep	special	shade
slot	soup	soil	sled
shut	step		

Ongoing Assessment

If… children make an error,	**then…** tell them the letter name and sound. Have children repeat the letter name and sound and write the correct letter.

Review Sounds /m/, /p/, /f/, /s/, /d/, /l/, /a/, /o/

Key Phonologic Skill Isolate Initial and Final Sounds

Phonological Awareness and Alphabetic Understanding

Activity	Materials	Time
1. Alphabetic Review o/o/	Alphabet Card: o	1–2 minutes
New **2. Phonologic** Initial Sound/Final Sound Discrimination	Picture Cards: *mop, duck, lamb, bed, ant, sock* 3-Square Strip	4–5 minutes
3. Integrated Phonologic/Alphabetic Sound Match with Letter Tiles: /o/, /a/, /d/, /l/	Letter Tiles: *o, a, d, l* (one of each per child) Sound Match Cards: 34a–34e (one card per child) Teacher Resource Package 1 Sound Production Cue Card	4–5 minutes
4. Integrated Phonologic/Alphabetic Review o/o/; Pictures to Letters Game	Alphabet Card: *o* Picture Cards: *ant, doll, fan, leg, mop, ox, pen* Sound Production Cue Card Letter Cards: *a, f, d, l, m, o, p, s* (one of each per child) paper bag (not provided)	4–5 minutes

Writing and Spelling

Activity	Materials	Time
5. Writer's Warm-Up Review *o, a, l, d, s, t, c, f, p, m*	Writer's Warm-Up (one per child) Student Activity Book 1, p. 59	2–3 minutes
6. Integrated Phonologic/Alphabetic Match a Picture's Last Sound: /d/, /f/	Picture Cards: *mud, leaf, red, bed, loaf, roof* Letter Cards: *d, f, m, o, l*	2–3 minutes
7. Phonologic/Spelling Final Sounds Dictation: *d, s, t, f, m*	Alphabet Cards: *d, s, t, f, m* Write-On/Wipe-Off Cards (one per child) markers (one per child/not provided)	6–8 minutes

Activity 1 — Review Letter Name and Sound

Review o/o/

Objective: Children identify letter name and sound.

Time: 1–2 minutes

	To Do	**To Say**
Test letter name and sound	Hold up the *o* Alphabet Card. Test the group.	**Test** **What is the <u>name</u> of this letter? What is the <u>sound</u> for this letter?**

Ongoing Assessment

If...children make an error,	then...tell them the letter name or sound, have them repeat the name or sound, and return to the letter a second time.

	To Do	**To Say**
	Continue holding up the *o* Alphabet Card. Give individual turns.	**Test** **What is the <u>name</u> of this letter? What is the <u>sound</u> for this letter?**

Phonological Awareness/Alphabetic Understanding

Identify Initial and Final Sounds

New

Initial Sound/Final Sound Discrimination

Objective: Children use a 3-Square Strip to identify initial and final sounds.

Time: 4–5 minutes

	To Do		**To Say**	
Introduce and model the activity	Display the 3-Square Strip so all children can see it. Place the *mop* Picture Card on the table.	**Model**	**Watch and listen. I'll say the sounds in *mop* and point to a square as I say each sound: /mmm/ /ooo/ /p/.** Point to a square for each sound. **We have a new game today. I'll say the sounds in *mop* and point to a square as I say each sound. Then I'll touch a square, and you'll say which sound I am touching. Watch: /mmm/ /ooo/ /p/.** Go back and touch the first box on the strip: **/mmm/; the first sound in *mop* is /mmm/.** Model the activity again with *mop*. Touch the last box on the strip: **/p/; the last sound in *mop* is /p/.**	
Test initial and final sounds	Place the *duck* Picture Card on the table. Have the 3-Square Strip ready.	**Test**	**Now let's do some together. I'll say the sounds in *duck*: /d/ /uuu/ /k/.** Point to a square as you say each sound. **Listen again. I'll say the sounds in *duck* and point to a square as I say each sound. Then I'll touch a square, and you'll say the sound I am touching. Watch: /d/ /uuu/ /k/.** Go back and touch the last box on the strip. **Everybody, what sound am I touching?** Say the sound with children: **/k/.** Confirm the correct answer: **Good. The last sound in *duck* is /k/.** Repeat with *lamb, bed, ant, sock*. Alternate touching the first and last box on the strip.	

 **Activity** **Identify Initial Sound**

Sound Match with Letter Tiles:
/o/, /a/, /d/, /l/

Objective: Children isolate initial sound and connect to letter.   Time: 4–5 minutes

	To Do	**To Say**
Introduce the game Sound Match with Letter Tiles	Gather the Sound Match cards and letter tiles.	**We're going to play Sound Match with Letter Tiles. I'll say a sound. You'll find the letter tile for that sound and place it on a picture that has that first sound. Everyone has a different Sound Match card, so you won't know who will win.**
Model the game	Place Sound Match Card 34c on the table.	**Model** **It's my turn to show you how to play Sound Match with Letter Tiles. Listen: /ooo/. I'll find the letter for the sound /ooo/.** Hold up the *o* Letter Tile. **O is the letter for the sound /ooo/. Everybody, what is the sound for the letter o? Now I'll find a picture on my Sound Match card that has the first sound /ooo/.** Name the pictures on your Sound Match card. Then have children name each picture with you. Model how to choose the correct picture: **My turn. I'll find the picture that has the first sound /ooo/.** Point to the letter tile for *o*. Tell the picture that begins with /ooo/: **ox. Ox has the first sound /ooo/. /ooo/, ox. I'll place my o Letter Tile on ox because ox has the first sound /ooo/.** Model one more example, using target sound /lll/. Then clear off your Sound Match card and tell children it's their turn to play.
Play the game to test initial sounds: /o/, /a/, /d/, /l/	Distribute to each child a Sound Match card and one of each letter tile: *o, a, d, l.*	**Test** **Listen: /d/. Find the letter tile for the sound /d/ and hold it up. Yes, d is the letter for the sound /d/. What is the sound for the letter d?**

Ongoing Assessment

If... children hold up the wrong letter tile,	then... model the correct answer. Have children hold up the correct letter tile. Review the sound production cue using the Sound Production Cue Card.

280

To Do

To Say

Ask children to whisper the name of each picture to themselves and to raise their hand if they don't know one. (The picture names are given below.) **Now find a picture with the first sound /d/ and place your _d_ Letter Tile on it.** Point to the letter tile for _d_. Go around the table and have children state the picture they placed the letter tile on. Confirm correct responses and have the whole group repeat each word. For example: **Yes, _duck_ has the first sound /d/. Everybody, say /d/, _duck_.**

Ongoing Assessment

If…children answer incorrectly,	then…model the correct answer, review the sound production cue using the Sound Production Cue Card, and have children repeat the correct answer.

Repeat the above procedures with target sounds /ooo/, /lll/, and /aaa/. Remind children to say "Sound Match!" as soon as they fill up a whole row or column. When a child wins, have the children clear off their cards. Collect the cards, mix them, and redistribute them. This time, start with the target sound /lll/ and then continue with /aaa/, /d/, and /ooo/.

Sound Match Picture Names
34a: _tail, saw, fin; octopus, apple, doughnut; moon, lid, cane_
34b: _fork, ant, tire; sick, log, olive; coat, desk, pool_
34c: _sit, man, alligator; foot, cone, tape; deer, lock, ox_
34d: _light, doughnut, cut; apple, peas, soap; otter, fin, tie_
34e: _pin, seal, doll; leaf, toe, ox; can, fire, ant_

Phonological Awareness/Alphabetic Understanding

Review o/o/;
Pictures to Letters Game

Objective: Children practice letter name and sound: o/o/.   Time: 4–5 minutes

	To Do		**To Say**	
Review o/o/	Hold up the *o* Alphabet Card. Give individual turns on letter name and sound.	**Test**	**What is the <u>name</u> of this letter? What is the <u>sound</u> for this letter?**	

Ongoing Assessment

If...children make an error,	then...tell them the letter name or sound, have them repeat the name or sound, and return to the letter a second time.

Introduce the game Pictures to Letters	Place the picture cards in a bag. Give each child a letter card for *m, p, f, s, d, l, a, o.*	**We're going to play a game with these letters. I'll pull a picture from the bag. Then you'll say the first sound of the picture and find the letter for that sound. When I say "One, two, three, go!" you'll hold up your letter card. Remember to wait until I say "go" to hold up your letter card.**
Model the game	Model how to play the game.	**Model** **My turn. I'll show you how to play the game.** Line up a set of letter cards on the table in front of you. Pull a picture from the bag. For example, say: **This is mop. What is this? I'll say the first sound in mop: /mmm/. Say the first sound in mop. Yes, /mmm/. Put your lips together and say /mmm/, mop. I'll find the letter for /mmm/.** Look at your letter cards. **One, two, three, go!** Hold up your *m* Letter Card. **See, I found m for the /mmm/ in mop.** Return your *m* Letter Card to the table. Set the *mop* Picture Card next to your *m* Letter Card.

	To Do	To Say

Play the game to test knowledge of /m/, /p/, /f/, /s/, /d/, /l/, /a/, /o/

Test

Your turn to play the game. Pull a picture from the bag. For example, say: **This is octopus. What is this? Say the first sound in octopus. Yes, /ooo/. Remember, when you say /ooo/ your mouth is open and your jaw drops. Open your mouth and say /ooo/, octopus.** Note: Use the Sound Production Cue Card to prompt sound production of the various initial sounds.

Ongoing Assessment

If... children cannot correctly identify the first sound of a picture,

then... tell them the first sound and have them repeat it. Prompt children on sound production using the Sound Production Cue Card.

Look for the letter that's for /ooo/. One, two, three, go! Everybody, what letter are you holding up? Yes, o because o is the letter for /ooo/ like the /ooo/ in octopus. Now place your o Letter Card back on the table. Place the picture of *octopus* by your *o* Letter Card. Continue until all picture cards have been pulled from the bag. Then give individual turns.

Ongoing Assessment

If... children hold up the wrong letter card,

then... repeat the sound and hold up the correct letter card. Have children find their correct letter card, hold it up, and say the sound with you.

Phonological Awareness/Alphabetic Understanding

Activity 5 — Writer's Warm-Up

Review: o, a, l, d, s, t, c, f, p, m
Objective: Children write review letters.

Time: 2–3 minutes

	To Do	**To Say**
Review  **letter names**	Give each child a Writer's Warm-Up.	**Place your finger on the first letter. What is the <u>name</u> of this letter?** Continue the procedure for all the letters on the Writer's Warm-Up.
Write letters	Have children trace and write each review letter one time.	**Trace the first letter with your finger. Now write the letter with your pencil. Remember to begin at the dot.** Continue the procedure for all the letters on the Writer's Warm-Up. Then say: **Now look at all the letters you wrote and circle your best ones.**

Ongoing Assessment

If...children make an error,	**then**...have them write the letter again. If they still need assistance, place your hand over their hand and guide them to write the letter. Then have children write the letter on their own. Repeat this procedure if necessary.

  **Connect Sound to Letter**

Match a Picture's Last Sound: /d/, /f/

Objective: Children connect final sound to letter: d/d/, f/f/.   Time: 2–3 minutes

	To Do	To Say	
Introduce the activity	Gather the picture cards and letter cards.	**You're going to choose the letter that goes with the last sound of some pictures.**	
Model the activity	Place the *mud* Picture Card on the table. Place the *d* and *f* Letter Cards under the picture.	Model	**This is *mud*. The last sound in *mud* is /d/.** **I'm going to choose the letter that matches this picture's last sound.** Point to the correct letter: ***d* is the letter for /d/ like the /d/ in *mud*.**
Test knowledge of final sound	Display the *leaf* Picture Card. Place the *f* and *m* Letter Cards on the table.	Model	**This is *leaf*. What is this? The last sound in *leaf* is /fff/. What is the last sound in *leaf*? That's right; /fff/ is the last sound in *leaf*. Your turn. Choose the letter that matches this picture's last sound. Which letter has the same sound as the /fff/ in *leaf*? Do you know?** Call on a child to point to the correct letter. **What's the <u>name</u> of the letter you pointed to? What is the <u>sound</u> for that letter? That's right; *f* is the letter for /fff/ like the /fff/ in *leaf*. Everyone, what's the <u>name</u> of this letter? What's the <u>sound</u> for this letter?** Continue with at least three more examples.

Ongoing Assessment

If...children make an error,	then...model the answer, have them repeat it, and return to the picture card a second time.

Activity **7** Connect Sound to Letter

Final Sounds Dictation: d, s, t, f, m

Objective: Children connect final sound to letter.

Time: 6–8 minutes

	To Do	**To Say**
Review letter names and sounds	Hold up each Alphabet Card, one at a time.	**What's the <u>name</u> of this letter? What's the <u>sound</u> for this letter?**
Introduce the activity	Distribute a Write-On/Wipe-Off Card and marker to each child.	**I'm going to say a word. You are going to write the letter for the last sound in the word on your Write-On/ Wipe-Off Card.**
Model the activity	Use a Write-On/ Wipe-Off Card and marker.	**Model** **My turn. The first word is** *sad*. **The last sound in** *sad* **is /d/. Now I'll write the letter that has the same sound as the /d/ in** *sad*. Write the letter on your card: ***d* is the letter for the sound /d/. It's your turn to write the letter for the sound /d/. That's right;** *d* **is the letter for the sound /d/ like the /d/ in** *sad*.
Test children on final sounds	For each final sound, dictate at least two words from the Word Bank. Vary the order.	**Test** **The next word is** *sniff*. **What's the last sound in** *sniff*? **That's right; /fff/ is the last sound in** *sniff*. **Now write the letter that has the same sound as the /fff/ in** *sniff*. Reinforce the group on the letter name and sound: **Everyone, what's the <u>name</u> of the letter you wrote? What's the <u>sound</u> for the letter?**

Word Bank

sit	stuff	Sam	sled	snakes
salt	scarf	stem	salad	skates
spot	stiff	same	seed	socks
seat		slim		skirts

Ongoing Assessment

If...children write the wrong letter or don't remember a letter,   **then**...show them the correct alphabet card, model tracing the letter, and say the letter sound.

Writing/Spelling

Review Sounds /m/, /p/, /f/, /k/, /t/, /l/, /a/, /o/
Key Phonologic Skills Isolate Initial and Final Sounds

Phonological Awareness and Alphabetic Understanding

Activity	Materials		Time
1. Alphabetic Review o/o/	Alphabet Card: o		1–2 minutes
2. Phonologic Initial Sound/Final Sound Discrimination	3-Square Strip	Picture Cards: *ant, pot, cap, mat, cat, top, map, lock, tape*	4–5 minutes
New **3. Phonologic** If You Land on Me, Say My First Sound	Game Board 2 number cube (not provided)	game markers (one per child/not provided) Sound Production Cue Card	4–5 minutes
4. Alphabetic Review o/o/; Be the Teacher Game	Alphabet Cards: o, m, p, f, c, t, l, a		4–5 minutes

Writing and Spelling

Activity	Materials		Time
5. Writer's Warm-Up Review o, a, l, d, s, t, c, f, p, m	Writer's Warm-Up (one per child) Student Activity Book 1, p. 60 Tracing Cards: o, a, l, d, s, t, c, f, p, m		2–3 minutes
6. Integrated Phonologic/Alphabetic Match a Picture's Last Sound: /m/	Picture Cards: *jam, gum, worm, ham, dime, lamb, game*	Letter Cards: t, m, c, o, l	2–3 minutes
7. Phonologic/Spelling Tic-Tac-Toe: Final Sounds for l, d, s, t, f, p, m	Tic-Tac-Toe (one per child) Student Activity Book 1, p. 61		6–8 minutes

Activity 1 — Review Letter Name and Sound

Review o/o/

Objective: Children review letter name and sound: o/o/.

Time: 1–2 minutes

	To Do	**To Say**	
Review letter name and sound	Hold up the *o* Alphabet Card. Test the group.	**Test**	**What is the name of this letter? What is the sound for this letter?**

Ongoing Assessment

If...children make an error,   **then**...tell them the letter name or sound, have them repeat the name or sound, and return to the letter a second time.

	To Do	**To Say**	
	Give individual turns.	**Test**	**What is the name of this letter? What is the sound for this letter?**

Phonological Awareness/Alphabetic Understanding

Activity **2** Identify Initial and Final Sounds

Initial Sound/Final Sound Discrimination

Objective: Children use a 3-Square Strip to identify sounds.   Time: 4–5 minutes

	To Do		To Say
Introduce and model the activity	Display the 3-Square Strip so all children can see it. Place the *ant* Picture Card on the table.	Model	**Watch and listen. I'll say the sounds in *ant* and point to a square as I say each sound: /aaa/ /nnn/ /t/.** Point to a square for each sound. **I will say each sound and point to a square. Then I'll touch a square, and you'll say which sound I am touching. Watch: /aaa/ /nnn/ /t/.** Go back and touch the first box on the strip: **/aaa/; the first sound in *ant* is /aaa/.** Model the activity again with *pot.* Touch the last box on the strip: **/t/; the last sound in *pot* is /t/.**
Lead the activity	Place the *cap* Picture Card on the table. Display the 3-Square Strip.	Lead	**Now let's do some together. I'll say the sounds in *cap*: /k/ /aaa/ /p/.** Point to a square as you say a sound. **Listen again. I'll say the sounds in *cap* and point to a square as I say each sound. Then I'll touch a square, and you'll say the sound I am touching: /k/ /aaa/ /p/.** Go back and touch the last box on the card. **Everybody, what sound am I touching?** Say the sound with children: **/p/.** Confirm the correct answer: **Good. The last sound in *cap* is /p/.** Repeat with *mat.* This time touch the first box.
Test initial and final sounds	Place the *cat* Picture Card on the table. Display the 3-Square Strip.	Test	**Your turn. I'll say the sounds in *cat*: /k/ /aaa/ /t/.** Point to a square as you say each sound. **Listen again. I'll say the sounds in *cat* and point to a square as I say each sound. Then I'll touch a square and you'll tell me the sound I'm touching: /k/ /aaa/ /t/.** Point to the first box. **Everybody, what sound am I touching?** Confirm the correct response: **Good, the first sound in *cat* is /k/.** Repeat with *top, map, lock, tape.*

Activity **3** Isolate Initial Sound

If You Land on Me, Say My First Sound

Objective: Children isolate initial sounds.

Time: 4–5 minutes

	To Do	**To Say**	
Introduce the game	Display Game Board 2. Point to each picture on the game board and name it.	**This is *foot, mop, bed, cat, read, lid, pool, fire, sun, mitt, doughnut, boat, coat, leaf, ant, rake, mouse, tub.*** Have children repeat picture names after you.	
Model the game		**Model**	**I'll show you how to play the game. I'll roll the number cube and move my marker for as many dots as there are on the number cube. Next, I'll say the name of the picture I land on and then its first sound.** Example: ***Foot*; /fff/ is the first sound in *foot*.**
Play the game to test initial sounds	Give each child a game marker to place on *Start*.	**Test**	**Let's play!** Have children play the game until someone reaches the finish line.

Ongoing Assessment

If ... a child makes an error,	**then** ... model the correct answer and have the whole group repeat the answer. Prompt sound production using the Sound Production Cue Card. The child who made the error does not move his or her marker. The next child takes a turn.

This activity was modified from Blevins's (1977) *Phonemic Awareness Activities for Early Reading Progress.*

Activity 4 Review Letter Name and Sound

Review o/o/; Be the Teacher Game

Objective: Children practice letter name and sound: o/o/.   Time: 4–5 minutes

	To Do	**To Say**	
Review o/o/	Hold up the *o* Alphabet Card.	**Test**	**What is the name of this letter? What is the sound for this letter?**

> ### Ongoing Assessment
> **If**...children make an error,   **then**...tell them the letter name or sound, have them repeat the name or sound, and return to the letter a second time.

	To Do	
Introduce the game Be the Teacher with o/o/, m/m/, p/p/, f /f/, c/k/, t/t/, l/l/, a/a/	Choose a child to be the "teacher." Give the "teacher" the alphabet cards.	Tell the "teacher" to hold up the first alphabet card. Then prompt the "teacher" to ask: **What is the name of this letter? What is the sound for this letter?** Allow the group to respond to each question. If the group answers correctly, have the "teacher" place the alphabet card on the table.

> ### Ongoing Assessment
> **If**...the group makes an error,   **then**...prompt the "teacher" to tell the letter name or sound and place the alphabet card at the bottom of the pile.

Continue until all letters and sounds have been identified correctly. When the game is completed, have the "teacher" give individual turns.

Activity 5 Writer's Warm-Up

Review: o, a, l, d, s, t, c, f, p, m

Objective: Children write review letters.

Time: 2–3 minutes

	To Do	**To Say**
Review letter names	Give each child a Writer's Warm-Up.	**Place your finger on the first letter. What is the <u>name</u> of this letter?** Continue procedure for all the letters on the Writer's Warm-Up.
Trace and write letters	Have children trace and write each review letter one time.	**Trace the first letter with your finger. Now write the letter with your pencil. Remember to start on the dot.** Continue procedure for all the letters on the Writer's Warm-Up. (If necessary, use the tracing cards to model tracing and writing the letters.) Then say: **Now look at all the letters you wrote and circle your best ones.**

Ongoing Assessment

If...children make an error,

then...have them write the letter again. If they still need assistance, place your hand over their hand and guide them to write the letter. Then have children write the letter on their own. Repeat this procedure if necessary.

Writing/Spelling

Activity 6 Connect Sound to Letter

Match a Picture's Last Sound: /m/

Objective: Children connect final sound to letter: *m/m/*.   Time: 2–3 minutes

	To Do	**To Say**	
Introduce the activity	Gather the picture cards and letter cards.		**You're going to choose the letter that goes with the last sound of some pictures.**
Model the activity	Place the *jam* Picture Card on the table. Place the *t* and *m* Letter Cards under the picture.	Model	**This is *jam*. The last sound in *jam* is /mmm/.** **I'm going to choose the letter that matches this picture's last sound.** Point to the correct letter: **m is the letter for the sound /mmm/ like the /mmm/ in *jam*.**
Test knowledge of final sounds	Display the *gum* Picture Card. Place the *m* and *o* Letter Cards on the table.	Test	**This is *gum*. What is this? The last sound in *gum* is /mmm/. What is the last sound in *gum*? That's right; /mmm/ is the last sound in *gum*. Your turn. Choose the letter that matches this picture's last sound. Which letter has the same sound as the /mmm/ in *gum*? Do you know?** Call on a child to point to the correct letter. **What's the <u>name</u> of the letter you pointed to? What is the <u>sound</u> for that letter? That's right; m is the letter for /mmm/ like the /mmm/ in *gum*. Everyone, what's the <u>name</u> of this letter? What's the <u>sound</u> for this letter?** Continue with at least three more examples.

Ongoing Assessment

If...children make an error,	then...model the answer, have them repeat it, and return to the picture card a second time.

293

Writing/Spelling

Activity 7 Identify Final Sound

Tic-Tac-Toe: Final Sounds for
l, d, s, t, f, p, m

Objective: Children connect final sound to letter.

Time: 6–8 minutes

	To Do	To Say
Introduce the game	Distribute a Tic-Tac-Toe to each child.	**We're going to play Tic-Tac-Toe. When I say a word, you will make an *x* over the letter that goes with the word's last sound. Let's see if we can cross out three letters in a row to get Tic-Tac-Toe!** Show children how they can get three letters in a row across and down.
Model the game	Model one example.	**Model** **Let's do one together on the first Tic-Tac-Toe. The first word is *miss*. The last sound in *miss* is /sss/. I'm going to make an *x* over the letter for the same sound as the /sss/ in *miss*.** Mark an *x* over one of the letter *s*'s on your Tic-Tac-Toe. **Now you cross out the letter for the same sound as the /sss/ in *miss*. That's right; *s* is the letter for the sound /sss/ like the /sss/ in *miss*.**
Play the game to test knowledge of final *l, d, s, t, f, p, m*	Play three games. For each game, dictate words from the Word Bank in the order given.	**Test** **The next word is *mud*. What is the last sound in *mud*? That's right, /d/ is the last sound in *mud*. Now make an *x* over the letter for the sound /d/ like the /d/ in *mud*. Everyone, what's the <u>name</u> of the letter you crossed out? What is the <u>sound</u> for the letter?** Continue playing until someone wins. Then play the second and third games.

Word Bank

Square 1: miss, mud, mess, mail, map, mom

Square 2: pass, put, pot, puff, pop, pail

Square 3: dot, dime, did, dial, doughnut, drip |

Ongoing Assessment

If... children make an error,	then... point to the correct letter and model the letter sound. Have children repeat the sound and cross out the correct letter.

LESSON 36

Review Sounds /m/, /p/, /f/, /k/, /t/, /l/, /a/, /o/

Key Phonologic Skills Isolate Initial and Final Sounds

Phonological Awareness and Alphabetic Understanding

Activity	Materials		Time
1. Alphabetic Review *o*/o/	Alphabet Card: *o*		1–2 minutes
New **2. Phonologic** Find the Picture with the Last Sound /t/, /p/, or /d/	Picture Cards: *cat, cap, cup, ant, bed, jeep, can, man, map, dog, pot*	3-Square Strip Letter Tiles: *t, p, d*	4–5 minutes
New **3. Integrated Phonologic/Alphabetic** Oral First Sound Mix-Up Game: *d*/d/, *l*/l/, *a*/a/, *o*/o/	Letter Cards: *d, l, a, o* (one set per child)	Sound Production Cue Card	4–5 minutes
4. Alphabetic Review *o*/o/; Partners Game: *o, m, p, f, c, t, s, d*	Alphabet Card: *o*	Letter Cards: *o, m, p, f, c, t, s, d* (one set per pair of children)	4–5 minutes

Writing and Spelling

Activity	Materials		Time
5. Writer's Warm-Up Letter Mission: Review *o, l, d, f, p, c, a, t, s*	Letter Mission (one per child) Student Activity Book 1, p. 62	Tracing Cards: *o, l, d, f, p, c, a, t, s*	2–3 minutes
6. Integrated Phonologic/Alphabetic Match a Picture's Last Sound: /p/, /l/	Picture Cards: *nail, cap, mop, cup, tape, soap, pail, doll, well, seal*	Letter Cards: *l, f, s, p, c*	2–3 minutes
New **7. Phonologic/Spelling** Letter Writing Game: Final *l, s, t, p, m*	Letter Writing Game (one per child) Student Activity Book 1, p. 63 game marker (one per child/not provided)	Game Board 3 number cube (not provided)	6–8 minutes

295

Lesson 36 Overview

Activity 1 Review Letter Name and Sound

Review o/o/

Objective: Children identify letter name and sound.

Time: 1–2 minutes

	To Do	**To Say**	
Test letter name and sound	Hold up the *o* Alphabet Card. Test the group.	**Test**	**What is the name of this letter? What is the sound for this letter?**

Ongoing Assessment

If...children make an error,	then...tell them the letter name or sound, have them repeat the name or sound, and return to the letter a second time.

	Give individual turns.	**Test**	**What is the name of this letter? What is the sound for this letter?**

Activity 2 Isolate Final Sound

Find the Picture with the Last Sound /t/, /p/, or /d/

Objective: Children isolate final sounds: /t/, /p/, /d/.　　Time: 4–5 minutes

	To Do	To Say
Introduce the game Find the Picture with the Last Sound /t/, /p/, or /d/		**Today you're going to listen for the last sounds in some words. I'll show you two pictures and tell you a last sound. You'll tell me which picture has the last sound I say.**
Model the game	Display the 3-Square Strip. Place the pictures of *cat* and *cap* above the strip. Model two examples.	**Model** **I'll show you how to play. I'll find the picture that has the last sound /t/.** Place the *t* Letter Tile in the last box on the card. Point to *cat* and say: **This picture is cat. I'll say the sounds in cat.** Point to each box as you say the sounds: **/k/ /aaa/ /t/.** Then point to *cap* and say: **This is cap. I'll say the sounds in cap.** Point to each box as you say the sounds: **/k/ /aaa/ /p/. Cat has the last sound /t/.** Point to each box as you say the sounds and then keep pointing to the last box as you say the last sound: **/k/ /aaa/ /t/.** Model again with *cup* and *ant* and the last sound /p/.
Play the game to test knowledge of final /t/, /p/, /d/	Test the activity with five examples.	**Test** **Your turn.** Display *bed* and *jeep* above the 3-Square Strip. **Find the picture that has the last sound /d/.** Place the letter tile for *d* in the last box on the strip. Point to *bed*: **This is bed. What is this? I'll say the sounds in bed.** Point to each box as you say the sounds: **/b/ /eee/ /d/.** Point to *jeep*: **This is jeep. What is this? I'll say the sounds in jeep.** Point to each box as you say the sounds: **/j/ /ēēē/ /p/. Everybody, which picture has the last sound /d/? Good, bed has the last sound /d/.** Point to each box as you say the sounds, keeping your finger on the last box: **/b/ /eee/ /d/.** Continue to test with the following examples: *can* and *ant* with /t/, *man* and *map* with /p/, *dog* and *pot* with /t/, *cap* and *can* with /p/.
	Give individual turns.	**Ongoing Assessment** **If...children make an error,** **then...**tell them the picture name that has the last sound. Say the sounds in the word as you touch each box. Repeat the last sound and tap the last box. Have children repeat the task.

Activity **3** Connect Initial Sound to Letter

Oral First Sound Mix-Up Game:
d/d/, l/l/, a/a/, o/o/

Objective: Children isolate initial sound and connect to letter.   Time: 4–5 minutes

	To Do	**To Say**	
Introduce the game Oral First Sound Mix-Up	Distribute letter cards to each child.	*Have children line up their letter cards in front of them and do so yourself.* **We have a new game today. I'll say a word. You'll tell me the first sound of the word and point to the letter for the sound. Listen carefully because I won't show you any pictures!**	
Model the game	Model the first word.	**Model**	**My turn.** *Otter.* **The first sound in** *otter* **is /ooo/.** *Touch the o Letter Card.* **The sound for this letter is /ooo/; /ooo/ for** *otter.*
Play the game to test knowledge of initial sounds: d/d/, l/l/, a/a, o/o/		**Test**	**Your turn. Here's your first word:** *deer.* **What's the word? Everybody, say the first sound in** *deer.* **Yes, /d/.**

Ongoing Assessment

If…children make an error identifying the first sound,	**then**…tell them the answer and have them repeat it. Prompt sound production using the Sound Production Cue Card. Return to the word a second time.

Find the letter for /d/ on the table and touch it. Everybody, what letter are you touching? What is the sound for that letter? Say /d/ for *deer.* *Continue the game with the words* ox, line, dive, octopus, leaf, ax.

Ongoing Assessment

If…children make an error identifying the letter,	**then**…hold up the correct letter card. Say: **This is the letter for the <u>sound</u> /_/. Everyone, touch the letter for the <u>sound</u> /_/.** Give at least two more words that begin with that sound as you continue to play the game.

Phonological Awareness/Alphabetic Understanding

Activity 4 Review Letter Name and Sound

Review o/o/; Partners Game:
o, m, p, f, c, t, s, d

Objective: Children review letter names and sounds.   Time: 4–5 minutes

	To Do	**To Say**	
Test letter name and sound	Hold up the *o* Alphabet Card. Test the group.	Test	**What is the name of this letter? What is the sound for this letter?**

> ### Ongoing Assessment
>
> **If** . . . children make an error,   **then** . . . tell them the letter name or sound, have them repeat the name or sound, and return to the letter a second time.

	To Do	**To Say**	
	Give individual turns.	Test	**What is the name of this letter? What is the sound for this letter?**
Introduce the Partners Game with *o, m, p, f, c, t, s, d*	Assign each child a partner. Give each pair a set of letter cards.	Lead	**Now we're going to play a game. You will show a letter card to your partner. Your partner will tell you the name and sound for that letter. If your partner says the correct letter name and sound, you will give him or her the letter card. If your partner makes a mistake, you will tell him or her the correct letter name and sound and then place the card on the bottom of your pile. You will continue playing until your partner has all the cards. Then you will switch roles.** Have children play the game.

Phonological Awareness/Alphabetic Understanding

Activity 5 — Writer's Warm-Up

Letter Mission: Review *o, l, d, f, p, c, a, t, s*

Objective: Children write review letters.

Time: 2–3 minutes

	To Do	To Say	
Introduce the activity	Distribute a Letter Mission to each child.		We're going on a letter mission. I'm going to tell you the name of a letter and you're going to write it. Let's see if we can help the dog get the bone!
Model the activity	Model writing the letter *o* on your Letter Mission.	Model	The first letter is *o*. Watch as I start at the dot and write the letter *o*.
		Lead	Now you write the letter *o*. Start at the dot and write the letter.
		Test	What is the <u>name</u> of the letter you wrote?
Lead the activity to test writing *l, d, f, p, c, a, t, s*	Continue naming letters for children to write.	Test	Now write the letter *l*. What is the <u>name</u> of the letter you just wrote? Continue with the following: *d, f, p, c, a, t, s.*

Ongoing Assessment

If...children write the wrong letter or don't remember a letter,	then...show them the tracing card of the correct letter and model tracing the letter. Have them write the letter again.

Writing/Spelling

Match a Picture's Last Sound: /p/, /l/

Objective: Children connect final sound to letter: p/p/, l/l/.   Time: 2–3 minutes

	To Do	**To Say**	
Introduce the activity	Gather picture cards and letter cards.		**You're going to choose the letter that goes with the last sound of some pictures.**
Model the activity	Place the *nail* Picture Card on the table. Place the *l* and *f* Letter Cards under the picture.	Model	**This is *nail*. The last sound in *nail* is /lll/.** **I'm going to choose the letter that matches this picture's last sound.** Point to the correct letter: **l is the letter for the sound /lll/ like the /lll/ in *nail*.**
Test knowledge of final sound	Display the *cap* Picture Card. Place the *s* and *p* Letter Cards on the table.	Test	**This is *cap*. What is this? The last sound in *cap* is /p/. What is the last sound in *cap*? That's right; /p/ is the last sound in *cap*. Your turn. Choose the letter that matches this picture's last sound. Which letter has the same sound as the /p/ in *cap*? Do you know?** Call on a child to point to the correct letter. **What's the <u>name</u> of the letter you pointed to? What is the <u>sound</u> for that letter? That's right; p is for /p/ like the /p/ in *cap*. Everyone, what's the <u>name</u> of this letter? What's the <u>sound</u> for this letter?** Continue with at least three more examples.

Ongoing Assessment

If…children make an error,   **then**…model the answer, have them repeat it, and return to the picture card a second time.

Activity **7** Connect Sound to Letter

Letter Writing Game:
Final l, s, t, p, m

Objective: Children identify final sound and connect to letter.   Time: 6–8 minutes

	To Do	**To Say**
Review letter names and sounds	Hold up a Letter Writing Game. Point to each letter.	For each letter, ask: **What is the <u>name</u> of this letter? What is the <u>sound</u> for this letter?**
Introduce the Letter Writing Game	Distribute a Letter Writing Game to each child.	**We're going to play a letter writing game. I'll say a word and you'll write the letter that goes with the word's last sound. Then someone will roll the number cube and move his or her marker on the game board.**
Model the game	Place a Letter Writing Game on the table.	Model **Let's do one together. The first word is** *call.* **The last sound in** *call* **is /lll/. I'm going to write the letter that has the same sound as the /lll/ in** *call.* Write the letter in the correct place. **Now you write the letter for the sound /lll/. Start at the dot and write the letter. That's right;** *l* **is the letter for the sound /lll/ like the /lll/ in** *call.*
Play the game to test children on knowledge of *l, s, t, p, m*	Dictate words from the Word Bank below. Vary the order.	Test **The next word is** *cap.* **What is the last sound in** *cap?* **That's right; /p/ is the last sound in** *cap.* **Now write the letter for the same sound as the /p/ in** *cap.* **Start at the dot and write the letter. Everyone, what's the <u>name</u> of the letter you wrote? What's the <u>sound</u> for that letter?** After children have written the letter, have one child roll the number cube and advance his or her marker on the game board. Continue the game until all the letters are written.

Word Bank

class	cat	cup	come	curl
case	coat	clap	clam	crawl
crease	carrot	cape	cream	cool
clowns	cart		crumb	

Ongoing Assessment

If...children make an error,	**then**...model the letter name and sound, have children repeat them, and have children write the correct letter.

302

Writing/Spelling

New Sound /r/
Review Sounds /f/, /k/, /t/, /s/, /d/, /l/, /a/, /o/
Key Phonologic Skills Isolate Initial and Final Sounds

Phonological Awareness and Alphabetic Understanding

Activity	Materials		Time
1. Alphabetic Introduce *r*/r/	Alphabet Card: *r* Letter Card: *r* (one per child)		1–2 minutes
2. Phonologic Does It Begin with /r/?	Picture Cards: *rake, can, ring, rabbit, rose, top*	Alphabet Card: *r*	4–5 minutes
3. Integrated Phonologic/Alphabetic Find the Picture with the Last Sound /t/, /d/, or /p/	Picture Cards: *cat, can; man, mud; leg, lip; coat, cup; sun, soap*	3-Square Strip Letter Tiles: *t, d, p*	4–5 minutes
4. Alphabetic Reintroduce *r*/r/; Play Who Has the Star?	Alphabet Card: *r* Game Cards: "star," *f, c, t, s, d, l, a, o* (two of each letter) sticky note (not provided)		4–5 minutes

New (for Activity 4)

Writing and Spelling

Activity	Materials		Time
5. Writer's Warm-Up Introduce *r*	Writer's Warm-Up (one per child) Student Activity Book 1, p. 64	Tracing Cards: *r, a, d, o, c, s, t*	2–3 minutes
6. Integrated Phonologic/Alphabetic Practice Session: First and Last Sounds	3-Square Strip	Letter Tiles: *d, s, t, c, p, m*	2–3 minutes
7. Phonologic/Spelling First and Last Sounds: *l, d, t, f, p, m*	First and Last Sounds (one per child) Student Activity Book 1, p. 65		6–8 minutes

New (for Activity 6)

303

Lesson 37 Overview

Activity **1** Introduce Letter Name and Sound

Introduce r/r/

Objective: Children learn letter name and sound: r/r/.

Time: 1–2 minutes

	To Do	To Say	
Introduce letter name	Hold up the *r* Alphabet Card.	Model	The <u>name</u> of this letter is *r*.
		Lead	Say the <u>name</u> with me: *r*.
		Test	What is the <u>name</u> of this letter?
Introduce letter sound	Continue holding up the *r* Alphabet Card.	Model	The <u>sound</u> for this letter is /rrr/. When you say /rrr/, your voice box is on and the tip of your tongue goes up toward the roof of your mouth. Say /rrr/ and feel the tip of your tongue go up toward the roof of your mouth. Put your hand on your throat to see if your voice box is on when you say /rrr/; /rrr/. Yes, your voice box is on when you say /rrr/.
		Lead	Say the <u>sound</u> with me: /rrr/.
		Test	What is the <u>sound</u> for this letter?
Test knowledge of letter name and sound	Continue holding up the *r* Alphabet Card.	Test	What is the <u>name</u> of this letter? What is the <u>sound</u> for this letter?
	Give individual turns on letter name and sound.		**Ongoing Assessment**
			If...children make an error, then...tell them the name or sound, have them repeat the name or sound, and return to the letter a second time.
Model tracing *r*	Distribute the *r* Letter Cards. Hold up the *r* Alphabet Card.	Model	Everyone, watch. I'll trace the letter *r*.
			Have children trace the *r* on their letter cards three times. Tell them to say /rrr/ each time they trace the letter.
			Ongoing Assessment
			If...children make an error, then...put your hand over their hand and guide them to trace the letter. Then have them try to trace the letter on their own. Repeat as necessary.

Activity 2 Isolate Initial Sound

Does It Begin with /r/?

Objective: Children isolate initial /r/.

Time: 4–5 minutes

	To Do		**To Say**
Model names of pictures	Gather the picture cards. Place *rake* on the table.	**Model**	**This is *rake*. What is this?** Continue with the remaining cards. Test children on the picture names by placing the cards on the table one at a time and asking: **What is this?**
Introduce the game Does It Begin with /r/?	Hold up the *r* Alphabet Card.		**We're going to play a game. I'll show you a picture. You'll tell whether the picture begins with /rrr/.** **Let's say /rrr/. Remember, when you say /rrr/, your voice box is on and the tip of your tongue goes up toward the roof of your mouth. Say /rrr/ and feel the tip of your tongue go up toward the roof of your mouth. Put your hand on your throat to see if your voice box is on when you say /rrr/; /rrr/. Yes, your voice box is on when you say /rrr/.**
Model the game	Place the *rake* Picture Card on the table. Place the *can* Picture Card on the table.	**Model**	**My turn. I'll say the name of the picture and then tell if it begins with /rrr/:** *rake* (exaggerate the first sound). ***Rake* begins with /rrr/. My voice box is on and the tip of my tongue goes up and back when I say /rrr/, *rake*.** **Next picture:** *can* (exaggerate the first sound). ***Can* does not begin with /rrr/.**
Play the game to test knowledge of initial /r/	Place the *ring* Picture Card on the table. Give individual turns.	**Test**	**This is *ring*. What is this? Does *ring*** (exaggerate the first sound) **begin with /rrr/?** Confirm correct responses and prompt sound production: **Yes, *ring* begins with /rrr/. Let's say /rrr/. Remember, when you say /rrr/, the tip of your tongue goes up toward the roof of your mouth and your voice box is on. Say /rrr/, *ring*.** Continue with *rabbit, rose,* and *top*.

Ongoing Assessment

If... children make an error,	**then...** model the correct answer. Review the sound production cue. Have children repeat the correct answer. Go back to the example a second time.

Activity **3** Isolate Final Sound

*Find the Picture with
the Last Sound /t/, /d/, or /p/*

Objective: Children isolate final /t/, /d/, and /p/.

Time: 4–5 minutes

	To Do		**To Say**
Introduce the activity	Gather the picture cards, the 3-Square Strip, and the letter tiles.		**You're going to listen for the last sound in some words. I'll show you two pictures and tell you a last sound. You'll tell me which picture has the last sound I say.**
Model the activity	Display the 3-Square Strip. Place the *cat* and *can* Picture Cards above the strip.	Model	**My turn. I'll show you how to play.** Place the *t* Letter Tile in the last square of the strip. **The last sound is /t/. I'll find the picture that has the last sound /t/.** Point to *cat*. **This is *cat*. I'll say the sounds in *cat*: /k/ /aaa/ /t/.** Point to each square as you say the sounds. **Next picture: *can*. I'll say the sounds in *can*: /k/ /aaa/ /nnn/.** Point to each square as you say the sounds. **Cat has the last sound /t/: /k/ /aaa/ /t/.** Point to each square as you say the sounds, keeping your finger on the last square as you say the last sound.
Test knowledge of final sound	Place the *d* Letter Tile in the last square of the strip. Place the *man* and *mud* Picture Cards above the strip.	Test	**Your turn. The last sound is /d/. Find the picture that has the last sound /d/.** Point to *man* and ask: **What is this? I'll say the sounds in *man*: /mmm/ /aaa/ /nnn/.** Point to each square as you say the sounds. Point to *mud* and ask: **What is this? I'll say the sounds in *mud*: /mmm/ /uuu/ /d/.** Point to each square as you say the sounds. **Everyone, which picture has the last sound /d/?** Confirm correct responses: **Yes, *mud* has the last sound /d/: /mmm/ /uuu/ /d/.**
			Continue with *leg* and *lip* for /p/, *coat* and *cup* for /t/, and *sun* and *soap* for /p/.
	Give individual turns.		

Ongoing Assessment

If...children make an error,	then...tell them which picture has the last sound. Say the sounds in the word as you touch each square. Repeat the last sound and tap the last square. Have children repeat the task.

Activity 4 — Reintroduce Letter Name and Sound

Reintroduce r/r/; Play Who Has the Star?
Objective: Children practice letter name and sound: r/r/.   Time: 4–5 minutes

	To Do	To Say	
Introduce letter name	Hold up the *r* Alphabet Card.	Model	The <u>name</u> of this letter is *r*.
		Lead	Say the <u>name</u> with me: *r*.
		Test	What is the <u>name</u> of this letter?
Introduce letter sound	Continue holding up the *r* Alphabet Card.	Model	The <u>sound</u> for this letter is /rrr/. When you say /rrr/, your voice box is on and the tip of your tongue goes up toward the roof of your mouth. Say /rrr/ and feel the tip of your tongue go up toward the roof of your mouth. Put your hand on your throat to see if your voice box is on when you say /rrr/; /rrr/. Yes, your voice box is on when you say /rrr/.
		Lead	Say the <u>sound</u> with me: /rrr/.
		Test	What is the <u>sound</u> for this letter?
Test knowledge of letter name and sound	Continue holding up the *r* Alphabet Card.	Test	What is the <u>name</u> of this letter? What is the <u>sound</u> for this letter?

Ongoing Assessment

If...children make an error,	then...tell them the name or sound, have them repeat the name or sound, and return to the letter a second time.

Play the game Who Has the Star?	Gather the "star" Game Card and two game cards each for *f, c, t, s, d, l, a,* and *o*.

Write the letter *m* on a sticky note and place it on the "star" card. Then mix the cards and distribute them to children. Have children take turns choosing a card from the person on the left. The child who chooses tells the name and sound of the letter on the card. The child who draws the "star" card tells the name and sound of the letter on the sticky note. Children who have pairs of matching cards place the pairs on the table. Play continues until there are no more cards. The child who is left holding the "star" card wins.

Ongoing Assessment

If...a child makes an error,	then...tell the child the name or sound and have the child repeat it.

Activity 5 Writer's Warm-Up

Introduce r

Objective: Children trace and write *r* and review writing *a*, *d*, *o*, *s*, *t*, and *c*.

Time: 2–3 minutes

	To Do	**To Say**
Review letter name and sound	Hold up the *r* Tracing Card.	**What is the <u>name</u> of this letter? What is the <u>sound</u> for this letter?**
Model tracing *r*	Distribute a Writer's Warm-Up to each child. Hold up the *r* Tracing Card.	**Model** **Everyone, watch as I trace the letter *r* with my finger.** **Lead** **Now you trace the first two *r*'s on your warm-up sheet.**
	Model tracing *r* again.	**Model** **Everyone, watch as I trace *r* again.** **Lead** **Now use your pencil to trace the next two *r*'s on your warm-up sheet.**
Model writing *r*	Hold up the lined side of the *r* Tracing Card.	**Model** **Everyone, watch as I write the letter *r*. I start at the dot and write the letter.** Have children write *r* two times on their warm-up sheets. Remind them to write their letters carefully.

Ongoing Assessment

If...children make an error,	then...put your hand over their hand and guide them to write the letter. Then have them write the letter on their own. Repeat as necessary.

Test knowledge of writing *r*	Model writing *r* again.	Have children cover the letters they traced and wrote. Have them write *r* two times from memory. Then have them uncover their papers and compare the letters. **Do your letters look the same? Circle the *r* that is your best work.**

Review *a, d, o, s, t, c*		Have children trace and write each review letter on their warm-up sheets.

Ongoing Assessment

If...children make an error,	then...use the tracing card to model tracing the letter. If needed, put your hand over their hand and guide them to write the letter. Then have them write the letter on their own. Repeat as necessary.

Activity 6 — Connect Sound to Letter

 New

Practice Session: First and Last Sounds

Objective: Children connect initial and final sounds to letters: d/d/, s/s/, t/t/, c/k/, p/p/, m/m/.

Time: 2–3 minutes

	To Do	To Say	
Introduce the activity	Gather the 3-Square Strip and the letter tiles.		**Today we're going to listen for first and last sounds. We're going to say the sounds in some words. Then we'll choose the letters that go with the first and last sounds.**
Lead the activity	Lead segmenting a word.	**Lead**	**The first word is *mat*. Listen. I'll say the sounds in *mat*: /mmm/ /aaa/ /t/.**
			Say the sounds in *mat* with me: /mmm/ /aaa/ /t/. Now you say the sounds in *mat*. Have the group say the sounds together. Then give individual turns.
	Display the 3-Square Strip. Lead children in isolating the first sound.		**I'll say the sounds in *mat* and point to a square as I say each sound: /mmm/ /aaa/ /t/.** Point to the first square. **What is the first sound in *mat*? That's right; /mmm/ is the first sound in *mat*.** Have the group say the sound together. Then give individual turns.
	Lay out two letter tiles, *m* and one other. Lead children in identifying the letter for the first sound.		**You're going to choose the letter for the sound /mmm/ like the /mmm/ in *mat*.** Point to the first square. **Does everyone know?** Call on a child to choose the correct letter and place it in the first square. Reinforce the group on the letter name and sound: **Everyone, what's the <u>name</u> of the letter? What's the <u>sound</u> for the letter?**
	Lead children in isolating the last sound.		**Watch again as I say the sounds in *mat* and point to a square as I say each sound: /mmm/ /aaa/ /t/.** Point to the last square: **/t/ is the last sound in *mat*. What is the last sound in *mat*?** Have the group say the sound together. Then give individual turns.
	Lay out two letter tiles, *t* and one other. Lead children in identifying the letter for the last sound.		**You're going to choose the letter for the sound /t/ like the /t/ in *mat*.** Point to the last square. **Does everyone know?** Call on a child to choose the correct letter and place it in the last square. Reinforce the group on the letter name and sound: **Everyone, what's the <u>name</u> of the letter? What's the <u>sound</u> for the letter?**

Practice with *pat, cat, cop,* and *sad,* as time allows.

Ongoing Assessment

If...children make an error,	then...model the answer, have them repeat it, and return to the sound and letter a second time.

Activity 7 Connect Sound to Letter

First and Last Sounds: l, d, t, f, p, m

Objective: Children connect initial and final sounds to letters: Time: 6–8 minutes
l/l/, d/d/, t/t/, f/f/, p/p/, m/m/.

	To Do	**To Say**	
Introduce the activity	Gather the picture cards. Distribute a First and Last Sounds page to each child.	Tell children that they are going to write the letters that go with the first and last sounds of some pictures.	
Model the activity	Hold up a First and Last Sounds page. Point to the first picture.	Model	This is *map*. Listen. I'll say the sounds in *map* slowly: **/mmm/ /aaa/ /p/.**
		Lead	Say the sounds in *map* slowly with me: **/mmm/ /aaa/ /p/.**
		Model	Now I'll say the sounds in *map* slowly and point to a letter space as I say each sound: **/mmm/ /aaa/ /p/.** Point to the first space: **/mmm/ is the first sound in *map*. I'm going to write the letter for the sound /mmm/ like the /mmm/ in *map*.** Write the letter *m* in the first space.
		Lead	Now you write the letter for the sound /mmm/ like the /mmm/ in *map*. Start at the dot and write the letter in the first space. That's right; *m* is the letter for the sound /mmm/.
	Continue to hold up a First and Last Sounds page.	Model	Listen again to the sounds in *map*: **/mmm/ /aaa/ /p/.**
		Lead	Say the sounds in *map* slowly with me: **/mmm/ /aaa/ /p/.**
		Model	Watch again as I point to the letter spaces and say *map* slowly: **/mmm/ /aaa/ /p/.** Point to the last space: **/p/ is the last sound in *map*. I'm going to write the letter for the sound /p/ like the /p/ in *map*.** Write the letter *p* in the last space.
		Lead	Now you write the letter for the sound /p/ like the /p/ in *map*. Start at the dot and write the letter in the last space. That's right; *p* is the letter for the sound /p/.

Test knowledge of initial and final sounds	**To Do**	**To Say**
	Continue to hold up a First and Last Sounds page. Point to the picture of *mitt*.	**Model** — This is *mitt*. What is this? Listen. I'll say the sounds in *mitt* slowly: /mmm/ /iii/ /t/.
		Lead — Say the sounds in *mitt* slowly with me: /mmm/ /iii/ /t/.
		Model — Now I'll say the sounds in *mitt* slowly and point to a letter space as I say each sound: /mmm/ /iii/ /t/. Point to the first space.
		Test — What is the <u>first</u> sound in *mitt*? That's right; /mmm/ is the <u>first</u> sound in *mitt*. Everyone, write the letter for the sound /mmm/ like the /mmm/ in *mitt*. Start at the dot and write the letter in the first space. Reinforce the group on the letter name and sound: Everyone, what's the <u>name</u> of the letter you wrote? What's the <u>sound</u> for that letter?
	Continue to hold up a First and Last Sounds page.	**Model** — Listen again as I say *mitt* slowly: /mmm/ /iii/ /t/.
		Lead — Say the sounds in *mitt* slowly with me: /mmm/ /iii/ /t/.
		Model — Now I'll say the sounds in *mitt* slowly and point to a letter space as I say each sound: /mmm/ /iii/ /t/. Point to the last space.
		Test — What is the <u>last</u> sound in *mitt*? That's right; /t/ is the <u>last</u> sound in *mitt*. Everyone, write the letter for the sound /t/ like the /t/ in *mitt* in the last space. Reinforce the group on the letter name and sound: Everyone, what's the <u>name</u> of the letter you wrote? What's the <u>sound</u> for that letter?
		Continue with the remaining pictures.

Ongoing Assessment

If...children make an error,	then...model the letter name and sound and have children repeat them. Have children write the correct letter.

New Sound /r/
Review Sounds /m/, /p/, /s/, /d/, /l/, /a/, /o/
Key Phonologic Skills Isolate Initial and Final Sounds

Phonological Awareness and Alphabetic Understanding

Activity	Materials		Time
1. Alphabetic Introduce *r*/r/	Alphabet Card: *r* Letter Card: *r* (one per child)		1–2 minutes
2. Phonologic Which Picture Begins with /r/?	Picture Choices: 38-1, 38-2, 38-3 Teacher Resource Package 1	Alphabet Card: *r*	4–5 minutes
3. Integrated Phonologic/Alphabetic Find the Picture with the Last Sound /d/, /p/, or /t/	Picture Cards: *pan, mud; cup, dog; pot, man; can, lip; mop, fin; cat, fan; map, sun; top, pin*	3-Square Strip Letter Tiles: *d, p, t*	4–5 minutes
New **4. Alphabetic** Reintroduce *r*/r/; Play Concentration	Alphabet Card: *r*	Game Cards: *m, p, s, d, l, a, o, r* (two of each letter)	4–5 minutes

Writing and Spelling

Activity	Materials		Time
5. Writer's Warm-Up Introduce *r*	Writer's Warm-Up (one per child) Student Activity Book 1, p. 66	Tracing Cards: *r, o, a, d, s, t, c*	2–3 minutes
6. Integrated Phonologic/Alphabetic Practice Session: First and Last Sounds	3-Square Strip	Letter Tiles: *s, t, c, p, m*	2–3 minutes
New **7. Phonologic/Spelling** Tic-Tac-Toe: First and Last Sounds	Tic-Tac-Toe (one per child) Student Activity Book 1, p. 67		6–8 minutes

Activity 1 — Introduce Letter Name and Sound

Introduce r/r/

Objective: Children learn letter name and sound: r/r/.

Time: 1–2 minutes

	To Do	To Say	
Introduce letter name	Hold up the *r* Alphabet Card.	Model	The <u>name</u> of this letter is *r*.
		Lead	Say the <u>name</u> with me: *r*.
		Test	What is the <u>name</u> of this letter?
Introduce letter sound	Continue holding up the *r* Alphabet Card.	Model	The <u>sound</u> for this letter is /rrr/. When you say /rrr/, your voice box is on and the tip of your tongue goes up toward the roof of your mouth. Say /rrr/ and feel the tip of your tongue go up toward the roof of your mouth. Put your hand on your throat to see if your voice box is on when you say /rrr/; /rrr/. Yes, your voice box is on when you say /rrr/.
		Lead	Say the <u>sound</u> with me: /rrr/.
		Test	What is the <u>sound</u> for this letter?
Test knowledge of letter name and sound	Continue holding up the *r* Alphabet Card.	Test	What is the <u>name</u> of this letter? What is the <u>sound</u> for this letter?

Ongoing Assessment

If... children make an error,   then... tell them the name or sound, have them repeat the name or sound, and return to the letter a second time.

Test knowledge of letter name and sound *(continued)*	Give individual turns on letter name and sound.		
Model tracing *r*	Distribute the *r* Letter Cards. Hold up the *r* Alphabet Card.	Model	Everyone, watch. I'll trace the letter *r*.

Have children trace the *r* on their letter cards three times. Tell them to say /rrr/ each time they trace the letter.

Ongoing Assessment

If... children make an error,   then... put your hand over their hand and guide them to trace the letter. Then have them try to trace the letter on their own. Repeat as necessary.

Phonological Awareness/Alphabetic Understanding

Activity 2 — Isolate Initial Sound

Which Picture Begins with /r/?

Objective: Children isolate initial /r/.

Time: 4–5 minutes

	To Do	To Say	
Model names of pictures	Gather the picture choices. Display Picture Choice 38-1. Point to *ant*.	Model	**This is *ant*. What is this?** Continue with the remaining pictures *(dime, run; rain, olive, soap)*. Test children on the picture names by pointing to the pictures one at a time and asking: **What is this?** Repeat for Picture Choices 38-2 *(ox, rug, apple; rake, sun, dot)* and 38-3 *(sick, dog, read; ant, rug, octopus)*.
Introduce the game Which Picture Begins with /r/?	Hold up the *r* Alphabet Card.		**We're going to play another game with our new sound /rrr/. I'll show you three pictures. You'll find the picture that has the first sound /rrr/.** **Let's say /rrr/. Remember, when you say /rrr/, your voice box is on and the tip of your tongue goes up toward the roof of your mouth. Say /rrr/ and feel the tip of your tongue go up toward the roof of your mouth. Put your hand on your throat to see if your voice box is on when you say /rrr/; /rrr/. Yes, your voice box is on when you say /rrr/.**
Model the game	Display Picture Choice 38-1. Cover the bottom row.	Model	**It's my turn to show you how to play the game. This is *ant, dime, run*. I'll find the picture that has the first sound /rrr/: *run*** (exaggerate the first sound). **Run has the first sound /rrr/.** Exaggerate the first sound and say the word: **/rrr/, run.** Model again with the bottom row of pictures: *rain, olive, soap.*
Play the game to test knowledge of initial /r/	Display Picture Choice 38-2. Cover the bottom row.		Have children name each picture. **Which picture has the first sound /rrr/?** Confirm correct responses and prompt sound production: **Yes, *rug* has the first sound /rrr/. Let's say /rrr/. Remember, when you say /rrr/, the tip of your tongue goes up toward the roof of your mouth and your voice box is on. Say /rrr/, rug.** Continue with the bottom row of pictures and Picture Choice 38-3.
	Give individual turns.		**Ongoing Assessment** **If…** children make incorrect responses, **then…** model the correct answer. Review the sound production cue. Have children repeat the correct answer. Go back to the example a second time.

Activity **3** Isolate Final Sound

Find the Picture with the Last Sound /d/, /p/, or /t/

Objective: Children isolate final /d/, /p/, and /t/.

Time: 4–5 minutes

	To Do		**To Say**
Introduce the activity	Gather the picture cards, the 3-Square Strip, and the letter tiles.		**You're going to listen for the last sound in some words. I'll show you two pictures and tell you a last sound. You'll tell me which picture has the last sound I say.**
Model the activity	Display the 3-Square Strip. Place the *mud* and *pan* Picture Cards above the strip.	**Model**	**My turn. I'll show you how to play.** Place the *d* Letter Tile in the last square of the strip. **The last sound is /d/. I'll find the picture that has the last sound /d/.** Point to *mud*. **This is *mud*. I'll say the sounds in *mud*: /mmm/ /uuu/ /d/.** Point to each square as you say the sounds. **Next picture: *pan*. I'll say the sounds in *pan*: /p/ /aaa/ /nnn/.** Point to each square as you say the sounds. ***Mud* has the last sound /d/: /mmm/ /uuu/ /d/.** Point to each square as you say the sounds, keeping your finger on the last square as you say the last sound. Model again with *pot* and *man* for /t/.
Test knowledge of final /d/, /p/, and /t/	Place the *p* Letter Tile in the last square of the strip. Place the *cup* and *dog* Picture Cards above the strip.	**Test**	**Your turn. The last sound is /p/. Find the picture that has the last sound /p/.** Point to *cup*. **This is *cup*. What is this? I'll say the sounds in *cup*: /k/ /uuu/ /p/.** Point to each square as you say the sounds. Point to *dog*. **This is *dog*. What is this? I'll say the sounds in *dog*: /d/ /ȯȯȯ/ /g/.** Point to each square as you say the sounds. **Everyone, which picture has the last sound /p/?** Confirm correct responses: **Yes, *cup* has the last sound /p/: /k/ /uuu/ /p/.** Continue with *can* and *lip* for /p/, *mop* and *fin* for /p/, *cat* and *fan* for /t/, *map* and *sun* for /p/, and *top* and *pin* for /p/.
	Give individual turns.		### Ongoing Assessment **If**...children make an error, **then**...tell them which picture has the last sound. Say the sounds in the word as you touch each square. Repeat the last sound and tap the last square. Have children repeat the task.

Activity **4** Reintroduce Letter Name and Sound

Reintroduce r/r/; Play Concentration

Objective: Children practice letter name and sound: r/r/.   Time: 4–5 minutes

	To Do	**To Say**	
Introduce letter name	Hold up the *r* Alphabet Card.	Model	The <u>name</u> of this letter is *r*.
		Lead	Say the <u>name</u> with me: *r*.
		Test	What is the <u>name</u> of this letter?
Introduce letter sound	Continue holding up the *r* Alphabet Card.	Model	The <u>sound</u> for this letter is /rrr/. When you say /rrr/, your voice box is on and the tip of your tongue goes up toward the roof of your mouth. Say /rrr/ and feel the tip of your tongue go up toward the roof of your mouth. Put your hand on your throat to see if your voice box is on when you say /rrr/; /rrr/. Yes, your voice box is on when you say /rrr/.
		Lead	Say the <u>sound</u> with me: /rrr/.
		Test	What is the <u>sound</u> for this letter?
Test knowledge of letter name and sound	Continue holding up the *r* Alphabet Card.	Test	What is the <u>name</u> of this letter? What is the <u>sound</u> for this letter?

Ongoing Assessment

Give individual turns on letter name and sound.	If...children make an error, then...tell them the name or sound, have them repeat the name or sound, and return to the letter a second time.

Play the game Concentration

Gather two game cards each for *m, p, s, d, l, a, o,* and *r*.

Mix the cards and arrange them face down on the table in rows of four. Have children take turns choosing two cards, turning them over, and telling the name and sound of the letter on each card. If the two cards match, the child keeps the pair and takes another turn. If the cards do not match, the child returns the cards to their face down positions and play proceeds to the next child. Play continues until all cards have been matched. The child with the most pairs wins.

Ongoing Assessment

If...children make an error,   then...tell them the letter name and sound and have children repeat them.

Activity 5 — Writer's Warm-Up

Introduce r

Objective: Children trace and write *r* and review writing *a, d, o, c, s,* and *t.*

Time: 2–3 minutes

	To Do	To Say	
Review letter name and sound	Hold up the *r* Tracing Card.		**What is the <u>name</u> of this letter? What is the <u>sound</u> for this letter?**
Model tracing *r*	Distribute a Writer's Warm-Up to each child. Hold up the *r* Tracing Card.	Model	**Everyone, watch as I trace the letter *r* with my finger.**
		Lead	**Now you trace the first two *r*'s on your warm-up sheet.**
	Model tracing *r* again.	Model	**Everyone, watch as I trace *r* again.**
		Lead	**Now use your pencil to trace the next two *r*'s on your warm-up sheet.**
Model writing *r*	Hold up the lined side of the *r* Tracing Card.	Model	**Everyone, watch as I write the letter *r*. I start at the dot and write the letter.** Have children write *r* two times on their warm-up sheets. Remind them to write their letters carefully.

Ongoing Assessment

If...children make an error,	**then**...put your hand over their hand and guide them to write the letter. Then have them write the letter on their own. Repeat as necessary.

| **Test knowledge of writing *r*** | Model writing *r* again. | Have children cover the letters they traced and wrote. Have them write *r* two times from memory. Then have them uncover their papers and compare the letters.

Do your letters look the same? Circle the *r* that is your best work. |
|---|---|---|

Review *a, d, o, c, s, t*		Have children trace and write each review letter on their warm-up sheets.

Ongoing Assessment

If...children make an error,	**then**...use the tracing card to model tracing the letter. If needed, put your hand over their hand and guide them to write the letter. Then have them write the letter on their own. Repeat as necessary.

Practice Session: First and Last Sounds

Objective: Children connect initial and final sounds to letters: s/s/, t/t/, c/k/, p/p/, m/m/.

Time: 2–3 minutes

	To Do	To Say	
Introduce the activity	Gather the 3-Square Strip and the letter tiles.		**Today we're going to practice for Tic-Tac-Toe. We're going to say the sounds in some words slowly. Then we'll choose the letters that go with the first and last sounds.**
Lead the activity	Model segmenting a word.	Model	**The first word is *sit*. Listen. I'll say the sounds in *sit* slowly: /sss/ /iii/ /t/.**
		Lead	**Say the sounds in *sit* slowly with me: /sss/ /iii/ /t/. Now you say the sounds in *sit* slowly.** Have the group say the sounds together. Then give individual turns.
	Display the 3-Square Strip. Lead children in isolating the first sound.		**I'll say the sounds in *sit* slowly and point to a square as I say each sound: /sss/ /iii/ /t/.** Point to the first square. **What is the first sound in *sit*? That's right; /sss/ is the first sound in *sit*.** Have the group say the sound together. Then give individual turns.
	Lay out two letter tiles, *s* and one other. Lead children in identifying the letter for the first sound.		**You're going to choose the letter for the sound /sss/ like the /sss/ in *sit*.** Point to the first square. **Does everyone know?** Call on a child to choose the correct letter and place it in the first square. Reinforce the group on the letter name and sound: **Everyone, what's the <u>name</u> of the letter? What's the <u>sound</u> for the letter?**
	Lead children in isolating the last sound.		**Watch again as I say the sounds in *sit* slowly and point to a square as I say each sound: /sss/ /iii/ /t/.** Point to the last square: **/t/ is the last sound in *sit*. What is the last sound in *sit*?** Have the group say the sound together. Then give individual turns.
	Lay out two letter tiles, *t* and one other. Lead children in identifying the letter for the last sound.		**You're going to choose the letter for the sound /t/ like the /t/ in *sit*.** Point to the last square. **Does everyone know?** Call on a child to choose the correct letter and place it in the last square. Reinforce the group on the letter name and sound: **Everyone, what's the <u>name</u> of the letter? What's the <u>sound</u> for the letter?**

Practice with *mat, top, put,* and *cup,* as time allows.

Ongoing Assessment

If...children make an error,	then...model the answer, have them repeat it, and return to the sound and letter a second time.

319

Writing/Spelling

 **Connect Sound to Letter**

Tic-Tac-Toe: First and Last Sounds

Objective: Children connect sound to letter: /l/, p/p/, s/s/, t/t/, c/k/, m/m/.

Time: 6–8 minutes

	To Do	**To Say**	
Introduce the activity	Distribute a Tic-Tac-Toe to each child.		We're going to play Tic-Tac-Toe. I'll tell you a word. You'll find the word's first and last sounds. Let's see if we can cross out a row to get Tic-Tac-Toe!
Model the activity	Hold up a Tic-Tac-Toe. Point to Square 1. Model identifying the letter for the first sound in *lap*.	Model	Let's do one together. The first word is *lap*. Listen. I'll say the sounds in *lap* slowly: /lll/ /aaa/ /p/.
		Lead	Say the sounds in *lap* slowly with me: /lll/ /aaa/ /p/.
		Model	The first sound in *lap* is /lll/. I'm going to make an X over the letter for the sound /lll/ like the /lll/ in *lap*. Make an X over the letter *l*.
		Lead	Now you make an X over the letter for the sound /lll/ like the /lll/ in *lap*. That's right; *l* is the letter for the sound /lll/ like the /lll/ in *lap*.
	Model identifying the letter for the last sound in *lap*.	Model	Listen again to the sounds in *lap*: /lll/ /aaa/ /p/.
		Lead	Say the sounds in *lap* slowly with me: /lll/ /aaa/ /p/.
		Model	The last sound in *lap* is /p/. I'm going to make an X over the letter for the sound /p/ like the /p/ in *lap*. Make an X over the letter *p*.
		Lead	Now you make an X over the letter for the sound /p/ like the /p/ in *lap*. That's right; *p* is the letter for the sound /p/ like the /p/ in *lap*. Look, we have Tic-Tac-Toe!

	To Do	**To Say**	
Test knowledge of initial and final sounds	Continue to hold up a Tic-Tac-Toe. Point to Square 2. Test children on identifying the letter for the first sound in *coat*.	**Model**	**Next game. The word is *coat*. Listen. I'll say the sounds in *coat* slowly: /k/ /ōōō/ /t/.**
		Lead	**Say the sounds in *coat* slowly with me: /k/ /ōōō/ /t/.**
		Test	**What is the <u>first</u> sound in *coat*? That's right; /k/ is the <u>first</u> sound in *coat*. Everyone, make an X over the letter for the sound /k/ like the /k/ in *coat*.** Reinforce the group on the letter name and sound: **Everyone, what's the <u>name</u> of the letter? What's the <u>sound</u> for the letter?**
	Test children on identifying the letter for the last sound in *coat*.	**Model**	**Listen again as I say *coat* slowly: /k/ /ōōō/ /t/.**
		Lead	**Say the sounds in *coat* slowly with me: /k/ /ōōō/ /t/.**
		Test	**What is the <u>last</u> sound in *coat*? That's right; /t/ is the <u>last</u> sound in *coat*. Everyone, make an X over the letter for the sound /t/ like the /t/ in *coat*.** Reinforce the group on the letter name and sound: **Everyone, what's the <u>name</u> of the letter? What's the <u>sound</u> for the letter?**

Continue with Square 3: *meat*; Square 4: *sit*; Square 5: *soap*; and Square 6: *cup*.

Ongoing Assessment

If...children make an error,	**then**...point to the correct letter and say its sound. Have children repeat the sound and make an X over the correct letter.

New Sound /r/

Review Sounds /m/, /p/, /f/, /k/, /t/, /s/, /d/, /l/, /a/, /o/

Key Phonologic Skills Isolate Initial and Final Sounds

Phonological Awareness and Alphabetic Understanding

Activity	Materials		Time
1. Alphabetic Introduce *r*/r/	Alphabet Card: *r* Letter Card: *r* (one per child)		1–2 minutes
2. Integrated Phonologic/Alphabetic Which Picture Begins with /r/?	Alphabet Card: *r* Picture Choices: 39-1, 39-2, 39-3 Teacher Resource Package 1		4–5 minutes
New 3. Phonologic Say the Last Sound of a Picture	Picture Cards: *ant, pail, pot,* *seal, carrot, doll, mat*	3-Square Strip	4–5 minutes
New 4. Alphabetic Reintroduce *r*/r/; Play Letter Match	Alphabet Card: *r* Letter Match Cards: 39a–39e	game markers (not provided)	4–5 minutes

Writing and Spelling

Activity	Materials		Time
5. Writer's Warm-Up Memory Review: *r, o, a, d, s, t*	Write-On/Wipe-Off Cards (one per child) markers and eraser (not provided) Tracing Cards: *r, o, a, d, s, t*		2–3 minutes
6. Integrated Phonologic/Alphabetic Practice Session: First and Last Sounds	3-Square Strip	Letter Tiles: *l, d, t, c,* *f, p, m*	2–3 minutes
New 7. Phonologic/Spelling Word Writing Game: First and Last Sounds	Word Writing Game (one per child) Student Activity Book 1, p. 68 Game Board 3	number cube (not provided) markers (not provided)	6–8 minutes

Activity 1 Introduce Letter Name and Sound

Introduce r/r/

Objective: Children learn letter name and sound: r/r/.

Time: 1–2 minutes

	To Do	**To Say**	
Introduce letter name	Hold up the *r* Alphabet Card.	Model	The <u>name</u> of this letter is *r*.
		Lead	Say the <u>name</u> with me: *r*.
		Test	What is the <u>name</u> of this letter?
Introduce letter sound	Continue holding up the *r* Alphabet Card.	Model	The <u>sound</u> for this letter is /rrr/. When you say /rrr/, your voice box is on and the tip of your tongue goes up toward the roof of your mouth. Say /rrr/ and feel the tip of your tongue go up toward the roof of your mouth. Put your hand on your throat to see if your voice box is on when you say /rrr/; /rrr/. Yes, your voice box is on when you say /rrr/.
		Lead	Say the <u>sound</u> with me: /rrr/.
		Test	What is the <u>sound</u> for this letter?
Test knowledge of letter name and sound	Continue holding up the *r* Alphabet Card.	Test	What is the <u>name</u> of this letter? What is the <u>sound</u> for this letter?
	Give individual turns on letter name and sound.		**Ongoing Assessment** **If**...children make an error, **then**...tell them the name or sound, have them repeat the name or sound, and return to the letter a second time.
Model tracing *r*	Distribute an *r* Letter Card to each child. Hold up the *r* Alphabet Card.	Model	**Everyone, watch. I'll trace the letter *r*.** Have children trace the *r* on their letter cards three times. Tell them to say /rrr/ each time they trace the letter. **Ongoing Assessment** **If**...children make an error, **then**...put your hand over their hand and guide them to trace the letter. Then have them try to trace the letter on their own. Repeat as necessary.

Phonological Awareness/Alphabetic Understanding

Activity 2 · Isolate Initial Sound

Which Picture Begins with /r/?

Objective: Children isolate initial /r/.

Time: 4–5 minutes

	To Do	**To Say**	
Model names of pictures	Gather the picture choices. Display Picture Choice 39-1. Point to *apple*.	Model	**This is *apple*. What is this?** Continue with the remaining pictures *(rose, dock, olive, sit, read)*. Test children on the picture names by pointing to the pictures one at a time and asking: **What is this?** Repeat for Picture Choices 39-2 *(roof, astronaut, pan, sandwich, rug, otter)* and 39-3 *(pig, ant, rain, ring, peas, seal)*.
Introduce the game Which Picture Begins with /r/?			**We're going to play a game. I'll show you a letter. Then I'll show you three pictures. You'll find the picture that begins with the sound for the letter.**
	Hold up the *r* Alphabet Card.	Model	**The <u>name</u> of this letter is *r*. The <u>sound</u> for this letter is /rrr/. Remember, when you say /rrr/, the tip of your tongue goes up toward the roof of your mouth and your voice box is on. Say /rrr/. Is the tip of your tongue up toward the roof of your mouth? Is your voice box on?**
		Test	**What is the <u>sound</u> for this letter?**
Model the game	Hold up Picture Choice 39-1. Cover the bottom row.	Model	**My turn. I'll show you how to play the game. This is *apple, rose, dock*. I'll find the picture that has the first sound /rrr/: *rose*** (exaggerate the first sound). ***Rose* has the first sound /rrr/.** Exaggerate the first sound and say the word: **/rrr/, *rose*.** Model again with the bottom row of pictures: *olive, sit, read*.
Play the game to test knowledge of /r/	Hold up the *r* Alphabet Card. Display Picture Choice 39-2. Cover the bottom row.	Test	**What is the <u>sound</u> for this letter?** Have children name each picture. **Which picture has the first sound /rrr/?** Confirm correct responses and prompt sound production: **Yes, *roof* has the first sound /rrr/. Let's say /rrr/. Remember, when you say /rrr/, the tip of your tongue goes up toward the roof of your mouth and your voice box is on. Say /rrr/, *roof*.** Continue with the bottom row of pictures and Picture Choice 39-3.
	Give individual turns.		

Ongoing Assessment

If... children make incorrect responses,	then... model the correct answer. Review the sound production cue. Have children repeat the correct answer. Go back to the example a second time.

Phonological Awareness/Alphabetic Understanding

Activity 3 Isolate Final Sound

Say the Last Sound of a Picture
Objective: Children isolate final /t/ and /l/.

Time: 4–5 minutes

	To Do	To Say	
Model names of pictures	Gather the picture cards. Place the *ant* Picture Card on the table.	**Model**	**This is *ant*. What is this?** Continue with the remaining cards. Test children on the picture names by placing the cards on the table one at a time and asking: **What is this?**
Introduce the activity			**We're going to play a new game. I'm going to show you a picture and tell you its name. You're going to listen for the last sound in the name and then tell me the last sound.**
	Set out the 3-Square Strip. Display the *ant* Picture Card.	**Model**	**This is *ant*.** Point to the last square on the strip. **The last sound in *ant* is /t/.**
		Lead	**Say the last sound in *ant* with me: /t/.** Put the strip away. **I'm going to put the strip away now because today you're going to tell me the last sound without using the strip.**
Model the activity	Display the *ant* Picture Card.	**Model**	**My turn. I'll show you how to play the game. I'll say the name of this picture: *ant*** (emphasize the last sound). **Now I'll say the last sound in *ant*: /t/.**
	Display the *pail* Picture Card.		**Next picture: *pail*. I'll say the last sound in *pail*: /lll/. I'll do one more picture before we do some pictures together. Listen carefully.**
	Display the *pot* Picture Card.		**This is *pot*. I'll say the last sound in *pot*: /t/.**
Test knowledge of final /t/ and /l/	Display the *seal* Picture Card.	**Test**	**This is *seal*. What is this? Everyone, say the last sound in *seal* with me: /lll/. That's right; the last sound in *seal* is /lll/.** Continue with *carrot, doll,* and *mat*.

326

Phonological Awareness/Alphabetic Understanding

Activity 4 Reintroduce Letter Name and Sound

Reintroduce r/r/; Play Letter Match

Objective: Children practice letter name and sound: r/r/.

Time: 4–5 minutes

	To Do	**To Say**	
Introduce letter name	Hold up the *r* Alphabet Card.	Model	The <u>name</u> of this letter is *r*.
		Lead	Say the <u>name</u> with me: *r*.
		Test	What is the <u>name</u> of this letter?
Introduce letter sound	Continue holding up the *r* Alphabet Card.	Model	The <u>sound</u> for this letter is /rrr/. When you say /rrr/, your voice box is on and the tip of your tongue goes up toward the roof of your mouth. Say /rrr/ and feel the tip of your tongue go up toward the roof of your mouth. Put your hand on your throat to see if your voice box is on when you say /rrr/; /rrr/. Yes, your voice box is on when you say /rrr/.
		Lead	Say the <u>sound</u> with me: /rrr/.
		Test	What is the <u>sound</u> for this letter?
Test knowledge of letter name and sound	Continue holding up the *r* Alphabet Card.	Test	What is the <u>name</u> of this letter? What is the <u>sound</u> for this letter?

Ongoing Assessment

	Give individual turns on letter name and sound.	If...children make an error,	then...tell them the name or sound, have them repeat the name or sound, and return to the letter a second time.

Play the Letter Match Game for r, o, a, l, d, s, t, c, f, p, and m	Give each child a Letter Match card and several markers.	Call out the sound for one of the letters *r, o, a, l, d, s, t, c, f, p,* or *m*. Have children repeat the sound as they place a marker on the corresponding letter on their cards. Continue until someone gets three in a row. If time permits, play the game again, substituting the letter name for the letter sound.

Activity 5 — Writer's Warm-Up

Memory Review: *r, o, a, d, s, t*

Objective: Children review writing *r, o, a, d, s,* and *t*.

Time: 2–3 minutes

	To Do	**To Say**
Introduce the activity	Gather the *r, o, a, d, s,* and *t* Tracing Cards. Distribute a Write-On/Wipe-Off Card and a marker to each child.	**Today we're going to practice writing the letters *r, o, a, d, s,* and *t*. I'm going to say the name of a letter. You're going to write the letter on your card.** Use the tracing cards to review the letter names.
Model the activity	Hold up a Write-On/Wipe-Off Card.	**Model** **My turn. I'll show you how this activity works. The first letter is *r*. Now I'll write the letter *r* on my card.** Write an *r* on your card.
Test children on writing *r, o, a, d, s,* and *t*		Dictate a letter name and have children write the letter on their cards. Reinforce the group on the letter name: **Everyone, what's the <u>name</u> of the letter you wrote?** Dictate each letter twice, or as time allows. Erase the cards between letters.

Ongoing Assessment

If…children write the wrong letter or don't remember a letter,	**then**…show them the tracing card for the correct letter. Trace the letter and say its name.

Activity 6 Connect Sound to Letter

Practice Session: First and Last Sounds

Objective: Children connect initial and final sounds to letters: /l/, /d/d/, /f/f/, /p/p/, /t/t/, /c/k/, /m/m/.

Time: 2–3 minutes

	To Do	**To Say**
Introduce the activity	Gather the 3-Square Strip and the letter tiles.	**Today we're going to practice for the Word Writing Game. We're going to say the sounds in some words. Then we'll choose the letters that go with the first and last sounds.**
Lead the activity	Lead children in segmenting a word.	**Lead** **The first word is _lid_. Listen. I'll say the sounds in _lid_: /lll/ /iii/ /d/.**
		Say the sounds in _lid_ with me: /lll/ /iii/ /d/. Now you say the sounds in _lid_. Have the group say the sounds together. Then give individual turns.
	Display the 3-Square Strip. Lead children in isolating the first sound.	**I'll say the sounds in _lid_ and point to a square as I say each sound: /lll/ /iii/ /d/.** Point to the first square. **What is the first sound in _lid_? That's right; /lll/ is the first sound in _lid_.** Have the group say the sound together. Then give individual turns.
	Lay out two letter tiles, _l_ and one other. Lead children in identifying the letter for the first sound.	**You're going to choose the letter for the sound /lll/ like the /lll/ in _lid_.** Point to the first square. **Does everyone know?** Call on a child to choose the correct letter and place it in the first square. Reinforce the group on the letter name and sound: **Everyone, what's the <u>name</u> of the letter? What's the <u>sound</u> for the letter?**
	Lead children in isolating the last sound.	**Watch again as I say the sounds in _lid_ and point to a square as I say each sound: /lll/ /iii/ /d/.** Point to the last square: **/d/ is the last sound in _lid_. What is the last sound in _lid_?** Have the group say the sound together. Then give individual turns.
	Lay out two letter tiles, _d_ and one other. Lead children in identifying the letter for the last sound.	**You're going to choose the letter for the sound /d/ like the /d/ in _lid_.** Point to the last square. **Does everyone know?** Call on a child to choose the correct letter and place it in the last square. Reinforce the group on the letter name and sound: **Everyone, what's the <u>name</u> of the letter? What's the <u>sound</u> for the letter?**

Practice with _cut, feed, dim,_ and _tap,_ as time allows.

Ongoing Assessment

If... children make an error,	**then...** model the answer, have them repeat it, and return to the letter a second time.

 **Connect Sound to Letter**

Word Writing Game: First and Last Sounds

Objective: Children connect sound to letter: m/m/, t/t/, p/p/, s/s/.

Time: 6–8 minutes

	To Do	To Say	
Introduce the activity	Distribute a Word Writing Game to each child.	**We're going to play a word writing game. I'll say a word. You'll write the letters that go with the word's first and last sounds. Every time we write a word, someone will roll the number cube and move a marker on the game board.**	
Model the activity	Hold up a Word Writing Game. Model identifying the letter for the first sound.	Model	**My turn. I'll show you how to play the game. The first word is *mat*. Listen. I'll say the sounds in *mat* slowly: /mmm/ /aaa/ /t/.**
		Lead	**Say the sounds in *mat* slowly with me: /mmm/ /aaa/ /t/.**
		Model	**Now I'll say the sounds in *mat* slowly and point to a letter space as I say each sound: /mmm/ /aaa/ /t/.** Point to the first space: **/mmm/ is the first sound in *mat*. I'm going to write the letter for the sound /mmm/ like the /mmm/ in *mat*.** Write the letter *m* in the first space.
		Lead	**Now you write the letter for the sound /mmm/ like the /mmm/ in *mat*. Start at the dot and write the letter in the first space. That's right; *m* is the letter for the sound /mmm/.**
	Model identifying the letter for the last sound.	Model	**Listen again to the sounds in *mat*: /mmm/ /aaa/ /t/.**
		Lead	**Say the sounds in *mat* slowly with me: /mmm/ /aaa/ /t/.**
		Model	**Watch again as I point to the letter spaces and say *mat* slowly: /mmm/ /aaa/ /t/.** Point to the last space: **/t/ is the last sound in *mat*. I'm going to write the letter for the sound /t/ like the /t/ in *mat*.** Write the letter *t* in the last space.
		Lead	**Now you write the letter for the sound /t/ like the /t/ in *mat*. Start at the dot and write the letter in the last space. That's right; *t* is the letter for the sound /t/.**

	To Do	**To Say**	
Test knowledge of initial and final sounds	Continue to hold up a Word Writing Game.	**Model**	**The next word is *pat*. Listen. I'll say the sounds in *pat* slowly: /p/ /aaa/ /t/.**
		Lead	**Say the sounds in *pat* slowly with me: /p/ /aaa/ /t/.**
		Model	**Now I'll say the sounds in *pat* slowly and point to a letter space as I say each sound: /p/ /aaa/ /t/.**
		Test	**What is the <u>first</u> sound in *pat*?** Point to the first space. **That's right; /p/ is the <u>first</u> sound in *pat*. Everyone, write the letter for the sound /p/ like the /p/ in *pat* in the first space.** Reinforce the group on the letter name and sound: **Everyone, what's the <u>name</u> of the letter? What's the <u>sound</u> for the letter?**
		Model	**Listen again to the sounds in *pat*: /p/ /aaa/ /t/.**
		Lead	**Say the sounds in *pat* slowly with me: /p/ /aaa/ /t/.**
		Model	**Watch again as I point to the letter spaces and say *pat* slowly: /p/ /aaa/ /t/.**
		Test	**What is the <u>last</u> sound in *pat*?** Point to the last space. **That's right; /t/ is the <u>last</u> sound in *pat*. Everyone, write the letter for the sound /t/ like the /t/ in *pat* in the last space.** Reinforce the group on the letter name and sound: **Everyone, what's the <u>name</u> of the letter? What's the <u>sound</u> for the letter?**
			Continue with *map, sat, pot, mom,* and *mop*. After each word, have a child roll the number cube and move a marker on the game board.

Ongoing Assessment

If...children make an error,	**then**...model the letter name and sound and have children repeat them. Have children write the correct letter.

Review Sounds /f/, /d/, /t/, /s/, /k/, /l/, /o/, /r/
Key Phonologic Skills Isolate Initial and Final Sounds

Phonological Awareness and Alphabetic Understanding

Activity	Materials		Time
1. Alphabetic Review *r*/r/	Alphabet Card: *r*		1–2 minutes
New **2. Phonologic** Where Is the Sound?	Picture Cards: *lip, soap, pail, mouse, lamb, seal, mat, tape*	3-Square Strip (one per child)	4–5 minutes
3. Phonologic Say the Last Sound of a Picture	Picture Cards: *seal, cup, pail, mop, coat, doll, tape, pot, soap, ant*	3-Square Strip	4–5 minutes
New **4. Alphabetic** Review *r*/r/; Play Go Fish!	Alphabet Card: *r*	Game Cards: *f, d, t, s, c, l, o, r* (two of each letter)	4–5 minutes

Writing and Spelling

Activity	Materials		Time
5. Writer's Warm-Up Review: *p, c, f, m, r, l, t, a, d, o, s*	Writer's Warm-Up (one per child) Student Activity Book 1, p. 69	Tracing Cards: *p, c, f, m, r, l, t, a, d, o, s*	2–3 minutes
6. Integrated Phonologic/Alphabetic Practice Session: First and Last Sounds	3-Square Strip	Letter Tiles: *m, d, l, p, t*	2–3 minutes
New **7. Phonologic/Spelling** Word Maze: First and Last Sounds	Word Maze (one per child) Student Activity Book 1, p. 70		6–8 minutes

Review r/r/

Objective: Children review letter name and sound: r/r/.

Time: 1–2 minutes

	To Do	**To Say**	
Test knowledge of letter name and sound	Hold up the *r* Alphabet Card.	**Test**	**What is the <u>name</u> of this letter? What is the <u>sound</u> for this letter?**
	Give individual turns on letter name and sound.		

Ongoing Assessment

If . . . children make an error,	**then** . . . tell them the name or sound, have them repeat the name or sound, and return to the letter a second time.

Activity  2 Isolate Initial and Final Sounds

Where Is the Sound?

Objective: Children locate position of a sound on a 3-Square Strip.

Time: 4–5 minutes

	To Do		**To Say**
Introduce the activity	Gather the picture cards. Distribute a 3-Square Strip to each child.		We're going to play a new game today. I'll say a sound in a word. You'll show me where the sound is on your strip.
Model the activity	Display a 3-Square Strip. Place the *lip* Picture Card on the table.	**Model**	My turn. I'll show you how to play the game. This is *lip*. I'll say the sounds in *lip*: /lll/ /iii/ /p/. Point to the squares on your strip as you say each sound. I'll show you /p/. Touch the last square on the strip: /p/ is the last sound in *lip*.
	Place the *soap* Picture Card on the table.		New picture. This is *soap*. I'll say the sounds in *soap*: /sss/ /ōōō/ /p/. Point to the squares as you say each sound. I'll show you /sss/. Touch the first square on the strip: /sss/ is the first sound in *soap*.
	Place the *pail* Picture Card on the table.		New picture. This is *pail*. I'll say the sounds in *pail*: /p/ /āāā/ /lll/. Point to the squares as you say each sound. I'll show you /lll/. Touch the last square on the strip: /lll/ is the last sound in *pail*.
Test knowledge of first and last sounds	Place the *mouse* Picture Card on the table.	**Test**	This is *mouse*. What is this? I'll say the sounds in *mouse*. We'll all point to a square as I say each sound: /mmm/ /ou/ /sss/. Point to the squares as you say each sound. Let's all find /mmm/. Point to the first square. That's right; /mmm/ is the first sound in *mouse*.
			Continue with *lamb, seal, mat,* and *tape*. Alternate between first and last sounds.

Phonological Awareness/Alphabetic Understanding

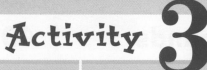

Say the Last Sound of a Picture

Objective: Children isolate final /p/, /l/, and /t/.

Time: 4–5 minutes

	To Do	To Say	
Model names of pictures	Gather the picture cards. Place the *seal* Picture Card on the table.	**Model**	**This is *seal*. What is this?** Continue with the remaining cards. Test children on the picture names by placing the cards on the table one at a time and asking: **What is this?**
Introduce the activity			**We're going to play a game. I'm going to show you a picture and tell you its name. You're going to listen for the last sound in the name and then tell me the sound.**
	Set out the 3-Square Strip. Display the *cup* Picture Card.	**Model**	**This is *cup*. What is this?** Point to the last square on the strip. **The last sound in *cup* is /p/. What is the last sound in *cup*? That's right; the last sound in *cup* is /p/.**
		Lead	**Say the last sound in *cup* with me: /p/.** Put the strip away. **I'm going to put the strip away now because today you're going to tell me the last sound without using the strip.**
Model the activity	Display the *seal* Picture Card.	**Model**	**My turn. I'll show you how to play the game. I'll say the name of this picture: *seal*** (exaggerate the last sound). **Now I'll say the last sound in *seal*: /lll/.**
	Display the *soap* Picture Card.	**Lead**	**Let's try one together. This is *soap*. What is this? Now say the last sound in *soap* with me: /p/. That's right; the last sound in *soap* is /p/.**
Test knowledge of final /p/, /l/, and /t/	Display the *pail* Picture Card.	**Test**	**Your turn to listen for the last sound. This is *pail*. What is this? Say the last sound in *pail*. That's right; /lll/ is the last sound in *pail*.**
			Continue with *mop, coat, doll, tape, pot,* and *ant*.

Ongoing Assessment

If... children make an error,

then... repeat the word and tell them the last sound. Have children repeat the task.

If... children continue to make errors,

then... go back to using the 3-Square Strip. Have children touch each square as you say the sounds in each word. Touch the last square and have children say the last sound.

Activity 4 Review Letter Name and Sound

Review r/r/; Play Go Fish!

Objective: Children practice letter name and sound: r/r/.

Time: 4–5 minutes

	To Do	**To Say**
Test knowledge of letter name and sound	Hold up the *r* Alphabet Card.	**Test** **What is the <u>name</u> of this letter? What is the <u>sound</u> for this letter?**

Ongoing Assessment

If... children make an error,	then... tell them the name or sound, have them repeat the name or sound, and return to the letter a second time.

	To Do	**To Say**
Play Go Fish!	Gather the game cards. Give two cards to each child. Place the remaining cards in a pile face down on the table.	**We are going to play the game Go Fish! We will try to collect matching pairs of letters. You will take turns asking another child if he or she has the card you need to make a match.**
	Model the game.	**Model** **My turn. I need a *t* to make a match. I will ask ____ if he has one. If he has that card, he will give it to me. Then I can have another turn. If he does not have the card I need, he will say, "Go fish!" Then I will take a card from the pile. The first person to have all matching pairs wins the game.**
	Play the game.	Guide children as needed. The first child to have all matching pairs wins the game. Repeat the game as time allows.

Activity 5 Writer's Warm-Up

Review: p, c, f, m, r, l, t, a, d, o, s

Objective: Children practice writing letters.

Time: 2–3 minutes

	To Do	To Say
Review writing *p, c, f, m, r, l, t, a, d, o,* and *s*	Hold up a Writer's Warm-Up. Distribute a Writer's Warm-Up to each child.	Review the name of each letter and how to write the letter. Have children trace and write each letter. Then have them circle their best letters.

Ongoing Assessment

If... children make an error,

then... have them write the letter again. If needed, put your hand over their hand and guide them to write the letter. Then have them write the letter on their own. Repeat as necessary.

Writing/Spelling

Activity 6 Connect Sound to Letter

Practice Session: First and Last Sounds

Objective: Children connect initial and final sounds to letters: Time: 2–3 minutes
m/m/, d/d/, l/l/, p/p/, t/t/.

	To Do	**To Say**
Introduce the activity	Gather the 3-Square Strip and the letter tiles.	**Today we're going to practice for the Word Maze. We're going to say the sounds in some words slowly. Then we'll choose the letters that go with the first and last sounds.**
Lead the activity	Model segmenting a word.	**Model** **The first word is** *mud.* **Listen. I'll say the sounds in** *mud* **slowly: /mmm/ /uuu/ /d/.**
		Lead **Say the sounds in** *mud* **slowly with me: /mmm/ /uuu/ /d/. Now you say the sounds in** *mud* **slowly.** Have the group say the sounds together. Then give individual turns.
	Display the 3-Square Strip. Lead children in isolating the first sound.	**I'll say the sounds in** *mud* **slowly and point to a square as I say each sound: /mmm/ /uuu/ /d/.** Point to the first square. **What is the first sound in** *mud?* **That's right; /mmm/ is the first sound in** *mud.*
	Lay out two letter tiles, *m* and one other. Lead children in identifying the letter that goes with the first sound.	**You're going to choose the letter for the sound /mmm/ like the /mmm/ in** *mud.* Point to the first square. **Does everyone know?** Call on a child to choose the correct letter and place it in the first square. Reinforce the group on the letter name and sound: **Everyone, what's the <u>name</u> of the letter? What's the <u>sound</u> for the letter?**
	Lead children in isolating the last sound.	**Watch again as I say the sounds in** *mud* **slowly and point to a square as I say each sound: /mmm/ /uuu/ /d/.** Point to the last square: **/d/ is the last sound in** *mud.* **What is the last sound in** *mud?*
	Lay out two letter tiles, *d* and one other. Lead children in identifying the letter that goes with the last sound.	**You're going to choose the letter for the sound /d/ like the /d/ in** *mud.* Point to the last square. **Does everyone know?** Call on a child to choose the correct letter and place it in the last square. Reinforce the group on the letter name and sound: **Everyone, what's the <u>name</u> of the letter? What's the <u>sound</u> for the letter?**
		Practice with *lip, lit, dim,* and *tip,* as time allows.

Ongoing Assessment

If...children make an error,	**then**...model the answer, have them repeat it, and return to the letter a second time.

Activity 7 **Connect Sound to Letter**

Word Maze: First and Last Sounds

Objective: Children connect initial and final sounds to letters: /l/l/, d/d/, m/m/, p/p/, t/t/.

Time: 6–8 minutes

	To Do	**To Say**	
Introduce the activity	Distribute a Word Maze to each child. Hold up a maze. Point to the top arrow and move your finger through the maze. Stop at the first word space, above the two sheep.		Today we have a word maze. I'm going to say a word. *You're going to write the letters that go with the word's first and last sounds. Let's see if we can get through the maze!* Watch as I move my finger through the maze. This is where the first word will go.
Model the activity	Hold up a Word Maze. Model identifying the letter for the first sound.	Model	The first word is at the beginning of the maze. The first word is *lid*. Listen. I'll say the sounds in *lid:* /lll/ /iii/ /d/.
		Lead	Say the sounds in *lid* with me: /lll/ /iii/ /d/.
		Model	Now I'll say the sounds in *lid* and point to a square as I say each sound: /lll/ /iii/ /d/. Point to the first square: /lll/ is the first sound in *lid*. I'm going to write the letter for the sound /lll/ like the /lll/ in *lid*. Write the letter *l* in the first square.
		Lead	Now you write the letter for the sound /lll/ like the /lll/ in *lid*. Start at the dot and write the letter in the first square. That's right; *l* is the letter for the sound /lll/.
	Model identifying the letter for the last sound.	Model	Watch again as I point to the squares and say the sounds in *lid:* /lll/ /iii/ /d/. Point to the last square: /d/ is the last sound in *lid*. I'm going to write the letter for the sound /d/ like the /d/ in *lid*. Write the letter *d* in the last square.
		Lead	Now you write the letter for the sound /d/ like the /d/ in *lid*. Start at the dot and write the letter in the last square. That's right; *d* is the letter for the sound /d/.

	To Do	**To Say**	
Test knowledge of initial and final sounds	Continue to hold up a Word Maze.	Model	**Find your way through the maze to the next word. The next word is** *map*. **Listen. I'll say the sounds in** *map* **slowly: /mmm/ /aaa/ /p/.**
		Lead	**Say the sounds in** *map* **slowly with me: /mmm/ /aaa/ /p/.**
		Model	**Now I'll say the sounds in** *map* **slowly and point to a square as I say each sound: /mmm/ /aaa/ /p/.**
		Test	**What is the <u>first</u> sound in** *map*? Point to the first square. **That's right; /mmm/ is the <u>first</u> sound in** *map*. **Everyone, write the letter for the sound /mmm/ like the /mmm/ in** *map* **in the first square.** Reinforce the group on the letter name and sound: **Everyone, what's the <u>name</u> of the letter? What's the <u>sound</u> for the letter?**
	Continue to hold up a Word Maze.	Model	**Watch again as I point to the squares and say** *map* **slowly: /mmm/ /aaa/ /p/.**
		Test	**What is the <u>last</u> sound in** *map*? Point to the last square. **That's right; /p/ is the <u>last</u> sound in** *map*. **Everyone, write the letter for the sound /p/ like the /p/ in** *map* **in the last square.** Reinforce the group on the letter name and sound: **Everyone, what's the <u>name</u> of the letter? What's the <u>sound</u> for the letter?**

Continue with *late* and *time*. After each word, have children find their way through the maze to the next word.

Ongoing Assessment

If...children make an error,	then...model the letter name and sound and have children repeat them. Have children write the correct letter.

Review Sounds /m/, /p/, /s/, /d/, /l/, /a/, /o/, /r/
Key Phonologic Skills Isolate Initial and Final Sounds

Phonological Awareness and Alphabetic Understanding

Activity	Materials		Time
1. Alphabetic Review *r*/r/	Alphabet Card: *r*		1–2 minutes
New **2. Integrated Phonologic/Alphabetic** Where Is the Sound?	Picture Cards: *cup, pot, mop, lip, map, cat, cap* 3-Square Strips (one per child)	Letter Tiles: *c, t, m, p* (one set per child)	4–5 minutes
3. Phonologic Say the Last Sound of a Picture	Picture Cards: *seal, mat, soap, doll, tape, cup, pot, mud, red*		4–5 minutes
New **4. Alphabetic** Review *r*/r/; Play Mystery Square	Alphabet Card: *r* Game Cards: "star," *m, p, s, d, l, a, o, r*	sticky notes (not provided)	4–5 minutes

Writing and Spelling

Activity	Materials		Time
5. Writer's Warm-Up Ready, Set, Go!	Writer's Warm-Up (one per child) Student Activity Book 1, p. 71	Tracing Cards: *p, t, m, o, a, l, d, f, c, s*	2–3 minutes
6. Integrated Phonologic/Alphabetic Practice Session: First and Last Sounds	3-Square Strip	Letter Tiles: *f, c, s, r, t*	2–3 minutes
7. Phonologic/Spelling Letter Tag	Letter Tag (one per child) Student Activity Book 1, p. 72		6–8 minutes

Activity **1** Review Letter Name and Sound

Review r/r/

Objective: Children review letter name and sound: *r/r/*.

Time: 1–2 minutes

	To Do		**To Say**	
Test knowledge of letter name and sound	Hold up the *r* Alphabet Card.	**Test**	**What is the <u>name</u> of this letter? What is the <u>sound</u> for this letter?**	
	Give individual turns on letter name and sound.			

Ongoing Assessment

If... children make an error,

then... tell them the name or sound, have them repeat the name or sound, and return to the letter a second time.

Activity 2 Isolate Initial and Final Sounds

Where Is the Sound?

Objective: Children locate position of a sound on a
3-Square Strip and place the corresponding letter tile.

Time: 4–5 minutes

	To Do	**To Say**	
Introduce the activity	Gather the picture cards. Give each child a 3-Square Strip and letter tiles for *c, t, m,* and *p.* Have children place the letter tiles below the 3-Square Strip so that they can see the letters.	**We're going to play the game in which you find the sound on the strip. But today we're also going to put letter tiles on the strip. I'll show you how.**	
Model the activity	Display a 3-Square Strip. Place the *cup* Picture Card on the table.	**Model**	**My turn. This is *cup*. I'll say the sounds in *cup*: /k/ /uuu/ /p/.** Point to the squares on your strip as you say each sound. **I'll show you /k/.** Touch the first square: **/k/ is the first sound in *cup*. I'll put the letter for the sound /k/ in the first square.** Place the *c* Letter Tile in the first square. Clear off your strip and model again for *pot* (last sound /t/) and *mop* (first sound /m/).
Test knowledge of first and last sounds	Place the *lip* Picture Card on the table.	**Test**	**Now let's do it together. This is *lip*. What is this? I'll say the sounds in *lip*. We'll all point to a square as I say each sound: /lll/ /iii/ /p/.** Point to the squares as you say each sound. **Let's all find /p/.** Point to the last square. **That's right; /p/ is the last sound in *lip*. Let's put the letter for the sound /p/ in the last square.** Place the *p* Letter Tile in the last square. Continue with *map* (first sound /m/), *cat* (last sound /t/), and *cap* (last sound /p/).

345

Phonological Awareness/Alphabetic Understanding

 **Activity 3 Isolate Final Sound**

Say the Last Sound of a Picture
Objective: Children isolate final /l/, /t/, /p/, and /d/.   Time: 4–5 minutes

	To Do	**To Say**	
Model names of pictures	Gather the picture cards. Place the *seal* Picture Card on the table.	Model	**This is *seal*. What is this?** Continue with the remaining cards. Test children on the picture names by placing the cards on the table one at a time and asking: **What is this?**
Introduce the activity			**We're going to play a game. I'm going to show you a picture and tell you its name. You're going to listen for the last sound in the name and then tell me the sound.**
Model the activity	Display the *seal* Picture Card. Display the *mat* Picture Card.	Model Lead	**My turn. I'll say the name of this picture: *seal*. Now I'll say the last sound in *seal*: /lll/.** **Let's try one together. This is *mat*. What is this? Now say the last sound in *mat* with me: /t/. That's right; the last sound in *mat* is /t/.**
Test knowledge of final /l/, /t/, /p/, and /d/	Display the *soap* Picture Card. Give individual turns.	Test	**Now it's your turn to listen for the last sound. This is *soap*. What is this? Say the last sound in *soap*. That's right; the last sound in *soap* is /p/.** Continue with *doll, tape, cup, pot, mud,* and *red*.

Ongoing Assessment

If...children make an error,	**then**...repeat the word and tell them the last sound. Have children repeat the task.
If...children continue to make errors,	**then**...go back to using the 3-Square Strip. Have children touch a square for each sound in the word. Touch the last square and have children say the last sound.

Phonological Awareness/Alphabetic Understanding

Review r/r/; Play Mystery Square
Objective: Children review letter name and sound: /r/.

Time: 4–5 minutes

	To Do		**To Say**
Test knowledge of letter name and sound	Hold up the *r* Alphabet Card. Give individual turns on letter name and sound.	**Test**	**What is the <u>name</u> of this letter? What is the <u>sound</u> for this letter?**

Ongoing Assessment

If...children make an error,	**then**...tell them the name or sound, have them repeat the name or sound, and return to the letter a second time.

	To Do		**To Say**
Play the game Mystery Square	Gather the game cards. Place a small sticky note on half of the cards, leaving the letter on the card visible. Mix the cards and arrange them face down in a 3-by-3 configuration on the table.	**Lead**	**We are going to play the game Mystery Square. You are going to choose a card. If you can name the letter on the card, you will earn one point. If there is a sticky note on the card you choose, you can earn two points by naming the letter and its sound. If you choose the "star" card, you will earn three points and another turn. I will keep track of the points.** After all the cards have been turned over, play a second round of the game if time permits.

Activity **5** Writer's Warm-Up

Ready, Set, Go!

Objective: Children practice writing *p, t, m, o, a, l, d, f, c,* and *s.*

Time: 2–3 minutes

	To Do	**To Say**	
Introduce the activity	Give each child a Ready, Set, Go! sheet.	**Today you're going to practice writing some of the letters you've learned. You're going to write your best letters as fast as you can.**	
Model the activity	Hold up a Ready, Set, Go! sheet. Point to the first row.	Model	**My turn. I'll show you how this activity works. The letters in the first row are *p, t, m,* and *o.* Watch as I trace each letter with my pencil.** Trace each letter in the first row.
		Lead	**Now it's your turn to trace the letters in the first row.** Watch as children trace the letters.
		Model	**After I say "Ready, set, go," I'll write my best *p, t, m,* and *o* as fast as I can on the second row. Watch me try. Ready, set, go!** Write the letters on the second row and then put your pencil down.
		Lead	**Now it's your turn to write your best *p, t, m,* and *o* as fast as you can. Ready, set, go!** Tell children to put their pencils down when they have finished.
Test knowledge of writing *a, l, d, f, c,* and *s*	Continue to hold up the activity sheet. Point to the next row of letters.	Test	**The letters in the next row are *a, l, d,* and *f.* Warm up by tracing each letter with your pencil. Put your pencil down when you have finished.**
			Now it's your turn to write your best *a, l, d,* and *f* as fast as you can. Ready, set, go! Remind children to put their pencils down when they have finished.
			Repeat for the last row of letters. Then have children look over their papers and circle their best letters: **Now look over your paper and circle your very best letters.**

Ongoing Assessment

If... children write the wrong letter or don't remember how to write a letter,	then... show them the tracing card for the correct letter. Trace the letter and say its name.

Writing/Spelling

Activity 6 — Connect Sound to Letter

Practice Session: First and Last Sounds

Objective: Children connect initial and final sounds to letters: Time: 2–3 minutes
r/r/, t/t/, c/k/, s/s/, f/f/.

	To Do	To Say	
Introduce the activity	Gather the 3-Square Strip and the letter tiles.	**Today we're going to practice for Letter Tag. We're going to say the sounds in some words slowly. Then we'll choose the letters that go with the first and last sounds.**	
Lead the activity	Model segmenting a word.	Model	**The first word is *rat*. Listen. I'll say the sounds in *rat* slowly: /rrr/ /aaa/ /t/.**
		Lead	**Say the sounds in *rat* slowly with me: /rrr/ /aaa/ /t/. Now you say the sounds in *rat* slowly.** Have the group say the sounds together. Then give individual turns.
	Display the 3-Square Strip. Lead children in isolating the first sound.		**I'll say the sounds in *rat* slowly and point to a square as I say each sound: /rrr/ /aaa/ /t/.** Point to the first square. **What is the first sound in *rat*? That's right; /rrr/ is the first sound in *rat*.** Have the group say the sound together. Then give individual turns.
	Lay out two letter tiles, *r* and one other. Lead children in identifying the letter that goes with the first sound.		**You're going to choose the letter for the sound /rrr/ like the /rrr/ in *rat*.** Point to the first square. **Does everyone know?** Call on a child to choose the correct letter and place it in the first square. Reinforce the group on the letter name and sound: **Everyone, what's the <u>name</u> of the letter? What's the <u>sound</u> for the letter?**
	Lead children in isolating the last sound.		**Watch again as I say the sounds in *rat* slowly and point to a square as I say each sound: /rrr/ /aaa/ /t/.** Point to the last square: **/t/ is the last sound in *rat*. What is the last sound in *rat*?**
	Lay out two letter tiles, *t* and one other. Lead children in identifying the letter that goes with the last sound.		**You're going to choose the letter for the sound /t/ like the /t/ in *rat*.** Point to the last square. **Does everyone know?** Call on a child to choose the correct letter and place it in the last square. Reinforce the group on the letter name and sound: **Everyone, what's the <u>name</u> of the letter? What's the <u>sound</u> for the letter?**
			Practice with *case, fire, safe,* and *cut,* as time allows.

Ongoing Assessment

If... children make an error,	then... model the answer, have them repeat it, and return to the letter a second time.

349

Writing/Spelling

Activity 7 — Connect Sound to Letter

Letter Tag

Objective: Children connect initial and final sounds to letters:
/l/l/, p/p/, s/s/, f/f/, m/m/, t/t/.

Time: 6–8 minutes

	To Do	**To Say**
Introduce the activity	Distribute a Letter Tag to each child.	**Today we're going to play Letter Tag. I'm going to tell you a word. You're going to tag the word's first and last sounds.**
Model the activity	Hold up a Letter Tag. Model identifying the letter for the first sound.	**Model** **My turn. I'll show you how to play Letter Tag. The first word is *lip*. Listen. I'll say the sounds in *lip* slowly: /lll/ /iii/ /p/.**
		Lead **Say the sounds in *lip* slowly with me: /lll/ /iii/ /p/.**
		Model **The first sound in *lip* is /lll/. I'm going to start at the arrow and tag the letter for the sound /lll/ like the /lll/ in *lip*.** Use a pencil to draw a line from the arrow to the letter *l*.
		Lead **Now it's your turn to tag the letter for the sound /lll/ like the /lll/ in *lip*. Put your pencil on the first arrow and tag the letter. That's right; *l* is the letter for the sound /lll/.**
	Model identifying the letter for the last sound.	**Model** **Listen again to the sounds in *lip*: /lll/ /iii/ /p/. The last sound in *lip* is /p/. I'm going to start at the first arrow again and tag the letter for the sound /p/ like the /p/ in *lip*.** Draw a line from the arrow to the letter *p*.
		Lead **Now it's your turn to tag the letter for the sound /p/ like the /p/ in *lip*. Put your pencil on the first arrow and tag the letter. That's right; *p* is the letter for the sound /p/.**

	To Do	**To Say**	
Test knowledge of initial and final sounds	Continue to hold up a Letter Tag. Point to the next box.	**Model**	The next word is *safe*. Listen. I'll say the sounds in *safe* slowly: /sss/ /āāā/ /fff/.
		Lead	**Say the sounds in *safe* slowly with me: /sss/ /āāā/ /fff/.**
		Test	**What is the <u>first</u> sound in *safe*? That's right; /sss/ is the <u>first</u> sound in *safe*. Put your pencil on the arrow and tag the letter for the sound /sss/ like the /sss/ in *safe*.** Reinforce the group on the letter name and sound: **Everyone, what's the <u>name</u> of the letter? What's the <u>sound</u> for the letter?**

Listen again as I say *safe* slowly: /sss/ /āāā/ /fff/. What is the <u>last</u> sound in *safe*? That's right; /fff/ is the <u>last</u> sound in *safe*. Everyone, put your pencil on the same arrow and tag the letter for the sound /fff/ like the /fff/ in *safe*. Reinforce the group on the letter name and sound: **Everyone, what's the <u>name</u> of the letter? What's the <u>sound</u> for the letter?**

Continue with 3. feet: /fff/, /t/; 4. mope: /mmm/, /p/; 5. sit: /sss/, /t/; 6. tell: /t/, /lll/. Follow the boxes left to right across the page.

Ongoing Assessment

If...children make an error,	**then**...model the letter name and sound and have children repeat them. Have children tag the correct letter.

351

Writing/Spelling

Review Sounds /m/, /p/, /f/, /k/, /t/, /a/, /o/, /r/
Key Phonologic Skills Isolate Initial and Final Sounds

Phonological Awareness and Alphabetic Understanding

Activity	Materials		Time
1. Alphabetic Review *r*/r/	Alphabet Card: *r*		1–2 minutes
2. Integrated Phonologic/Alphabetic Where Is the Sound?	Picture Cards: *pot, cup, cat, soup, mud, mat, lip, seal* 3-Square Strips (one per child)	Letter Tiles: *p, t, s, m, l* (one set per child)	4–5 minutes
3. Phonologic Say the Last Sound of a Picture	Picture Cards: *carrot, map, mud, pail, pot, mop, red, doll, coat, soap*		4–5 minutes
New **4. Alphabetic** Review *r*/r/; Diz Chooses a Sound Game	Alphabet Card: *r* Game Cards: "star," *m, p, f, c, t, a, o, r* (two of each letter)	Diz puppet	4–5 minutes

Writing and Spelling

Activity	Materials		Time
New **5. Writer's Warm-Up** Treasure Hunt: *o, l, s, f, r, a, d, c*	Treasure Hunt (one per child) Student Activity Book 1, p. 73	Tracing Cards: *o, l, s, f, r, a, d, c*	2–3 minutes
6. Integrated Phonologic/Alphabetic Practice Session: First and Last Sounds	3-Square Strip	Letter Tiles: *r, m, s, p, f*	2–3 minutes
New **7. Phonologic/Spelling** Rhyme Time	Rhyme Time (one per child) Student Activity Book 1, p. 74		6–8 minutes

Review r/r/

Objective: Children review letter name and sound: r/r/.

Time: 1–2 minutes

	To Do	**To Say**
Test knowledge of letter name and sound	Hold up the *r* Alphabet Card.	**Test** **What is the name of this letter? What is the sound for this letter?**

Ongoing Assessment

If...children make an error,	then...tell them the name or sound, have them repeat the name or sound, and return to the letter a second time.

Give individual turns on letter name and sound.

Where Is the Sound?

Objective: Children locate position of a sound on a
3-Square Strip and place the corresponding letter tile.

Time: 4–5 minutes

	To Do	To Say
Introduce the activity	Gather the picture cards. Give each child a 3-Square Strip and letter tiles.	**We're going to play the game in which you find the sound on the strip. But today we're also going to put letter tiles on the strip. I'll show you how. First, place your letter tiles below your 3-Square Strip so that you can see all of the letters.**
Model the activity	Display a 3-Square Strip. Place the *pot* Picture Card on the table.	**Model** **My turn. This is *pot*. I'll say the sounds in *pot*: /p/ /ooo/ /t/.** Point to the squares on your strip as you say each sound. **I'll show you /p/.** Touch the first square: **/p/ is the first sound in *pot*. I'll put the letter for the sound /p/ in the first square.** Place the *p* Letter Tile in the first square. *Clear off the strip and model again for* cup *(last sound /p/).*
	Place the *cat* Picture Card on the table.	**Lead** **Now let's do one together. This is *cat*. What is this? I'll say the sounds in *cat*. We'll all point to a square as I say each sound: /k/ /aaa/ /t/.** Point to the squares as you say each sound. **Let's all find /t/.** Point to the last square. **That's right; /t/ is the last sound in *cat*. Let's put the letter for the sound /t/ in the last square.** *Clear off the strips and repeat for* soup *(first sound /s/).*
Test knowledge of first and last sounds	Place the *mud* Picture Card on the table.	**Test** **Now it's your turn. I'll say the sounds in *mud*. You'll point to a square as I say each sound: /mmm/ /uuu/ /d/.** Have children point to a square as you say each sound. **Show me /mmm/. That's right; /mmm/ is the first sound in *mud*. Put the letter for the sound /mmm/ in the first square.** *Repeat for* mat *(last sound /t/),* lip *(first sound /l/), and* seal *(first sound /s/).*
	Give individual turns.	

Ongoing Assessment

If...	then...
If... children make an error in identifying the position of the sound,	then... say the sounds in the word again as you touch each square. Point to the square that represents the sound.
If... children select the wrong letter tile for the square,	then... show them the letter tile they should select. Have them repeat the task.

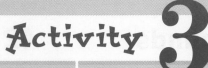

Activity **3** Isolate Final Sound

Say the Last Sound of a Picture

Objective: Children isolate final /t/, /p/, /d/, and /l/.

Time: 4–5 minutes

	To Do		**To Say**	
Model names of pictures	Gather the picture cards. Place the *carrot* Picture Card on the table.	Model	**This is *carrot*. What is this?** Continue with the remaining cards. Test children on the picture names by placing the cards on the table one at a time and asking: **What is this?**	
Introduce the activity			**We're going to play a game. I'm going to show you a picture and tell you its name. You're going to listen for the last sound in the name and then tell me the sound.**	
Model the activity	Display the *carrot* Picture Card.	Model	**My turn. I'll show you how to play the game. I'll say the name of this picture: *carrot*** (exaggerate the last sound). **Now I'll say the last sound in *carrot*: /t/.**	
	Display the *map* Picture Card.	Lead	**Let's try one together. This is *map*. What is this? Say the last sound in *map* with me: /p/. That's right; the last sound in *map* is /p/.**	
Test knowledge of final /t/, /p/, /d/, and /l/	Display the *mud* Picture Card.	Test	**Now it's your turn to listen for the last sound. This is *mud*. What is this? Say the last sound in *mud*. That's right; the last sound in *mud* is /d/.** Continue with *pail, pot, mop, red, doll, coat,* and *soap*.	

Ongoing Assessment

If...children make an error,	**then**...repeat the word and tell them the last sound. Have children repeat the task.
If...children continue to make errors,	**then**...go back to using the 3-Square Strip. Have children touch each square as you say the sounds in each word. Touch the last square and have children say the last sound.

Phonological Awareness/Alphabetic Understanding

Review r/r/; Diz Chooses a Sound Game

Objective: Children review letter name and sound: r/r/.

Time: 4–5 minutes

	To Do		**To Say**
Test knowledge of letter name and sound	Hold up the *r* Alphabet Card. Give individual turns on letter name and sound.	**Test**	**What is the <u>name</u> of this letter? What is the <u>sound</u> for this letter?**

Ongoing Assessment

If... children make an error,	**then...** tell them the name or sound, have them repeat the name or sound, and return to the letter a second time.

	To Do		**To Say**
Play the game Diz Chooses a Sound	Gather the Diz puppet and the game cards. Mix the cards and give an equal number to each child.	**Lead**	**We are going to play a sound matching game with Diz, our puppet. When it is your turn to hold Diz, you will ask another child for a card by saying, "Do you have a /p/?" If the person has the card, he or she will repeat the sound and give you the card. If that person doesn't have the card, you will give Diz to the child sitting next to you and it will be his or her turn to ask someone for a card.**
			Continue until all cards have been paired.

**Activity**  **5** **Writer's Warm-Up**

New

Treasure Hunt: o, l, s, f, r, a, d, c

Objective: Children practice writing *o, l, s, f, r, a, d,* and *c*.

Time: 2–3 minutes

	To Do	**To Say**	
Introduce the activity	Give each child a Treasure Hunt sheet.	**We're going to go on a treasure hunt. I'm going to tell you the name of a letter, and you're going to write it. Let's see if we can get past the monsters and find the hidden treasure!**	
Model the activity	Hold up a Treasure Hunt.	Model	**Let's do one together. The first letter is *o*. Watch as I start at the dot and write the letter *o*.** Write an *o* on the first line.
		Lead	**Now you write the letter *o*. Start at the dot and write the letter.**
Test children on writing *l, s, f, r, a, d,* and *c*		Test	**The next letter is *l*. Write the letter *l*. Start at the dot and write the letter.** Reinforce the group on the letter name: **Everyone, what's the <u>name</u> of the letter you wrote?**
			Continue with *s, f, r, a, d,* and *c*.

Ongoing Assessment

If...children write the wrong letter or don't remember a letter,	**then**...show them the tracing card for the letter and model tracing the letter.

Practice Session: First and Last Sounds

Objective: Children connect initial and final sounds
to letters: r/r/, m/m/, s/s/, p/p/, f/f/.

Time: 2–3 minutes

	To Do	**To Say**
Introduce the activity	Gather the 3-Square Strip and the letter tiles.	**Today we're going to practice for Rhyme Time. We're going to say the sounds in some words slowly. Then we'll choose the letters that go with the first and last sounds.**
Lead the activity	Model segmenting a word.	**Model** **The first word is *rim*. Listen. I'll say the sounds in *rim* slowly: /rrr/ /iii/ /mmm/.**
		Lead **Say the sounds in *rim* slowly with me: /rrr/ /iii/ /mmm/. Now you say the sounds in *rim* slowly.** Have the group say the sounds together. Then give individual turns.
	Display the 3-Square Strip. Lead children in isolating the first sound.	**I'll say the sounds in *rim* slowly and point to a square as I say each sound: /rrr/ /iii/ /mmm/.** Point to the first square. **What is the first sound in *rim*? That's right; /rrr/ is the first sound in *rim*.** Have the group say the sound together. Then give individual turns.
	Lay out two letter tiles, *r* and one other. Lead children in identifying the letter that goes with the first sound.	**You're going to choose the letter for the sound /rrr/ like the /rrr/ in *rim*.** Point to the first square. **Does everyone know?** Call on a child to choose the correct letter and place it in the first square. Reinforce the group on the letter name and sound: **Everyone, what's the <u>name</u> of the letter? What's the <u>sound</u> for the letter?**
	Lead children in isolating the last sound.	**Watch again as I say the sounds in *rim* slowly and point to a square as I say each sound: /rrr/ /iii/ /mmm/.** Point to the last square: **/mmm/ is the last sound in *rim*. What is the last sound in *rim*?**
	Lay out two letter tiles, *m* and one other. Lead children in identifying the letter that goes with the last sound.	**You're going to choose the letter for the sound /mmm/ like the /mmm/ in *rim*.** Point to the last square. **Does everyone know?** Call on a child to choose the correct letter and place it in the last square. Reinforce the group on the letter name and sound: **Everyone, what's the <u>name</u> of the letter? What's the <u>sound</u> for the letter?**
		Practice with *soap, fair, mop,* and *foam,* as time allows.

Ongoing Assessment

If…children make an error, then…model the answer, have them repeat it, and return to the sound and letter a second time.

Rhyme Time

Objective: Children write the first and last sounds of words that go with a rhyme.

Time: 6–8 minutes

	To Do	**To Say**
Introduce the activity	Distribute a Rhyme Time to each child.	**Today you're going to write the first and last sounds of some words that go with a rhyme.**
Model the activity		**I'll show you how Rhyme Time works. I'll say a rhyme like "The fat old <u>cat</u> sat on the _____."** Emphasize the word to rhyme (e.g., *cat*). **You'll tell me the word that finishes the rhyme. *Mat* finishes this rhyme: "The fat old <u>cat</u> sat on the <u>mat</u>."**
	Hold up a Rhyme Time. Model identifying the letter for the first sound in *mat*.	**Model** **Listen. I'll say the sounds in *mat*: /mmm/ /aaa/ /t/.**
		Lead **Say the sounds in *mat* with me: /mmm/ /aaa/ /t/.**
		Model **Now I'll say the sounds in *mat* and point to a square as I say each sound: /mmm/ /aaa/ /t/.** Point to the first square: **/mmm/ is the first sound in *mat*. I'm going to write the letter for the sound /mmm/ like the /mmm/ in *mat*.** Write the letter *m* in the first box.
		Lead **Now you write the letter for the sound /mmm/ like the /mmm/ in *mat*. Start at the dot and write the letter in the first box. That's right; *m* is the letter for the sound /mmm/.**
	Model identifying the letter for the last sound in *mat*.	**Model** **Watch again as I point to the squares and say the sounds in *mat*: /mmm/ /aaa/ /t/.** Point to the last square: **/t/ is the last sound in *mat*. I'm going to write the letter for the sound /t/ like the /t/ in *mat*.** Write the letter *t* in the last box.
		Lead **Now you write the letter for the sound /t/ like the /t/ in *mat*. Start at the dot and write the letter in the last box. That's right; *t* is the letter for the sound /t/.**

	To Do	**To Say**	
Test knowledge of initial and final sounds		**Test**	Here's the next rhyme. "To clean up the <u>pop</u>, he took out a _____." What word finishes this rhyme? That's right; *mop. Mop* finishes this rhyme: "To clean up the <u>pop</u>, he took out a <u>mop</u>."

Hold up a Rhyme Time.

Listen. I'll say the sounds in *mop* slowly: /mmm/ /ooo/ /p/. Now I'll say the sounds in *mop* slowly and point to a square as I say each sound: /mmm/ /ooo/ /p/. Point to the first square. **What is the first sound in *mop*? Everyone, write the letter for the sound /mmm/ like the /mmm/ in *mop* in the first box.** Reinforce the group on the letter name and sound: **Everyone, what's the <u>name</u> of the letter? What's the <u>sound</u> for the letter?**

Continue to hold up a Rhyme Time.

Watch again as I point to the squares and say *mop* slowly: /mmm/ /ooo/ /p/. Point to the last square. **What is the last sound in *mop*? That's right; /p/ is the last sound in *mop*. Everyone, write the letter for the sound /p/ like the /p/ in *mop* in the last box.** Reinforce the group on the letter name and sound: **Everyone, what's the <u>name</u> of the letter? What's the <u>sound</u> for the letter?**

Continue with these rhymes: 3. Please do not <u>tap</u> on my <u>cap</u>. 4. This is <u>Tom</u> and his <u>mom</u>. 5. The fat rat <u>sat</u> near the <u>cat</u>.

Ongoing Assessment

If... children make an error,	**then...** model the letter name and sound and have children repeat them. Have children write the correct letter.